Human Body Systems

interactive
SCIENCE

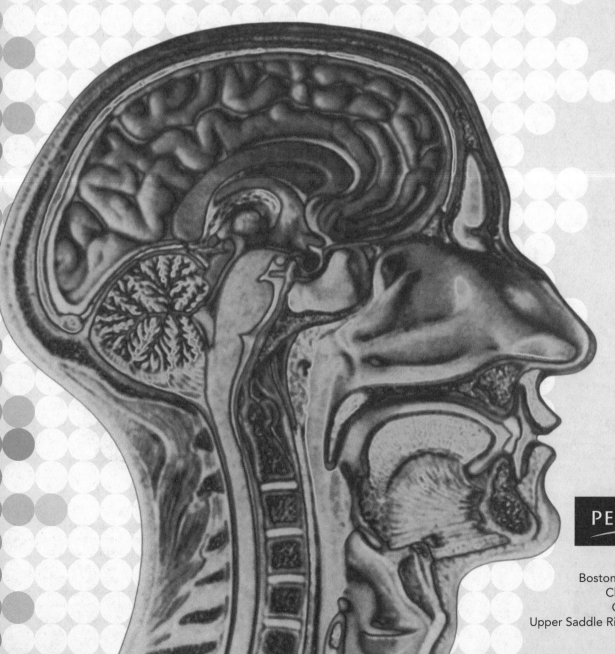

PEARSON

Boston, Massachusetts
Chandler, Arizona
Glenview, Illinois
Upper Saddle River, New Jersey

AUTHORS

You're an author!

As you write in this science book, your answers and personal discoveries will be recorded for you to keep, making this book unique to you. That is why you are one of the primary authors of this book.

✏️ **In the space below, print your name, school, town, and state. Then write a short autobiography that includes your interests and accomplishments.**

YOUR NAME

SCHOOL

TOWN, STATE

AUTOBIOGRAPHY

Your Photo

Acknowledgments appear on pages 309–311, which constitute an extension of this copyright page.

ISBN-13: 978-0-13-368491-9
ISBN-10: 0-13-368491-1
16 16

ON THE COVER
Seeing Inside
Magnetic resonance imaging (MRI) uses magnetism, radio waves, and a computer to produce images of structures inside a person's body. Scientists developed a way to add color to this MRI so that specific organs and tissues are easier to see than if they were in black and white.

Program Authors

DON BUCKLEY, M.Sc.
Information and Communications Technology Director, The School at Columbia University, New York, New York
Mr. Buckley has been at the forefront of K–12 educational technology for nearly two decades. A founder of New York City Independent School Technologists (NYCIST) and long-time chair of New York Association of Independent Schools' annual IT conference, he has taught students on two continents and created multimedia and Internet-based instructional systems for schools worldwide.

ZIPPORAH MILLER, M.A.Ed.
Associate Executive Director for Professional Programs and Conferences, National Science Teachers Association, Arlington, Virginia
Associate executive director for professional programs and conferences at NSTA, Ms. Zipporah Miller is a former K–12 science supervisor and STEM coordinator for the Prince George's County Public School District in Maryland. She is a science education consultant who has overseen curriculum development and staff training for more than 150 district science coordinators.

MICHAEL J. PADILLA, Ph.D.
Associate Dean and Director, Eugene P. Moore School of Education, Clemson University, Clemson, South Carolina
A former middle school teacher and a leader in middle school science education, Dr. Michael Padilla has served as president of the National Science Teachers Association and as a writer of the National Science Education Standards. He is professor of science education at Clemson University. As lead author of the *Science Explorer* series, Dr. Padilla has inspired the team in developing a program that promotes student inquiry and meets the needs of today's students.

KATHRYN THORNTON, Ph.D.
Professor and Associate Dean, School of Engineering and Applied Science, University of Virginia, Charlottesville, Virginia
Selected by NASA in May 1984, Dr. Kathryn Thornton is a veteran of four space flights. She has logged over 975 hours in space, including more than 21 hours of extravehicular activity. As an author on the *Scott Foresman Science* series, Dr. Thornton's enthusiasm for science has inspired teachers around the globe.

MICHAEL E. WYSESSION, Ph.D.
Associate Professor of Earth and Planetary Science, Washington University, St. Louis, Missouri
An author on more than 50 scientific publications, Dr. Wysession was awarded the prestigious Packard Foundation Fellowship and Presidential Faculty Fellowship for his research in geophysics. Dr. Wysession is an expert on Earth's inner structure and has mapped various regions of Earth using seismic tomography. He is known internationally for his work in geoscience education and outreach.

Instructional Design Author

GRANT WIGGINS, Ed.D.
President, Authentic Education, Hopewell, New Jersey
Dr. Wiggins is a co-author with Jay McTighe of *Understanding by Design, 2nd Edition* (ASCD 2005). His approach to instructional design provides teachers with a disciplined way of thinking about curriculum design, assessment, and instruction that moves teaching from covering content to ensuring understanding.
UNDERSTANDING BY DESIGN® and UbD™ are trademarks of ASCD, and are used under license.

Planet Diary Author

JACK HANKIN
Science/Mathematics Teacher, The Hilldale School, Daly City, California Founder, Planet Diary Web site
Mr. Hankin is the creator and writer of Planet Diary, a science current events Web site. He is passionate about bringing science news and environmental awareness into classrooms and offers numerous Planet Diary workshops at NSTA and other events to train middle and high school teachers.

ELL Consultant

JIM CUMMINS, Ph.D.
Professor and Canada Research Chair, Curriculum, Teaching and Learning department at the University of Toronto
Dr. Cummins focuses on literacy development in multilingual schools and the role of technology in promoting student learning across the curriculum. *Interactive Science* incorporates essential research-based principles for integrating language with the teaching of academic content based on his instructional framework.

Reading Consultant

HARVEY DANIELS, Ph.D.
Professor of Secondary Education, University of New Mexico, Albuquerque, New Mexico
Dr. Daniels is an international consultant to schools, districts, and educational agencies. He has authored or coauthored 13 books on language, literacy, and education. His most recent works are *Comprehension and Collaboration: Inquiry Circles in Action* and *Subjects Matter: Every Teacher's Guide to Content-Area Reading.*

REVIEWERS

Contributing Writers

Edward Aguado, Ph.D.
Professor, Department of Geography
San Diego State University
San Diego, California

Elizabeth Coolidge-Stolz, M.D.
Medical Writer
North Reading, Massachusetts

Donald L. Cronkite, Ph.D.
Professor of Biology
Hope College
Holland, Michigan

Jan Jenner, Ph.D.
Science Writer
Talladega, Alabama

Linda Cronin Jones, Ph.D.
Associate Professor of Science and Environmental Education
University of Florida
Gainesville, Florida

T. Griffith Jones, Ph.D.
Clinical Associate Professor of Science Education
College of Education
University of Florida
Gainesville, Florida

Andrew C. Kemp, Ph.D.
Teacher
Jefferson County Public Schools
Louisville, Kentucky

Matthew Stoneking, Ph.D.
Associate Professor of Physics
Lawrence University
Appleton, Wisconsin

R. Bruce Ward, Ed.D.
Senior Research Associate
Science Education Department
Harvard-Smithsonian Center for Astrophysics
Cambridge, Massachusetts

Content Reviewers

Paul D. Beale, Ph.D.
Department of Physics
University of Colorado at Boulder
Boulder, Colorado

Jeff R. Bodart, Ph.D.
Professor of Physical Sciences
Chipola College
Marianna, Florida

Joy Branlund, Ph.D.
Department of Earth Science
Southwestern Illinois College
Granite City, Illinois

Marguerite Brickman, Ph.D.
Division of Biological Sciences
University of Georgia
Athens, Georgia

Bonnie J. Brunkhorst, Ph.D.
Science Education and Geological Sciences
California State University
San Bernardino, California

Michael Castellani, Ph.D.
Department of Chemistry
Marshall University
Huntington, West Virginia

Charles C. Curtis, Ph.D.
Research Associate Professor of Physics
University of Arizona
Tucson, Arizona

Diane I. Doser, Ph.D.
Department of Geological Sciences
University of Texas
El Paso, Texas

Rick Duhrkopf, Ph.D.
Department of Biology
Baylor University
Waco, Texas

Alice K. Hankla, Ph.D.
The Galloway School
Atlanta, Georgia

Mark Henriksen, Ph.D.
Physics Department
University of Maryland
Baltimore, Maryland

Chad Hershock, Ph.D.
Center for Research on Learning and Teaching
University of Michigan
Ann Arbor, Michigan

Jeremiah N. Jarrett, Ph.D.
Department of Biology
Central Connecticut State University
New Britain, Connecticut

Scott L. Kight, Ph.D.
Department of Biology
Montclair State University
Montclair, New Jersey

Jennifer O. Liang, Ph.D.
Department of Biology
University of Minnesota–Duluth
Duluth, Minnesota

Candace Lutzow-Felling, Ph.D.
Director of Education
The State Arboretum of Virginia
University of Virginia
Boyce, Virginia

Cortney V. Martin, Ph.D.
Virginia Polytechnic Institute
Blacksburg, Virginia

Joseph F. McCullough, Ph.D.
Physics Program Chair
Cabrillo College
Aptos, California

Heather Mernitz, Ph.D.
Department of Physical Science
Alverno College
Milwaukee, Wisconsin

Sadredin C. Moosavi, Ph.D.
Department of Earth and Environmental Sciences
Tulane University
New Orleans, Louisiana

David L. Reid, Ph.D.
Department of Biology
Blackburn College
Carlinville, Illinois

Scott M. Rochette, Ph.D.
Department of the Earth Sciences
SUNY College at Brockport
Brockport, New York

Karyn L. Rogers, Ph.D.
Department of Geological Sciences
University of Missouri
Columbia, Missouri

Laurence Rosenhein, Ph.D.
Department of Chemistry
Indiana State University
Terre Haute, Indiana

Sara Seager, Ph.D.
Department of Planetary Sciences and Physics
Massachusetts Institute of Technology
Cambridge, Massachusetts

Tom Shoberg, Ph.D.
Missouri University of Science and Technology
Rolla, Missouri

Patricia Simmons, Ph.D.
North Carolina State University
Raleigh, North Carolina

William H. Steinecker, Ph.D.
Research Scholar
Miami University
Oxford, Ohio

Paul R. Stoddard, Ph.D.
Department of Geology and Environmental Geosciences
Northern Illinois University
DeKalb, Illinois

John R. Villarreal, Ph.D.
Department of Chemistry
The University of Texas–Pan American
Edinburg, Texas

John R. Wagner, Ph.D.
Department of Geology
Clemson University
Clemson, South Carolina

Jerry Waldvogel, Ph.D.
Department of Biological Sciences
Clemson University
Clemson, South Carolina

Donna L. Witter, Ph.D.
Department of Geology
Kent State University
Kent, Ohio

Edward J. Zalisko, Ph.D.
Department of Biology
Blackburn College
Carlinville, Illinois

Museum of Science.

Special thanks to the Museum of Science, Boston, Massachusetts, and Ioannis Miaoulis, the Museum's president and director, for serving as content advisors for the technology and design strand in this program.

CONTENTS

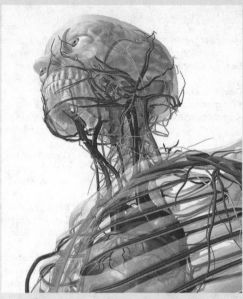

Enter the Lab zone for hands-on inquiry.

Chapter Lab Investigation:
• Directed Inquiry: A Look Beneath the Skin
• Open Inquiry: A Look Beneath the Skin

Inquiry Warm-Ups: • How Is Your Body
Organized? • How Does Your Body Respond?
• Out of Balance

Quick Labs: • Observing Cells and Tissues
• Working Together, Act I • Working Together,
Act II • Working to Maintain Balance

my science Online.com

**Go to MyScienceOnline.com to
interact with this chapter's content.
Keyword: The Human Body**

UNTAMED SCIENCE
• Keeping Cool and Staying Warm

PLANET DIARY
• The Human Body

INTERACTIVE ART
• Body Systems

ART IN MOTION
• Body Systems in Action

REAL-WORLD INQUIRY
• A Wrench in the System

Enter the Lab zone for hands-on inquiry.

Chapter Lab Investigation:
• Directed Inquiry: Sun Safety
• Open Inquiry: Sun Safety

Inquiry Warm-Ups: • Hard as a Rock?
• How Do Muscles Work? • What Can You
Observe About Skin?

Quick Labs: • The Skeleton • Observing
Joints • Soft Bones? • Observing Muscle
Tissue • Modeling How Skeletal Muscles Work
• Sweaty Skin

my science online.com

**Go to MyScienceOnline.com to
interact with this chapter's content.
Keyword: Bones, Muscles, and Skin**

> **UNTAMED SCIENCE**
• Feeling Just Spine, Thank You

> **PLANET DIARY**
• Bones, Muscles, and Skin

> **INTERACTIVE ART**
• The Skeletal and Muscular Systems • Build
a Skeleton

> **ART IN MOTION**
• Muscle Motion

> **VIRTUAL LAB**
• Up Close: Support Tissues

CONTENTS

Enter the Lab zone for hands-on inquiry.

Chapter Lab Investigation:
• Directed Inquiry: As the Stomach Churns
• Open Inquiry: As the Stomach Churns

Inquiry Warm-Ups: • Food Claims
• Calculating Calorie Content • Where Does Digestion Start? • Which Surface Is Larger?

Quick Labs: • Measuring Calories
• Predicting Starch Content • Classifying Foods • Calculating Percentage of Calories From Fat • How Can You Speed Up Digestion? • Break Up! • The Role of the Large Intestine

my science online.com

Go to MyScienceOnline.com to interact with this chapter's content. Keyword: Digestion

> **UNTAMED SCIENCE**
• Digestion Rocks

> **PLANET DIARY**
• Digestion

> **INTERACTIVE ART**
• Nutrients at Work

> **ART IN MOTION**
• Enzyme Action

> **REAL-WORLD INQUIRY**
• A Digestive Journey

Lab zone® **Enter the Lab zone for hands-on inquiry.**

Chapter Lab Investigation:
• Directed Inquiry: Heart Beat, Health Beat
• Open Inquiry: Heart Beat, Health Beat

Inquiry Warm-Ups: • Observing a Heart
• How Does Pressure Affect Blood Flow?
• What Kinds of Cells Are in Blood? • Which Foods Are "Heart Healthy"?

Quick Labs: • How Hard Does Your Heart Work? • Direction of Blood Flow • Observing Diffusion • Blood Pressure • Modeling Plasma • Do You Know Your A-B-Os? • Blocking the Flow • Heart-Healthy Activities

my science online.com

Go to MyScienceOnline.com to interact with this chapter's content. Keyword: Circulation

> **UNTAMED SCIENCE**
• Blood Lines

> **PLANET DIARY**
• Circulation

> **INTERACTIVE ART**
• The Heart • Arteries or Veins?

> **ART IN MOTION**
• The Adventures of an RBC

> **VIRTUAL LAB**
• Up Close: Components of Blood

CONTENTS

Enter the Lab zone for hands-on inquiry.

Chapter Lab Investigation:
• Directed Inquiry: A Breath of Fresh Air
• Open Inquiry: A Breath of Fresh Air

Inquiry Warm-Ups: How Big Can You Blow Up a Balloon? • A Smoker's Lungs • How Does Filtering a Liquid Change the Liquid?

Quick Labs: Modeling Respiration • What Do You Exhale? • Chemicals in Tobacco Smoke • Modeling a Health Checkup Procedure • Kidney Function • Perspiration

my science online.com

Go to MyScienceOnline.com to interact with this chapter's content.
Keyword: Respiration and Excretion

> **UNTAMED SCIENCE**
• Zen Diving

> **PLANET DIARY**
• Respiration and Excretion

> **INTERACTIVE ART**
• The Respiratory System • Waste on the Way Out

> **ART IN MOTION**
• Gas Exchange

> **REAL-WORLD INQUIRY**
• Is Smoking Really That Bad for You?

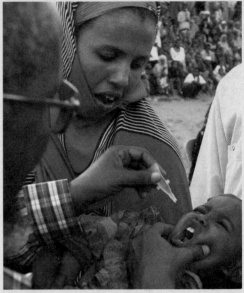

CHAPTER 6

Fighting Disease *T.LS.4*

Enter the Lab zone for hands-on inquiry.

Chapter Lab Investigation:
• Directed Inquiry: The Skin as a Barrier
• Open Inquiry: The Skin as a Barrier

Inquiry Warm-Ups: • The Agents of Disease • Which Pieces Fit Together? • How Does HIV Spread? • Types of Immunity • Causes of Death, Then and Now

Quick Labs: • How Do Pathogens Cause Disease? • How Does a Disease Spread? • Stuck Together • How Does HIV Attack? • What Will Spread HIV? • Modeling Active and Passive Immunity • What Substances Can Kill Pathogens? • What Happens When Air Flow Is Restricted? • What Does Sunlight Do to the Beads?

my science online.com

**Go to MyScienceOnline.com to interact with this chapter's content.
Keyword: Fighting Disease**

› PLANET DIARY
• Fighting Disease

› INTERACTIVE ART
• Immune Response

› ART IN MOTION
• How Do Vaccines Work?

› REAL-WORLD INQUIRY
• Diagnosis Please, Doctor

› VIRTUAL LAB
• Up Close: Pathogens

CONTENTS

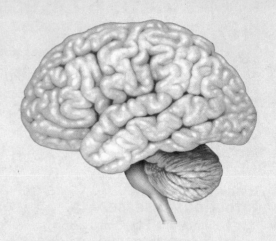

Enter the Lab zone for hands-on inquiry.

Chapter Lab Investigation:
• Directed Inquiry: Ready or Not!
• Open Inquiry: Ready or Not!

Inquiry Warm-Ups: • How Simple Is a Simple Task? • What Are the Parts of the Nervous System? • Eyes and Ears • Can You Feel It? • How Can You Best Say No?

Quick Labs: • Modeling a Neuron • Getting the Message Across • Making Models of the Brain • How Does Your Knee React? • When Things Go Wrong • Working Together • Making Models of the Ear • Taste and Smell • What's in the Bag? • Effects of Drugs • Over-the-Counter Medication Labels • Demonstrating BAC

my science online.com

Go to MyScienceOnline.com to interact with this chapter's content.
Keyword: The Nervous System

> **UNTAMED SCIENCE**
• Think Fast!

> **PLANET DIARY**
• The Nervous System

> **INTERACTIVE ART**
• The Nervous System • Are Drugs Really That Bad for You?

> **ART IN MOTION**
• How a Nerve Impulse Travels

> **REAL-WORLD INQUIRY**
• Sensing the World

 Enter the Lab zone for hands-on inquiry.

Chapter Lab Investigation:
• Directed Inquiry: Modeling Negative Feedback
• Open Inquiry: Modeling Negative Feedback

Inquiry Warm-Ups: • What's the Signal?
• What's the Big Difference? • Prenatal Growth • A Precious Bundle

Quick Labs: • Making Models
• Reproductive Systems • Looking at Hormone Levels • Way to Grow! • Egg-cellent Protection • Labor and Delivery • Growing Up

my science online.com

Go to MyScienceOnline.com to interact with this chapter's content.
Keyword: The Endocrine System and Reproduction

> **UNTAMED SCIENCE**
• Wow, I Look Old!

> **PLANET DIARY**
• The Endocrine System and Reproduction

> **INTERACTIVE ART**
• Negative Feedback in the Endocrine System • Reproductive Anatomy

> **ART IN MOTION**
• Stages of Prenatal Development

> **REAL-WORLD INQUIRY**
• Are They Growing up Normally?

interactive SCIENCE

This is your book. You can write in it!

Get Engaged!
At the start of each chapter, you will see two questions: an Engaging Question and the Big Question. Each chapter's Big Question will help you start thinking about the Big Ideas of Science. Look for the Big Q symbol throughout the chapter!

HOW CAN WIND KEEP YOUR LIGHTS ON?

THE BIG Q What are some of Earth's energy sources?

This man is repairing a wind turbine at a wind farm in Texas. Most wind turbines are at least 30 meters off the ground where the winds are fast. Wind speed and blade length help determine the best way to capture the wind and turn it into power. **Develop Hypotheses** Why do you think people are working to increase the amount of power we get from wind?

Wind energy collected by the
turbine does not cause air pollution.

> UNTAMED SCIENCE Watch the Untamed Science video to learn more about energy resources.

174 Energy Resources

Untamed Science

Follow the Untamed Science video crew as they travel the globe exploring the Big Ideas of Science.

Interact with your textbook. **Interact with inquiry.** **Interact online.**

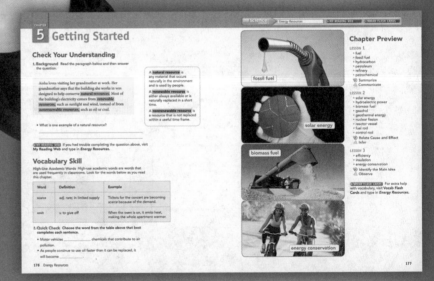

Build Reading, Inquiry, and Vocabulary Skills

In every lesson you will learn new ✏ Reading and ▲ Inquiry skills. These skills will help you read and think like a scientist. Vocabulary skills will help you communicate effectively and uncover the meaning of words.

my science online.com

Go Online!

Look for the MyScienceOnline.com technology options. At MyScienceOnline.com you can immerse yourself in amazing virtual environments, get extra practice, and even blog about current events in science.

Explore the Key Concepts.

Each lesson begins with a series of Key Concept questions. The interactivities in each lesson will help you understand these concepts and Unlock the Big Question.

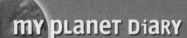

MY PLANET DIARY

At the start of each lesson, My Planet Diary will introduce you to amazing events, significant people, and important discoveries in science or help you to overcome common misconceptions about science concepts.

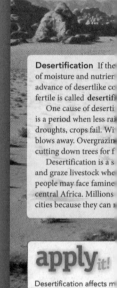

Desertification If the of moisture and nutrier advance of desertlike c fertile is called desertifi

One cause of deserti is a period when less rai droughts, crops fail. Wi blows away. Overgrazin cutting down trees for f

Desertification is a s and graze livestock whe people may face famine central Africa. Millions cities because they can

apply it!

Desertification affects m areas around the world.

❶ **Name** Which contine has the most existing de

❷ **Interpret Maps** Whe the United States is the risk of desertification?

❸ **Infer** Is desertificati is existing desert? Expla your answer.

❹ **CHALLENGE** If an area things people could do

132 Land, Air, and Wat

LESSON 2 Friction and Gravity

☐ What Factors Affect Friction?
☐ What Factors Affect Gravity?

MY PLANET DIARY CAREERS

Space Athletes

Have you ever seen pictures of astronauts playing golf on the moon or playing catch in a space station? Golf balls and baseballs can float or fly farther in space, where gravitational forces are weaker than they are on Earth. Imagine what professional sports would be like in reduced gravity!

You may not have to imagine much longer. At least one company specializes in airplane flights that simulate a reduced gravity environment. Similar to NASA training flights that astronauts use when preparing to go into space, these flights allow passengers to fly around the cabin. In environments with reduced gravity, athletes can perform jumps and stunts that would be impossible on Earth. As technology improves, permanent stadiums could be built in space for a whole new generation of athletes.

Communicate Discuss these questions with a partner and then answer them below.

1. Sports can be more fun in reduced gravity. What jobs could be harder or less fun to do in space? Why?

2. What kinds of sports do you think could be more fun in space? Why?

PLANET DIARY Go to Planet Diary to learn more about everyday forces.

Lab zone Do the Inquiry Warm-Up Observing Friction.

my science online | Frictions | PLANET DIARY | ART IN MOTION

Vocabulary
• friction • sliding friction • static friction
• fluid friction • rolling friction • gravity
• mass • weight

Skills
▲ Reading: Identify Supporting Evidence
▲ Inquiry: Design Experiments

What Factors Affect Friction?

When you ride a bike on the road, the surface of the tires rubs against the surface of the road. The force that two surfaces exert on each other when they rub against each other is called friction.

☐ Two factors that affect the force of friction are the types of surfaces involved and how hard the surfaces are pushed together. The biker in **Figure 1** would have an easier time pedaling on a newly paved road than on a rugged gravel road. In general, smooth surfaces produce less friction than rough surfaces. It may surprise you to know that even the smoothest objects—like a patch of ice or a countertop—have irregular, bumpy surfaces. When the irregularities of one surface come into contact with those of another surface, friction occurs.

What would happen if you switched to a much heavier bike? You would find the heavier bike harder to pedal because the tires push down harder against the road. Similarly, if you rubbed your hands together forcefully, there would be more friction than if you rubbed your hands together lightly. Friction increases when surfaces push harder against each other.

Friction acts in a direction opposite to the direction of the object's motion. Without friction, a moving object will not stop until it strikes another object.

Vocabulary Latin Word Origins Friction comes from the Latin word fricare. Based on the definition of friction, what do you think fricare means?
○ to burn
○ to rub
○ to melt

FIGURE 1
ART IN MOTION Friction and Different Surfaces
The strength of friction depends on the types of surfaces involved. Sequence Rank the surfaces above by how hard it would be to pedal over them, from easiest (1) to hardest (3). (Each surface is flat.) What does this ranking tell you about the amount of friction over these surfaces?

Explain what you know.

Look for the pencil. When you see it, it's time to interact with your book and demonstrate what you have learned.

apply it!

Elaborate further with the Apply It activities. This is your opportunity to take what you've learned and apply those skills to new situations.

Lab Zone

Look for the Lab zone triangle. This means it's time to do a hands-on inquiry lab. In every lesson, you'll have the opportunity to do a hands-on inquiry activity that will help reinforce your understanding of the lesson topic.

becomes depleted
desert. The
previously were
(KAY shun).
example, a **drought**
area. During
osed soil easily
nd sheep and
fication, too.
annot grow crops
curred. As a result,
cation is severe in
moving to the
elves on the land.

Key
- Existing desert
- High-risk area
- Moderate-risk area

where there
map to support

, what are some
s?

Land Reclamation Fortunately, it is possible to replace land damaged by erosion or mining. The process of restoring an area of land to a more productive state is called **land reclamation**. In addition to restoring land for agriculture, land reclamation can restore habitats for wildlife. Many different types of land reclamation projects are currently underway all over the world. But it is generally more difficult and expensive to restore damaged land and soil than it is to protect those resources in the first place. In some cases, the land may not return to its original state.

FIGURE 4
Land Reclamation
These pictures show land before and after it was mined.
✎ **Communicate** Below the pictures, write a story about what happened to the land.

_____

_____

🖿 Assess Your Understanding

1a. Review Subsoil has (less/more) plant and animal matter than topsoil.

b. Explain What can happen to soil if plants are removed?

_____

_____

c. Apply Concepts
that could prev
land reclama

_____

got it?

○ I get it! Now I know that soil management is important becau

_____

○ I need extra help with _____

Go to **MY SCIENCE COACH** online for help with this subject.

Lab zone — Do the Quick Lab Modeling S...

got it?

Evaluate Your Progress.

After answering the Got It question, think about how you're doing. Did you get it or do you need a little help? Remember, **MY SCIENCE COACH** is there for you if you need extra help.

Explore the Big Question.

At one point in the chapter, you'll have the opportunity to take all that you've learned to further explore the Big Question.

Pollution and Solutions

EXPLORE THE BIG

What can people do to use resources wisely?

FIGURE 4 ....
▶ REAL-WORLD INQUIRY All living things depend on land, air, and water. Conserving these resources for the future is important. Part of resource conservation is identifying and limiting sources of pollution.

✎ **Interpret Photos** On the photograph, write the letter from the key into the circle that best identifies the source of pollution.

Land
Describe at least one thing your community could do to reduce pollution on land.

Air
Describe at least one thing your community could do to reduce air pollution.

Water
Describe at least one thing your community could do to reduce water pollution.

Pollution Sources
A. Sediments
B. Municipal solid waste
C. Runoff from development

Assess You

1a. **Define** What are s

b. **Explain** How can spill in the ocean?

c. **ANSWER** What can resources

d. **CHALLENGE** Why to recycle the wa would reduce wa

got it? ....
○ I get it! Now I can be reduced

○ I need extra he

Go to my science with this subject.

ANSWER THE BIG

Answer the Big Question.

Now it's time to show what you know and answer the Big Question.

Review What You've Learned.

Use the Chapter Study Guide to review the Big Question and prepare for the test.

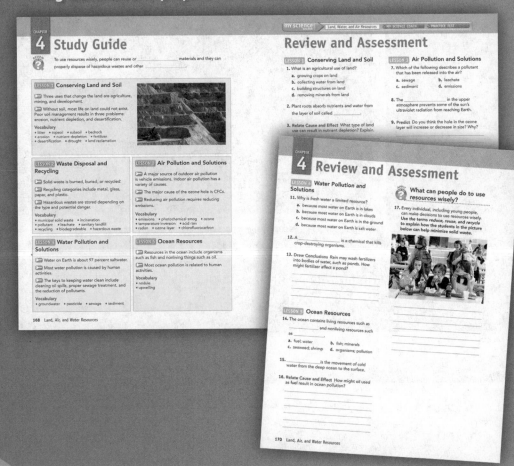

Practice Taking Tests.

Apply the Big Question and take a practice test in standardized test format.

INTERACT... WITH YOUR TEXTBOOK...

Go to **MyScienceOnline.com** and immerse yourself in amazing virtual environments.

THE BIG QUESTION

Each online chapter starts with a Big Question. Your mission is to unlock the meaning of this Big Question as each science lesson unfolds.

VOCAB FLASH CARDS

Practice chapter vocabulary with interactive flash cards. Each card has an image, definitions in English and Spanish, and space for your own notes.

INTERACTIVE ART

At MyScienceOnline.com, many of the beautiful visuals in your book become interactive so you can extend your learning.

interactive SCIENCE
GO ONLINE

> ## PLANET DIARY

My Planet Diary online is the place to find more information and activities related to the topic in the lesson.

Still Growing! Mount Everest in the Himalayas is the highest mountain on Earth. Climbers who reach the peak stand 8,850 meters above sea level. You might think that mountains never change. But forces inside Earth push Mount Everest at least several millimeters higher each year. Over time, Earth's forces slowly but constantly lift, stretch, bend, and break Earth's crust in dramatic ways!

> Planet Diary Go to Planet Diary to learn more about forces in the Earth's crust.

> ## VIRTUAL LAB

Get more practice with realistic virtual labs. Manipulate the variables on-screen and test your hypothesis.

C + http://www.myscienceonline.com/

Find Your Chapter

1 Go to www.myscienceonline.com.

2 Log in with username and password.

3 Click on your program and select your chapter.

Keyword Search

1 Go to www.myscienceonline.com.

2 Log in with username and password.

3 Click on your program and select Search.

4 Enter the keyword (from your book) in the search box.

Other Content Available Online

> UNTAMED SCIENCE Follow these young scientists through their amazing online video blogs as they travel the globe in search of answers to the Big Questions of Science.

> MY SCIENCE COACH Need extra help? My Science Coach is your personal online study partner. My Science Coach is a chance for you to get more practice on key science concepts. There you can choose from a variety of tools that will help guide you through each science lesson.

> MY READING WEB Need extra reading help on a particular science topic? At My Reading Web you will find a choice of reading selections targeted to your specific reading level.

? BIG IDEAS OF SCIENCE

Have you ever worked on a jigsaw puzzle? Usually a puzzle has a theme that leads you to group the pieces by what they have in common. But until you put all the pieces together you can't solve the puzzle. Studying science is similar to solving a puzzle. The big ideas of science are like puzzle themes. To understand big ideas, scientists ask questions. The answers to those questions are like pieces of a puzzle. Each chapter in this book asks a big question to help you think about a big idea of science. By answering the big questions, you will get closer to understanding the big idea.

✎ Before you read each chapter, write about what you know and what more you'd like to know.

BIGIDEA

Living things maintain constant conditions inside their bodies.

What do you already know about your body temperature regardless of how warm or cold it is outside? ✎ **What more would you like to know?**

_____

_____

_____

Big Questions:

? How does your body work? Chapter 1

? Why do you sometimes get sick? Chapter 6

✎ **After reading the chapters, write what you have learned about the Big Idea.**

_____

_____

_____

_____

Like a rock climber who carefully adjusts to changing conditions on the mountain, your body adjusts to changes in your surroundings.

Structures in living things are related to their functions.

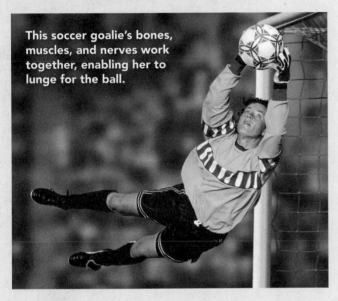

This soccer goalie's bones, muscles, and nerves work together, enabling her to lunge for the ball.

What do you already know about how your body systems perform their functions? ✎ **What more would you like to know?**

_____

_____

Big Questions:

❓ What holds your body together? Chapter 2

❓ How does food become materials your body can use? Chapter 3

❓ How does your body's transport system work? Chapter 4

❓ How do you breathe? Chapter 5

❓ How does your body sense and react to your surroundings? Chapter 7

✎ **After reading the chapters, write what you have learned about the Big Idea.**

_____

_____

_____

Living things grow, change, and reproduce during their lifetimes.

As people age, their appearance changes.

What do you already know about how children grow into adults? ✎ **What more would you like to know?**

_____

_____

Big Question:

❓ What changes happen in your body over your lifetime? Chapter 8

✎ **After reading the chapter, write what you have learned about the Big Idea.**

_____

_____

_____

_____

WHAT CAN THESE BODY PARTS DO?

How does your body work?

Your body is an amazingly complex mass of trillions of cells. These cells work together, doing all the functions that keep you alive. On average, an adult has 206 bones, 96,500 kilometers of blood vessels, and a brain with a mass of 1.4 kilograms. Your nerves can send signals at speeds of up to 120 meters per second. Your smallest muscle is in your ear.

 Infer What jobs do some of these body parts do?

_____

_____

_____

_____

_____

> **UNTAMED SCIENCE** Watch the **Untamed Science** video to learn more about body systems.

The Human Body

CHAPTER 1

Check Your Understanding

1. Background Read the paragraph below and then answer the question.

Fara is learning how to build and fix bicycles. First, she learned to change a tire using a tire lever. This tool's **structure**—a lever with a curved end—matches its **function**—to pry a tire off a metal rim. She's also learning about the **interactions** between the different bike parts—how the chain, gears, wheels, and brakes all work together as a **system.**

- Circle the structure below that best matches the function of helping a fish to swim.

  scales   gills   fins   eyes

An object's **structure** is its shape or form.

An object's **function** is the action it performs or the role it plays.

An **interaction** occurs when two or more things work together or affect one another.

A **system** is a group of parts that work together to perform a function or produce a result.

> **MY READING WEB** If you had trouble completing the question above, visit **My Reading Web** and type in *The Human Body.*

Vocabulary Skill

Suffixes A suffix is a word part that is added to the end of a word to change its meaning. For example, the suffix *-tion* means "process of." If you add the suffix *-tion* to the verb *digest,* you get the noun *digestion.* *Digestion* means "the process of digesting." The table below lists some other common suffixes and their meanings.

Suffix	Meaning	Example
-al	of, like, or suitable for	epithelial, *adj.* describes a tissue that covers inner and outer surfaces of the body
-ive	of, relating to, belonging to, having the nature or quality of	connective, *adj.* describes a tissue that provides support for the body and connects all of its parts

2. Quick Check Circle the suffix in each of the terms below.

skeletal   digestive   internal

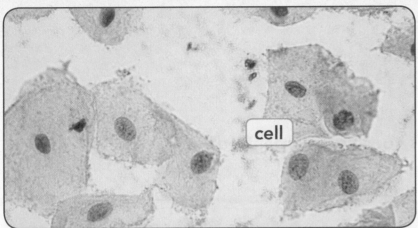

cell

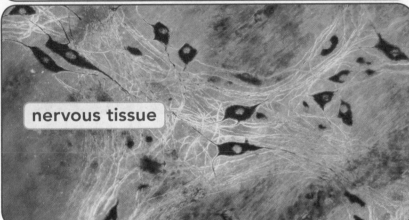

nervous tissue

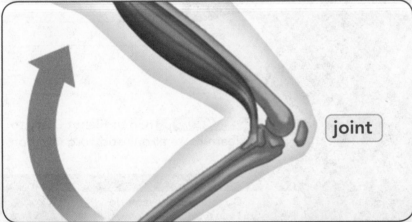

joint

stress

Chapter Preview

LESSON 1
- cell
- cell membrane
- nucleus
- cytoplasm
- tissue
- muscle tissue
- nervous tissue
- connective tissue
- epithelial tissue
- organ
- organ system
- ⟳ **Identify the Main Idea**
- △ **Make Models**

LESSON 2
- skeleton
- skeletal muscle
- joint
- nutrient
- absorption
- gland
- stimulus
- response
- hormone
- ⟳ **Summarize**
- △ **Develop Hypotheses**

LESSON 3
- homeostasis
- stress
- ⟳ **Relate Cause and Effect**
- △ **Communicate**

▷ VOCAB FLASH CARDS For extra help with vocabulary, visit **Vocab Flash Cards** and type in *The Human Body.*

Body Organization

UNLOCK
THE BIG
?

🔑 How Is Your Body Organized?

my planet Diary

CAREER

Medical Illustrator

Who made the colorful drawings of human body structures in this book? The drawings are the work of specialized artists called medical illustrators. These artists use their drawing skills and knowledge of human biology to make detailed images of body structures. Many artists draw images, such as the one on this page, using 3-D computer graphics. The work of medical illustrators appears in textbooks, journals, magazines, videos, computer learning programs, and many other places.

Communicate Answer the question below. Then discuss your answer with a partner.

Why do you think medical illustrations are important to the study of human biology?

_____

_____

_____

▷ PLANET DIARY Go to **Planet Diary** to learn more about body organization.

Lab zone® Do the Inquiry Warm-Up *How Is Your Body Organized?*

How Is Your Body Organized?

The bell rings—lunchtime! You hurry to the cafeteria, fill your tray, and pay the cashier. You look around the cafeteria for your friends. Then you walk to the table, sit down, and begin to eat.

Think about how many parts of your body were involved in the simple act of getting and eating your lunch. Every minute of the day, whether you are eating, studying, walking, or even sleeping, your body is busily at work. Each part of the body has a specific job to do. And all these different parts usually work together so smoothly that you don't even notice them.

Vocabulary

- cell • cell membrane • nucleus • cytoplasm • tissue
- muscle tissue • nervous tissue • connective tissue
- epithelial tissue • organ • organ system

Skills

- Reading: Identify the Main Idea
- Inquiry: Make Models

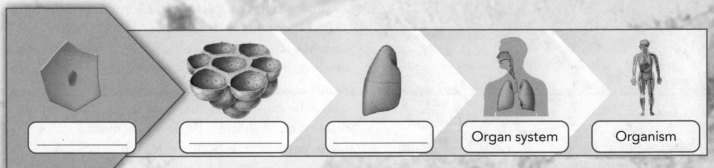

_____ | _____ | _____ | Organ system | Organism

FIGURE 1 ....

Body Organization

You will see this diagram three more times in this lesson. It will help you track the levels of organization in the body.

✏ **Name Fill in the missing terms in the diagram above.**

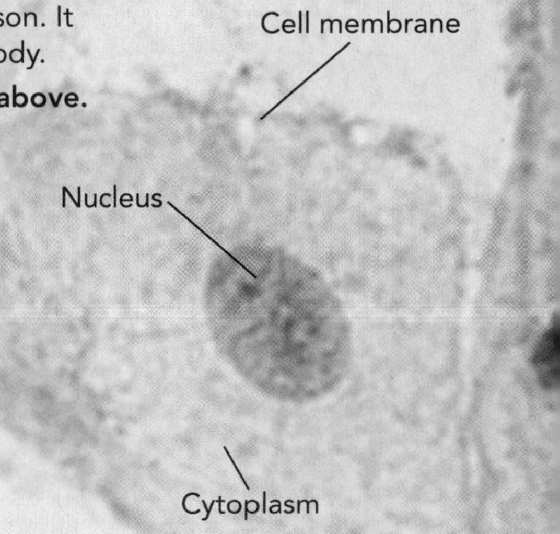

The smooth functioning of your body is due partly to how the body is organized. ⚷ **The levels of organization in the human body consist of cells, tissues, organs, and organ systems.** The smallest unit of organization is a cell. The next largest unit is a tissue, then an organ. Finally, an organ system is the largest unit of organization in an organism. **Figure 1** shows body organization.

Cells A **cell** is the basic unit of structure and function in a living thing. Complex organisms are made up of many cells in the same way that your school is made up of many rooms. The human body contains about 100 trillion tiny cells. Most cells cannot be seen without a microscope.

Structures of Cells Almost all cells in the human body have the same basic parts, as shown in **Figure 2.** The **cell membrane** forms the outside border of a cell. The **nucleus** directs the cell's activities and holds information that controls a cell's function. The rest of the cell, called the **cytoplasm** (SYT oh plaz um), is made of a clear, jellylike substance that contains many cell structures. Each of these structures has a specific job, or function.

Functions of Cells Cells carry on the processes that keep organisms alive. Inside cells, for example, molecules from digested food undergo changes that release energy that the cells can use. Cells also grow, reproduce, and get rid of the waste products that result from these activities.

Cell membrane

Nucleus

Cytoplasm

FIGURE 2 ....

Cell Structure

A microscope reveals some of the parts of a human cheek cell.

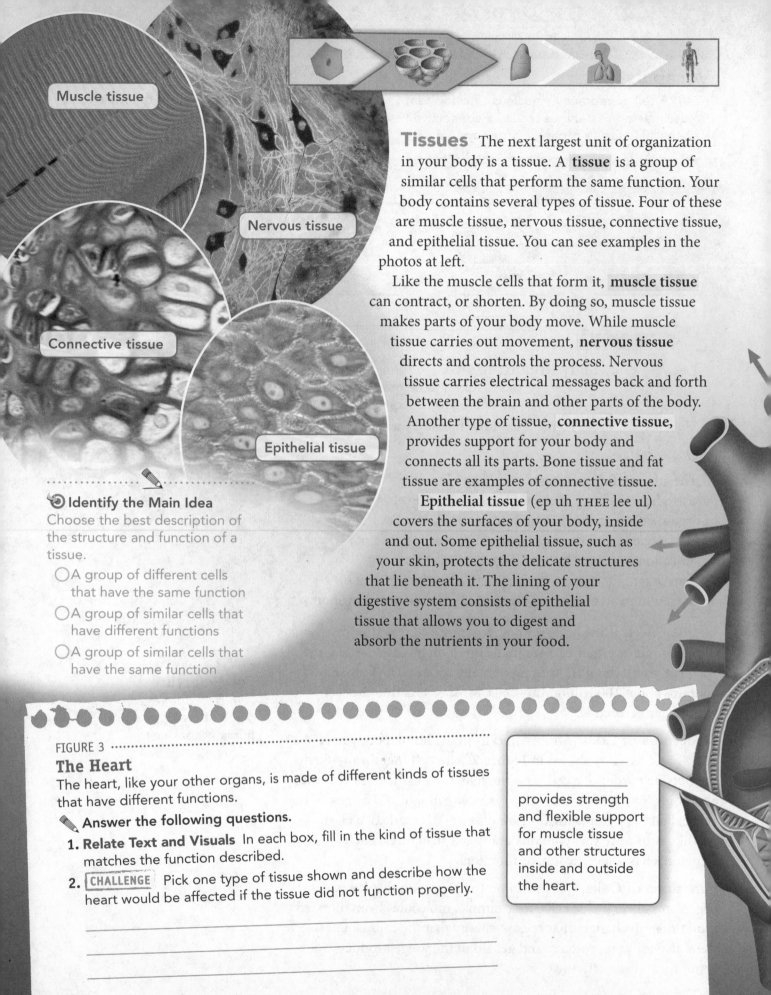

Muscle tissue

Nervous tissue

Connective tissue

Epithelial tissue

Tissues The next largest unit of organization in your body is a tissue. A **tissue** is a group of similar cells that perform the same function. Your body contains several types of tissue. Four of these are muscle tissue, nervous tissue, connective tissue, and epithelial tissue. You can see examples in the photos at left.

Like the muscle cells that form it, **muscle tissue** can contract, or shorten. By doing so, muscle tissue makes parts of your body move. While muscle tissue carries out movement, **nervous tissue** directs and controls the process. Nervous tissue carries electrical messages back and forth between the brain and other parts of the body. Another type of tissue, **connective tissue,** provides support for your body and connects all its parts. Bone tissue and fat tissue are examples of connective tissue.

Epithelial tissue (ep uh THEE lee ul) covers the surfaces of your body, inside and out. Some epithelial tissue, such as your skin, protects the delicate structures that lie beneath it. The lining of your digestive system consists of epithelial tissue that allows you to digest and absorb the nutrients in your food.

✏️ **Identify the Main Idea**
Choose the best description of the structure and function of a tissue.

◯ A group of different cells that have the same function

◯ A group of similar cells that have different functions

◯ A group of similar cells that have the same function

FIGURE 3
The Heart
The heart, like your other organs, is made of different kinds of tissues that have different functions.

✏️ **Answer the following questions.**

1. **Relate Text and Visuals** In each box, fill in the kind of tissue that matches the function described.

2. **CHALLENGE** Pick one type of tissue shown and describe how the heart would be affected if the tissue did not function properly.

_____ provides strength and flexible support for muscle tissue and other structures inside and outside the heart.

Organs Your stomach, heart, brain, and lungs are all organs. An **organ** is a structure that is made up of different kinds of tissue. Like a tissue, an organ performs a specific job. The job of an organ, however, is usually more complex than that of a tissue. For example, the heart pumps blood through your body over and over again. The heart contains muscle, connective, and epithelial tissues. In addition, nervous tissue connects to the heart and helps control heart function. **Figure 3** shows a diagram of a human heart and describes how some of the heart's tissues work. Each type of tissue contributes in a different way to the organ's job of pumping blood.

_____
covers the inside surfaces of the heart and of the blood vessels that lead into and out of the heart.

_____
carries electrical messages from the brain to the heart but is not shown in this diagram.

_____
contracts, squeezing the heart so blood moves through the heart's chambers and then into blood vessels that lead to the body.

apply it!

Books are a nonliving model of levels of organization. Find out how a book is organized.

STEP ① Observe Examine this book to see how its chapters, lessons, and other parts are related.

STEP ② Make Models Next, compare levels of organization in this book to those in the human body. Draw lines to show which part of this book best models a level in the body.

Organism   Lessons

Organ systems   Book

Organs   Words

Tissues   Chapters

Cells   Paragraphs

STEP ③ Make Models Where in the book model do you think this Apply It fits? What level of organization in the body does the Apply It represent?

_____
_____
_____
_____
_____

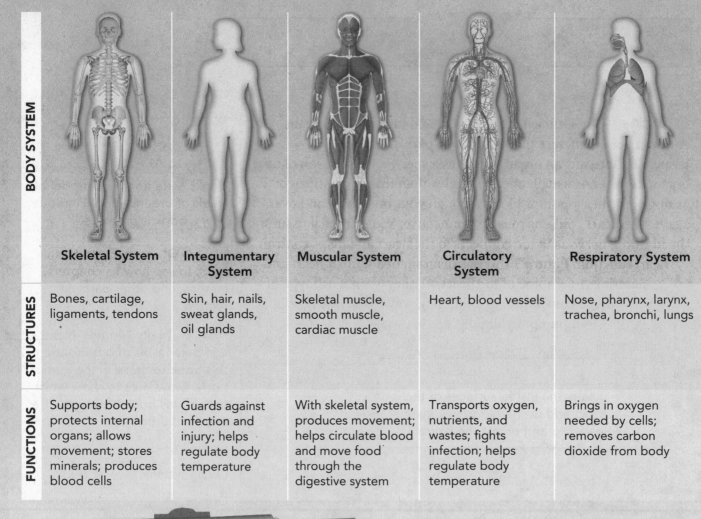

	Skeletal System	Integumentary System	Muscular System	Circulatory System	Respiratory System
STRUCTURES	Bones, cartilage, ligaments, tendons	Skin, hair, nails, sweat glands, oil glands	Skeletal muscle, smooth muscle, cardiac muscle	Heart, blood vessels	Nose, pharynx, larynx, trachea, bronchi, lungs
FUNCTIONS	Supports body; protects internal organs; allows movement; stores minerals; produces blood cells	Guards against infection and injury; helps regulate body temperature	With skeletal system, produces movement; helps circulate blood and move food through the digestive system	Transports oxygen, nutrients, and wastes; fights infection; helps regulate body temperature	Brings in oxygen needed by cells; removes carbon dioxide from body

*(Row label on far left: **BODY SYSTEM**)*

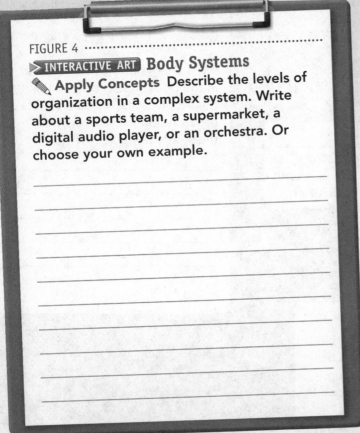

FIGURE 4 ···

> INTERACTIVE ART **Body Systems**

✎ **Apply Concepts** Describe the levels of organization in a complex system. Write about a sports team, a supermarket, a digital audio player, or an orchestra. Or choose your own example.

_____

_____

_____

_____

_____

_____

_____

_____

_____

Systems Each organ in your body is part of an **organ system,** which is a group of organs that work together, carrying out major functions. For example, your heart is part of your circulatory system, which carries oxygen and other materials throughout your body. The circulatory system also includes blood vessels and blood. **Figure 4** shows most of the organ systems in the human body.

Organisms Starting with cells, the levels of organization in an organism become more and more complex. A tissue is more complex than a cell, an organ is more complex than a tissue, and so on. You, as an organism, are the next level of organization. And all organisms are part of levels of organization within the environment.

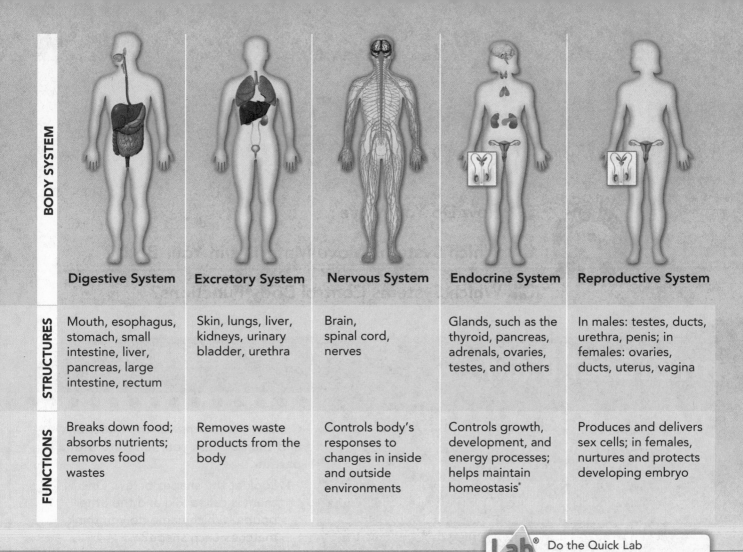

BODY SYSTEM	Digestive System	Excretory System	Nervous System	Endocrine System	Reproductive System
STRUCTURES	Mouth, esophagus, stomach, small intestine, liver, pancreas, large intestine, rectum	Skin, lungs, liver, kidneys, urinary bladder, urethra	Brain, spinal cord, nerves	Glands, such as the thyroid, pancreas, adrenals, ovaries, testes, and others	In males: testes, ducts, urethra, penis; in females: ovaries, ducts, uterus, vagina
FUNCTIONS	Breaks down food; absorbs nutrients; removes food wastes	Removes waste products from the body	Controls body's responses to changes in inside and outside environments	Controls growth, development, and energy processes; helps maintain homeostasis*	Produces and delivers sex cells; in females, nurtures and protects developing embryo

Lab zone® Do the Quick Lab *Observing Cells and Tissues.*

🔑 Assess Your Understanding

1a. Review How are cells, tissues, and organs related?

_____

_____

_____

b. Infer What systems of the body are involved in preparing and eating a sandwich?

_____

_____

_____

c. Make Judgments How does learning about body systems help you make informed decisions about your health?

_____

_____

_____

_____

_____

_____

_____

got it? ....

○ **I get it!** Now I know that the body's levels of organization, from least complex to most complex, are

_____

○ I need extra help with _____

Go to MY SCIENCE COACH online for help with this subject.

System Interactions

 UNLOCK THE BIG ?

🔑 **How Do You Move?**

🔑 **Which Systems Move Materials in Your Body?**

🔑 **Which Systems Control Body Functions?**

MY PLANET DIARY

Do you hear in color?

What color is the letter *b* or the roar of a tiger? You might not see colors when you hear sounds, but some people do. In people with synesthesia (sin us THEE zhuh), their senses overlap. Some people with synesthesia may taste a shape or hear music in colors. Others may hear a sound when they see motion. Even people without synesthesia experience some connections between their senses. You can explore how your own senses overlap in the first question on this page.

FUN FACTS

Communicate Answer the questions and then discuss your answers with a partner.

1. Look at the shapes below. One of them is called kiki and the other bouba. Which name do you think matches each shape?

A  B

_____

_____

2. Most people call the rounded shape bouba and the pointed shape kiki. Why do you think that is?

_____

_____

_____

> PLANET DIARY Go to **Planet Diary** to learn more about how body systems interact.

 Lab zone® Do the Inquiry Warm-Up *How Does Your Body Respond?*

Vocabulary

- skeleton • skeletal muscle • joint • nutrient
- absorption • gland • stimulus • response • hormone

Skills

⟳ Reading: Summarize

△ Inquiry: Develop Hypotheses

How Do You Move?

Carefully coordinated movements let you thread a needle, ride a bicycle, brush your teeth, and dance. These movements—and all of your body's other movements—happen as a result of the interactions between body systems. Your muscular system is made up of all the muscles in your body. Your skeletal system, or **skeleton,** includes all the bones in your body. ⟲ **Muscles and bones work together, making your body move. The nervous system tells your muscles when to act.**

Muscles and Bones

Skeletal muscles are attached to the bones of your skeleton and provide the force that moves your bones. Muscles contract and relax. When a muscle contracts, it shortens and pulls on the bones to which it is attached, as shown in **Figure 1.**

FIGURE 1 ·······························

Muscles Moving Bones

As this dancer's muscles pull on his leg bones, he can make rapid, skillful moves.

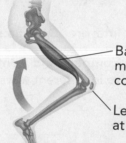

Back thigh muscles contract.

Leg bends at knee.

Front thigh muscles contract.

Leg extends.

△ **Develop Hypotheses** An octopus has no bones. Explain how you think it moves.

_____

_____

_____

_____

✏️ **Summarize** In your own words, describe which of your systems work together when you write in this book.

_____

_____

_____

_____

Bones and Joints What happens when you wiggle your fingers or touch your toes? Even though your bones are rigid, your body can bend in many ways. Your skeleton bends at its joints. A **joint** is a place in the body where two bones come together. For example, your elbow and your shoulder are two joints that move when you raise your hand.

Making Movement Happen Muscles make bones move at their joints. Try standing on one leg and bending the other leg at the knee. Hold that position. You can feel that you are using the muscles at the back of your thigh. Now straighten your leg. You can feel the muscles in the back of your leg relax, but the muscles in the front of your leg are at work. Your nervous system controls when and how your muscles act on your bones. You will read more about the nervous system later in this lesson.

apply it!

❶ **Interpret Diagrams** Circle three of the football player's joints.

❷ **Compare and Contrast** Describe how your shoulder and elbow move in different ways.

_____

_____

_____

❸ **CHALLENGE** From a standing position, bend down and grab your ankles. List six places or joints where your skeleton bends.

_____

_____

Lab zone® Do the Lab Investigation *A Look Beneath the Skin.*

🔑 Assess Your Understanding

got it? ....

○ **I get it!** Now I know that _____ and _____ work together to make the body move.

○ **I need extra help with** _____

Go to **my science** 🔵 **coach** *online for help with this subject.*

Which Systems Move Materials in Your Body?

The trillions of cells that make up your body need materials to function. Cells also produce wastes that must be removed. If the processes of moving these materials were made into a movie, your nervous system would be the director. The movie set would include the muscular and skeletal systems. And the main characters would be some of your other systems. 🔑 **The circulatory, respiratory, digestive, and excretory systems play key roles in moving materials in your body.**

Transporting Materials

Your circulatory system includes your heart, blood vessels, and blood. Blood vessels are found throughout your body. Blood that flows through these vessels carries materials such as water, oxygen, and food to every cell, as shown in **Figure 2**. Materials that your cells must get rid of, such as carbon dioxide and other cell wastes, are also moved through the body in the blood.

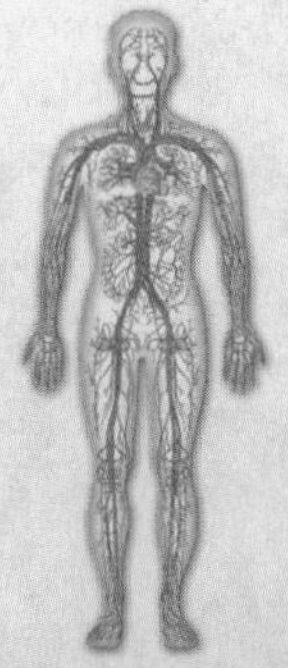

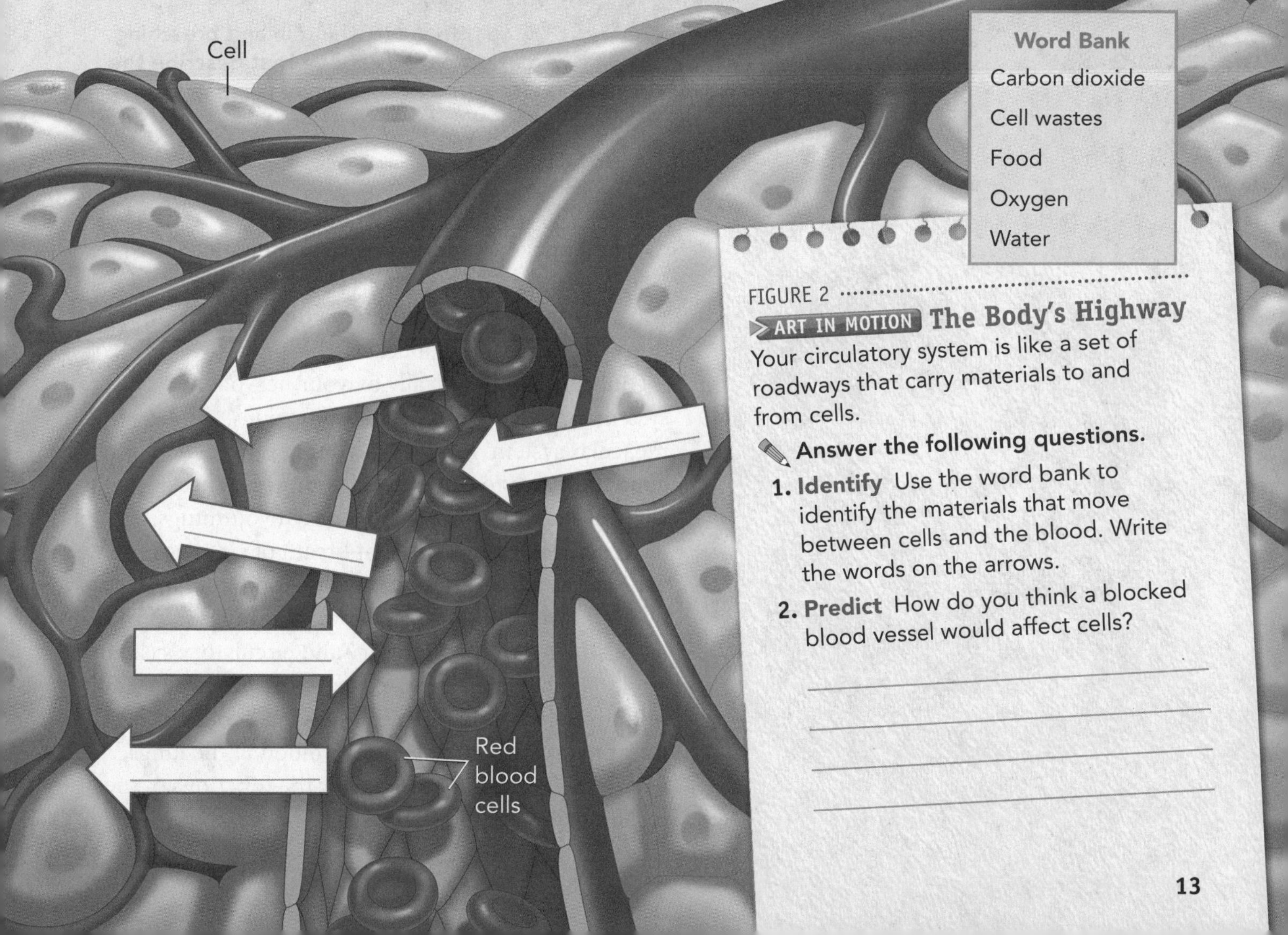

Blood vessel

Cell

Red blood cells

Word Bank

Carbon dioxide

Cell wastes

Food

Oxygen

Water

FIGURE 2 ....

> ART IN MOTION **The Body's Highway**

Your circulatory system is like a set of roadways that carry materials to and from cells.

✏️ **Answer the following questions.**

1. **Identify** Use the word bank to identify the materials that move between cells and the blood. Write the words on the arrows.

2. **Predict** How do you think a blocked blood vessel would affect cells?

_____

_____

_____

13

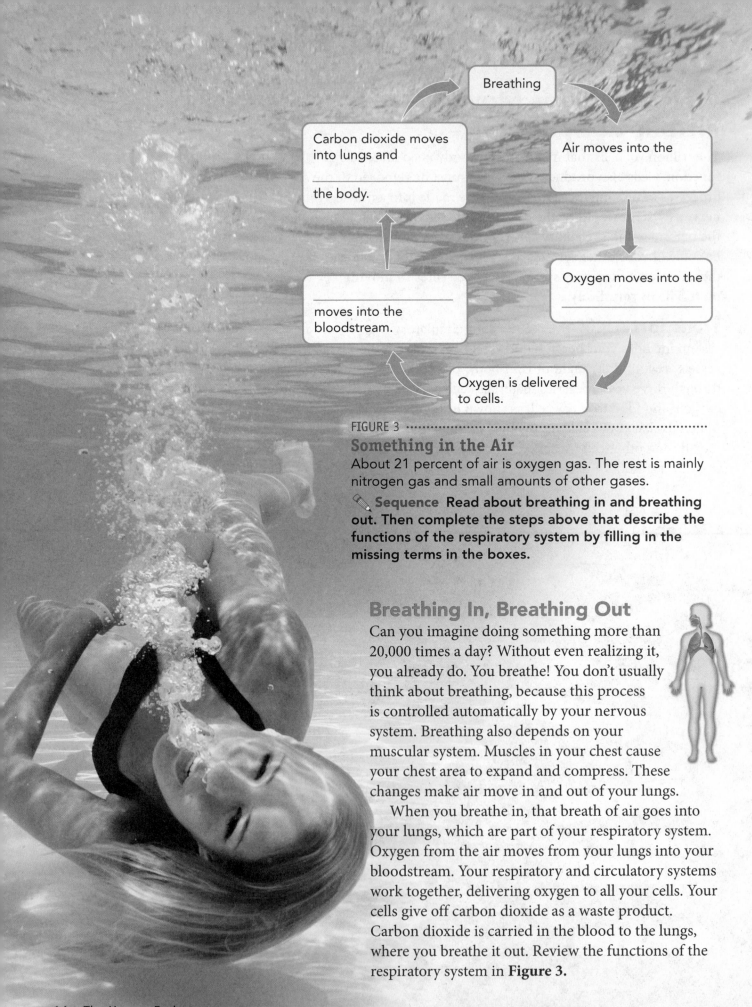

Breathing

Carbon dioxide moves into lungs and
_____
the body.

Air moves into the
_____

_____
moves into the bloodstream.

Oxygen moves into the
_____

Oxygen is delivered to cells.

FIGURE 3 ···

Something in the Air
About 21 percent of air is oxygen gas. The rest is mainly nitrogen gas and small amounts of other gases.

✎ **Sequence Read about breathing in and breathing out. Then complete the steps above that describe the functions of the respiratory system by filling in the missing terms in the boxes.**

Breathing In, Breathing Out

Can you imagine doing something more than 20,000 times a day? Without even realizing it, you already do. You breathe! You don't usually think about breathing, because this process is controlled automatically by your nervous system. Breathing also depends on your muscular system. Muscles in your chest cause your chest area to expand and compress. These changes make air move in and out of your lungs.

When you breathe in, that breath of air goes into your lungs, which are part of your respiratory system. Oxygen from the air moves from your lungs into your bloodstream. Your respiratory and circulatory systems work together, delivering oxygen to all your cells. Your cells give off carbon dioxide as a waste product. Carbon dioxide is carried in the blood to the lungs, where you breathe it out. Review the functions of the respiratory system in **Figure 3**.

Getting Food

Your respiratory system takes in oxygen, and your circulatory system delivers it to your cells. Oxygen is used in cells to release energy from sugar molecules that come from the food you eat. But how do sugar molecules get to your cells? Your digestive system helps to break down foods into sugars and other nutrient molecules that your body can use. A **nutrient** is a substance that you get from food and that your body needs to carry out processes, such as contracting muscles. Through a process called **absorption,** nutrients move from the digestive system into the bloodstream. The circulatory system then delivers the nutrients to all the cells in your body. In this way, your digestive system and circulatory system work together to get food to your cells.

Moving Wastes

The excretory system eliminates wastes from your body. Your respiratory, circulatory, and digestive systems all have roles in the excretory system. You already read that carbon dioxide passes from the circulatory system into the respiratory system and leaves the body when you exhale. Other cellular wastes also pass into the blood. These wastes are filtered out of the blood by the kidneys. This process produces urine, which then carries the wastes out of your body. Materials that are not used by the digestive system leave the body as solid waste.

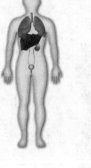

Vocabulary Suffixes The names of three body systems contain the suffix *-atory* or *-etory*, which both mean "of, or pertaining to." Circle the name of each of these systems once in the text on this page. Then underline sentences that describe what these systems do.

Lab zone® Do the Quick Lab *Working Together, Act I.*

🔑 Assess Your Understanding

1a. List Name four body systems that are involved in getting oxygen to your cells.

_____

_____

b. Explain How is absorption an important function of the digestive system?

_____

_____

_____

c. Draw Conclusions How does the circulatory system help other systems function?

_____

_____

_____

_____

_____

_____

_____

got it? ....

O **I get it!** Now I know that materials are moved within my body by the _____

_____

O I need extra help with _____

Go to MY SCIENCE ⓢ COACH *online for help with this subject.*

Which Systems Control Body Functions?

To function properly, each part of your body must be able to communicate with other parts of your body. For example, if you hear a phone ring, that message must be sent to your brain. Your brain then directs your muscles to move your bones so you can answer the phone. These actions are controlled by the nervous system, which is made up of the brain, spinal cord, and nerves. In your nervous system, information travels through nerve cells.

Other messages are sent by chemical signals that are produced by the endocrine system. The endocrine system is made up of organs called **glands** that release chemical signals directly into the bloodstream. For example, when you exercise, your endocrine system sends signals that make you perspire, or sweat. As sweat evaporates, it helps you cool down. 🔑 **The nervous system and the endocrine system work together to control body functions.**

Nervous System Your eyes, ears, skin, nose, and taste buds send information about your environment to your nervous system. Your senses let you react to bright light, hot objects, and freshly baked cookies. A signal in the environment that makes you react is called a **stimulus** (plural *stimuli*). A **response** is what your body does in reaction to a stimulus. Responses are directed by your nervous system but often involve other body systems. For example, your muscular and skeletal systems help you reach for a cookie. And your digestive system releases saliva before the cookie even reaches your mouth.

FIGURE 4 ·······································

Stimulus and Response
Have you ever been startled by something unexpected?

✏️ **Use the pictures to complete these tasks.**

1. **Sequence** Use numbers 1, 2, and 3 to put the pictures in order.

2. **Explain** Use the terms *stimulus* and *response* to explain what happened.

_____

_____

_____

_____

_____

apply it!

Among the drugs that affect the nervous system, caffeine is one of the most commonly used worldwide. Caffeine is found in coffee, tea, soda, other beverages, and even in chocolate.

①Explain How does caffeine reach the brain after someone drinks a cup of coffee or tea? In your answer, be sure to identify the systems involved.

_____

_____

_____

②Infer Caffeine is addictive, which means that the body can become physically dependent on the drug. Which body system do you think would be most involved in an addiction? Explain your answer.

_____

_____

_____

Endocrine System The chemical signals released by the endocrine system are called **hormones.** Hormones are transported through your body by the circulatory system. These chemicals affect many body processes. For example, one hormone interacts with the excretory system and the circulatory system to control the amount of water in the bloodstream. Another hormone interacts with the digestive system and the circulatory system to control the amount of sugar in the bloodstream. Hormones also affect the reproductive systems of both males and females.

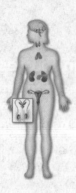

Lab zone® Do the Quick Lab
Working Together, Act II.

🔑 Assess Your Understanding

2a. Compare and Contrast How are the nervous system and the endocrine system different?

_____

_____

_____

_____

b. Apply Concepts Describe an example of a stimulus and response that involves your sense of hearing.

_____

_____

_____

_____

got it? ....

○ **I get it!** Now I know that the _____ system and _____ system work

together to _____

○ **I need extra help with** _____

Go to **MY SCIENCE ⑤ COACH** *online for help with this subject.*

Homeostasis

UNLOCK
THE BIG
?

🔑 **How Does Your Body Stay in Balance?**

my planet Diary

SCIENCE STATS

Worried Sick—Not Just an Expression

Starting in the 1980s, scientists began to gather
evidence that stress can affect the immune system.
For example, the graph below shows the relationship
between the length of time a person is stressed and the
risk of catching a cold when exposed to a virus. Today,
scientists know that high levels of stress and long periods
of stress can increase a person's risk for many diseases.
Therefore, managing stress is an important part of a healthy
lifestyle. Many activities, including hanging out with friends,
getting enough sleep, and exercising moderately, can help
lower stress levels.

Read Graphs Use the graph to answer the questions.

1. Summarize the information given in the graph.

_____

_____

_____

2. What do you do to manage stress?

_____

_____

▷ PLANET DIARY Go to **Planet Diary** to learn more about
homeostasis.

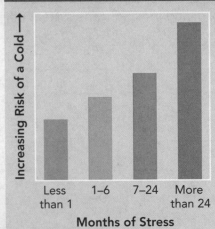

Stress and Catching a Cold

Increasing Risk of a Cold →

| Less than 1 | 1–6 | 7–24 | More than 24 |

Months of Stress

Lab®zone Do the Inquiry Warm-Up
Out of Balance.

Vocabulary
- homeostasis
- stress

Skills
- Reading: Relate Cause and Effect
- Inquiry: Communicate

How Does Your Body Stay in Balance?

It may be summer or winter. You may be indoors or outdoors. You may be running or sitting still. Regardless, your internal body temperature is almost exactly 37°C. The conditions outside your body may change. But the conditions inside your body stay stable, or steady. Most of these conditions, including the chemical makeup of your cells, their water content, and your body temperature, stay about the same.

Homeostasis The condition in which an organism's internal environment is kept stable in spite of changes in the outside environment is called **homeostasis**. Keeping this balance is necessary for an organism to function properly and survive. **All of your body systems working together maintain homeostasis and keep the body in balance.**

FIGURE 1 ·····················

Keeping Warm in the Cold
The clothes on this snowboarder help keep him warm. But his body is working hard, too. His nervous, circulatory, and muscular systems work together, keeping his body warm.

Describe Think of a time when you were really hot or really cold. Describe the changes you felt as your body adjusted to that condition.

_____

_____

_____

_____

_____

_____

_____

Maintaining Homeostasis
You experience homeostasis in action when you shiver, sweat, or feel hungry, full, or thirsty. Your nervous and endocrine systems control these responses. Other systems, including the digestive, respiratory, circulatory, and muscular systems, also play roles in your body's responses.

Regulating Temperature When you are cold, your nervous system signals your muscles to make you shiver. Shivering produces heat that helps keep you warm. As explained in the diagram below, when you warm up, shivering stops. When you are too warm, your endocrine system releases hormones that make you perspire. As the sweat evaporates, your body cools. The circulatory system and skin also help regulate temperature. Changes in the amount of blood flow in the skin can help prevent heat loss or carry heat away. In this way, your body temperature stays steady.

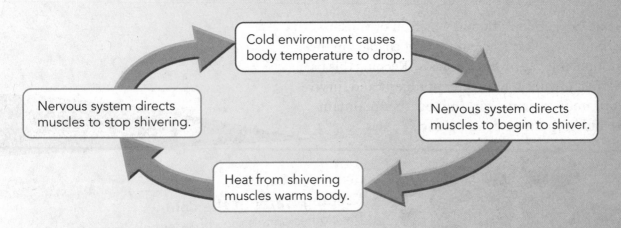

Cold environment causes body temperature to drop.

Nervous system directs muscles to begin to shiver.

Heat from shivering muscles warms body.

Nervous system directs muscles to stop shivering.

Meeting Energy Needs If your body needs more energy, hormones from the endocrine system signal the nervous system to make you feel hungry. After you eat, other hormones tell your brain to make you feel full. Other body systems are also involved. For example, your muscular system helps move food through your digestive system. Your respiratory system takes in the oxygen that is used in cells to release energy from food.

FIGURE 2 ·······························

Hungry or Not?
Signals between your nervous system and your digestive system control your feelings of hunger.

✎ **Sequence** Fill in the missing steps in the cycle diagram.

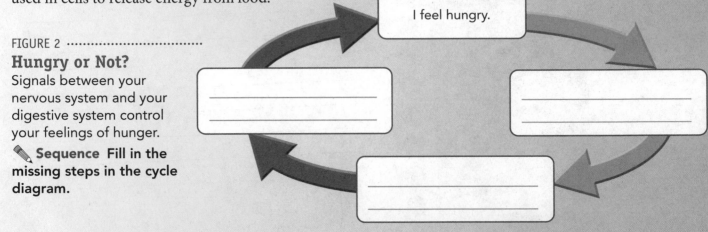

I feel hungry.

Maintaining Water Balance Life depends on water. All the chemical reactions that keep you alive happen within the watery environment of your cells. If your body needs more water, you feel thirsty. The water you drink passes from your digestive system into your circulatory system. Excess water leaves your body through your excretory system when you exhale, sweat, and urinate.

Keeping Your Balance You know that you hear with your ears. But did you know your ears also help you keep your balance? Structures in your inner ear sense the position of your head. They send this information to your brain, which interprets the signals. If your brain senses that you are losing your balance, it sends messages to your muscles to move in ways that help you stay steady, as in **Figure 3**.

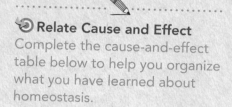

Relate Cause and Effect
Complete the cause-and-effect table below to help you organize what you have learned about homeostasis.

Cause	Effect
_____ _____	Shivers
Body gets overheated.	_____
Body needs more energy.	_____
_____ _____ _____	Thirst

FIGURE 3 ·······

Balancing Act
Signals from this diver's ears to her brain lead to movements that help her balance on the edge of the diving board.

✎ **Name** What systems of the diver's body play a role in keeping her balanced on her toes?

_____

_____

_____

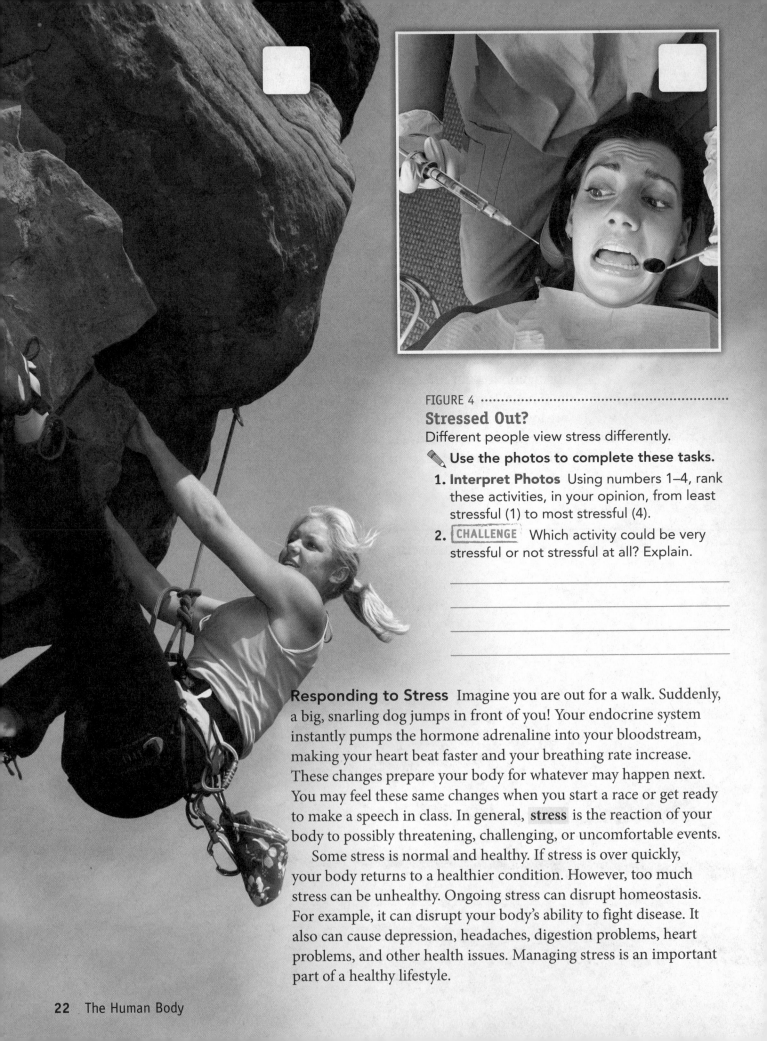

FIGURE 4 ···

Stressed Out?

Different people view stress differently.

✎ **Use the photos to complete these tasks.**

1. **Interpret Photos** Using numbers 1–4, rank these activities, in your opinion, from least stressful (1) to most stressful (4).

2. **CHALLENGE** Which activity could be very stressful or not stressful at all? Explain.

_____

_____

_____

_____

Responding to Stress Imagine you are out for a walk. Suddenly, a big, snarling dog jumps in front of you! Your endocrine system instantly pumps the hormone adrenaline into your bloodstream, making your heart beat faster and your breathing rate increase. These changes prepare your body for whatever may happen next. You may feel these same changes when you start a race or get ready to make a speech in class. In general, **stress** is the reaction of your body to possibly threatening, challenging, or uncomfortable events.

Some stress is normal and healthy. If stress is over quickly, your body returns to a healthier condition. However, too much stress can be unhealthy. Ongoing stress can disrupt homeostasis. For example, it can disrupt your body's ability to fight disease. It also can cause depression, headaches, digestion problems, heart problems, and other health issues. Managing stress is an important part of a healthy lifestyle.

apply it!

△ Communicate A soccer game, a music recital, a class presentation, and many other events can cause stress. Think of an event from your life when you felt stress. Describe how your body responded during the event, and then after the event or when the stress went away.

_____

_____

_____

_____

_____

_____

_____

_____

_____

_____

_____

_____

_____

_____

Fighting Disease When your body systems are in balance, you are healthy. However, bacteria and viruses that cause disease can disrupt homeostasis and make you sick. Think about the last time you had a cold or influenza (the flu). You may have had a fever and less energy. You also may have slept more than usual. Over a few days, your immune system probably fought off the disease.

The immune system includes specialized cells that can attack and destroy viruses. When you are sick, these cells temporarily increase in number. Fighting infection sometimes causes your body temperature to go up. It also uses extra energy. As you get well, your fever goes away and your energy comes back. If you are sick for more than a few days, you may need medical attention to help your body fight the infection and become healthy again.

Systems in Action

How does your body work?

FIGURE 5 ··

> **REAL-WORLD INQUIRY** The body systems of this runner work together as she pushes herself to excel.

✎ **Apply Concepts** Read the descriptions of functions happening in the runner's body. Then identify the main systems involved.

Sweat appears on the surface of the runner's skin, and carbon dioxide moves rapidly out of her lungs. Cell wastes move into her blood and are filtered by her kidneys.

_____

_____

_____

Food from the runner's breakfast has been broken down into nutrients and is delivered to cells.

_____

_____

_____

The runner's brain interprets what her eyes see and directs her movements.

_____

_____

_____

Hormones move through the runner's bloodstream, stimulating her body systems to work harder.

_____

_____

The runner's breathing rate and heart rate increase, supplying more oxygen to her muscle cells.

_____

_____

_____

The runner's legs lift her off the ground and over the hurdle.

_____

_____

_____

Lab zone ® Do the Quick Lab *Working to Maintain Balance.*

🔑 Assess Your Understanding

1a. Define What is homeostasis?

_____

_____

_____

_____

b. List Give four examples of conditions in your body that are related to maintaining homeostasis.

_____

_____

_____

c. Relate Cause and Effect Give an example of how stress can affect homeostasis.

_____

_____

_____

_____

d. ANSWER THE BIG **?** How does your body work? Use what you have learned about how your body systems function to write your answer.

_____

_____

_____

_____

_____

got it? ······························

○ **I get it!** Now I know that maintaining

homeostasis depends on _____

_____

○ **I need extra help with** _____

Go to MY SCIENCE ⑤ COACH *online for help with this subject.*

Study Guide

REVIEW THE BIG ?

Cells, tissues, and organs make up organ _____ , which constantly

help maintain _____ .

LESSON 1 Body Organization

🔑 The levels of organization in the human body consist of cells, tissues, organs, and organ systems.

Vocabulary
- cell • cell membrane • nucleus
- cytoplasm • tissue • muscle tissue
- nervous tissue • connective tissue
- epithelial tissue • organ • organ system

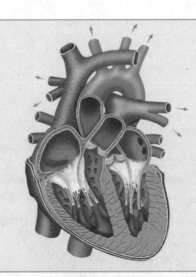

LESSON 2 System Interactions

🔑 Muscles, bones, and nerves work together to make your body move.
🔑 The circulatory, respiratory, digestive, and excretory systems play key roles in moving materials in your body.
🔑 The nervous system and the endocrine system work together to control body functions.

Vocabulary
- skeleton • skeletal muscle • joint • nutrient
- absorption • gland • stimulus • response
- hormone

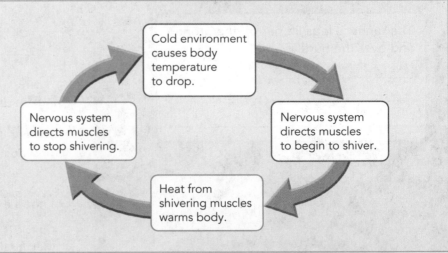

LESSON 3 Homeostasis

🔑 All of your body systems working together maintain homeostasis and keep the body in balance.

Vocabulary
- homeostasis
- stress

Cold environment causes body temperature to drop.

Nervous system directs muscles to begin to shiver.

Heat from shivering muscles warms body.

Nervous system directs muscles to stop shivering.

Review and Assessment

LESSON 1 **Body Organization**

1. Bone tissue and fat tissue are examples of

   a. muscle tissue.   **b.** nervous tissue.

   c. epithelial tissue.   **d.** connective tissue.

2. The _____ forms the

outside border of a cell.

3. Sequence Use numbers 1 through 5 to label the diagrams below in order of smallest to largest levels of organization.

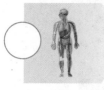

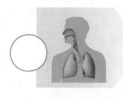

4. Compare and Contrast How is a tissue different from an organ? How are they similar?

_____

_____

_____

_____

_____

5. [Write About It] Scientists classify blood as connective tissue. On a separate paper, explain why you think blood is classified as a tissue.

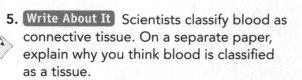

LESSON 2 **System Interactions**

6. Signals from the _____

make skeletal muscles move.

   a. nervous system   **b.** digestive system

   c. respiratory system   **d.** muscular system

7. A _____ is a chemical

signal that can control one or more body

processes.

8. Infer Your knee is called a hinge joint. What is another joint that works like a hinge?

_____

9. Apply Concepts Pick one material that is moved within the body by the organ systems. Describe which systems are involved and how they work together.

_____

_____

_____

_____

_____

10. Interpret Diagrams Describe how the nervous system functions in the situation shown below.

_____

_____

_____

_____

27

Review and Assessment

Homeostasis

11. Under what circumstances would your endocrine system release adrenaline?

a. sleep   **b.** sudden stress

c. absorption   **d.** homeostasis

12. Your body systems work together to maintain internal conditions, or

_____

13. Read Graphs According to the graph below, how do changes in environmental temperature affect skin temperature and internal body temperature?

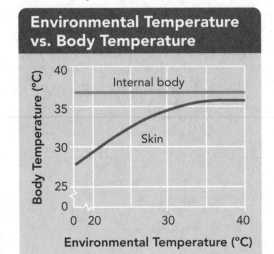

Environmental Temperature vs. Body Temperature

_____
_____
_____
_____

14. [**Write About It**] Imagine you are leading a workshop to help students deal with stress. Tell why managing stress matters, and describe three suggestions for stress management.

How does your body work?

15. Describe how the body systems of this boy function during and after the time he eats his lunch. Use at least four different body systems in your answer.

_____
_____
_____
_____
_____
_____
_____
_____
_____
_____
_____
_____
_____
_____

Standardized Test Prep

Multiple Choice

Circle the letter of the best answer.

1. Which term best fits the level of organization pictured in the diagram below?

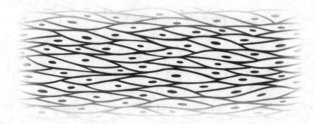

   A organ
   B tissue
   C single cell
   D organ system

2. What is one way that stress can affect homeostasis?

   A disrupts ability to fight disease
   B increases water balance
   C maintains constant internal temperature
   D decreases signals from the inner ear to the brain to help with balance

3. Which two systems work together to respond to internal and external conditions and to control body functions?

   A skeletal and muscular systems
   B endocrine and nervous systems
   C muscular and digestive systems
   D respiratory and circulatory systems

4. When the muscles at the back of your thigh contract, your leg is _____, and when the muscles in the front of your thigh contract, your leg is _____.

   A bent; bent
   B straight; straight
   C bent; straight
   D straight; bent

5. Which body systems are involved in the maintenance of homeostasis?

   A all organ systems
   B nervous and endocrine systems only
   C nervous, endocrine, and respiratory systems only
   D nervous, endocrine, excretory, and respiratory systems only

Constructed Response

Copy the flowchart below on a separate piece of paper. Use your knowledge of body organization to help you answer Question 6.

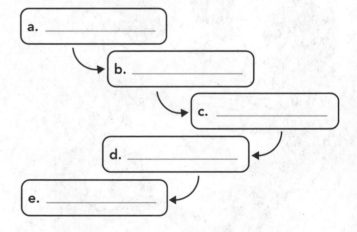

6. Construct a flowchart showing the levels of organization in an organism from the least complex to the most complex. Then explain how the terms in your flowchart are related.

ON PINS AND NEEDLES

It happens all the time—you are watching a movie, or sitting in class, and you realize your leg has "fallen asleep." At first it's numb, and you may have trouble moving it. But gradually, the sensation of feeling comes back—painfully. Your leg feels like it's being poked with pins and needles!

When a body part, such as your arm or leg, falls asleep, your nervous system is not working properly. A nerve or several nerves have been compressed. The pins and needles are a sort of warning sign. Eventually, a compressed nerve could become damaged.

How does this warning sign work? Nerves carry sensory information to your brain. They also carry signals that control the movement of body parts. When your leg or arm is compressed, these signals are disrupted and your limb "falls asleep."

At first, nerve cells send confused sensory information to the brain. But gradually, the nerve cells stop sending signals, making your limb numb. When you move and the pathways between your brain and your limb start working again, your nerves become very excitable. The more you stimulate them—by moving or shaking a sleeping limb—the more excitable the nerves become. The very excitable nerves cause the feeling of "pins and needles."

Research It Pins and needles can sometimes be a sign of more serious nervous system problems. Research one condition, such as carpal tunnel syndrome, that can cause this symptom. Make a pamphlet describing prevention, warning signs, and treatment of the condition.

THE BIG CHILL

When a person's body temperature falls dramatically for long enough, the body loses its ability to maintain homeostasis. The body's core temperature then begins to drop—a condition called hypothermia.

When the body loses more heat than it can generate, it starts to shiver. Shivering generates some heat and may bring the body's temperature back up. But shivering uses a lot of energy. If the body's temperature keeps falling, the person will stop shivering and lose consciousness.

To protect the organs, the body slows down all its systems. Less blood circulates to the arms and legs, metabolism in the cells slows down, and the heart beats more slowly. Hypothermia can be deadly. If the person keeps losing body heat, the heart eventually stops. But doctors are now realizing that hypothermia can also save lives!

When a person suffers a heart attack, blood is blocked from circulating, so it cannot carry oxygen to cells. Oxygen starvation can damage the body's tissues—including tissues in the brain—permanently. But when a person has hypothermia, the person's core body temperature drops, and the person's cells use less oxygen. Doctors are using this knowledge to protect brain cells during a heart attack. Doctors lower a patient's body temperature, giving the patient hypothermia. As a result, the cells need less oxygen and may suffer less damage. So, if doctors can induce, or cause hypothermia on purpose, they might just be able to save the cells—and the patient!

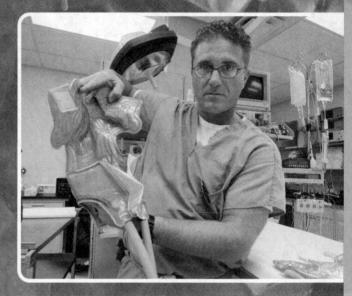

▲ As part of the process of causing hypothermia, doctors use a helmet filled with cooling gel to wrap a patient's head and neck.

Research It Doctors must be very careful when they induce hypothermia in a patient. List three questions you think doctors must consider before they begin the process. Research the answers and report them on a poster.

HOW CAN THE GYMNAST HOLD THIS POSITION?

THE BIG ?

What holds your body together?

Years of training are required to perfect a pose like this L-cross on the still rings. Once in position, this athlete must hold his pose without moving for two seconds. That doesn't seem like a long time, but it requires tremendous strength and endurance.

Infer Look at the photo. What parts of the athlete's body work together to hold this difficult position?

_____

_____

_____

_____

_____

_____

_____

> **UNTAMED SCIENCE** Watch the **Untamed Science** video to learn more about bones, muscles, and skin.

Bones, Muscles, and Skin

2 Getting Started

Check Your Understanding

1. Background Read the paragraph below and then answer the question.

Cid is late. He hastily dresses and sprints to the bus. To make it, the organ systems in his body must work efficiently. But as he is getting on the bus, he trips and falls. Fortunately, when he gently moves his arm to test his bones and muscles, they feel sore but function without pain.

An **organ system** is a group of organs that work together, performing major jobs.

Muscle is the type of tissue that makes it possible for your body to move.

To **function** is to serve a certain purpose or perform a certain role.

- How did Cid determine that the fall did not harm the functioning of his bones and muscles?

_____

_____

_____

> MY READING WEB If you had trouble completing the question above, visit **My Reading Web** and type in *Bones, Muscles, and Skin*.

Vocabulary Skill

Latin Word Parts Some terms in this chapter contain word parts with Latin origins. The table below lists some of the Latin words that terms in this chapter come from.

Latin Word	Meaning of Latin Word	Term
in-	not	involuntary, *adj.* not consciously controlled
voluntas	free will	voluntary, *adj.* controlled by one's mind or will

2. Quick Check The terms *involuntary* and *voluntary* both come from the Latin word *voluntas*. Circle the meaning of *voluntas* in the table above.

joint

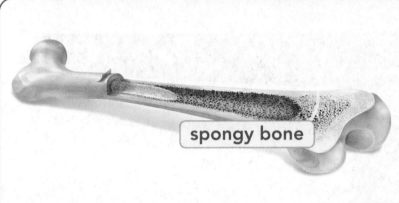
spongy bone

smooth muscle

epidermis

Chapter Preview

LESSON 1
- skeleton
- vertebrae
- joint
- ligament
- compact bone
- spongy bone
- marrow
- cartilage
- osteoporosis
- ↻ **Summarize**
- △ **Classify**

LESSON 2
- involuntary muscle
- voluntary muscle
- skeletal muscle
- tendon
- smooth muscle
- cardiac muscle
- striated muscle
- ↻ **Compare and Contrast**
- △ **Infer**

LESSON 3
- epidermis
- melanin
- dermis
- pore
- follicle
- cancer
- ↻ **Relate Cause and Effect**
- △ **Observe**

> **VOCAB FLASH CARDS** For extra help with vocabulary, visit **Vocab Flash Cards** and type in *Bones, Muscles, and Skin.*

The Skeletal System

UNLOCK THE BIG ?

🔑 **What Does the Skeleton Do?**

🔑 **What Role Do Joints Play?**

🔑 **What Are the Characteristics of Bones?**

my pLaneT DiaRY

FUN FACTS

Know Your Bones!

Here are some fascinating facts you may not know about your bones.

- You have the same number of bones in your neck as a giraffe. However, a single bone in the neck of a giraffe can be as long as 25 centimeters.

- You have 27 bones in each hand and 26 bones in each foot. They account for 106 of the 206 bones in your body.

- You do not have a funny bone. You have a sensitive spot on your elbow where a nerve passes close to the skin. If you hit this spot, the area feels funny.

- No one is truly "double-jointed." People who are able to twist in weird directions have very flexible joints.

Communicate Discuss the question with a partner. Then write your answer below.

Why do you think it is helpful for your hand to have 27 bones?

_____

_____

_____

_____

_____

_____

> PLANET DIARY Go to **Planet Diary** to learn more about bones.

Lab zone Do the Inquiry Warm-Up *Hard as a Rock?*

Vocabulary
- skeleton • vertebrae • joint • ligament
- compact bone • spongy bone • marrow
- cartilage • osteoporosis

Skills
- ↻ Reading: Summarize
- △ Inquiry: Classify

What Does the Skeleton Do?

If you have ever visited a construction site, you have seen workers assemble steel pieces into a rigid frame for a building. Once the building is finished, this framework is invisible.

Like a building, you have an inner framework. Your framework, or **skeleton,** is made up of all the bones in your body. Just as a building would fall without its frame, you would collapse without your skeleton. 🔑 **Your skeleton has five major functions. It provides shape and support, enables you to move, and protects your organs. It also produces blood cells and stores minerals and other materials until your body needs them.**

Shape and Support Your skeleton shapes and supports your body. It is made up of about 206 bones of different shapes and sizes. Your backbone, or vertebral column, is the center of your skeleton. A total of 26 small bones, or **vertebrae** (VUR tuh bray) (singular *vertebra*), make up your backbone. **Figure 1** shows how vertebrae connect to form the backbone or vertebral column.

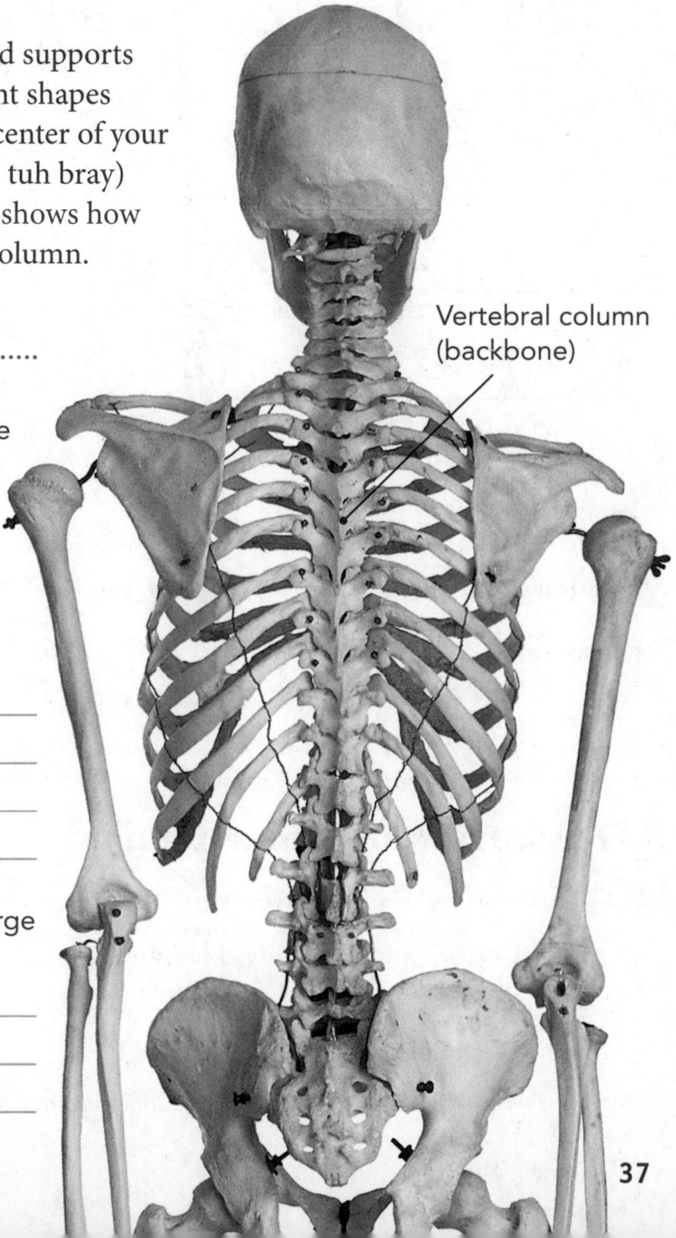

FIGURE 1 ···

The Vertebral Column

Just like a flexible necklace of beads, your vertebrae move against each other, allowing you to bend and twist.

✏️ **Use the photo to answer the questions about your vertebrae.**

1. **Interpret Photos** Which body parts does the vertebral column support?

_____

_____

_____

2. CHALLENGE What is the advantage of having large vertebrae at the base of the vertebral column?

_____

_____

_____

Vertebral column (backbone)

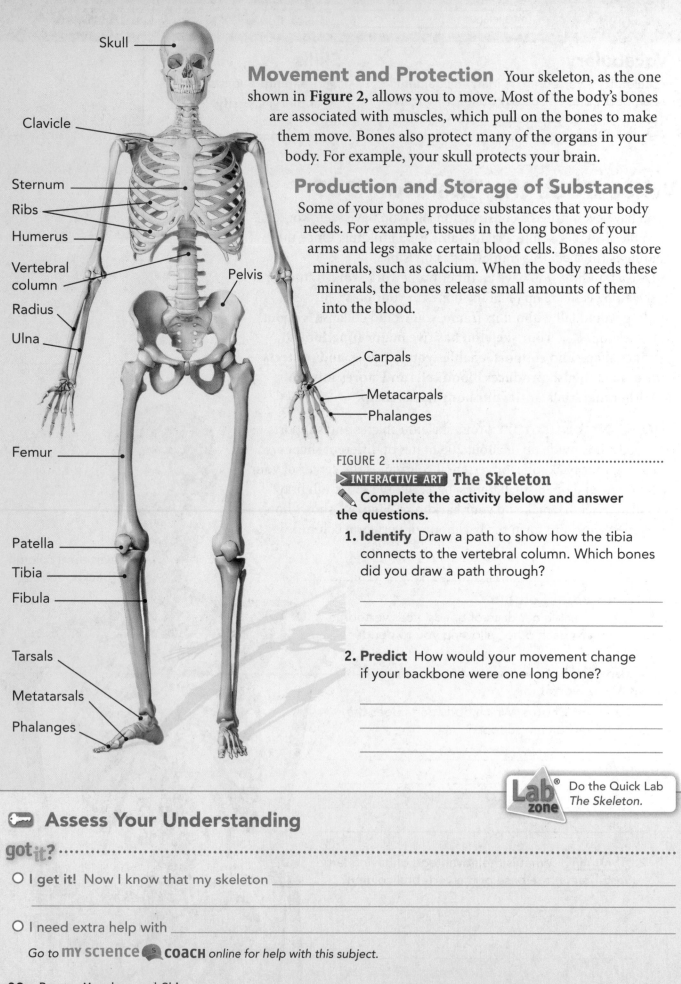

Skull

Clavicle

Sternum

Ribs

Humerus

Vertebral column

Radius

Ulna

Pelvis

Carpals

Metacarpals

Phalanges

Femur

Patella

Tibia

Fibula

Tarsals

Metatarsals

Phalanges

Movement and Protection
Your skeleton, as the one shown in **Figure 2**, allows you to move. Most of the body's bones are associated with muscles, which pull on the bones to make them move. Bones also protect many of the organs in your body. For example, your skull protects your brain.

Production and Storage of Substances
Some of your bones produce substances that your body needs. For example, tissues in the long bones of your arms and legs make certain blood cells. Bones also store minerals, such as calcium. When the body needs these minerals, the bones release small amounts of them into the blood.

FIGURE 2 ···

> INTERACTIVE ART The Skeleton

✎ **Complete the activity below and answer the questions.**

1. **Identify** Draw a path to show how the tibia connects to the vertebral column. Which bones did you draw a path through?

_____

_____

2. **Predict** How would your movement change if your backbone were one long bone?

_____

_____

_____

Lab zone® Do the Quick Lab *The Skeleton.*

🔑 Assess Your Understanding

got it? ···

○ **I get it!** Now I know that my skeleton _____

_____

○ **I need extra help with** _____

Go to MY SCIENCE ⓢ COACH online for help with this subject.

What Role Do Joints Play?

If your leg had only one long bone, how would you get out of bed? Luckily, your leg has many bones so you can move it easily. A **joint** is a place where two bones come together. 🗝 **Joints allow bones to move in different ways.** You have two kinds of joints: immovable and movable.

Immovable Joints Immovable joints connect bones but allow little or no movement. The bones of the skull are held together by immovable joints.

Movable Joints Most joints are movable. They allow the body to make many different movements such as those shown in **Figure 3.** The bones in movable joints are held together by **ligaments,** which are made of strong connective tissue.

Infer What would happen if your skull bones had movable joints?

_____

_____

_____

_____

FIGURE 3 ·······················

▷ **INTERACTIVE ART** **Movable Joints**
Movable joints allow you to move in different ways.

✎ **Classify** **Write the name of another joint of each type on the line in each box.**

Ball-and-Socket Joint
This joint allows the greatest range of motion. Your hip has a ball-and-socket joint that allows you to swing your leg in a circle.

_____

Hinge Joint
This joint allows forward or backward motion. Your knee is a hinge joint that allows you to bend and straighten your leg.

_____

Pivot Joint
This joint allows one bone to rotate around another bone. You use this joint to turn your arm at your elbow side-to-side.

_____

Gliding Joint
This joint allows one bone to slide over another. Your wrist has a gliding joint that allows it to bend and flex.

_____

Without movable joints, your body would be as stiff as a board.

1 Observe Perform each activity below. Write the type of joint you use.

Move your arm from the shoulder in a circle. _____

Move your wrist to wave. _____

Turn your head from side to side. _____

2 Classify In the chart, write the name of the type of joint each object has.

3 Apply Concepts What type of joint do you have in your toes? Explain your answer.

_____

_____

Object	Type of Joint
Book	_____
Sliding Door	_____
Steering Wheel	_____

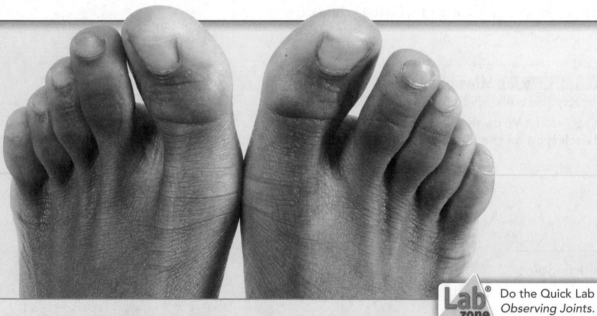

Lab zone® Do the Quick Lab
Observing Joints.

🔑 Assess Your Understanding

1a. Explain Why does your body need both immovable and movable joints?

_____

_____

_____

_____

b. Relate Cause and Effect How would your legs move if your knees were ball-and-socket joints?

_____

_____

_____

_____

got it? ....

○ **I get it!** Now I know that joints _____

_____

○ **I need extra help with** _____

   Go to **my science COACH** *online for help with this subject.*

What Are the Characteristics of Bones?

The word *skeleton* comes from the Greek words meaning "a dried body." This suggests that a skeleton is dead, but bones are not dead at all. 🔑 **Bones are complex living structures that grow, develop, and repair themselves. Bones are also strong and lightweight.**

Bones are made up of bone tissue, blood vessels, and nerves. A thin, tough outer membrane covers all of a typical bone except the ends. Beneath the membrane is a thick layer of **compact bone,** which is hard and dense but not solid. Compact bone contains minerals that give bones strength. Small canals in the compact bone carry blood vessels and nerves from the bone's surface to its living cells.

Long bones, such as the femur in **Figure 4,** have a layer of spongy bone at the ends and under the compact bone. The small spaces within **spongy bone** make it lightweight but still strong. Bone also has two types of soft connective tissue called **marrow.** Red bone marrow fills the spaces in some of your spongy bone. It produces most of your blood cells. Yellow bone marrow is found in a space in the middle of the bone. It stores fat.

FIGURE 4 ·······················

Bone Structure

Many tissues make up the femur, the body's longest bone.

✎ **Relate Text and Visuals** Write notes to describe each part of the bone and what it does.

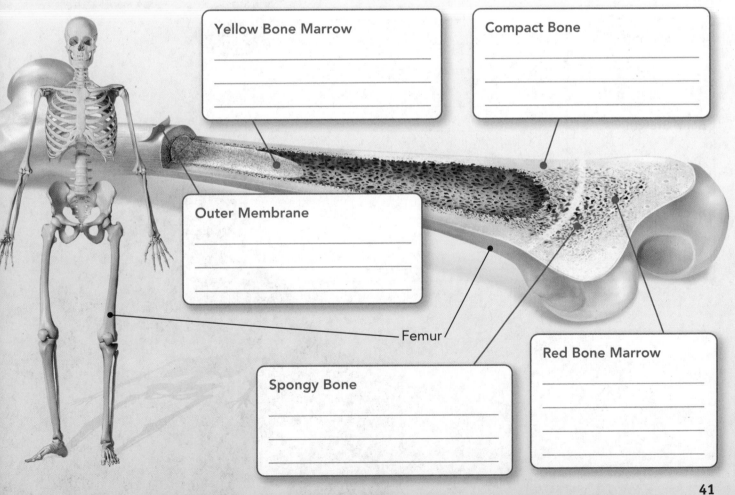

Yellow Bone Marrow
_____
_____
_____

Compact Bone
_____
_____
_____

Outer Membrane
_____
_____
_____

Femur

Spongy Bone
_____
_____
_____

Red Bone Marrow
_____
_____
_____
_____

41

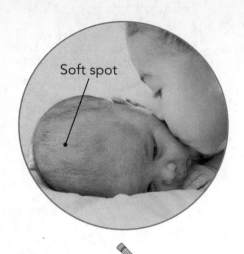

Soft spot

Infer Infants are born with soft spots in their skull made out of cartilage. What do you think happens to soft spots over time?

_____

_____

⊘ Summarize Write a summary about the characteristics of bones.

Bone Strength Bone is both strong and lightweight. Bones can absorb more force without breaking than concrete or granite rock can. Yet bones weigh much less than those materials. In fact, only about 20 percent of an average adult's body weight is bone. Bone feels as hard as a rock because it is made of tightly packed minerals—mainly phosphorus and calcium.

Bone Growth Because bones are alive, they form new bone tissue as you grow. Your bones are growing longer now, making you taller. Even after you are fully grown, bone tissue continues to form. For example, every time you play soccer or basketball, some of your bones absorb the force of your weight. They respond by making new bone tissue. New bone tissue also forms when a bone breaks.

Bone Development When you were born, most of your bones were cartilage. **Cartilage** is a strong connective tissue that is more flexible than bone. As you grew, most of that cartilage was replaced with bone. Some cartilage still protects the ends of your bones. You also have cartilage in your ears and at the tip of your nose.

Bone Strength	_____
	_____
	_____
Bone Growth	_____
	_____
	_____
Bone Development	_____
	_____
	_____

Healthy Bones A combination of a balanced diet and regular exercise are important for healthy bones. A balanced diet includes foods that contain enough calcium and phosphorus to keep your bones strong while they are growing. You should eat dairy products; meats; whole grains; and green, leafy vegetables.

Exercise helps build and maintain strong bones. During activities such as running and dancing, your bones support the weight of your entire body. These weight-bearing activities help your bones grow stronger. However, to prevent injury, always wear appropriate safety equipment when exercising.

As you age, your bones start to lose some minerals. This mineral loss can lead to **osteoporosis** (ahs tee oh puh ROH sis), a condition in which bones become weak and break easily. You can see how osteoporosis causes the spaces in a bone to become larger, reducing its density and strength in **Figure 5**.

FIGURE 5 ·······························

Osteoporosis

Regular exercise and a diet rich in calcium with vitamin D can help prevent osteoporosis later in life.

✏ **Compare and Contrast**
The photos show two bones. Label the healthy bone and the bone with osteoporosis. Then explain your choices.

_____

_____

_____

_____

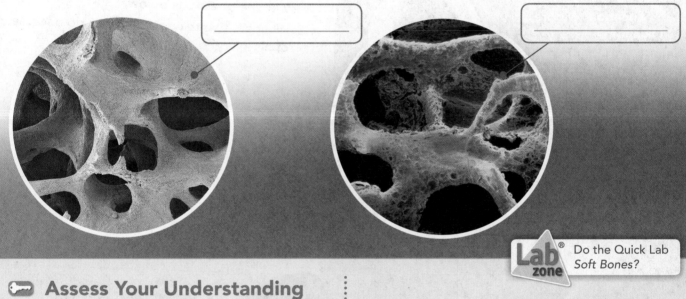

Lab zone®   Do the Quick Lab
Soft Bones?

🔑 Assess Your Understanding

2a. Explain How do eating a balanced diet and exercising regularly help your bones?

_____

_____

_____

b. Apply Concepts How do you know that bone is living tissue?

_____

_____

_____

got it?

O **I get it!** Now I know that my bones are _____

_____

_____

_____

_____

_____

O **I need extra help with** _____

Go to **MY SCIENCE** 🔵 **COACH** online for help with this subject.

The Muscular System

🔑 **What Muscles Are in Your Body?**

🔑 **How Do Skeletal Muscles Work?**

MY PLANET DIARY

BLOG

Posted by: Will

Location: Moore, Oklahoma

I hurt my shoulder while participating in tackling drills during football practice. The doctor said I had a deep muscle contusion, which is a bruise deep in a muscle. I was unable to lift my right arm for more than a week because of the injury. I had to take three tablets of ibuprofen every day for two weeks because it helped the swelling go down. I missed playing in only one game, and the pain eventually went away.

Answer the questions below.

1. What are two things Will had to do because of his injury?

_____

_____

_____

2. What can you do to avoid being injured when playing sports?

_____

_____

_____

_____

▶ PLANET DIARY Go to **Planet Diary** to learn more about muscles.

Lab zone® Do the Inquiry Warm-Up *How Do Muscles Work?*

Vocabulary

- involuntary muscle
- voluntary muscle
- skeletal muscle
- tendon
- smooth muscle
- cardiac muscle
- striated muscle

Skills

↺ Reading: Compare and Contrast

△ Inquiry: Infer

What Muscles Are in Your Body?

Try to sit without moving any muscles. Can you do it? First, you probably need to breathe, so your chest expands to let air in. Then you swallow. Breathing and swallowing involve muscles, so it is impossible to sit still without any muscle movement.

Involuntary and Voluntary Muscles Some body movements, such as smiling, are easy to control. Other movements, such as breathing, are impossible to control completely. That is because some of your muscles are not under your conscious control. Those muscles are **involuntary muscles.** Involuntary muscles are responsible for other activities such as digesting food. The muscles under your conscious control are **voluntary muscles.** Smiling, writing, and getting out of your seat when the bell rings are all actions controlled by voluntary muscles.

FIGURE 1 ·······················

Muscle Use
Some muscles are voluntary and others are involuntary.

✎ **Relate Text and Visuals**
Write how the person in each frame is using involuntary and voluntary muscles.

	Frame 1	Frame 2	Frame 3
Involuntary			
Voluntary			

45

Types of Muscle Tissue

Your body has skeletal, smooth, and cardiac muscle tissues. Some of these muscle tissues are involuntary, and some are voluntary.

Skeletal muscles provide the force that moves your bones. A strong connective tissue called a **tendon** attaches the muscle to a bone. Because you have conscious control of skeletal muscles, they are classified as voluntary muscles. In contrast, the inside of many internal body organs, such as the stomach and blood vessels, contain **smooth muscle** tissue. These are involuntary muscles. They work to control certain movements inside your body, such as moving food through your digestive system. The tissue called **cardiac muscle** is found only in your heart. Like smooth muscle, cardiac muscle is involuntary. Look at **Figure 2.**

FIGURE 2 ·································

Muscle Tissue

You have three types of muscle tissue: skeletal, smooth, and cardiac.

✎ **Classify** In the table, identify the type of muscle tissue in each body structure.

Skeletal Muscle Skeletal muscle cells appear banded, or striated, so they are sometimes called **striated muscle** (STRY ay tid). Skeletal muscle allows your body to react quickly. However, it also tires quickly.

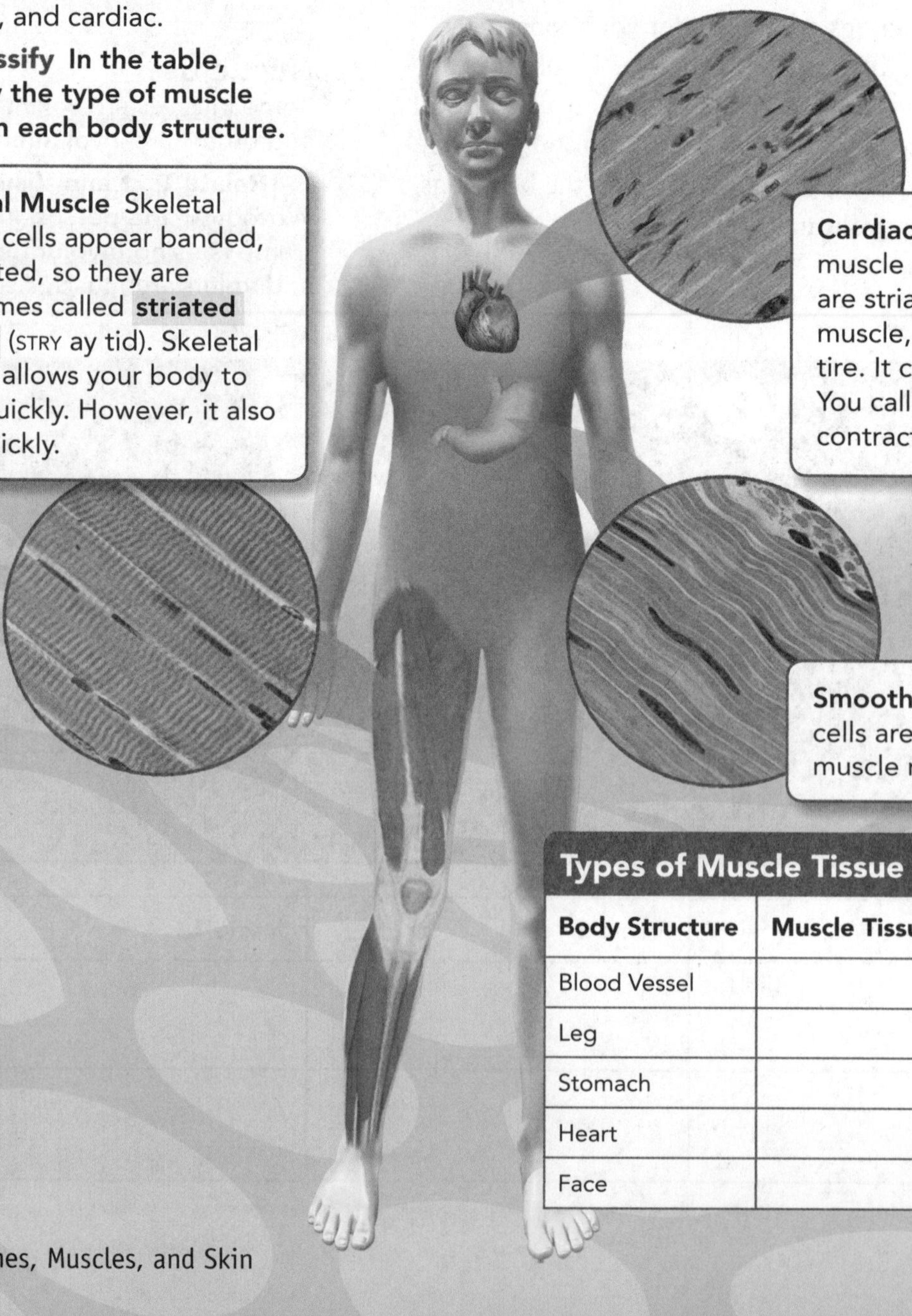

Cardiac Muscle Like skeletal muscle cells, cardiac muscle cells are striated. But unlike skeletal muscle, cardiac muscle does not tire. It can contract repeatedly. You call those repeated contractions heartbeats.

Smooth Muscle Smooth muscle cells are not striated. This type of muscle reacts and tires slowly.

Types of Muscle Tissue	
Body Structure	**Muscle Tissue**
Blood Vessel	
Leg	
Stomach	
Heart	
Face	

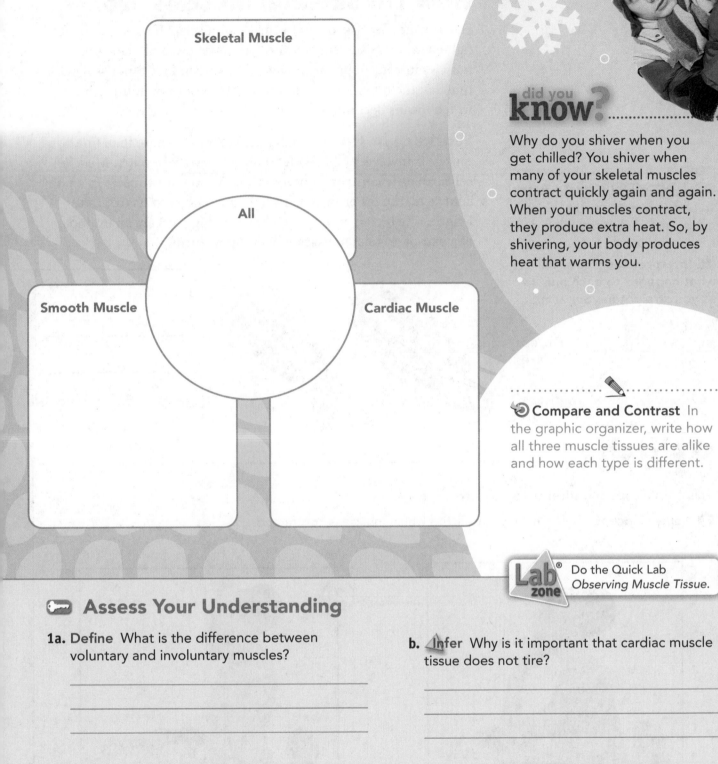

Skeletal Muscle

All

Smooth Muscle

Cardiac Muscle

..........................✏..........................

⟲ **Compare and Contrast** In the graphic organizer, write how all three muscle tissues are alike and how each type is different.

Lab zone® Do the Quick Lab *Observing Muscle Tissue.*

🔑 **Assess Your Understanding**

1a. Define What is the difference between voluntary and involuntary muscles?

_____

_____

_____

b. Infer Why is it important that cardiac muscle tissue does not tire?

_____

_____

_____

got it?...

○ **I get it!** Now I know that the muscles in my body are _____

_____

○ **I need extra help with** _____

Go to **MY SCIENCE** ⓢ **COACH** online for help with this subject.

How Do Skeletal Muscles Work?

Has anyone ever asked you to "make a muscle"? If so, you probably tightened your fist, bent your arm at the elbow, and made the muscles in your upper arm bulge, or contract. Like other skeletal muscles, the muscles in your arm do their work by contracting, which means becoming shorter and thicker.

Working in Pairs Each time you move, more than one muscle is involved. 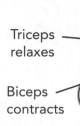 **Skeletal muscles work in pairs. Muscle cells can only contract, not lengthen. While one muscle in a pair contracts, the other muscle in the pair relaxes to its original length.** The biceps and triceps shown in **Figure 3** are an example of a pair of sketetal muscles in your upper arm.

FIGURE 3 ·····································

> ART IN MOTION **Muscle Pairs**
To bend your arm at the elbow, the biceps contracts while the triceps relaxes.

✎ **Interpret Diagrams** Tell what happens to each muscle as you straighten your arm.

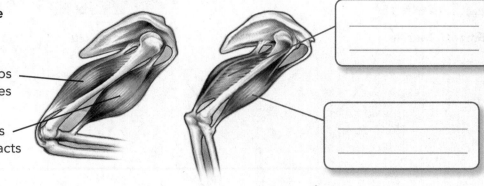

Triceps relaxes

Biceps contracts

 apply it!

This girl's biceps and triceps work as a pair.

❶ **Apply Concepts** Below each photo, write which muscle is contracted.

① ②

_____   _____

❷ **Infer** What might happen if the biceps could not contract?

_____

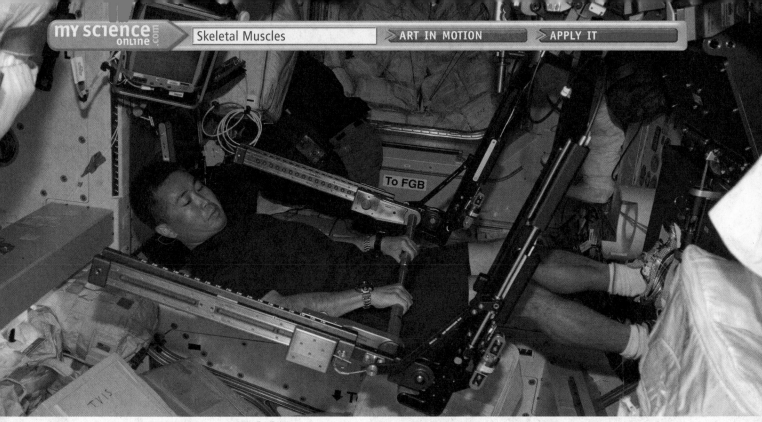

To FGB

Keeping Muscles Healthy
Regular exercise is important for maintaining the strength and flexibility of muscles. Exercise makes individual muscle cells grow bigger, so the whole muscle becomes thicker and stronger. Warming up before exercising increases the blood flow to your muscles. Stretching as you warm up helps your muscles become more flexible and prepares them for exercise. Exercise is important even in space, as shown in **Figure 4**.

Sometimes, muscles can become injured. A muscle strain can occur when muscles are overworked or overstretched. After a long period of exercise, a skeletal muscle can cramp, or contract and stay contracted. If you injure a muscle, be sure to follow medical instructions and rest the injured area so it can heal properly.

FIGURE 4 ·······
Muscle Loss
Without gravity, astronauts in space can lose muscle mass. Therefore, they need to exercise daily.

✎ CHALLENGE **Explain why a lack of gravity might cause muscles to weaken.**

_____

_____

_____

Lab® zone | Do the Quick Lab *Modeling How Skeletal Muscles Work*.

🔑 Assess Your Understanding

2a. Review How do muscles work in pairs?

_____

_____

_____

b. Make Generalizations Why is it important to exercise both muscles in a pair?

_____

_____

_____

got it?·······

○ **I get it!** Now I know that skeletal muscles work _____

_____

○ I need extra help with _____

Go to MY SCIENCE 🅢 COACH online for help with this subject.

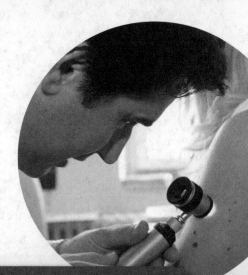

LESSON

3 The Skin

🔑 **What Are the Functions and Structures of the Skin?**

🔑 **How Can You Have Healthy Skin?**

MY PLANET DiARY

Would You Like to Be a Skin Doctor?

Did you know that there is a special type of doctor who studies and treats skin? This type of doctor, a dermatologist, specializes in caring for skin, hair, and nails. Dermatologists diagnose and treat a variety of skin problems ranging from acne to psoriasis to dangerous cancers.

To become a dermatologist, you need a lot of education. You may spend about ten years in schooling and training after you graduate high school. Then you must pass a certification test. Although becoming a dermatologist is not easy, it can be a rewarding career!

Psoriasis

CAREER

Communicate Discuss the question with a partner. Then write down your answer.

Why do you think dermatologists are important?

_____

_____

_____

_____

_____

_____

_____

▶ PLANET DIARY Go to **Planet Diary** to learn more about your skin.

 Do the Inquiry Warm-Up *What Can You Observe About Skin?*

Vocabulary
- epidermis • melanin • dermis
- pore • follicle • cancer

Skills
- ⟳ Reading: Relate Cause and Effect
- △ Inquiry: Observe

What Are the Functions and Structures of the Skin?

If an adult's skin were stretched out flat, it would cover an area about the size of a mattress on a twin bed. The skin is part of the integumentary system (in teg yoo MEN tur ee). In addition to the skin, this system includes hair, nails, sweat glands, and oil glands.

Functions of the Skin Your skin helps you in many ways. **The skin has two layers that protect the body. Skin helps regulate body temperature, eliminate wastes, gather information about the environment, and produce vitamin D.**

Protecting the Body The skin forms a barrier that keeps harmful substances outside the body. It also keeps important substances such as water and other fluids inside the body.

Maintaining Temperature The skin helps the body maintain a steady temperature. When you become too warm, like the runner in **Figure 1,** blood vessels in your skin enlarge. This widening of the vessels allows more blood to flow through them and body heat to escape into the environment. In addition, sweat glands produce perspiration in response to excess heat. As perspiration evaporates from your skin, your skin is cooled. When you get cold, blood vessels in your body contract. This reduces blood flow to the skin and helps your body conserve heat.

FIGURE 1 ···

Amazing Skin

As this runner exercises, his skin helps to cool him off.

✎ **Describe** On the notebook page, describe a time that your skin protected you, maintained your body temperature, or both.

Eliminating Wastes Perspiration contains dissolved waste materials that come from the breakdown of chemical processes. Your skin helps eliminate wastes whenever you perspire.

Gathering Information Nerves in your skin gather information from the environment. They provide information about things such as pressure, temperature, and pain. Pain messages warn you that something in your surroundings can injure you.

Producing Vitamin D Some skin cells produce vitamin D in the presence of sunlight. Vitamin D is important for healthy bones because it helps your body absorb the calcium in your food. Your skin cells need sunlight each day to produce enough vitamin D.

⊘ **Relate Cause and Effect**
Describe the possible effect of not getting enough sunlight each day.

_____
_____
_____

FIGURE 2

Skin at Work
You may not notice that your skin is constantly working.

✎ **Complete the activity and answer the questions below.**

1. **Interpret Photos** Write below each photo the functions that the skin performs.

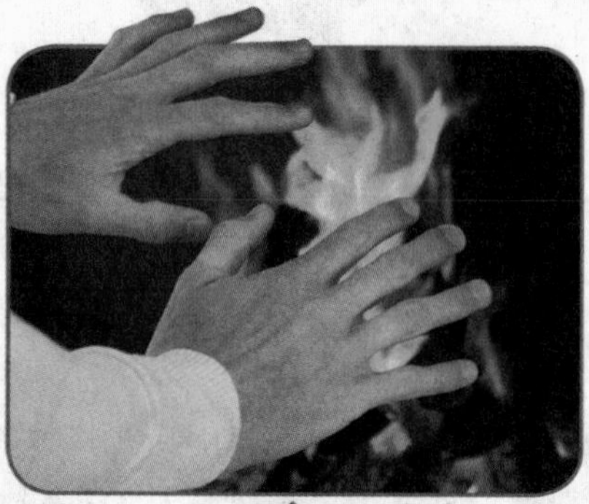

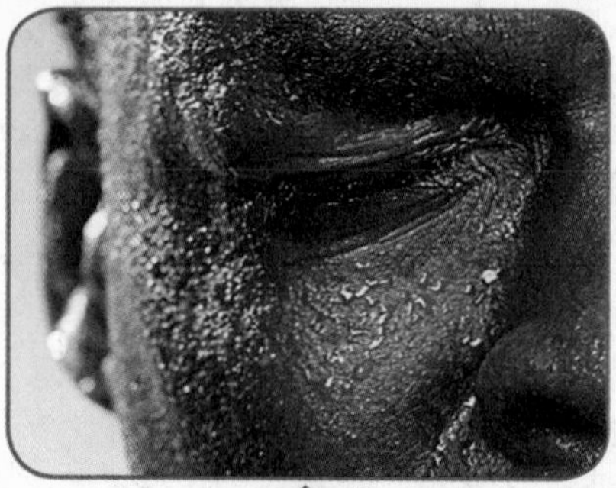

2. ◭ **Observe** Press down firmly on your arm with your fingertips. Then lightly pinch yourself. What information did you receive?

3. [CHALLENGE] What might happen if the nerves in your skin did not gather information?

52 Bones, Muscles, and Skin

Structures of the Skin

The skin has two main layers, as shown in **Figure 3.** Together, these layers—an outer layer and an inner layer—perform all the skin's functions.

The **epidermis** is the outer layer of the skin. Deep in the epidermis, new cells form. As they mature, they move upward until they die. They then become part of the epidermal surface layer. This surface layer helps protect your skin. Cells stay in this layer for about two to three weeks until they are shed. Some cells deep in the epidermis produce **melanin,** a pigment that colors the skin.

The **dermis** is the inner layer of the skin. It is above a layer of fat. This fat layer pads the internal organs and helps keep heat in the body. The dermis includes nerves, blood vessels, sweat glands, hairs, and oil glands. **Pores** are openings that allow sweat to reach the surface. Strands of hair grow within the dermis in **follicles** (FAHL ih kulz). Oil produced in glands around the follicles keeps the surface of the skin moist and the hairs flexible.

Vocabulary Latin Word Origins
The Latin word *porus* means "passage." How does this meaning relate to the pores of the skin?

_____

_____

_____

FIGURE 3 ·

Structures of the Skin

✎ **Relate Text and Visuals** On the lines, write the functions of the epidermis, the nerves, and the sweat gland.

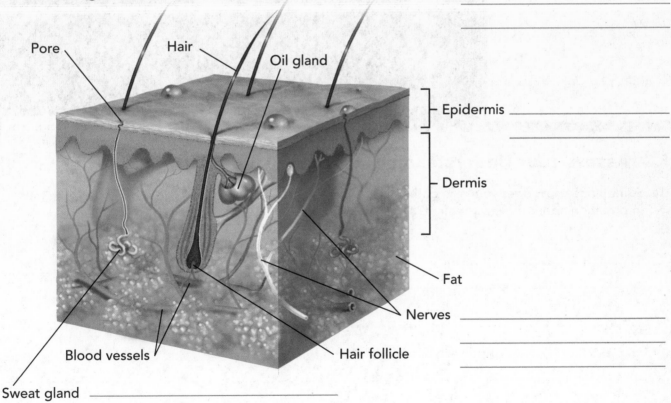

Pore

Hair

Oil gland

Epidermis _____

_____

Dermis

Fat

Nerves _____

_____

Blood vessels

Hair follicle

Sweat gland _____

_____

_____

53

YOUR SUPPORT SYSTEM

What holds your body together?

FIGURE 4 ....

> **VIRTUAL LAB** Your bones, muscles, and skin all support and protect your body.

✏ **Apply Concepts** Write in the boxes details about how this girl's bones, muscles, and skin are functioning.

Bones
_____
_____
_____
_____
_____

Muscles
_____
_____
_____
_____
_____

Skin
_____
_____
_____
_____
_____

Lab zone® Do the Quick Lab _Sweaty Skin._

🔑 Assess Your Understanding

1a. Summarize How does your skin gather information about the environment?

_____
_____
_____

b. ANSWER THE BIG ? What holds your body together?

_____
_____
_____

got_{it}? ....

○ **I get it!** Now I know that the skin has two layers that _____
_____
_____

○ **I need extra help with** _____

Go to MY SCIENCE COACH online for help with this subject.

How Can You Have Healthy Skin?

Taking care of your skin is important. 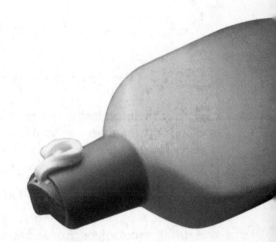 **Three habits can help you have healthy skin: eat a healthy diet, keep your skin clean, and limit your time in the sun.**

Eating a balanced diet provides the energy and raw materials needed for the growth and replacement of skin cells. A healthful diet also includes drinking plenty of water.

Washing your skin with mild soap gets rid of dirt and harmful bacteria. It also controls oiliness. When glands become clogged with oil, the blackheads and whiteheads of acne can form.

Too much sunlight can harm skin cells and cause skin cancer. **Cancer** is a disease in which some cells divide uncontrollably. To protect your skin, wear a hat, sunglasses, and sunscreen.

do the math!

Sunscreen Ratings

The graph shows how sunscreens with different sun protection factor (SPF) ratings affect the amount of time that two people can stay in the sun without beginning to sunburn.

Key
- No sunscreen
- SPF 4
- SPF 15

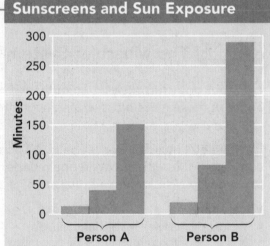

Sunscreens and Sun Exposure

Minutes (y-axis: 0, 50, 100, 150, 200, 250, 300)

Person A   Person B

❶ **Read Graphs** What does the height of each bar in the graph represent?

_____
_____
_____
_____

❷ **Calculate** How much longer can Person B spend in the sun wearing SPF 15 than Person A?

_____
_____

❸ **Infer** Which sunscreen should Person B apply at an all-day picnic? Explain.

_____
_____
_____
_____

Lab zone® Do the Lab Investigation *Sun Safety*.

Assess Your Understanding

got it? ....

○ **I get it!** Now I know that I can have healthy skin by _____

_____

_____

○ **I need extra help with** _____

Go to **my science** ⁵ **coach** *online for help with this subject.*

55

Study Guide

My _____, _____, and _____ work as a team to hold my body together.

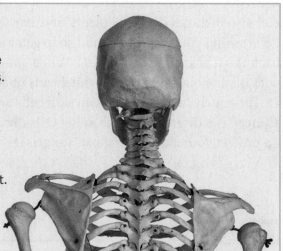

LESSON 1 The Skeletal System

🔑 Your skeleton has five major functions. It provides shape and support, enables you to move, and protects your organs. It also produces blood cells and stores minerals and other materials until your body needs them.

🔑 Joints allow bones to move in different ways.

🔑 Bones are complex living structures that grow, develop, and repair themselves. Bones are also strong and lightweight.

Vocabulary
• skeleton • vertebrae • joint • ligament • compact bone
• spongy bone • marrow • cartilage • osteoporosis

LESSON 2 The Muscular System

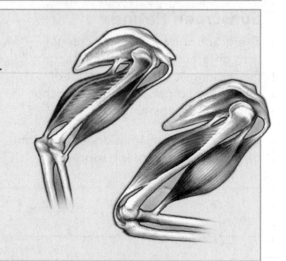

🔑 Your body has skeletal, smooth, and cardiac muscle tissues. Some of these muscle tissues are involuntary, and some are voluntary.

🔑 Skeletal muscles work in pairs. Muscle cells can only contract, not lengthen. While one muscle in a pair contracts, the other muscle in the pair relaxes to its original length.

Vocabulary
• involuntary muscle • voluntary muscle • skeletal muscle
• tendon • smooth muscle • cardiac muscle • striated muscle

LESSON 3 The Skin

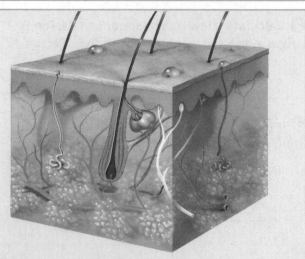

🔑 The skin has two layers that protect the body. Skin helps regulate body temperature, eliminate wastes, gather information about the environment, and produce vitamin D.

🔑 Three habits can help you have healthy skin: eat a healthful diet, keep your skin clean, and limit your time in the sun.

Vocabulary
• epidermis • melanin • dermis • pore
• follicle • cancer

Review and Assessment

LESSON 1 The Skeletal System

1. A soft connective tissue found inside bones is

   a. cytoplasm.   **b.** marrow.

   c. cartilage.   **d.** osteoporosis.

2. The _____ make up your backbone.

3. **Infer** Would jogging or swimming be a better exercise for building your bone strength? Why?

_____

_____

_____

_____

4. **Relate Cause and Effect** What makes bones both strong and lightweight?

_____

_____

_____

_____

_____

_____

_____

5. **Draw Conclusions** Does your body have more movable joints or immovable joints? Explain your answer.

_____

_____

_____

_____

6. **Write About It** Suppose you hear someone calling to you from behind. You turn your head around and see that it is your friend, so you wave. Describe the types of joints you use to perform these actions.

LESSON 2 The Muscular System

7. Muscles that help the skeleton move are

   a. cardiac muscles.   **b.** smooth muscles.

   c. skeletal muscles.   **d.** involuntary muscles.

8. Skeletal muscle must work in pairs because muscle cells can only _____

9. **Compare and Contrast** Write one similarity and one difference between skeletal muscle and cardiac muscle.

_____

_____

_____

_____

10. **Predict** What would happen if a tendon in your finger were cut?

_____

_____

_____

11. **Apply Concepts** Look at the photo. What would you say if one of these teammates suggested eliminating stretching from practice?

_____

_____

_____

_____

LESSON 3 The Skin

12. A pigment that colors the skin is

    a. the dermis.   **b.** the epidermis.

    c. a follicle.   **d.** melanin.

13. Hair grows in _____

14. Make Generalizations What skin layers are affected when a cut on your hand bleeds?

_____

_____

15. The graph below shows how environmental temperature affected one boy's skin and internal temperatures.

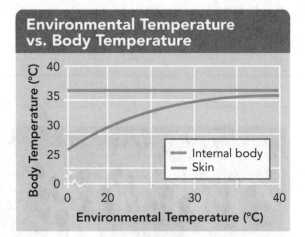

Environmental Temperature vs. Body Temperature

Internal body
Skin

Interpret Data What effect would going outdoors on a cold morning have on the boy's internal and skin temperatures?

_____

_____

_____

_____

16. Write About It Write a story about some friends who went to the beach for a day. Explain how they took good care of their skin.

 What holds your body together?

17. Imagine what the body would look like if it did not have any bones, muscles, or skin. Write about each situation and how it would make everyday life difficult and dangerous.

_____

_____

_____

_____

_____

_____

_____

_____

_____

_____

_____

_____

_____

_____

_____

_____

_____

_____

Standardized Test Prep

Multiple Choice

Circle the letter of the best answer.

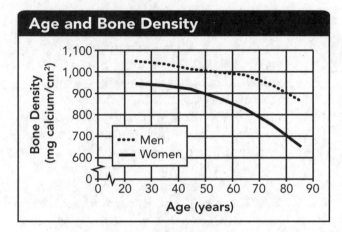

Age and Bone Density

1. Which statement below is true?

   A Bone density decreases with age.

   B Women have denser bones than men.

   C Men's bones have the least calcium.

   D Women who are 55 years old have stronger bones than men of the same age.

2. The muscles you use to lift a book are

   A cardiac muscles.

   B smooth muscles.

   C involuntary muscles.

   D skeletal muscles.

3. Which of the following is an important function of the integumentary system?

   A It produces blood cells.

   B It stores minerals until the body needs them.

   C It regulates body temperature.

   D It allows the body to move.

4. Which of the following are constantly forming in the epidermis?

   A follicles

   B skin cells

   C nerves

   D glands

5. Which of the following connects the bones in movable joints?

   A tendons

   B cartilage

   C marrow

   D ligaments

Constructed Response

Use the diagram and your knowledge of science to help you answer Question 6. Write your answer on a separate sheet of paper.

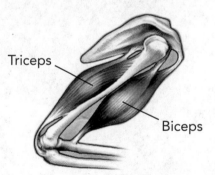

Triceps

Biceps

6. Explain how these muscles work to move the elbow joint.

STUDENT ATHLETIC TRAINERS:

MORE THAN COUNTING EXERCISES

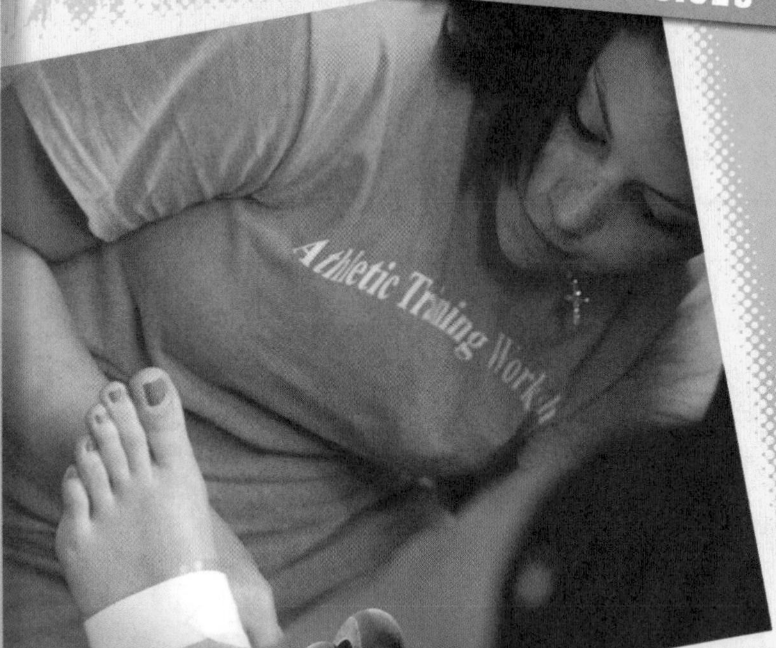

We all know of athletes such as basketball players, figure skaters, or swimmers, who have impressive physical skills. But even the most skilled athletes can use help getting into top form. Athletic trainers are some of the most important people to any sports team or individual athlete. If you are interested in medicine or sports, you don't have to wait until college to learn more. Being a student athletic trainer can give you an inside look into the world of sports medicine.

Student trainers gain basic first-aid skills and learn about anatomy and physiology, the study of the body's functions. Student trainers must understand how the skeletal and muscular systems work together. They also learn how to diagnose and treat common athletic injuries. Some student trainers visit college and professional sports training rooms.

Write About It Interview a coach and a trainer at your school. How do they use their knowledge of the muscular and skeletal systems to help athletes train and prevent injuries? How do they help athletes recover from injuries? Write an article for your school newspaper describing the interviews.

Seeing
THE
SKELETAL SYSTEM

Have you ever broken a bone? If you have, you may have gotten an X-ray. X-rays are just one example of the powerful tools that doctors use to look inside the human body without surgery.

X-rays can reveal a broken bone, but other tools such as bone scans help doctors determine how a patient's bones are growing. During a bone scan, tiny amounts of radioactive material are injected into the patient's bloodstream. This material contains elements whose molecules have unstable nuclei. As the nuclei of these elements in the radioactive material break down, they release radiation, including gamma rays. The radioactive material accumulates in areas of the bone where growth and cell division are taking place.

After a few hours, a special camera that detects gamma rays is used to scan the patient. The camera shows darker and lighter areas of the patient's bones. The darker areas show where more growth is taking place, while the lighter areas show less growth. These images help doctors figure out whether an area of bone is growing abnormally or if it has a tumor. Bone scans are also used to detect hidden fractures that may not appear on an X-ray.

Research It Research one other medical imaging technique, such as magnetic resonance imaging (MRI) or computed axial tomography (CAT) scans. Write a one-page explanation of how the technology works, and what impact it has had on medicine in the past 30 years.

61

WHY DO
HOT PEPPERS
BURN YOUR
MOUTH
BUT NOT YOUR
STOMACH?

THE BIG ?

How does food become materials your body can use?

> **UNTAMED SCIENCE** Watch the **Untamed Science** video to learn more about digestion.

When you eat nachos and get a bite of a jalapeño pepper, your mouth burns, your face turns red, and you may start to perspire. A compound in chili peppers, called capsaicin, acts on nerves in your mouth to cause the burning sensation. Eating hot peppers increases the saliva in your mouth, helping to break down the capsaicin before it enters the rest of the digestive system.

▷ Draw Conclusions Why do you think your stomach doesn't feel the same heat of the chili peppers as your mouth does?

_____

_____

_____

_____

Digestion

3 Getting Started

Check Your Understanding

1. Background Read the paragraph below and then answer the question.

Aretha's basketball team is entering the playoffs. The coach urges the team to eat a healthy **diet**, which will provide the energy team members need to win their games. Healthy food is **essential** for growth and physical activity, as well as for maintaining **homeostasis.**

Diet is the food that a person typically consumes.

Something that is necessary is **essential.**

The condition in which an organism's internal environment is kept stable is called **homeostasis.**

- How is a healthy diet essential for growth, physical activity, and homeostasis?

_____

_____

_____

> **MY READING WEB** If you had trouble completing the question above, visit **My Reading Web** and type in *Digestion.*

Vocabulary Skill

Identify Related Word Forms Increase your vocabulary by learning related forms of words. The table below lists verbs, nouns, and adjectives related to vocabulary in this chapter.

Verb	Noun	Adjective
absorb, *v.* to soak up a liquid or take in nutrients gradually	absorption, *n.* the movement of nutrients from the digestive system into the bloodstream	absorbent, *adj.* capable of soaking up liquid or nutrients
digest, *v.* to break down food	digestion, *n.* the process by which the body breaks down food	digestive, *adj.* helping to break down food

2. Quick Check Fill in the blanks with the correct form of the words.

- The _____ system breaks down food into substances

  that the bloodstream can _____

proteins

carbohydrates

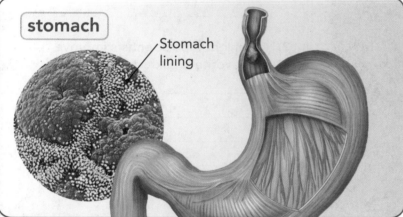
stomach
Stomach lining

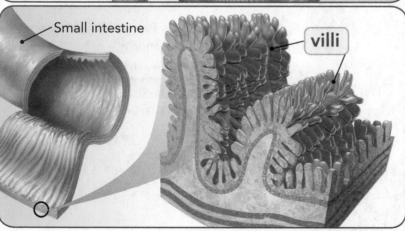
Small intestine
villi

Chapter Preview

LESSON 1
- calorie • nutrient
- carbohydrate
- glucose
- fats • protein
- amino acid
- vitamins
- mineral
- ↻ Outline
- △ Classify

LESSON 2
- Percent Daily Value
- Dietary Reference Intakes
- ↻ Ask Questions
- △ Draw Conclusions

LESSON 3
- digestion
- absorption
- saliva
- enzyme
- epiglottis
- esophagus
- mucus
- peristalsis
- stomach
- ↻ Sequence
- △ Infer

LESSON 4
- small intestine
- liver • bile
- gallbladder • pancreas
- villi • large intestine
- rectum • anus
- ↻ Identify the Main Idea
- △ Develop Hypotheses

▷ VOCAB FLASH CARDS For extra help with vocabulary, visit **Vocab Flash Cards** and type in *Digestion.*

65

Food and Energy

🔑 **Why Do You Need Food?**

🔑 **What Nutrients Do You Need?**

MY PLANET DiARY

The Science of Food

You know that you need to eat food every day. But did you know that for some people studying food is their job? People called food scientists research and improve the food products you buy at the grocery store. Sometimes, they even think up new foods!

Like other scientists, many food scientists spend a lot of time in a lab. They use what they know about biology and chemistry to test food for nutrition, taste, and shelf life, which is how long the food will last before it spoils. If you like science and food, being a food scientist might be the job for you!

CAREER

Communicate Discuss these questions with a partner. Then write your answers.

1. Why should food scientists test foods before the foods are sold?

_____

_____

_____

2. How might food scientists improve your favorite breakfast food?

_____

_____

_____

_____

_____

▷ **PLANET DIARY** Go to **Planet Diary** to learn more about food and energy.

 Do the Inquiry Warm-Up *Food Claims.*

Vocabulary

- calorie • nutrient • carbohydrate
- glucose • fat • protein
- amino acid • vitamins • minerals

Skills

↻ Reading: Outline

△ Inquiry: Classify

Why Do You Need Food?

All living things need food to stay alive. **Food provides your body with materials to grow and to repair tissues. It also provides energy for everything you do.** Exercising, reading, and sleeping require energy. Even maintaining homeostasis takes energy.

When food is used for energy, the amount of energy released is measured in calories. One **calorie** is the amount of energy needed to raise the temperature of one gram of water by one degree Celsius. The unit *Calorie*, with a capital *C*, is used to measure the energy in foods. One Calorie equals 1,000 calories. Everyone needs a certain number of Calories to meet their daily energy needs. However, the more active you are, the more Calories you need.

Erica's Journal

9am – 3pm: I rode the bus to school and chatted with friends at lunch.

4pm – 6pm: I did my homework.

8pm – 10pm: I read my book.

Yama's Journal

9am – 3pm: I rode my bike to school and played basketball after lunch.

4pm – 6pm: I did my homework.

8pm – 10pm: I watched TV.

FIGURE 1 ·····················

Energy Needs

The number of Calories you burn depends on your weight and level of activity.

✎ **Compare and Contrast** Read the journals. Do you think Erica and Yama have the same Calorie needs? Explain.

_____

_____

_____

_____

Do the Quick Lab
Measuring Calories.

⌐ Assess Your Understanding

got it? ···

○ **I get it!** Now I know that food provides _____

_____

○ **I need extra help with** _____

Go to **my science** ⟨s⟩ **coach** *online for help with this subject.*

What Nutrients Do You Need?

Your body breaks down the food you eat into nutrients it can use. **Nutrients** are the substances in food that provide the raw materials and energy the body needs to carry out all its essential processes. **People need six types of nutrients: carbohydrates, fats, proteins, vitamins, minerals, and water.**

Carbohydrates The nutrients known as **carbohydrates** (kahr boh HY drayts) are a major source of energy and made of carbon, oxygen, and hydrogen. Carbohydrates also provide raw materials to make cell parts. About 45 to 65 percent of your daily Calories should come from carbohydrates. Carbohydrates can be divided into simple carbohydrates and complex carbohydrates.

Simple Carbohydrates Simple carbohydrates are called sugars. Sugars can give you a quick burst of energy. Foods contain many kinds of sugars. However, one sugar, **glucose** (GLOO kohs), is the major source of energy for your body's cells. The body converts the different sugars in foods into glucose.

Complex Carbohydrates Complex carbohydrates are made up of many linked sugar molecules. Starch is a complex carbohydrate. Potatoes, rice, wheat, and corn contain starches. Your body breaks down starches into sugar molecules so their energy can be released. Starches provide a steady long-term energy source.

Fiber is another complex carbohydrate in plants. Fiber is not a nutrient because your body cannot digest it. Even so, you still need fiber because it helps keep your digestive system functioning properly. **Figure 2** shows foods containing carbohydrates.

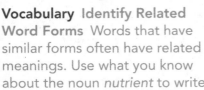

Vocabulary Identify Related Word Forms Words that have similar forms often have related meanings. Use what you know about the noun *nutrient* to write a definition for the adjective *nutritious*.

_____

_____

_____

_____

_____

Brownie (1 square)
Total Carbohydrates 18 g

Sugars	10 g
Starches	7 g
Fiber	1 g

Pasta (1 cup)
Total Carbohydrates 40 g

Sugars	1 g
Starches	37 g
Fiber	2 g

Yellow Corn (1 ear)
Total Carbohydrates 19 g

Sugars	2 g
Starches	15 g
Fiber	2 g

FIGURE 2 ···

Foods Containing Carbohydrates

One gram of carbohydrate provides your body with four Calories of energy.

✎ **Communicate** Working with a partner, explain which foods shown on these two pages would be good to eat before each activity below.

Sprinting

_____

_____

_____

Five-Mile Charity Walk

_____

_____

Basketball Tournament

_____

_____

_____

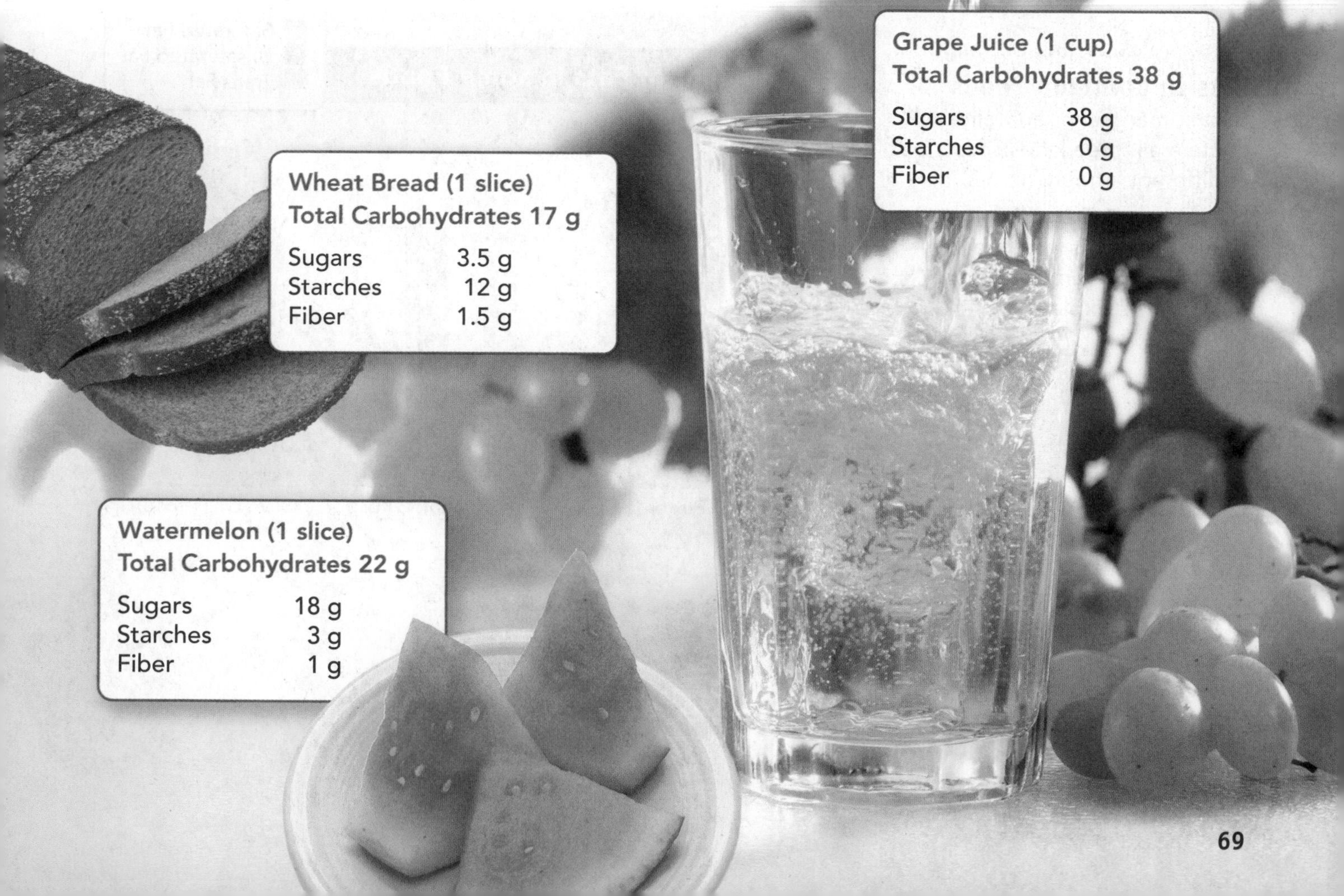

Grape Juice (1 cup)
Total Carbohydrates 38 g

Sugars	38 g
Starches	0 g
Fiber	0 g

Wheat Bread (1 slice)
Total Carbohydrates 17 g

Sugars	3.5 g
Starches	12 g
Fiber	1.5 g

Watermelon (1 slice)
Total Carbohydrates 22 g

Sugars	18 g
Starches	3 g
Fiber	1 g

Fats Like carbohydrates, **fats** are energy-containing nutrients composed of carbon, oxygen, and hydrogen. However, one gram of fat provides nine Calories of energy, while one gram of carbohydrate provides only four Calories. Fats form part of the cell membrane. In addition, fatty tissue protects your organs and insulates your body.

Kinds of Fats There are three kinds of fats in foods—saturated fat, unsaturated fat, and trans fat. Saturated fats, such as the fats in meat, are usually solid at room temperature. Unsaturated fats, such as cooking oils, are usually liquid at room temperature. Trans fats are made by adding hydrogen to vegetable oils. Unsaturated fats are helpful in proper amounts, but saturated and trans fats are not. Therefore, no more than 30 percent of your daily Calories should come from fats. **Figure 3** compares the amount of fats in three common foods.

Cholesterol Cholesterol (kuh LES tur awl) is a waxy, fatlike substance found in products from animals. Like fats, cholesterol is an important part of your body's cells. Because your liver makes all the cholesterol you need, you do not need to eat foods that contain it. A diet high in fat and cholesterol can lead to a buildup of fatty material in the blood vessels and may cause heart disease.

FIGURE 3 ·······························

Fats in Common Foods

Butter, margarine, and olive oil contain all three kinds of fats but in different amounts.

✎ **Interpret Data** Do you think olive oil is less healthy or healthier than butter and margarine? Explain.

_____

_____

_____

_____

_____

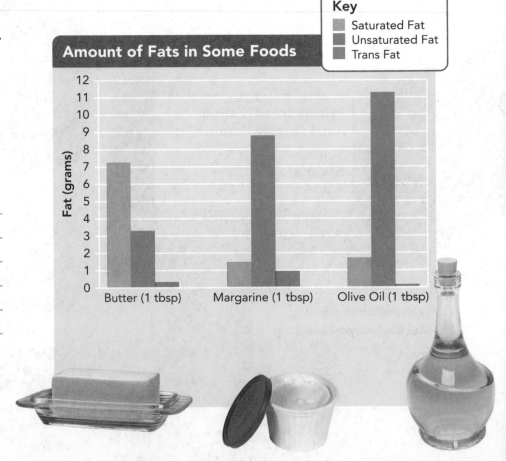

Amount of Fats in Some Foods

Key
▮ Saturated Fat
▮ Unsaturated Fat
▮ Trans Fat

Fat (grams): 0–12

Butter (1 tbsp)   Margarine (1 tbsp)   Olive Oil (1 tbsp)

Proteins **Proteins** are nutrients that contain nitrogen as well as carbon, oxygen, and hydrogen. Your body needs proteins for growth and tissue repair. In addition, proteins can be an energy source. About 10 to 35 percent of your daily Calorie intake should come from proteins.

Proteins are made up of small, linked units called **amino acids** (uh MEE noh). Thousands of different proteins are built from about 20 different amino acids. Your body can make about half of the amino acids it needs. The other half of the amino acids are called essential amino acids. They must come from your food.

Foods from both animals and plants contain protein. Proteins from animal sources, such as meat, fish, and eggs, contain all the essential amino acids, so they are called complete proteins. Proteins from plant sources do not contain all the essential amino acids. They are called incomplete proteins. Different plants lack different amino acids.

Outline Make an outline that will help you review the types of nutrients.

I. Carbohydrates

   A. _____

   B. _____

II. _____

   A. _____

   B. _____

   C. _____

III. _____

   A. _____

   B. _____

apply it!

Both meat and plant foods are sources of protein. To obtain the essential amino acids from plant sources alone, you need to eat a variety of plant foods.

1 Classify Put a check mark beside the foods that contain complete proteins. Circle the foods that contain incomplete proteins.

2 Explain How did you determine your choice for the eggs?

_____

3 List Write the names of three protein-rich animal foods not shown here.

_____

4 CHALLENGE What diet advice could you give a vegetarian?

_____

Fish

Peanuts

Beans

Beef

Chicken

Eggs

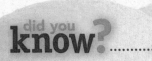

did you know?

In the 1700s, many sailors developed a disease called scurvy. Dr. James Lind put sailors with scurvy into groups and fed each group different foods. The sailors who were fed citrus fruits recovered from scurvy. Soon all sailors were eating citrus fruits and scurvy disappeared.

Today, scientists know that scurvy is caused by a lack of vitamin C, which is found in citrus fruits.

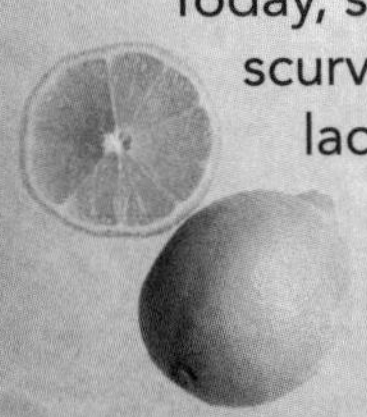

Vitamins Unlike some nutrients, vitamins do not provide the body with raw materials and energy. Instead, **vitamins** act as helper molecules in your body's chemical reactions. The body can make a few vitamins. For example, your skin can make vitamin D when exposed to sunlight. As shown in **Figure 4,** foods are the source of most vitamins.

Fat-Soluble Vitamins Some vitamins are fat-soluble, which means that they dissolve in fat and are stored in fatty tissues in the body. Your body can release these vitamins when they are needed. Examples of fat-soluble vitamins include vitamins A, D, E, and K.

Water-Soluble Vitamins Water-soluble vitamins dissolve in water and are not stored in the body. Therefore, you must include sources of water-soluble vitamins in your diet every day. Vitamin C and all the B vitamins are water-soluble.

FIGURE 4

Some Essential Vitamins

This table lists sources and functions of some of the 13 essential vitamins.

Identify Circle the fat-soluble vitamins. Underline the water-soluble vitamins. In the last column, put a check for each vitamin that the body stores.

Vitamin	Some Sources	Function	Stored in Body
A	Dairy products; eggs; liver; vegetables; fruits	Maintains skin, bones, teeth, and hair; aids vision	
B2 (riboflavin)	Dairy products; whole-grain foods; green, leafy vegetables	Needed for normal growth	
B3 (niacin)	Many protein-rich foods; whole-grain foods; nuts	Needed to release energy	
B12	Meats; fish; poultry; dairy products; eggs	Maintains nervous system; helps form red blood cells	
C	Citrus fruits; tomatoes; potatoes; dark green vegetables	Needed to form connective tissue and fight infection	
D	Fish; eggs; liver; made by skin cells in the presence of sunlight	Maintains bones and teeth	
E	Vegetable oils; margarine; green, leafy vegetables; whole-grain foods	Helps maintain red blood cells	
K	Green, leafy vegetables; milk; liver; made by bacteria in the intestines	Aids in blood clotting; needed for bone formation	

Minerals Nutrients that are not made by living things are called **minerals.** Like vitamins, minerals do not provide your body with raw materials and energy. However, your body still needs small amounts of minerals to carry out chemical processes. For example, you need calcium to build bones and teeth, iron to help red blood cells function, and magnesium to aid muscle and nerve function. Plant roots absorb minerals from the soil. You obtain minerals by eating plants or animals that have eaten plants. **Figure 5** shows foods that contain some important minerals you need.

Water Water is the most important nutrient because all the body's vital processes take place in water. In addition, water helps regulate body temperature and remove wastes. Water accounts for about 65 percent of the average healthy person's body weight because it makes up most of the body's fluids, including blood. Under normal conditions, you need to take in about 2 liters of water every day to stay healthy.

Sources of iron

Sources of magnesium

Sources of calcium

FIGURE 5 ···

> **INTERACTIVE ART** **Minerals**
Eating a variety of foods provides you with needed minerals.

✎ **Sequence** Fill in the boxes and draw arrows to show the order in which your body gets minerals from the soil.

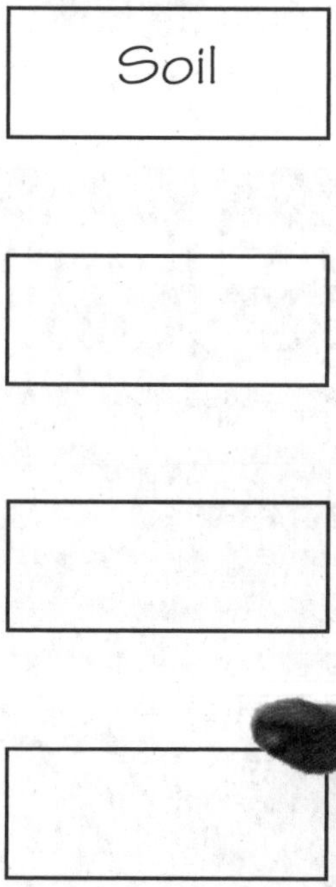

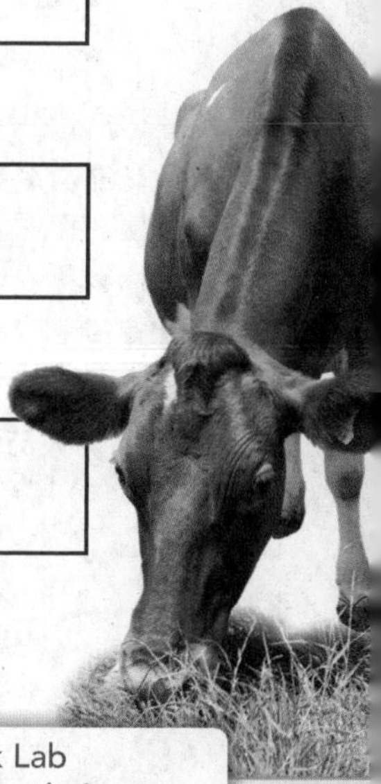

Soil

Lab **zone** Do the Quick Lab
Predicting Starch Content.

Assess Your Understanding

1a. Summarize Describe the role water plays in the body.

_____

_____

_____

b. Draw Conclusions Why do active teenagers have high energy needs?

_____

_____

_____

got it? ···

○ **I get it!** Now I know that the nutrients that the body needs are _____

_____

○ **I need extra help with** _____

Go to MY SCIENCE ⬤ COACH *online for help with this subject.*

2 Healthy Eating

🔑 How Can Food Guidelines Help You?

🔑 What Do Food Labels Tell You?

my planeT DiaRY

Garlic: Bad Breath? Good Health?

What does eating garlic do for you? If you answered that it adds flavor to the food you eat, you are correct. If you said that it gives you bad breath, you're also correct. But garlic is good for you, too! It contains both minerals and vitamins that your body needs, especially vitamin B6 and vitamin C. Throughout history, people have used garlic to prevent some diseases of the digestive system and the heart. So, don't get rid of the garlic in your diet!

Communicate Discuss the following questions with a partner. Then write your answers.

1. What foods do you eat that contain garlic?

_____

_____

_____

2. What do you think might happen if a person's diet lacked important nutrients?

_____

_____

_____

> PLANET DIARY Go to **Planet Diary** to learn more about healthy eating.

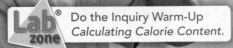

Do the Inquiry Warm-Up *Calculating Calorie Content.*

How Can Food Guidelines Help You?

What does healthy eating mean to you? Eating vegetables and fruits? Cutting down on soft drinks and chips? With so many foods available, it may seem difficult to establish a healthy diet. Luckily, nutritionists have developed dietary guidelines and food labels as a way to help you eat healthily.

Vocabulary
- Percent Daily Value
- Dietary Reference Intakes

Skills
- Reading: Ask Questions
- Inquiry: Draw Conclusions

Healthy Diet Guidelines
In 2005, the United States Department of Agriculture (USDA) introduced a new set of food guidelines. **The guidelines help people make healthy food choices based on their age, sex, and amount of physical activity.**

MyPlate In 2011, the USDA changed the symbol of its plan from a pyramid to a plate. The MyPlate icon reminds people that they should eat more of some food groups than others. For example, fruits and vegetables should make up half of a meal. The four colored triangles on the plate and the circle to the side of the plate represent the five food groups. Although important to a healthful diet, oils are not included because they are not recognized as a food group. For information about portion sizes, you can visit www.ChooseMyPlate.gov.

FIGURE 1 ·······················
Reading MyPlate
The size of each triangle on the plate shows the portion of that group to include in a healthful meal. The blue circle represents a portion of dairy.

✎ **Classify** In the chart, write a list of some foods you ate yesterday. Include the group each food belongs to.

ChooseMyPlate.gov

Food	Group

Grains	Vegetables	Fruits	Dairy	Protein
Choose whole grain products when you can. Good choices include breads, pasta, rice, couscous, and quinoa.	Vary your vegetable choices to get different nutrients. Good choices are broccoli, spinach, collard greens, carrots, sweet potatoes, and corn.	Enjoy many different fruits including fresh, frozen, canned, or 100% fruit juice. Good choices are apples, grapes, pineapples, oranges, kiwi, and berries.	This group contains milk products that contain a significant amount of calcium and calcium-fortified soy milk. Good choices include cheese, milk, and yogurt.	Choose low-fat or lean meats. Peas and beans belong to both the vegetable and protein groups. Other good choices include fish, eggs, nuts, and seeds.

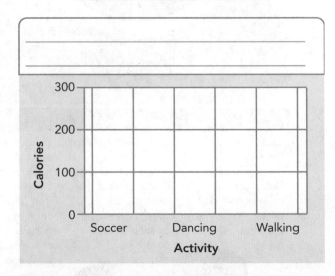

Ask Questions Write one question you have about personalizing MyPlate.

_____

_____

_____

Limiting Sugars and Fats Are you surprised that cookies and potato chips are not included in MyPlate? Foods like these have lots of sugar and are high in fat. They have many Calories but very few nutrients. Therefore, the USDA does not include them in their healthy eating guidelines. Instead, the USDA recommends that people limit their intake of foods with added sugars and extra fats.

Personalizing MyPlate
Dietary needs vary from person to person. For example, children who are growing need to eat more Calories than adults need to eat. Physically active people need to eat more Calories than less active people. Even among physically active people, their different activities burn different amounts of Calories.

do the math!

The USDA recommends that people do about 30 to 60 minutes of physical activity most days. The data table shows the amount of Calories a 13 year old weighing 45 kilograms burns during 30 minutes of each activity.

❶ **Graph** Use the data to draw a bar graph.

❷ **Name** Write a title for the bar graph.

❸ **CHALLENGE** Why does the type of physical activity change a person's dietary needs? Use the graph to explain your answer.

_____

_____

_____

_____

_____

_____

_____

_____

Activity	Calories Burned in 30 Minutes
Soccer	275
Dancing	115
Walking	75

apply it!

This log shows the food that a student ate in one day. Use the log to answer the questions.

1 Classify Write the name of each food that was eaten next to the correct food group.

Grains _____

Vegetables _____

Fruits _____

Dairy _____

Protein _____

2 Draw Conclusions Suggest three changes to the food log so this diet better follows the USDA guidelines. Explain how your changes improve the diet.

_____

_____

_____

_____

_____

Tuesday's Food Log

Meal	Food
Breakfast	Cereal, milk, yogurt
Lunch	Turkey, bread, lettuce
Snacks	Carrots, peanuts
Dinner	Chicken, beans, rice

Do the Quick Lab
Classifying Foods.

🔑 Assess Your Understanding

1a. Identify According to MyPlate, which two groups should you eat in the largest amounts?

_____

_____

b. Make Generalizations How does the USDA's MyPlate help people?

_____

_____

_____

_____

got it? ....

○ **I get it!** Now I know that food guidelines help_____

_____

○ **I need extra help with** _____

Go to MY SCIENCE ⓢ COACH online for help with this subject.

What Do Food Labels Tell You?

Suppose you are shopping for breakfast cereal. How do you choose the healthiest cereal? One thing you can do is read the food labels. 🔑 **Food labels help you evaluate a single food and compare the nutritional value of different foods.**

Food Labels Food labels, such as the one in **Figure 2**, provide information about the food in the container. The label includes the serving size, the Calories, and the Percent Daily Value. The ingredients are also listed in order by the amount that is in the food, starting with the main ingredient.

FIGURE 2 ·······································

Reading a Food Label
By law, specific nutritional information must be listed on food labels.

✎ **Interpret Photos** Draw a line from each box to the part of the label it describes. Then answer the questions.

Nutrition Facts

Serving Size	½ cup (30g)
Servings Per Container	About 10

Amount Per Serving

Calories 110	Calories from Fat 17

	% Daily Value*
Total Fat 2g	**3%**
Saturated Fat 0g	**0%**
Trans Fat 0.5g	
Cholesterol 0mg	**0%**
Sodium 130mg	**12%**
Total Carbohydrate 43g	**7%**
Dietary Fiber 3g	**12%**
Sugars 1g	
Protein 3g	

Vitamin A	25%	• Vitamin C	20%
Calcium	4%	• Iron	25%

* Percent Daily Values are based on a 2,000 Calorie diet. Your Daily Values may be higher or lower depending on your Calorie needs:

	Calories	2,000	2,500
Total Fat	Less than	65g	80g
Sat. Fat	Less than	20g	25g
Cholesterol	Less than	300mg	300mg
Sodium	Less than	2,400mg	2,400mg
Total Carbohydrate		300g	375g
Fiber		25g	30g

Calories per gram:
Fat 9 • Carbohydrate 4 • Protein 4

Ingredients: RICE, WHOLE GRAIN OATS, WHOLE GRAIN WHEAT, CORNSTARCH, HIGH FRUCTOSE CORN SYRUP, SUGAR, OAT BRAN, SALT, NATURAL AND ARTIFICIAL FLAVOR, VITAMIN A PALMITATE, SUCRALOSE, ZINC OXIDE, REDUCED IRON, FOLIC ACID, BHT (PRESERVATIVE), VITAMIN B12 AND VITAMIN D.

Serving Size is the size of a single serving in the container. The rest of the label's information is based on a single serving size.

Estimate If you eat one serving of cereal every morning, when would you run out of cereal?

_____

_____

Calories show how much energy you get from one serving of the food.

Identify How many Calories are from fat?

_____

_____

Percent (%) Daily Value shows how the nutrients in one serving fit into a diet of 2,000 Calories a day.

Calculate How many servings of this cereal would give you a 100 percent Daily Value for iron?

_____

_____

Ingredients include substances, called preservatives, that are added to a food to keep it from spoiling.

Name What preservative is added to this food?

_____

_____

Dietary Reference Intakes

The USDA has charts that show the amounts of nutrients needed every day. The charts are known as **Dietary Reference Intakes (DRIs).** DRIs provide guidelines based on the type of nutrient and the age and sex of a person. For example, DRIs for vitamins recommend that people your age get 45 milligrams of vitamin C every day.

DRIs tell how your daily Calories should be split among fats, carbohydrates, and proteins. DRI amounts are used to develop food labels like those in **Figure 3.** The Percent Daily Values on food labels can help you make sure that you meet the DRIs for different nutrients.

FIGURE 3 ·····························
Nutrition Facts

Food labels can help you make healthful food choices.

✎ **Compare and Contrast** These food labels are from two different snack foods. Which food is a healthier snack? Explain.

_____

_____

_____

_____

A

Nutrition Facts
Serving Size 7 pieces (42 g)
Servings Per Container about 6

Amount Per Serving	
Calories 250 Calories from Fat 110	
	% Daily Value*
Total Fat 12 g	17%
Saturated Fat 6 g	30%
Trans Fat 0 g	
Cholesterol 5 mg	2%
Sodium 80 mg	3%
Total Carbohydrate 35 g	8%
Dietary Fiber 1 g	4%
Sugars 45 g	
Protein 3 g	

B

Nutrition Facts
Serving size 1 box
Calories 130
Not a significant source of fat calories, sat fat, trans fat, and cholesterol.
* Percent Daily Values (DV) are based on a 2,000 Calorie diet.

Amount/Serving	% DV*	Amount/Serving	% DV*
Total Fat 0g	0%	Fiber 2g	10%
Sodium 10mg	0%	Sugars 20g	
Total Carb 25g	11%	**Protein** 1g	
Calcium	2%	Iron	6%

Do the Quick Lab
Calculating Percentage of Calories From Fat.

⚷ Assess Your Understanding

2a. Define What is Percent Daily Value?

_____

_____

b. Summarize How can you use food labels and DRIs to make sure you get enough iron?

_____

_____

_____

got it?

○ **I get it!** Now I know that food labels _____

_____

_____

_____

_____

○ **I need extra help with** _____

Go to MY SCIENCE coach *online for help with this subject.*

79

The Digestive Process Begins

🔑 **What Are the Functions of the Digestive System?**

🔑 **What Is the Role of the Mouth, the Esophagus, and the Stomach?**

my planet Diary

DISCOVERY

Watch Digestion Live

Often scientists make discoveries by accident. In 1822, Alexis St. Martin was wounded in the stomach. Dr. William Beaumont saved St. Martin's life but the surgery left him with a permanent opening in his stomach. By looking in this opening, Dr. Beaumont could observe food changing chemically! By analyzing liquid from St. Martin's stomach, Beaumont learned that the stomach liquid contains acid. He hypothesized that chemical reactions in the stomach broke down foods into very small particles. Today, scientists know Beaumont was right.

A healthy stomach lining

Write your answer to the question below.

What are some modern-day methods doctors use to see what happens inside the digestive system?

_____

_____

_____

_____

_____

_____

> **PLANET DIARY** Go to **Planet Diary** to learn more about digestion.

> **Lab zone** Do the Inquiry Warm-Up *Where Does Digestion Start?*

What Are the Functions of the Digestive System?

Your digestive system is about 9 meters long from beginning to end. **Figure 1** shows the organs of the digestive system. 🔑 **The organs of the digestive system have three main functions: digestion, absorption, and elimination.** These functions occur one after the other in an efficient, continuous process.

Vocabulary
- digestion • absorption • saliva • enzyme • epiglottis
- esophagus • mucus • peristalsis • stomach

Skills
↺ Reading: Sequence
△ Inquiry: Infer

Digestion The process by which your body breaks down food into small nutrient molecules is called **digestion.** Digestion can be mechanical or chemical. In mechanical digestion, bites of food are torn or ground into smaller pieces. This kind of digestion happens mostly in the mouth and stomach. In chemical digestion, chemicals break foods into their building blocks. Chemical digestion takes place in many parts of the digestive system. Substances made in the liver and pancreas help digestion occur.

Absorption and Elimination

Absorption occurs after digestion. **Absorption** is the process by which nutrient molecules pass through the wall of your digestive system into your blood. Most absorption occurs in the small intestine. The large intestine eliminates materials that are not absorbed.

FIGURE 1 ·····························
Digestive System Organs
Food passes directly through five of the organs of your digestive system.

✎ **Review** Circle the name(s) of the organ(s) where mechanical digestion occurs. Check the name(s) of the organ(s) where most absorption occurs. Underline the name(s) of the organ(s) where elimination occurs.

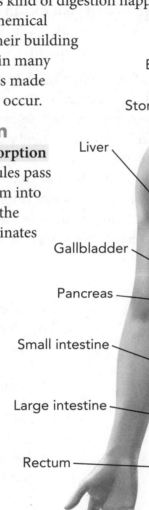

Mouth
Epiglottis
Salivary gland
Stomach
Esophagus
Liver
Gallbladder
Pancreas
Small intestine
Large intestine
Rectum

Lab zone Do the Quick Lab *How Can You Speed Up Digestion?*

🔑 Assess Your Understanding

got it? ···

O **I get it!** Now I know that the functions of the digestive system are _____

_____

O **I need extra help with** _____

Go to **my science** 🄢 **coach** *online for help with this subject.*

What Is the Role of the Mouth, the Esophagus, and the Stomach?

Your upper digestive system consists of the mouth, the esophagus, and the stomach. ⟶ **Your mouth, esophagus, and stomach are the organs in which mechanical digestion is completed and chemical digestion of your food begins.**

The Mouth Have you noticed that smelling food can be enough to start your mouth watering? This response happens because your mouth is where digestion begins. **Figure 2** shows the parts of your mouth.

Digestion When you bite off a piece of food, both mechanical and chemical digestion begin inside your mouth. Your teeth and tongue carry out mechanical digestion. Your teeth cut, tear, crush, and grind food into small pieces. Your tongue pushes food toward your teeth.

As your teeth work, your saliva (suh LY vuh) moistens food into a slippery mass. **Saliva** is the fluid released by salivary glands when you eat. Saliva contains a chemical that can break down starches into sugars. This begins the chemical digestion of your food.

FIGURE 2 ···
The Mouth
Digestion begins in your mouth.

✎ **Use the diagram of the mouth to complete the activities.**

1. **Name** Identify the type(s) of digestion that each part of your mouth is involved with. Write an **M** for mechanical digestion and a **C** for chemical digestion.

2. **Interpret Diagrams** How does saliva get from the salivary glands into the mouth?

_____

_____

3. [CHALLENGE] Identify two problems that a person without salivary glands might have.

_____

_____

_____

_____

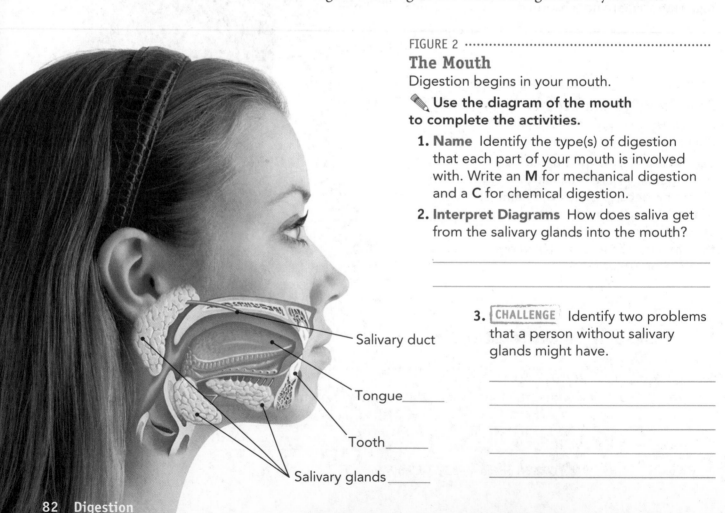

Salivary duct

Tongue_____

Tooth_____

Salivary glands_____

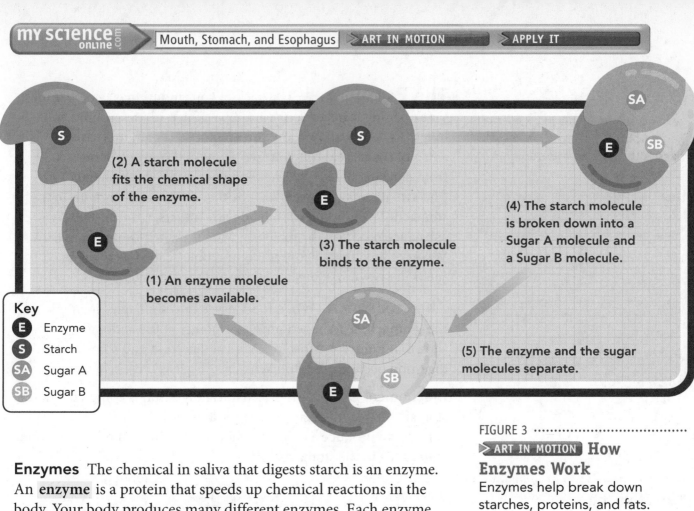

(2) A starch molecule fits the chemical shape of the enzyme.

(1) An enzyme molecule becomes available.

(3) The starch molecule binds to the enzyme.

(4) The starch molecule is broken down into a Sugar A molecule and a Sugar B molecule.

(5) The enzyme and the sugar molecules separate.

Key
- **E** Enzyme
- **S** Starch
- **SA** Sugar A
- **SB** Sugar B

Enzymes The chemical in saliva that digests starch is an enzyme. An **enzyme** is a protein that speeds up chemical reactions in the body. Your body produces many different enzymes. Each enzyme has a specific chemical shape that enables it to speed up only one kind of reaction. Different enzymes are needed to complete the process of digestion. **Figure 3** shows how enzymes work.

FIGURE 3 ·······················

> ART IN MOTION **How Enzymes Work**
Enzymes help break down starches, proteins, and fats.

✎ **Observe** Identify which molecule does not change.

_____

_____

_____

apply it!

You have four types of teeth. Each type has a specific function.

❶ **Name** Think about eating a carrot. Which type of teeth cuts the carrot into a bite-sized piece? _____

❷ **Identify** Which teeth at the back of your mouth crush and grind the carrot piece? _____ and _____

❸ **Interpret Diagrams** When people tear chicken off a bone, they use their pointed teeth called _____

❹ **Summarize** Write about all the teeth people use to eat an apple.

_____

_____

Molars

Premolars

Incisors

Canine

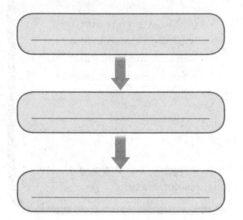

⟲**Sequence** Write in order the names of the organs that food passes through at the beginning of digestion.

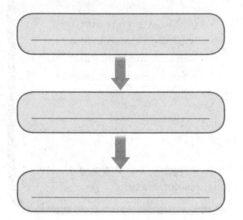

⬇

⬇

The Esophagus

The back of your mouth has two openings. One opening leads to your windpipe, which carries air into your lungs. As you swallow food, the **epiglottis** (ep uh GLAHT is), a flap of tissue, seals off your windpipe and prevents food from entering the lungs. The food goes into the **esophagus** (ih SAHF uh gus), a muscular tube that connects the mouth to the stomach. The esophagus is lined with **mucus,** a thick, slippery substance produced by the body. Mucus makes food move easily. Waves of involuntary muscle contractions, called **peristalsis** (pehr ih STAWL sis), push food toward the stomach.

The Stomach

When food leaves the esophagus, it enters the **stomach,** a J-shaped muscular pouch in the abdomen, shown in **Figure 4.** Most mechanical digestion and some chemical digestion occur in the stomach.

Mechanical Digestion Mechanical digestion is completed in the stomach. It occurs as layers of smooth muscle in the stomach wall contract to produce a churning motion. This action mixes the food with fluids in the stomach.

FIGURE 4 ···

The Stomach

The stomach wall has three muscle layers. The microscopic view shows you the cells that line the inside of the stomach.

✎ **Draw an arrow that points to where peristalsis is taking place. Label the arrow. Then answer the question.**

Infer Why do stomach muscles run in different directions?

_____

_____

_____

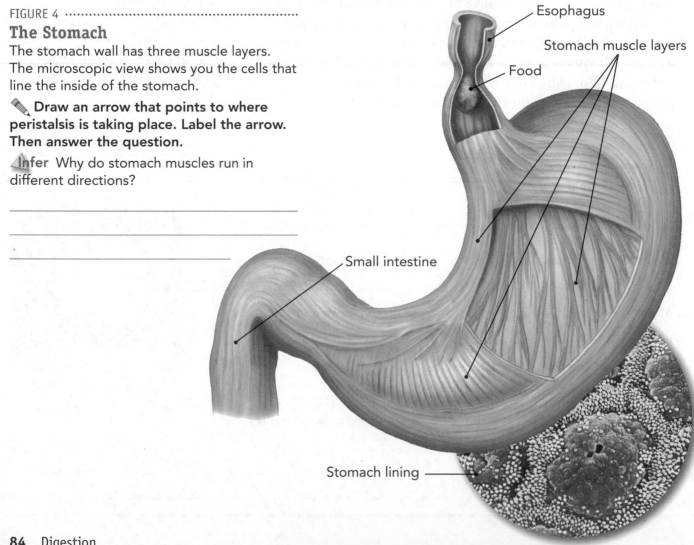

Esophagus

Stomach muscle layers

Food

Small intestine

Stomach lining

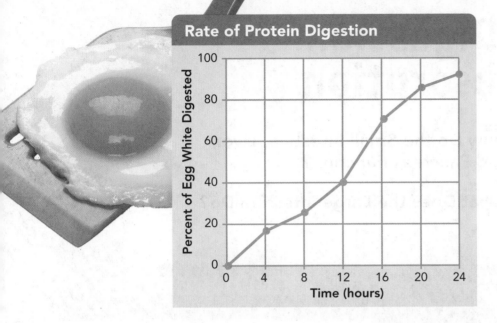

Rate of Protein Digestion

Percent of Egg White Digested (y-axis: 0, 20, 40, 60, 80, 100)

Time (hours) (x-axis: 0, 4, 8, 12, 16, 20, 24)

FIGURE 5 ·····················

Protein Digestion
The graph shows the results of an experiment that measured the rate at which protein in egg white was digested by pepsin in a mixture of hydrochloric acid.

✎ **Use the graph to answer the questions.**

1. **Infer** Would all the protein you eat be digested by the time it leaves the stomach? Explain.

_____

_____

_____

_____

2. **CHALLENGE** Draw a line on the graph that you think might show the results of an experiment on carbohydrate digestion. Explain.

_____

_____

_____

_____

_____

Chemical Digestion Chemical digestion occurs as the churning food mixes with digestive juice. Digestive juice is a fluid produced by cells that line the stomach. It contains the enzyme pepsin, which chemically digests proteins into short chains of amino acids. A graph of protein digestion is shown in **Figure 5.**

Digestive juice also contains hydrochloric acid, a strong acid that helps your stomach function in two ways. First, pepsin works best in an acid environment. Second, the acid kills many bacteria that you swallow with your food. Mucus, which lines the stomach, protects the stomach from the acid.

Food usually stays in your stomach for a few hours until mechanical digestion is complete. Then, the food you ate, now a thick liquid, enters the next part of the digestive system. That is where chemical digestion continues and absorption take place.

Lab ® Do the Lab Investigation
zone *As the Stomach Churns.*

🔑 **Assess Your Understanding**

1a. Review The _____ in your body speed up chemical reactions.

b. Compare and Contrast The stomach is similar to a washing machine because _____

_____

_____

_____

got it?

○ **I get it!** Now I know that the role of the mouth, esophagus, and stomach is _____

_____

_____

_____

○ **I need extra help with** _____

Go to **MY SCIENCE** 🅢 **COACH** *online for help with this subject.*

Final Digestion and Absorption

🔑 **How Do the Small Intestine, Liver, and Pancreas Function?**

🔑 **What Does the Large Intestine Do?**

my pLaneT DiaRY

Partnering with Bacteria

Misconception Bacteria are bad for you.

That isn't always true. In one experiment, scientists showed that some bacteria are actually good for your body! The scientists created "bacteria-free" mice. They found that these mice got sick more easily than mice with bacteria in them. The bacteria were actually good for the mice.

When you eat foods such as certain yogurts or cereals, you are not only satisfying your hunger. You're also making sure your body has enough good bacteria to keep your digestive system healthy. Good bacteria help protect you from harmful germs by either killing them or making your body an unfriendly environment for them to live in. So, if you want to keep your body healthy, let those good bacteria get to work!

Bacteria from an intestine

MISCONCEPTION

Communicate Discuss the questions with a partner. Write your answers below.

1. Why do you think the "bacteria-free" mice got sick more easily?

_____

_____

_____

_____

2. What else can you do to stay healthy?

_____

_____

_____

> **PLANET DIARY** Go to **Planet Diary** to learn more about digestion and absorption.

 Do the Inquiry Warm-Up *Which Surface Is Larger?*

Vocabulary

- small intestine • liver • bile • gallbladder • pancreas
- villi • large intestine • rectum • anus

Skills

- Reading: Identify the Main Idea
- Inquiry: Develop Hypotheses

How Do the Small Intestine, Liver, and Pancreas Function?

Think about how ticket takers help people enter an event in an orderly way. In some ways, the stomach is the "ticket taker" of the digestive system. After food becomes a thick liquid, the stomach releases a little of that liquid at a time into the small intestine, the next part of the digestive system.

The Small Intestine At about 6 meters—longer than some full-sized cars—the small intestine makes up two thirds of the length of the digestive system. Its small diameter, from 2 to 3 centimeters wide, gives the small intestine its name.

A great deal happens in the small intestine. The **small intestine** is the part of the digestive system where most chemical digestion takes place. When food reaches the small intestine, starches and proteins have been partially broken down, but fats have not been digested. **Most chemical digestion and the absorption of nutrients take place in the small intestine. Substances produced by the liver, pancreas, and lining of the small intestine help to complete chemical digestion.** The liver and the pancreas send their substances into the small intestine through small tubes.

Identify the Main Idea
Complete the graphic organizer by identifying the main idea and supporting details about the small intestine.

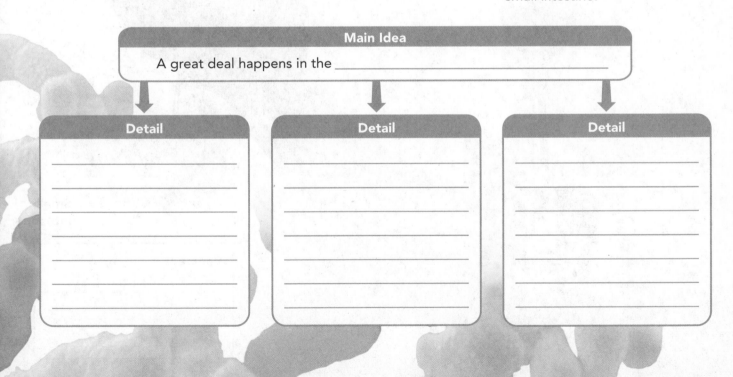

Main Idea

A great deal happens in the _____

Detail

Detail

Detail

FIGURE 1 ···

Organs of Digestion

The liver, pancreas, and gallbladder produce and store substances that aid digestion.

✏️ **Use the diagram to complete the activities below.**

1. **Explain** Describe each organ and its function.

2. **Develop Hypotheses** How might a blockage in the tube between the gallbladder and the small intestine affect digestion?

_____

_____

_____

_____

_____

_____

_____

The Liver and Gallbladder

Find the liver in **Figure 1.** The **liver** does many jobs in the body. One of its jobs is to make bile for the digestive system. **Bile** is a substance that breaks up fat particles. Once it is made, bile is stored in an organ called the **gallbladder.** It is released when food enters the small intestine. Bile does not aid in the chemical digestion of foods. It physically breaks up large fat particles into smaller fat droplets. The droplets are broken down by enzymes produced in the pancreas.

The Pancreas

Like the liver, the pancreas does many jobs in the body. The **pancreas** is a triangular organ located between the stomach and the first part of the small intestine. The pancreas produces digestive enzymes that help break down carbohydrates, proteins, and fats. But, these digestive enzymes cannot break down all food substances. For example, the enzymes are not able to break down the fiber in food.

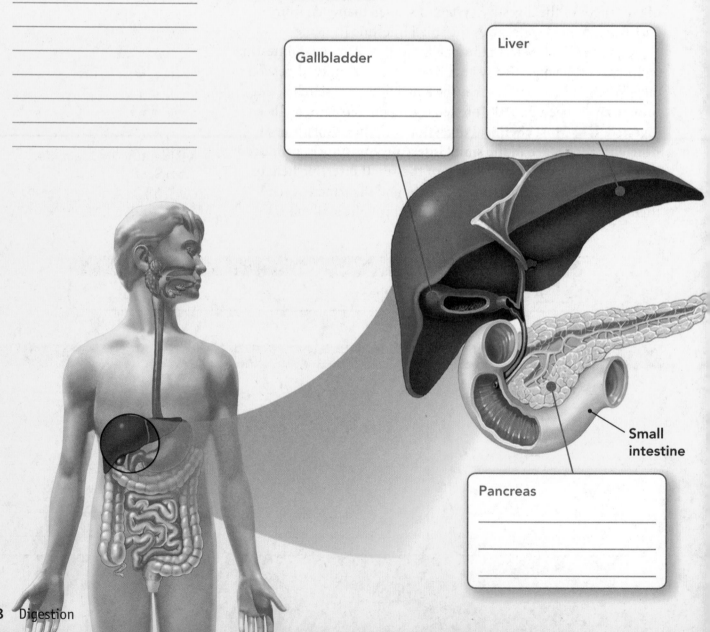

Gallbladder

_____

_____

_____

Liver

_____

_____

_____

Small intestine

Pancreas

_____

_____

_____

Absorption in the Small Intestine After chemical digestion takes place, the small nutrient molecules are ready for the body to absorb. The structure of the small intestine helps absorption occur. The inner surface of the small intestine is folded into millions of tiny finger-shaped structures called **villi** (VIL eye) (singular *villus*). Villi, shown in **Figure 2,** greatly increase the surface area of the small intestine. More surface area means that more nutrients can be absorbed. Nutrient molecules pass from cells on the surface of a villus into blood vessels and are then delivered to body cells.

FIGURE 2 ···
Villi
Tiny villi line the folds of the small intestine.

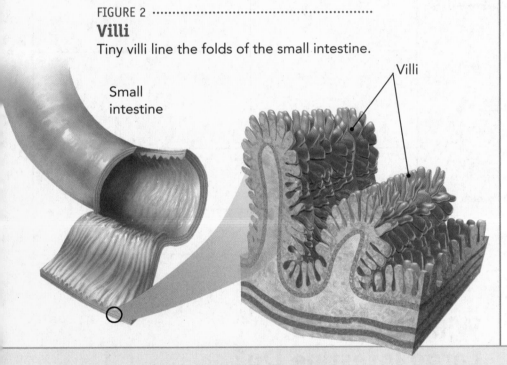

Small intestine

Villi

do the
math!
If the small intestine had smooth walls, its surface area would be 0.57 m². With villi, its surface area is about 250 m², about the size of a tennis court.

1 Calculate Divide to find how many times greater the surface area is with villi than it is without villi. Round your answer to the nearest whole number.

2 CHALLENGE Some people have a wheat allergy that results in villi being destroyed. What problems might they have?

_____
_____
_____
_____
_____

Do the Quick Lab
Break Up!

🔑 Assess Your Understanding

1a. Explain How are the liver and pancreas involved in digestion?

_____
_____
_____
_____

b. Relate Cause and Effect How do villi help the small intestine carry out its function?

_____
_____
_____
_____

got it? ···

○ **I get it!** Now I know that the small intestine, liver, and pancreas _____

○ **I need extra help with** _____

Go to **MY SCIENCE COACH** online for help with this subject.

Food for you

How does food become materials your body can use?

FIGURE 3 ·····················

REAL-WORLD INQUIRY There are many different parts to your body's digestive system.

✎ **Use what you've learned about digestion to complete the tasks.**

1. **Describe** Identify the different kinds of nutrients listed in the table and what each nutrient is needed for.

2. **Explain** In the boxes on the next page, write how each structure helps food become materials your body can use.

Three Groups of Nutrients

	Kinds	Needed for...
Carbohydrates		
Fats		
Proteins		

What Does the Large Intestine Do?

By the time material reaches the end of the small intestine, most nutrients have been absorbed. The water and undigested food that is left moves from the small intestine into the large intestine. As you can see in **Figure 3,** the **large intestine** is the last section of the digestive system. 🔑 **As the material moves through the large intestine, water is absorbed into the bloodstream. The remaining material is readied for elimination from the body.**

The large intestine is about 1.5 meters long. It contains bacteria that feed on the material passing through. These bacteria normally do not cause disease. In fact, they are helpful because they make certain vitamins, including vitamin K.

The large intestine ends in a short tube called the rectum. The **rectum** is where waste material is compressed into solid form. This waste material is eliminated from the body through the **anus,** a muscular opening at the end of the rectum.

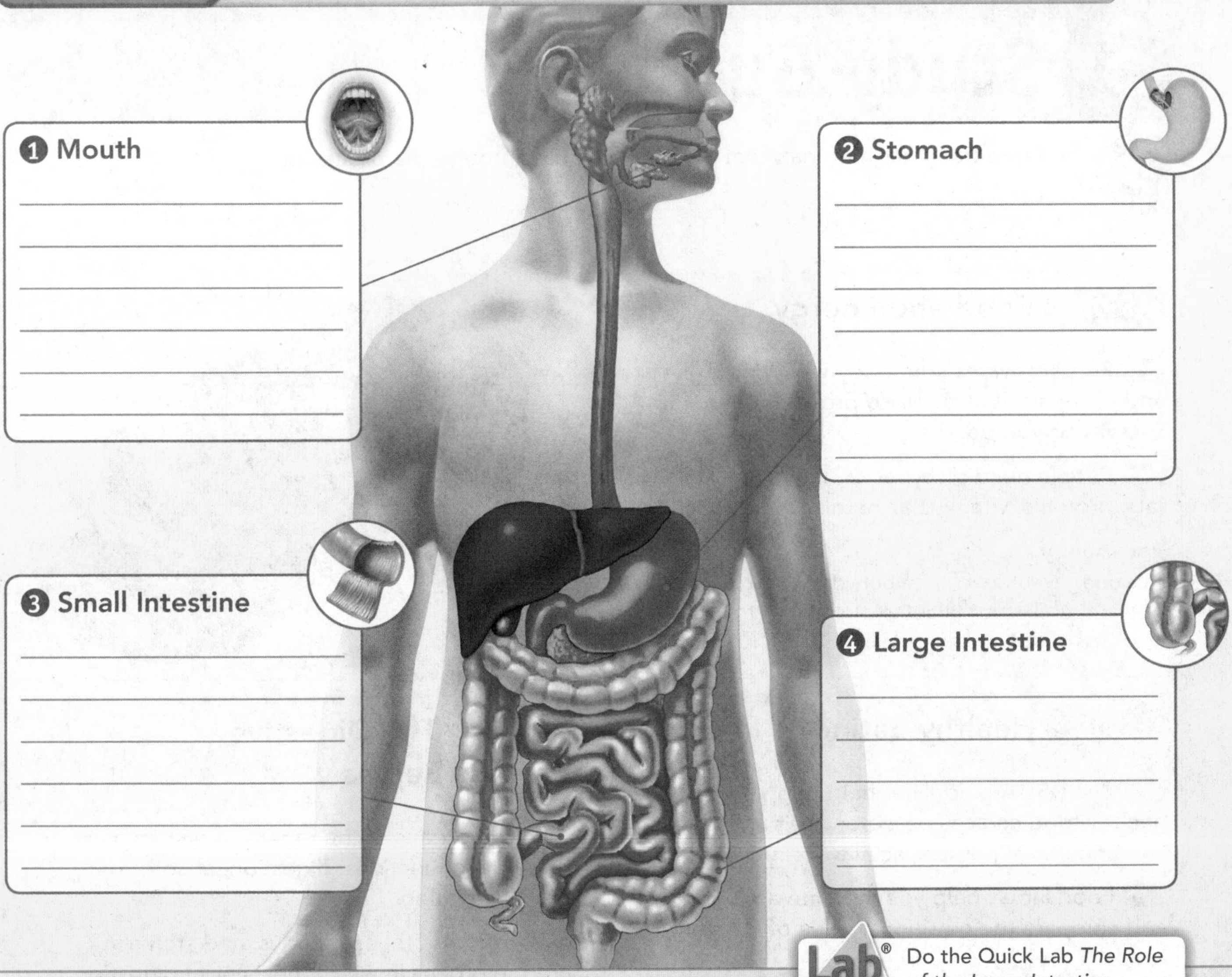

1 Mouth

2 Stomach

3 Small Intestine

4 Large Intestine

Lab® zone Do the Quick Lab *The Role of the Large Intestine.*

🔑 **Assess Your Understanding**

2a. Review What role do bacteria play in the large intestine?

_____
_____
_____
_____
_____

b. ANSWER THE BIG ? How does food become materials your body can use?

_____
_____
_____
_____
_____

got it? ....

○ **I get it!** Now I know that the large intestine's role is_____
_____
_____

○ **I need extra help with** _____

Go to my science 🔊 coach *online for help with this subject.*

Study Guide

Food becomes materials that my body can use through the processes

of _____ and _____.

LESSON 1 Food and Energy

🔑 Food provides your body with materials to grow and to repair tissues. It also provides energy for everything you do.

🔑 People need six types of nutrients: carbohydrates, fats, proteins, vitamins, minerals, and water.

Vocabulary
- calorie • nutrient • carbohydrate • glucose
- fats • protein • amino acid • vitamins • minerals

LESSON 2 Healthy Eating

🔑 The USDA guidelines help people make healthy food choices based on their age, sex, and amount of physical activity.

🔑 Food labels help you evaluate a single food and compare the nutritional value of different foods.

Vocabulary
- Percent Daily Value
- Dietary Reference Intakes

LESSON 3 The Digestive Process Begins

🔑 The organs of the digestive system have three main functions: digestion, absorption, and elimination.

🔑 Your mouth, esophagus, and stomach are the organs in which mechanical digestion is completed and chemical digestion of your food begins.

Vocabulary
- digestion • absorption • saliva • enzyme
- epiglottis • esophagus • mucus
- peristalsis • stomach

LESSON 4 Final Digestion and Absorption

🔑 Most chemical digestion and the absorption of nutrients take place in the small intestine. Substances produced by the liver, pancreas, and lining of the small intestine help to complete chemical digestion.

🔑 As material moves through the large intestine, water is absorbed into the bloodstream. The remaining material is readied for elimination from the body.

Vocabulary
- small intestine • liver • bile • gallbladder • pancreas
- villi • large intestine • rectum • anus

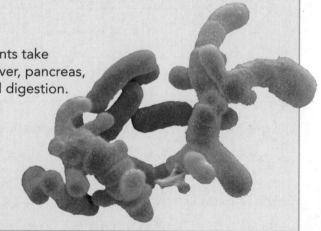

Review and Assessment

LESSON 1 Food and Energy

1. The building blocks of proteins are

a. vitamins.

b. minerals.

c. amino acids.

d. fats.

2. _____ are nutrients that are not made by living things.

3. Infer How does a person's level of physical activity affect his or her daily energy needs?

_____

_____

_____

_____

4. Calculate Your aunt eats 250 Calories of protein and 1,800 Calories total for the day. Did she get enough protein on that particular day? Show your calculations.

_____

_____

_____

_____

_____

_____

5. Apply Concepts Before winter, animals that hibernate often prepare by eating foods high in fat. How is this behavior helpful?

_____

_____

_____

_____

_____

6. **Write About It** List all the foods you ate yesterday for breakfast, lunch, dinner, and snacks. What nutrients did each food provide your body?

LESSON 2 Healthy Eating

7. The amount of nutrients you need each day can be found in the

a. serving size.

b. MyPlate.

c. Calories.

d. Dietary Reference Intakes.

8. The _____ on two food labels show which food has more iron.

Use the table to answer Questions 9–10.

Comparing Nutrient Data

Food (1 cup)	Calcium (% Daily Value)	Calories	Calories from Fat
Chocolate milk	30	230	80
Low-fat milk	30	110	20
Plain yogurt	35	110	35

9. Interpret Data How many cups of low-fat milk provide 100% of the day's Daily Value for calcium?

_____

10. Classify Which food group do these foods belong to? How can you find out how much food you need to consume from this group each day?

_____

_____

_____

_____

_____

_____

_____

The Digestive Process Begins

11. Mechanical digestion begins in the

    a. liver.   **b.** esophagus.

    c. mouth.   **d.** small intestine.

12. _____ is the involuntary contraction of muscles that pushes food forward.

13. Relate Cause and Effect How does mucus affect food in the digestive system?

_____

_____

_____

_____

14. Interpret Diagrams How do you think acid reflux, the condition illustrated in the diagram below, affects the esophagus?

_____

_____

_____

_____

Stomach acid

Esophagus

Stomach

15. Write About It Have you ever choked when eating? Explain what happens in a person's body when they choke. Describe some things people can do to avoid choking while eating.

Final Digestion and Absorption

16. Bile is produced by the

    a. liver.   **b.** pancreas.

    c. small intestine.   **d.** large intestine.

17. Most materials are absorbed into the blood in the _____ intestine.

18. Predict Suppose a medicine killed all the bacteria in your body. How might this affect vitamin production in your body?

_____

_____

_____

_____

_____

APPLY THE BIG ? **How does food become materials your body can use?**

19. Describe the journey of a piece of cheese through your digestive system. Start in the stomach and end with absorption. Include where the digestion of proteins and fats takes place.

_____

_____

_____

_____

_____

_____

_____

_____

Standardized Test Prep

Multiple Choice

Circle the letter of the best answer.

Use the table to answer Question 1.

Length of Time Food Usually Stays in Organs	
Organ	**Time**
Mouth	Less than 1 minute
Stomach	1 to 3 hours
Small Intestine	1 to 6 hours
Large Intestine	12 to 36 hours

1. If a person eats at noon, absorption cannot have begun by

   A 1 P.M.   **B** 7 P.M.

   C 9 P.M.   **D** noon the next day.

2. Which of the following nutrients provides the *most* energy for the body?

   A proteins

   B fats

   C carbohydrates

   D vitamins

3. A food label on a cereal box gives you the following information: a serving size equals one cup, and each serving has 110 Calories. You measure the amount of cereal you plan to eat. It measures $1\frac{1}{2}$ cups. How many Calories will you consume?

   A 110 Calories

   B 165 Calories

   C 220 Calories

   D 1,100 Calories

4. Which of the following parts of the digestive system is paired with its function?

   A esophagus—digests carbohydrates

   B stomach—digests fats

   C small intestine—begins mechanical digestion

   D large intestine—absorbs water

5. According to the USDA guidelines, the *most* healthful diet limits one's intake of

   A sugar and fats.

   B water.

   C grains.

   D fruits and vegetables.

Constructed Response

The diagram below uses a model to show how enzymes work. Use the diagram and your knowledge of science to help you answer Question 6. Write your answer on a separate sheet of paper.

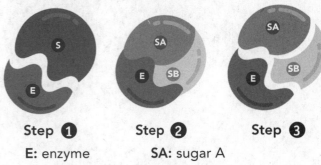

Step ❶   Step ❷   Step ❸

E: enzyme   SA: sugar A
S: starch   SB: sugar B

6. Look at each step of the process shown in the diagram. Use the steps to explain how enzymes are involved in the digestive process.

WHAT'S IN ENERGY DRINKS?

Have you ever looked closely at advertisements for energy drinks? They claim all sorts of things. Some say they will give you energy. Others say that they will replace vital nutrients. Will they turn you into a star athlete, as some claim?

Where does the "energy" come from? In almost all energy drinks, caffeine and sugar are what give you the "boost." Caffeine is a powerful stimulant. It excites your central nervous system. Some energy drinks have as much caffeine as three cups of coffee! Caffeine can cause your heart to beat faster. It can also cause nervousness, irritability, and insomnia, and make it difficult for you to concentrate. Sugars such as glucose and fructose provide a quick boost of energy that doesn't last long. These sugars can make you tired as you burn the energy they provide.

Design It Many energy drinks claim to have safe, natural ingredients that boost energy. Research some common ingredients in energy drinks to find out what their effects are. Are there risks involved in consuming these ingredients? Are the claims made about these energy drinks regulated in any way? Create a presentation for your class that compares the claims with the reality. How would you test the claims?

ROBOTIC PILLS

Imagine swallowing a robot! A new type of pill really is a tiny robot. Before it is swallowed, the robotic pill can be programmed with specific instructions, such as when to release the medication inside it. This robotic pill can be swallowed with a glass of water. When it reaches the target area inside the body, a miniature pump releases the medicine. Doctors can also use a radio transmitter to control the pill.

Robotic pills were developed to treat digestive tract disorders like Crohn's disease. Crohn's disease makes the intestines swollen and irritated. It causes pain and extreme weight loss. People with Crohn's disease have difficulty digesting a lot of food. Traditionally, doctors had to give patients huge doses of medication for enough of the medicine to survive the digestive system and help the patient. These huge doses caused side effects, such as headaches and fevers. The new pill can deliver smaller bursts of medication over longer periods of time. This reduces the medicine's side effects, so people don't get headaches or fevers. The pill could be the beginning of a new form of robotic medicine!

▲ This robotic pill contains a tiny camera that allows doctors to see video images of the patient's digestive system.

Design It Working in teams of two or three, consider other potential uses for this robotic pill technology. How else might doctors use a pill that can deliver medications or other chemicals throughout the body? Create a computer presentation of your proposal.

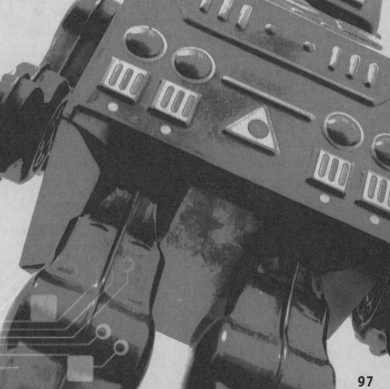

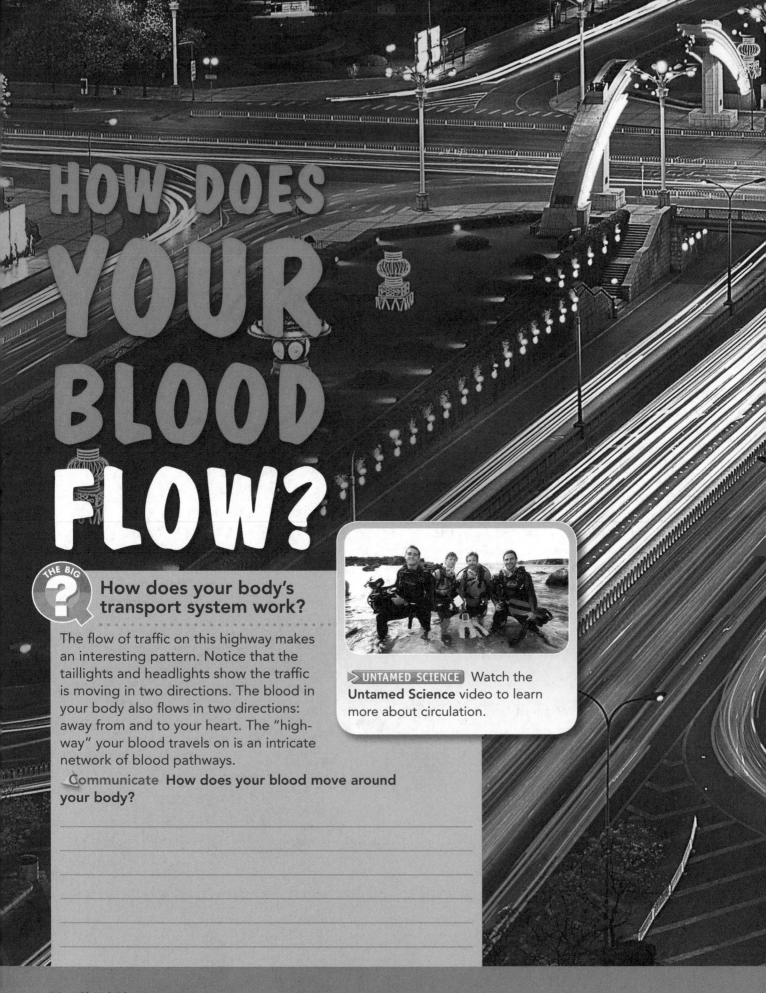

HOW DOES YOUR BLOOD FLOW?

THE BIG ?

How does your body's transport system work?

The flow of traffic on this highway makes an interesting pattern. Notice that the taillights and headlights show the traffic is moving in two directions. The blood in your body also flows in two directions: away from and to your heart. The "highway" your blood travels on is an intricate network of blood pathways.

Communicate How does your blood move around your body?

_____

_____

_____

_____

_____

> **UNTAMED SCIENCE** Watch the **Untamed Science** video to learn more about circulation.

Circulation

CHAPTER 4

Circulation   › UNTAMED SCIENCE   › THE BIG QUESTION

4 Getting Started

Check Your Understanding

1. **Background** Read the paragraph below and then answer the question.

Each day, Ken circulates from the food pantry to senior centers around the city and then returns to the pantry. He transports meals and juice to the seniors and collects their empty bottles. Similarly, your blood circulates in your body. From the heart, your blood carries oxygen and glucose to your body cells. It picks up wastes before returning to the heart.

> To **circulate** is to move in a circle and return to the same point.
>
> To **transport** is to carry something from one place to another.
>
> **Glucose** is a sugar that is the major source of energy for the body's cells.

• What materials does your blood transport to your body cells?

_____

_____

▶ **MY READING WEB** If you had trouble completing the question above, visit **My Reading Web** and type in *Circulation.*

Vocabulary Skill

Greek Word Origins Some science words contain word parts with Greek origins. The table below lists two Greek words that some English words come from.

Greek Word	Meaning of Greek Word	Example
haima	blood	hemoglobin, *n.* an iron-containing protein in red blood cells
kardia	heart	cardiovascular, *adj.* related to the heart, blood vessels, and blood

2. **Quick Check** The English word *vascular* means "having vessels or ducts." So, *cardiovascular* means "of the heart and blood vessels." In the table, circle the Greek word meaning "heart."

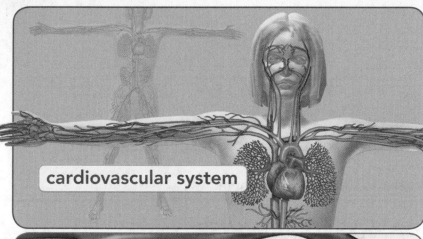

cardiovascular system

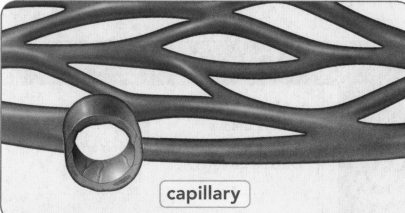

capillary

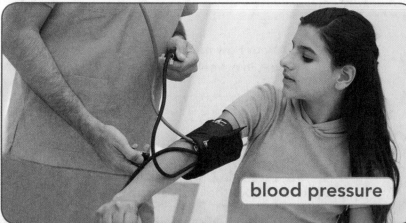

blood pressure

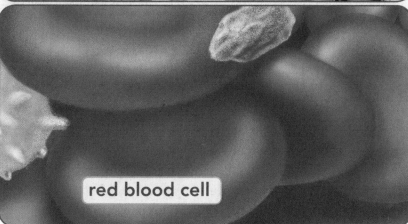

red blood cell

Chapter Preview

LESSON 1
- cardiovascular system
- heart
- atrium
- ventricle
- pacemaker
- valve
- artery
- aorta
- capillary
- vein
- ↻ Sequence
- △ Calculate

LESSON 2
- coronary artery
- diffusion
- blood pressure
- ↻ Summarize
- △ Infer

LESSON 3
- plasma
- red blood cell
- hemoglobin
- white blood cell
- platelet
- lymphatic system
- lymph
- lymph node
- ↻ Identify the Main Idea
- △ Draw Conclusions

LESSON 4
- atherosclerosis
- heart attack
- hypertension
- ↻ Relate Cause and Effect
- △ Communicate

> VOCAB FLASH CARDS For extra help with vocabulary, visit **Vocab Flash Cards** and type in *Circulation.*

The Body's Transport System

UNLOCK THE BIG Q?

- 🔑 What Is the Role of the Cardiovascular System?

- 🔑 What Is the Role of the Heart?

- 🔑 How Does Blood Travel Through Your Body?

my PLANET DiARY

Your Heart, Your Health

Here are some fascinating facts that you may not know about your heart.

- In one year, your heart pumps enough blood to fill more than 30 competition-sized swimming pools!

- A drop of blood makes the entire trip through your body in less than a minute.

- Your heart beats about 100,000 times a day.

- Your heart pushes blood through about 100,000 kilometers of vessels. They would circle Earth more than twice!

- A child's heart is about the size of a fist. An adult's heart is about the size of two fists.

FUN FACTS

Read the following questions. Write your answers below.

1. Why is it important for a person's heart to be healthy?

_____

_____

_____

2. About how many times does your heart beat in a week? In a year?

_____

_____

_____

> PLANET DIARY   Go to **Planet Diary** to learn more about the body's transport system.

Lab zone®   Do the Inquiry Warm-Up *Observing a Heart.*

What Is the Role of the Cardiovascular System?

As shown in **Figure 1,** the **cardiovascular system,** or circulatory system, is made up of the heart, blood vessels, and blood. 🔑 The cardiovascular system delivers needed substances to cells, carries wastes away from cells, and helps regulate body temperature. In addition, blood contains cells that fight disease.

Vocabulary
- cardiovascular system • heart • atrium
- ventricle • pacemaker • valve • artery
- aorta • capillary • vein

Skills
↻ **Reading:** Sequence
△ **Inquiry:** Calculate

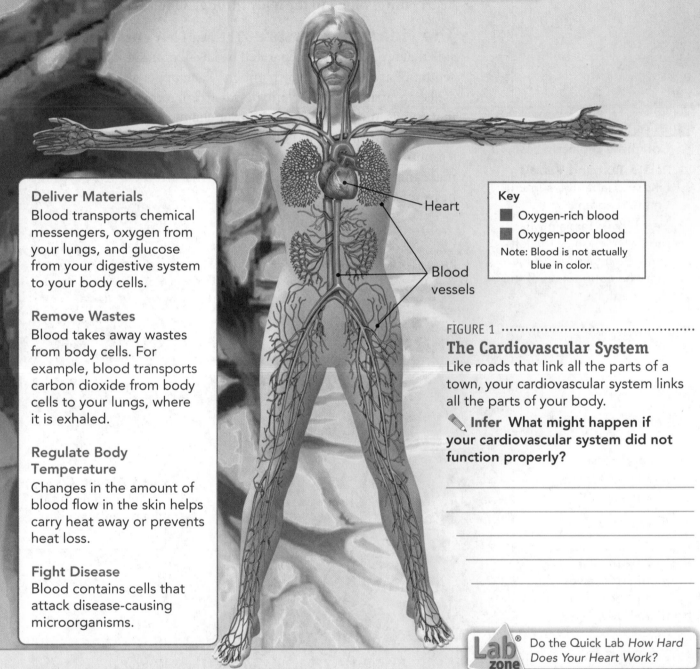

Heart

Blood vessels

Key
■ Oxygen-rich blood
■ Oxygen-poor blood
Note: Blood is not actually blue in color.

Deliver Materials
Blood transports chemical messengers, oxygen from your lungs, and glucose from your digestive system to your body cells.

Remove Wastes
Blood takes away wastes from body cells. For example, blood transports carbon dioxide from body cells to your lungs, where it is exhaled.

Regulate Body Temperature
Changes in the amount of blood flow in the skin helps carry heat away or prevents heat loss.

Fight Disease
Blood contains cells that attack disease-causing microorganisms.

FIGURE 1 ·····························
The Cardiovascular System
Like roads that link all the parts of a town, your cardiovascular system links all the parts of your body.

✎ **Infer** What might happen if your cardiovascular system did not function properly?

_____

_____

_____

_____

_____

Lab zone Do the Quick Lab *How Hard Does Your Heart Work?*

☞ Assess Your Understanding

got it? ·····························

○ **I get it!** Now I know that the cardiovascular system _____

_____

○ **I need extra help with** _____

Go to **MY SCIENCE** ⑤ **COACH** online for help with this subject.

What Is the Role of the Heart?

Without your heart your blood would not go anywhere. As **Figure 2** shows, the heart is a hollow, muscular organ. 🔑 **The heart pumps blood to the body through blood vessels.**

The Heart's Structure The heart has a right side and left side that are completely separated by a wall of tissue called the septum. Each side has two chambers. Each upper chamber, called an **atrium** (AY tree um; plural *atria*), receives blood that comes into the heart. Each lower chamber, called a **ventricle,** pumps blood out of the heart. The **pacemaker,** a group of cells in the right atrium, sends out signals that make the heart muscle contract. The signals regulate heart rate.

FIGURE 2 ·······························

▷ INTERACTIVE ART The Heart
✎ Complete the activities.

1. **Relate Text and Visuals** Find and label the septum on the diagram.

2. CHALLENGE Explain why the contraction of the left ventricle must be stronger than the contraction of the right ventricle.

_____

_____

_____

_____

_____

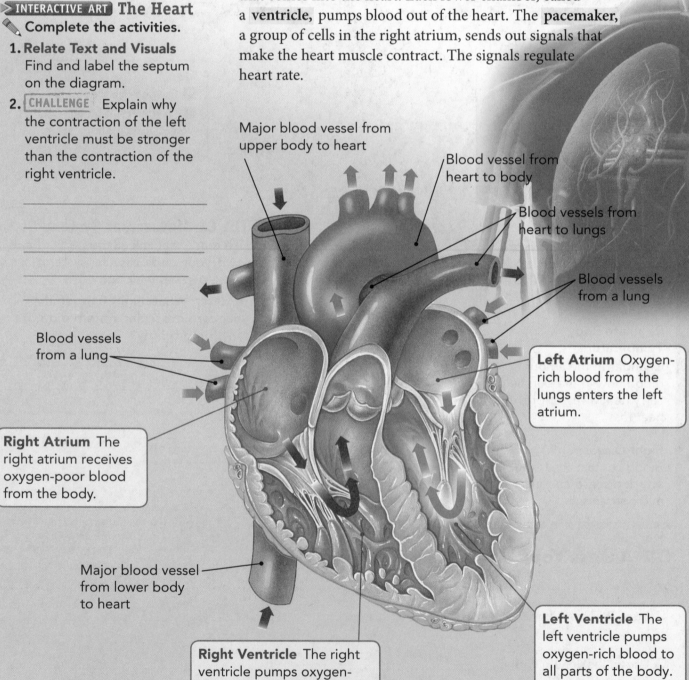

Major blood vessel from upper body to heart

Blood vessel from heart to body

Blood vessels from heart to lungs

Blood vessels from a lung

Blood vessels from a lung

Left Atrium Oxygen-rich blood from the lungs enters the left atrium.

Right Atrium The right atrium receives oxygen-poor blood from the body.

Major blood vessel from lower body to heart

Left Ventricle The left ventricle pumps oxygen-rich blood to all parts of the body.

Right Ventricle The right ventricle pumps oxygen-poor blood to the lungs.

How the Heart Works

Valves separate the atria from the ventricles. A **valve** is a flap of tissue that prevents blood from flowing backward. Valves also separate the ventricles and the large blood vessels that carry blood away from the heart.

A heartbeat sounds something like *lub-dup*. First, the heart muscle relaxes, and the atria fill with blood. Next, the atria contract, squeezing blood through valves, like those in **Figure 3.** Then the blood moves into the ventricles. The ventricles contract. This contraction closes the valves between the atria and ventricles, making the *lub* sound and squeezing blood into large blood vessels. Finally, the valves between the ventricles and blood vessels snap shut, making the *dup* sound. All this happens in less than one second.

✏️ **Sequence** In the text, underline each step involved in a heartbeat. Number the steps. Then write the steps in the table below.

FIGURE 3 ⋯⋯⋯⋯⋯⋯⋯⋯
Heart Valves
Like a faucet controls the flow of water, valves control the flow of blood through the heart.

Open Valve

Closed Valve

Step 1	
Step 2	
Step 3	
Step 4	
Step 5	
Step 6	

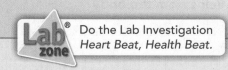
Lab zone® Do the Lab Investigation *Heart Beat, Health Beat.*

🔑 Assess Your Understanding

1a. Name The _____ sends out signals that make the heart muscle contract.

b. Predict What do you think would happen if a valve in the heart did not close?

_____

_____

got it?

○ **I get it!** Now I know that the heart _____

_____

○ **I need extra help with** _____

Go to **MY SCIENCE** ⬤ **COACH** *online for help with this subject.*

How Does Blood Travel Through Your Body?

As you can see in **Figure 4,** the overall pattern of blood flow through the body is similar to a figure eight. The heart is at the center where the two loops cross. **In the first loop, blood travels from the heart to the lungs and then back to the heart. In the second loop, blood travels from the heart throughout the body and then back to the heart.**

Your body has three kinds of blood vessels: arteries, capillaries, and veins. **Arteries** carry blood away from the heart. For example, blood in the left ventricle is pumped into the **aorta** (ay AWR tuh), the largest artery in the body. From the arteries, blood flows into tiny vessels called **capillaries.** In the capillaries, substances are exchanged between the blood and body cells. From capillaries, blood flows into **veins,** which carry blood back to the heart.

Vocabulary Greek Word Origins The Greek word *kardia* means "heart." The English word *cardiac* is based on this Greek root. What do you think the word *cardiology* means?

FIGURE 4

Two Loops

Your heart can pump 5 liters of blood through the two loops each minute.

✏ **Interpret Diagrams** In each box, write where the blood from the heart travels to. Then tell where blood travels after it leaves each part listed below.

Right atrium

Veins from the body

Arteries to the lungs

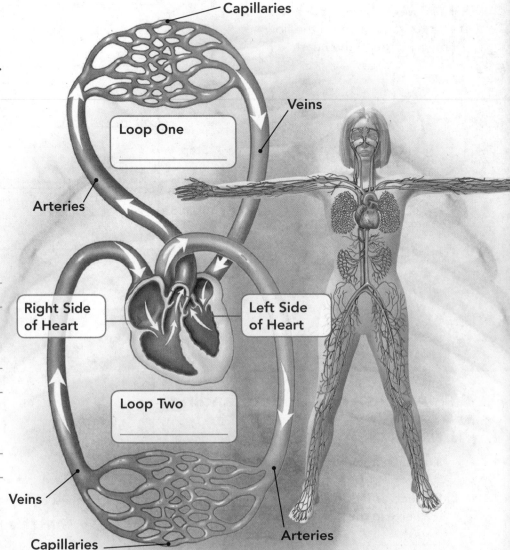

Capillaries

Veins

Loop One

Arteries

Right Side of Heart

Left Side of Heart

Loop Two

Veins

Capillaries

Arteries

do the math!

When you exercise, your heart pumps more blood through your body than when you are at rest.

1 Read Graphs About how much more blood flows through the body during exercise than at rest?

_____

_____

_____

2 Calculate About how much blood flows through the body each second at rest? During exercise?

_____

_____

_____

_____

_____

3 Infer Why do you think the rate that blood flows through the body is greater during exercise than it is at rest?

_____

_____

_____

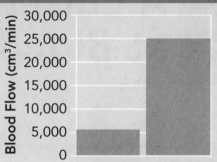

Average Rate of Blood Flow Through the Body

Blood Flow (cm³/min): 30,000 / 25,000 / 20,000 / 15,000 / 10,000 / 5,000 / 0

At Rest   During Exercise

🔑 Assess Your Understanding

2a. Identify Where does blood returning from the lungs enter the heart?

_____

_____

b. Draw Conclusions Why must your blood complete both loops to keep you healthy?

_____

_____

_____

 Do the Quick Lab
Direction of Blood Flow.

got it?

○ **I get it!** Now I know that blood travels _____

_____

_____

_____

○ **I need extra help with** _____

Go to MY SCIENCE COACH online for help with this subject.

A Closer Look at Blood Vessels

UNLOCK THE BIG ?

🔑 **What Is the Role of Blood Vessels?**

🔑 **What Causes Blood Pressure?**

my pLaneT DiaRY

What Color Is Your Blood?

Misconception: Blood can be blue.

You might think the blood flowing through your veins is blue because blue is what you see through your skin. However, no matter where blood is found in your body, it is always red. Blood found in most of your arteries is bright red because it is rich in oxygen. Blood found in most of your veins is oxygen poor, so it is dark red in color. Think about a time when you cut yourself. Did you bleed blue blood? Now that would be scary!

MISCONCEPTION

Read the following questions. Write your answers below.

1. Why is some blood bright red and some blood dark red?

_____

_____

_____

2. Why do you think you can see veins better than arteries in your wrist?

_____

_____

_____

_____

▷ PLANET DIARY Go to **Planet Diary** to learn more about blood vessels.

Lab zone® Do the Inquiry Warm-Up *How Does Pressure Affect Blood Flow?*

Vocabulary
- coronary artery
- diffusion
- blood pressure

Skills
- Reading: Summarize
- Inquiry: Infer

What Is the Role of Blood Vessels?

Like hallways in a large building, blood vessels run through all the tissues of your body. Although some blood vessels are as wide as your thumb, most of them are much finer than a human hair. If all the blood vessels in your body were hooked together end to end, they would stretch a distance of almost 100,000 kilometers. That's long enough to wrap around Earth twice—with a lot left over!

You know that you have three kinds of blood vessels—arteries, capillaries, and veins. These three kinds of vessels have different structures and functions. **Arteries are thick-walled, muscular vessels that carry blood away from the heart to the body's cells. Capillaries are tiny, thin-walled vessels where materials and wastes are exchanged between the blood and the body's cells. Veins are large vessels with walls thinner than artery walls that carry blood from the body cells back to the heart.**

Summarize Fill in the table with the information from this lesson about blood vessels. Then write a title for the table.

Blood Vessel	Function	Structure
Artery		
Capillary		
Vein		

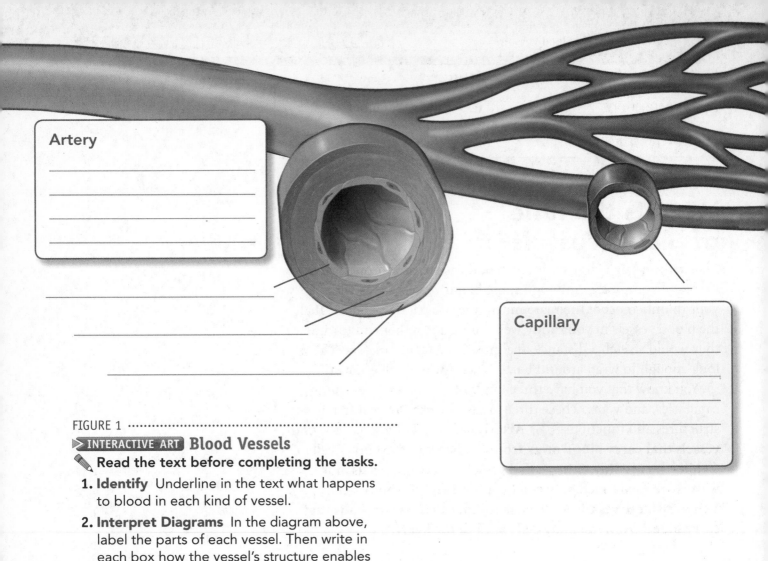

Artery

_____
_____
_____
_____

Capillary

_____
_____
_____
_____

FIGURE 1 ··

▷ **INTERACTIVE ART** **Blood Vessels**

✎ **Read the text before completing the tasks.**

1. **Identify** Underline in the text what happens to blood in each kind of vessel.

2. **Interpret Diagrams** In the diagram above, label the parts of each vessel. Then write in each box how the vessel's structure enables it to function.

···············✎···············

Observe The alternating relaxing and contracting of arteries as blood is forced through them results in a pulse. Touch the inside of your wrist and find your pulse. How many heartbeats do you count in one minute?

_____
_____

Arteries Arteries, shown in **Figure 1,** carry blood from the heart toward body organs. Two large arteries carry blood from the heart. One leaves the right ventricle and carries blood to the lungs. The other, the aorta, leaves the left ventricle and carries blood to the other organs. As these arteries move away from the heart, they branch into smaller arteries. The first branches off the aorta, called the **coronary arteries,** carry blood to the heart itself. Other branches carry blood to the other organs.

In general, the thick, elastic artery walls have three tissue layers. The innermost layer is epithelial tissue that enables blood to flow freely. The middle layer is mostly smooth muscle tissue that relaxes and contracts, allowing the artery to widen and narrow. This layer regulates the amount of blood sent to different organs. The outer layer is flexible connective tissue. These layers enable arteries to withstand the force of pumping blood.

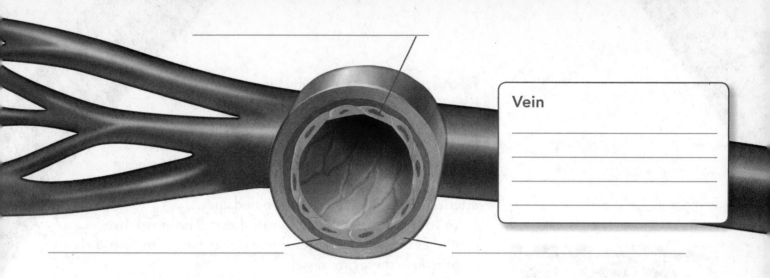

Vein

Capillaries

Blood flows from arteries into tiny capillaries. Capillary walls are made of a single layer of epithelial cells. Materials pass easily from the blood, through the capillary walls, and into the body cells. The waste products of cells travel in the opposite direction.

One way materials and wastes pass through capillary walls is by diffusion. In **diffusion,** molecules move from an area of higher concentration to an area of lower concentration. For example, blood contains more glucose than cells do. As a result, glucose diffuses from the blood into body cells.

Veins

Capillaries merge and form larger vessels called veins. From capillaries, blood enters veins and travels back to the heart. The walls of veins have the same tissue layers as arteries. However, the walls of veins are thinner than artery walls.

do the math!

The table shows percentages of total blood flow through skeletal muscles at rest and during exercise.

1 **Infer** What is the difference between the percentage of blood flow during rest and during exercise? Explain your reasoning.

_____

_____

_____

Percentage of Total Blood Flow Through Skeletal Muscles	
Skeletal Muscles at Rest	18%
Skeletal Muscles During Exercise	75%

2 **CHALLENGE** Which organ do you think also receives more blood during exercise than at rest? Explain.

_____

_____

Moving Blood

Moving blood through your body involves many factors. The contractions of your heart's ventricles force blood into and through your arteries. You can see an artery in **Figure 2.** As your arteries become smaller, the force from the heart lessens. However, the blood that continues to enter these arteries from behind pushes the blood ahead.

In your capillaries, blood moves slowly. The blood that continues to enter capillaries from arteries pushes the blood ahead of it through these tiny vessels.

Blood flows into veins with little pumping force of the heart behind it. So, many other factors must help the blood move. First, the volume of blood from the capillaries collecting in veins helps to push along the blood ahead of it. Second, the contraction of skeletal muscles helps push along the blood. Third, larger veins have valves that keep blood from flowing backward. Finally, breathing movements help force blood in the chest veins back toward the heart.

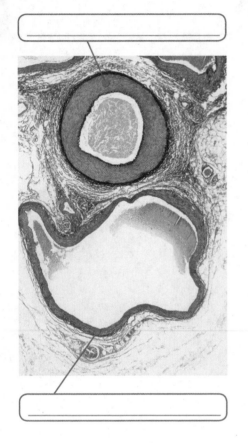

FIGURE 2 ·······································

An Artery and a Vein

This photo is a microscopic view of an artery and a vein.

✎ **Interpret Photos** Label the artery and the vein. Explain the evidence that supports each label.

_____

_____

_____

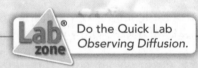
Do the Quick Lab
Observing Diffusion.

🔑 Assess Your Understanding

1a. Describe In which direction do arteries carry blood?

_____

_____

b. Compare and Contrast How are arteries and veins alike? How are they different?

_____

_____

_____

got it?

○ **I get it!** Now I know that the structure of blood vessels _____

_____

_____

_____

○ **I need extra help with** _____

Go to **MY SCIENCE** 🔵 **COACH** *online for help with this subject.*

What Causes Blood Pressure?

Similar to the way moving water exerts pressure on the walls of a hose, blood exerts a force called **blood pressure** against the walls of blood vessels. ⚯ **The force with which ventricles contract causes blood pressure.** In general, blood flowing through arteries near the heart exerts higher pressure on the vessel walls than blood flowing through arteries farther from the heart. Blood pressure in veins is always very low.

As shown in **Figure 3,** blood pressure is measured using a cuff that is wrapped around the upper arm. Air is pumped into the cuff until it stops the blood flowing through the artery. As the pressure is released, the examiner listens to the pulse and records two numbers. The first number is a measure of blood pressure when the ventricles contract. The second, lower number measures blood pressure while the ventricles relax. The two numbers are expressed as a fraction: the contraction pressure over the relaxation pressure. A typical blood pressure reading for a healthy adult is about 120 over 80. The reading is expressed as the fraction 120/80.

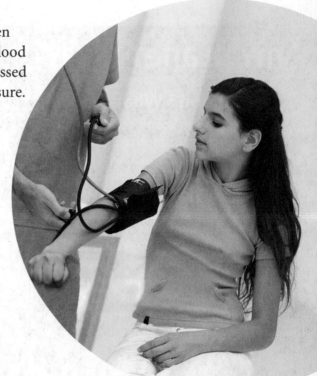

FIGURE 3 ⋯⋯⋯⋯⋯⋯⋯⋯⋯⋯⋯⋯⋯⋯⋯⋯⋯⋯

Measuring Blood Pressure

Blood pressure can be measured using an instrument called a sphygmomanometer (sfig moh muh NAHM uh tur).

✎ **Apply Concepts** Explain how this student's blood pressure reading would be different if the instrument were on her leg.

_____

_____

_____

Lab zone ® Do the Quick Lab *Blood Pressure.*

⚯ Assess Your Understanding

2a. Define What is blood pressure?

_____

_____

b. Relate Cause and Effect How might having low blood pressure affect your body?

_____

_____

_____

got it?

○ **I get it!** Now I know that blood pressure is

_____

_____

_____

○ **I need extra help with** _____

Go to **my science** ⬤ᔆ **coach** *online for help with this subject.*

113

Composition of Blood

UNLOCK THE BIG ?

🔑 **What Does Blood Contain?**

🔑 **What Is the Role of Blood Types in Transfusions?**

my planet Diary

DISCOVERY

Blood? What Blood?

If a crime scene seems to have no evidence, is it impossible to solve the crime? Not necessarily. Specialists known as forensic scientists help find evidence not visible to the naked eye. Forensic scientists use a chemical called luminol. This chemical was discovered in 1928 by a chemist named H.O. Albrecht. When luminol is sprayed on a surface with even microscopic amounts of blood, it reacts with the iron in red blood cells. The result is a glowing bluish-green light. At a crime scene, the glow of luminol can make evidence visible.

Read the question. Write your answer below.
How can luminol help solve crimes?

_____

_____

_____

▷ **PLANET DIARY** Go to **Planet Diary** to learn more about blood.

 Do the Inquiry Warm-Up *What Kinds of Cells Are in Blood?*

What Does Blood Contain?

While riding your bike, you fall off and scrape your knee. Your knee stings, and blood oozes from the open wound. You go inside to clean the scrape. As you do, you wonder, "Just what is blood?"

Blood is a complex tissue. 🔑 **Blood has four components: plasma, red blood cells, white blood cells, and platelets.** About 45 percent of the volume of blood is cells. The rest is plasma. The graph in **Figure 1** shows blood's components.

Vocabulary
- plasma • red blood cell • hemoglobin
- white blood cell • platelet • lymphatic system
- lymph • lymph node

Skills
↻ Reading: Identify the Main Idea
△ Inquiry: Draw Conclusions

Plasma Most materials transported in blood travel in the plasma. **Plasma** is the liquid part of the blood. Water makes up 90 percent of plasma. The other 10 percent is dissolved materials. Plasma carries nutrients, such as glucose, fats, vitamins, and minerals. Plasma also carries chemical messengers that direct body activities, such as how your cells use glucose. In addition, plasma carries away most of the carbon dioxide and many other wastes that cell processes produce.

If you looked at plasma, it would appear yellow because of protein molecules in it. There are three groups of proteins in plasma. One group helps regulate the amount of water in blood. The second group, produced by white blood cells, helps fight disease. The third group of proteins interacts with platelets to form blood clots.

List On the notebook, list and describe the materials that plasma carries.

FIGURE 1 ··········

Blood Components
Blood is a tissue. It contains plasma and specialized cells. In turn, plasma contains dissolved materials and water.

✎ **Relate Text and Visuals** On the graph, label the components of blood. Then write the percentages of each component.

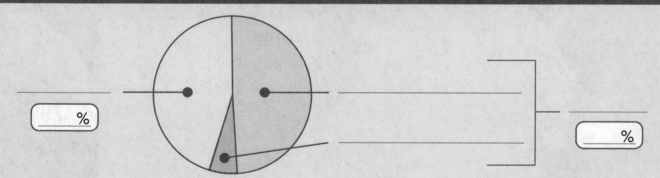

Blood's Components

did you know?

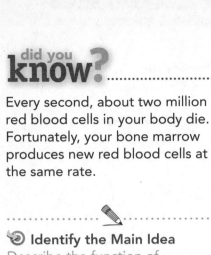

Every second, about two million red blood cells in your body die. Fortunately, your bone marrow produces new red blood cells at the same rate.

✏

⟲ Identify the Main Idea
Describe the function of hemoglobin in the blood.

_____

_____

_____

_____

_____

_____

FIGURE 2 ·······················

▶ VIRTUAL LAB Cells in Blood
In addition to red and white blood cells, blood contains platelets, the fragments of cells.
✏ **Relate Text and Visuals** In the boxes, write the function of each component. Include where the blood cells are produced.

Red Blood Cells Without red blood cells like those shown in **Figure 2,** your body could not use the oxygen in the air you breathe. **Red blood cells** take up oxygen in the lungs and deliver it to cells throughout the body. Red blood cells, like most blood cells, are produced in bone marrow. A red blood cell is made mostly of **hemoglobin** (HEE muh gloh bin), a protein that contains iron and binds chemically to oxygen molecules. When hemoglobin binds with oxygen, the cells become bright red. Without oxygen, the cells are dark red.

Hemoglobin picks up oxygen in the lungs. It releases oxygen as the blood travels through the body's capillaries. Hemoglobin also picks up some of the carbon dioxide that cells produce. However, plasma carries most of the carbon dioxide. Carbon dioxide is released from the lungs when you exhale.

Mature red blood cells have no nuclei. Without a nucleus, a red blood cell cannot reproduce or repair itself. Mature red blood cells live only about 120 days.

Red Blood Cells

_____

_____

_____

_____

_____

Platelets

_____

_____

_____

_____

_____

White Blood Cells

White Blood Cells Like red blood cells, white blood cells are produced in bone marrow. **White blood cells** are the body's disease fighters. Some white blood cells recognize disease-causing organisms, such as bacteria, and alert the body to the invasion. Other white blood cells produce chemicals to fight the invaders. Still others surround and kill the organisms.

White blood cells differ from red blood cells in several ways. There is about one white blood cell for every 500 to 1,000 red blood cells. White blood cells are larger than red blood cells and contain nuclei. They may live for days, months, or even years.

Platelets **Platelets** (PLAYT lits) are cell fragments that help form blood clots. When a blood vessel is cut, platelets collect and stick to the vessel at the site of the wound. The platelets release chemicals that produce a protein called fibrin (FY brin). Fibrin weaves a net of tiny fibers across the cut. Platelets and blood cells become trapped in the net, and a blood clot forms.

Apply Concepts What do you think happens to the number of white blood cells in the body when a person is fighting an infection? Explain.

_____

_____

_____

_____

_____

_____

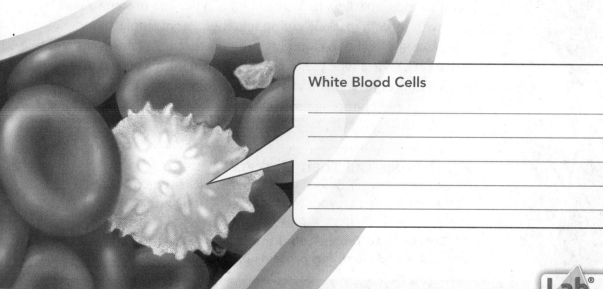

White Blood Cells

_____

_____

_____

_____

Lab ® Do the Quick Lab
zone *Modeling Plasma.*

🔑 Assess Your Understanding

1a. Define What is plasma?

_____

_____

b. Make Generalizations Why is it important for a person's blood to produce fibrin?

_____

_____

_____

_____

got it?

○ **I get it!** Now I know that blood is made of

_____

_____

_____

_____

○ **I need extra help with** _____

Go to **MY SCIENCE** 🅢 **COACH** *online for help with this subject.*

What Is the Role of Blood Types in Transfusions?

A blood transfusion is the transfer of blood from one person to another. Most early attempts at blood transfusion failed, but no one knew why. In the early 1900s, a physician named Karl Landsteiner tried mixing blood samples from two people. Sometimes the two blood samples blended smoothly. At other times, the red blood cells clumped together, clogging the capillaries and causing death.

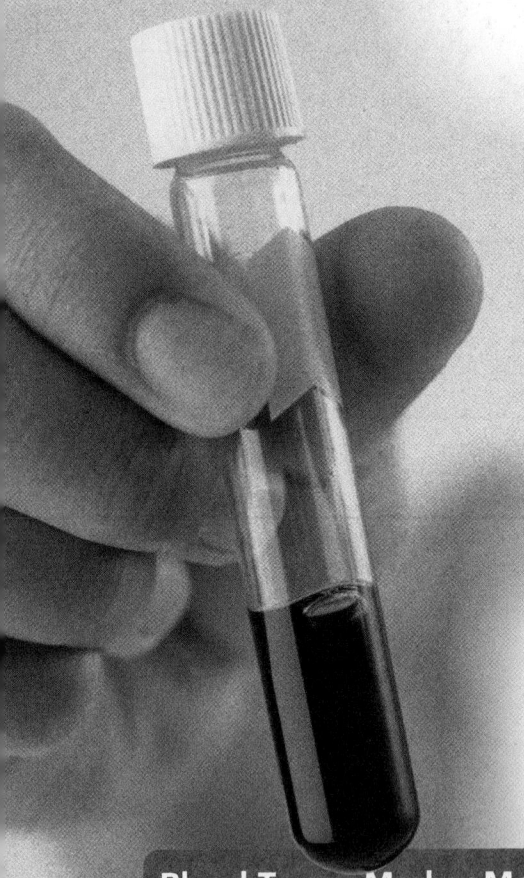

Marker Molecules Landsteiner identified the four major types of blood: A, B, AB, and O. Blood types are determined by marker molecules on red blood cells. If your blood type is A, you have the A marker. If your blood type is B, you have the B marker. People with type AB blood have both A and B markers. People with type O blood do not have A or B markers.

Clumping proteins in your plasma recognize red blood cells with "foreign" markers that are not your type. The proteins make cells with foreign markers clump together. For example, blood type A contains anti-B clumping proteins that act against cells with B markers. Blood type O has clumping proteins for both A and B markers. In **Figure 3,** you can see all the blood type marker molecules and clumping proteins.

FIGURE 3 ···

Blood Types and Their Markers

Depending on your blood type, you may have certain marker molecules on your red blood cells and certain clumping proteins in your plasma.

✎ **Create Data Tables** Label the rest of the marker molecules and clumping proteins in the table.

Blood Types, Marker Molecules, and Clumping Proteins

Blood Type Characteristic	Blood Type A	Blood Type B	Blood Type AB	Blood Type O
Marker Molecules on Red Blood Cells	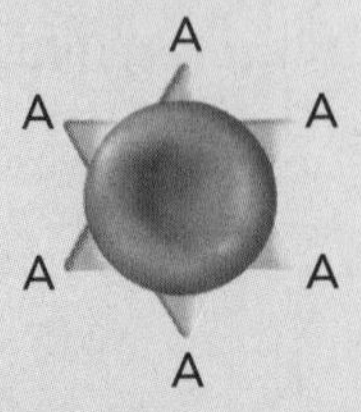 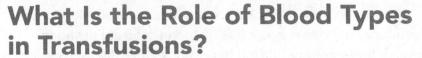			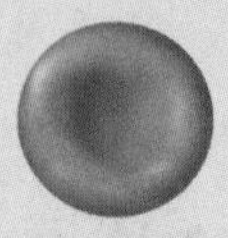
Clumping Proteins	anti-B			

Safe Transfusions Landsteiner's work led to a better understanding of transfusions. ⊙ **The marker molecules on your red blood cells determine your blood type and the type of blood you can safely receive in transfusions.** A person with type A blood can receive transfusions of either type A or type O blood. Neither of these blood types has B markers. Thus, these blood types would not be recognized as foreign by the clumping proteins in type A blood. A person with type AB blood can receive all blood types in transfusion because type AB blood has no clumping proteins.

If you ever receive a transfusion, your blood type will be checked first. Then donated blood that you can safely receive will be found. This process is called cross matching.

FIGURE 4 ······················
Blood Transfusions
Blood for transfusions is often collected at blood drives.

✎ **Complete the tasks about safe blood transfusion.**

1. **Summarize** In the graphic organizer, complete the main idea about safe transfusions. Then write the supporting details.

2. **CHALLENGE** Which blood type does a person have if that person can receive only the same blood type for a safe transfusion? Explain.

_____

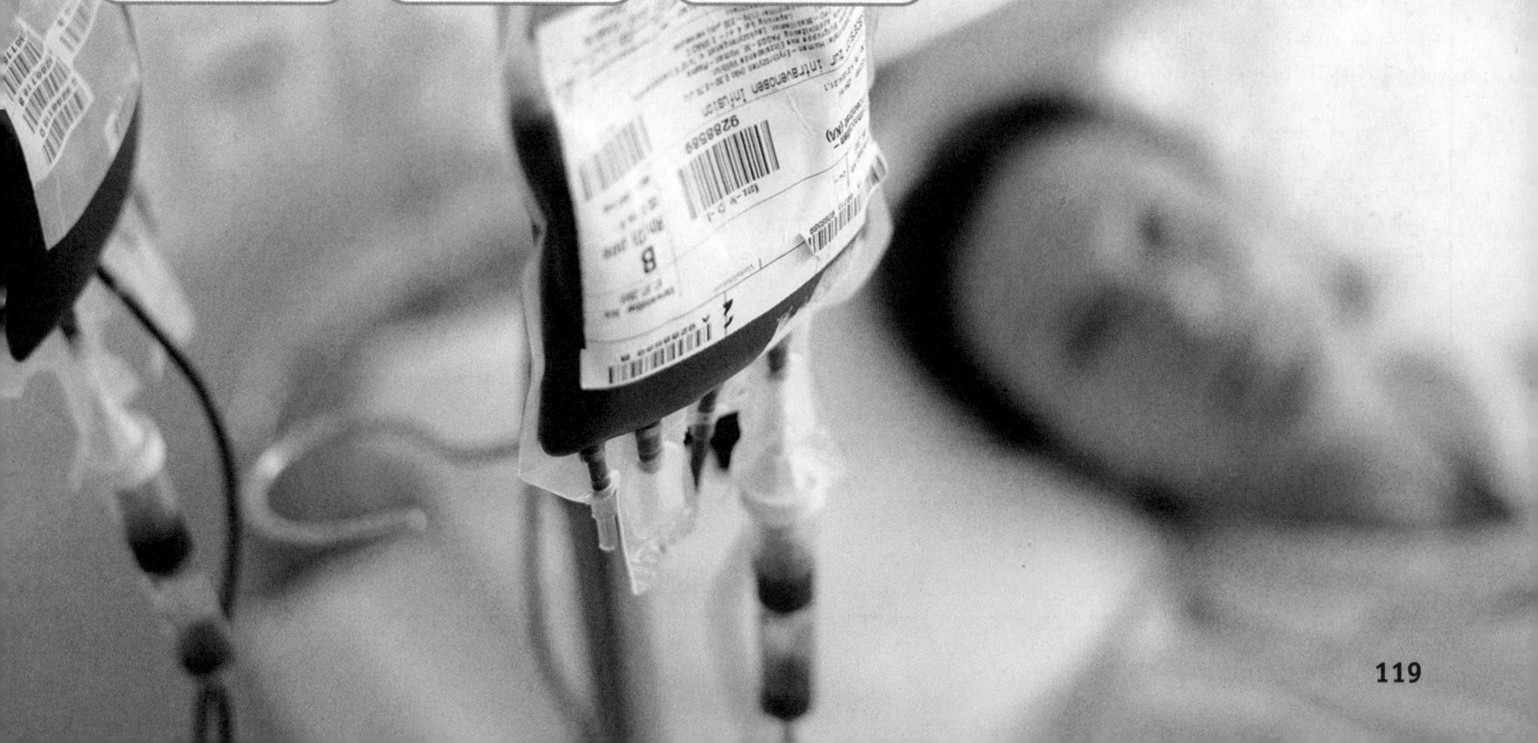

_____

_____

_____

_____

Main Idea

Marker molecules on your red blood cells

_____

_____

_____

Detail	**Detail**	**Detail**

119

Preparing blood for viewing under a microscope

Rh Factor Landsteiner also discovered a protein on red blood cells that he called *Rh factor*. About 85 percent of the people he tested had this protein. The rest did not. As with blood type, a marker molecule on the red blood cells determines the presence of Rh factor. An Rh-positive blood type has the Rh marker. An Rh-negative blood type does not. Clumping proteins will develop in Rh-negative people if they receive Rh-positive blood. This situation may be potentially dangerous.

The Lymphatic System As blood travels through the capillaries, some of the fluid moves into the surrounding tissues. This fluid carries materials that tissue cells need. After bathing the cells, this fluid moves into your body's drainage system, called the **lymphatic system** (lim FAT ik). This network of veinlike vessels returns the fluid to the bloodstream. The lymphatic system acts something like rain gutters during a rainstorm, carrying the excess fluid away.

apply it!

The circle graph shows the distribution of each blood type in the population of the United States.

❶ **Read Graphs** The four major blood types are A, B, AB, and O. Rank them from least common to most common. Include the percent of each blood type in the population.

_____

_____

❷ **Calculate** According to the graph, what percent of the population is Rh-positive? What percent is Rh-negative?

_____

_____

❸ **Draw Conclusions** Compare the percentages of Rh-positive and Rh-negative for each blood type. What can you conclude about the percentages of people with each type?

_____

_____

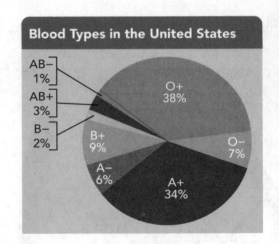

Blood Types in the United States

AB−
1%

AB+
3%

B−
2%

B+
9%

A−
6%

A+
34%

O+
38%

O−
7%

Lymph Once fluid is inside the lymphatic system, it is called **lymph.** Lymph consists of water and dissolved materials such as glucose. It also contains white blood cells that have left the capillaries. As you can see in **Figure 5,** the lymphatic system has no pump, so lymph moves slowly.

Lymph Nodes As lymph flows through the lymphatic system, it passes through small knobs of tissue called lymph nodes. **Lymph nodes** filter lymph, trapping bacteria and other disease-causing microorganisms in the fluid.

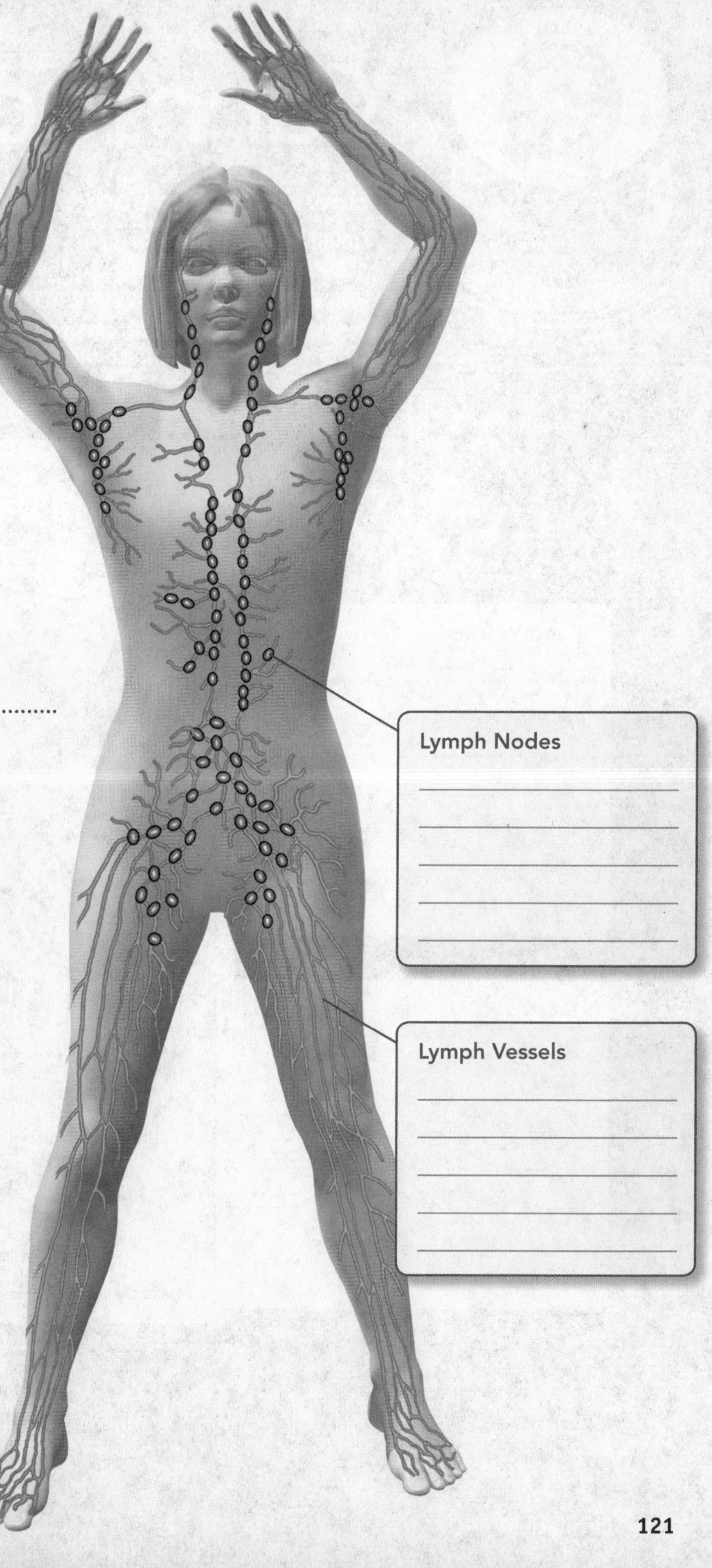

FIGURE 5 ··

The Lymphatic System

Fluid moves out of capillaries into the lymphatic system, and then returns to the bloodstream.

✎ **Complete these tasks.**

1. **Explain** In each box, describe the role of the parts of the lymphatic system.

2. **Infer** Why do you think lymph nodes sometimes swell when you have an infection?

_____
_____
_____
_____
_____

Lymph Nodes

_____
_____
_____
_____

Lymph Vessels

_____
_____
_____
_____

Carried Away

How does your body's transport system work?

FIGURE 6 ···

▶ **ART IN MOTION** The parts of the cardiovascular system transport materials throughout your body.

✎ **Summarize** Draw arrows to trace the path of blood and write the function of each labeled part.

Blood Vessels

_____
_____
_____
_____
_____
_____

Heart

_____
_____
_____
_____
_____
_____

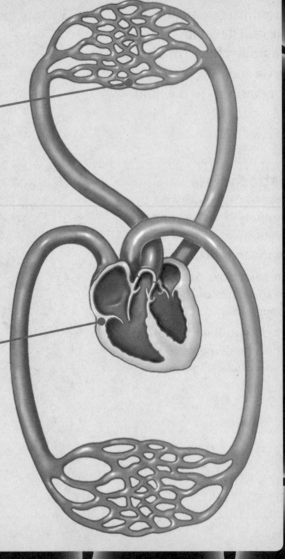

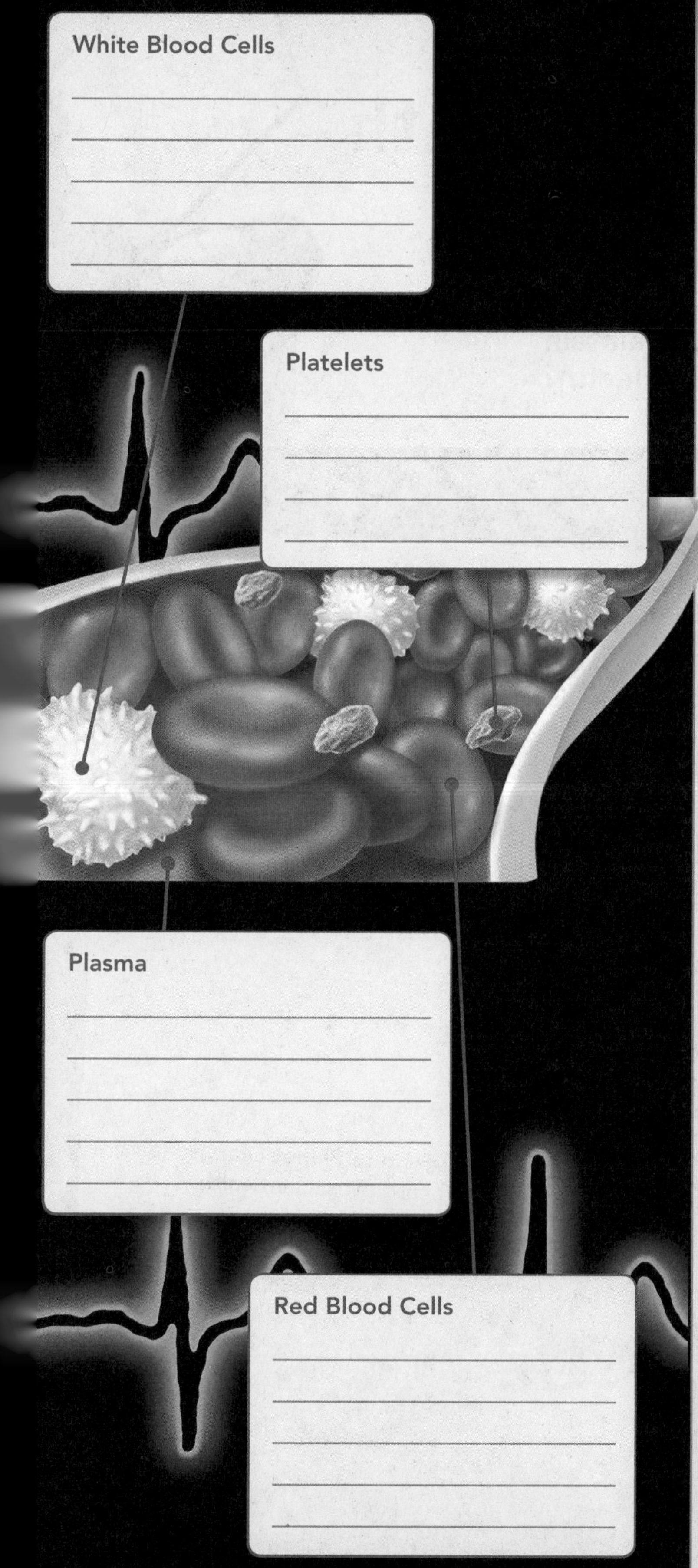

White Blood Cells

_____

_____

_____

_____

Platelets

_____

_____

_____

_____

Plasma

_____

_____

_____

_____

Red Blood Cells

_____

_____

_____

_____

Lab zone® Do the Quick Lab Do You Know Your A-B-Os?

🔑 Assess Your Understanding

2a. Review Why are the markers on blood cells important?

_____

_____

_____

_____

b. Predict Can a person with type AB– blood safely receive a transfusion of type O– blood? Explain.

_____

_____

_____

_____

_____

_____

c. ANSWER THE BIG **?** How does your body's transport system work?

_____

_____

_____

_____

_____

_____

_____

got **it?** ....

⭕ **I get it!** Now I know that blood type is determined by _____

_____

⭕ **I need extra help with** _____

Go to MY SCIENCE ⑤ COACH online for help with this subject.

Cardiovascular Health

UNLOCK THE BIG Q

🔑 **What Are Some Cardiovascular Diseases?**

🔑 **How Can You Maintain Cardiovascular Health?**

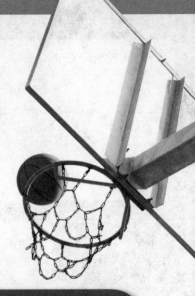

my planet Diary

PROFILE

Every Little Bit Counts

Winston School

Short Hills, New Jersey

You may think that heart disease affects only adults, but it can affect you, too. In 2008, students from more than 15,000 schools in the United States took an active role in fighting heart disease. They participated in Hoops For Heart. This fundraising program enables students to practice basketball skills, learn how to have a healthy, active lifestyle, and have fun—all at the same time.

Although their school is small, students from the Winston School in Short Hills, New Jersey, raised $9,044 to support heart disease research. The students were nationally recognized for their fundraising efforts.

Communicate Discuss the questions with a partner. Write your answers below.

1. Why is Hoops For Heart an important program?

_____

_____

2. How successful do you think your school might be if it participated in Hoops For Heart? Why?

_____

_____

_____

_____

▶ **PLANET DIARY** Go to **Planet Diary** to learn more about cardiovascular health.

Lab zone Do the Inquiry Warm-Up *Which Foods Are "Heart Healthy"?*

Vocabulary
- atherosclerosis
- hypertension
- heart attack

Skills
- Reading: Relate Cause and Effect
- Inquiry: Communicate

What Are Some Cardiovascular Diseases?

Did you know that cardiovascular disease is the leading cause of death in the United States today? One out of three teens has health issues that can lead to an increased risk of cardiovascular disease in the future. **Diseases of the cardiovascular system include atherosclerosis and hypertension.**

Atherosclerosis **Atherosclerosis** (ath uh roh skluh ROH sis) is a condition in which an artery wall thickens as a result of the buildup of fatty materials. You may have heard of one of these fatty materials—cholesterol, a substance naturally made by the body. A thickened artery wall results in a reduced flow of blood and, therefore, a decrease in oxygen moving through the artery. One artery in **Figure 1** shows atherosclerosis.

Atherosclerosis can develop in the coronary arteries, which supply blood to the heart muscle. It can eventually lead to a heart attack. A **heart attack** occurs when blood flow to part of the heart muscle is blocked, causing cells to die.

Treatment for mild atherosclerosis usually includes a low-fat diet and exercise. Medications to lower the levels of cholesterol and fats in the blood may be prescribed. Severe cases might require surgery or other procedures to unclog blocked arteries.

Relate Cause and Effect
In the text, circle the cause of atherosclerosis. Underline the effects of atherosclerosis.

FIGURE 1 ·······
Atherosclerosis
The photos show cross-sections of a healthy artery and an artery with atherosclerosis.

✎ **Use the artery photos to complete these tasks.**

1. **Interpret Photos** Label the artery that you think shows atherosclerosis. Explain your choice.

_____

_____

2. CHALLENGE Why do you think animal products are high in cholesterol?

_____

_____

_____

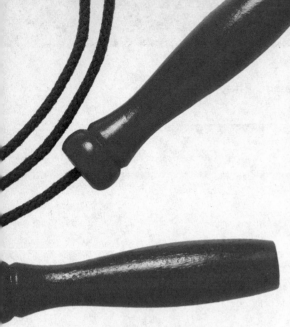

Hypertension High blood pressure, or **hypertension** (hy pur TEN shun), is a disease in which a person's blood pressure is consistently higher than normal—usually defined as greater than 140/90. Hypertension causes the heart to work harder. It also may damage the blood vessels. People with hypertension often have no obvious symptoms until the damage is severe. So, hypertension is sometimes called the "silent killer."

Hypertension and atherosclerosis are closely related. As the arteries narrow, blood pressure increases. For mild hypertension, regular exercise and careful food choices may lower blood pressure. People with hypertension may need to limit their intake of sodium, which can increase blood pressure. However, many people with hypertension require medication to lower their blood pressure.

apply it!

Many people in the United States have hypertension. The graph shows hypertension data collected by gender and age between 2003 and 2006.

❶ **Read Graphs** In what age group is the difference in blood pressure between women and men the lowest?

_____

_____

_____

❷ **Communicate** Discuss with a partner why you think more people have high blood pressure as they get older. Write your ideas below.

_____

_____

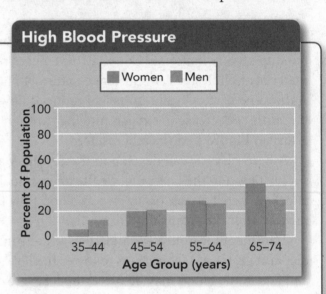

High Blood Pressure

 Do the Quick Lab
Blocking the Flow.

🔑 Assess Your Understanding

1a. Define What is atherosclerosis?

_____

_____

b. 🔄 Relate Cause and Effect How might atherosclerosis and hypertension be related?

_____

_____

got it?

○ **I get it!** Now I know that two cardiovascular diseases are _____

_____

○ **I need extra help with** _____

Go to MY SCIENCE 🅢 COACH online for help with this subject.

How Can You Maintain Cardiovascular Health?

People as young as 18 can show signs of atherosclerosis. **To help maintain cardiovascular health, people should exercise regularly; eat a balanced diet that is low in saturated fats, trans fats, cholesterol, and sodium; and avoid smoking.**

Every time you ride a bike, swim, or dance, you are helping strengthen your heart muscle and prevent atherosclerosis. Watching your diet also can help maintain healthy blood vessels. Foods that are high in cholesterol, saturated fats, and trans fats can lead to atherosclerosis. Red meats, eggs, and cheese are high in cholesterol. Butter, whole milk, and ice cream are high in saturated fats. Potato chips, and doughnuts are high in trans fat. Salty foods are high in sodium. Look for these foods in **Figure 2.**

Smokers are more than twice as likely to have a heart attack as nonsmokers are. If smokers quit, however, their risk of death from cardiovascular disease decreases.

FIGURE 2 ·······························

A Healthy Saturday?
A teenager wrote in a journal what he ate and did on a Saturday in the spring.

✎ **Apply Concepts Circle at least three things the teen should change. Suggest ways to change them.**

_____

_____

_____

_____

_____

11:00 A.M.—ate an omelet with cheese and salt
1:00 P.M.—played basketball for an hour
3:00 P.M.—ate 4 slices of pizza with pepperoni
5:00 P.M.—watched TV
7:00 P.M.—ate fish and vegetables
9:00 P.M.—ate ice cream

Lab® zone   Do the Quick Lab
Heart-Healthy Activities.

Assess Your Understanding

2a. Review Why is it important to exercise?

_____

_____

b. Explain How does eating a balanced diet help cardiovascular health?

_____

_____

got it?

○ **I get it!** Now I know that I can maintain cardiovascular health by _____

_____

_____

○ **I need extra help with** _____

Go to **MY SCIENCE** ⁵ **COACH** *online for help with this subject.*

REVIEW THE BIG ?

In the body's transport system, _____ pumped by the _____ transports materials through _____.

LESSON 1 The Body's Transport System

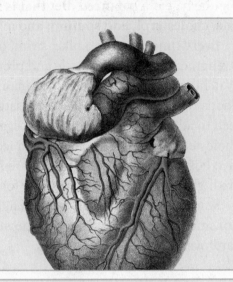

🔑 The cardiovascular system delivers needed substances to cells, carries wastes away from cells, and regulates body temperature. In addition, blood contains cells that fight disease.

🔑 The heart pumps blood to the body through blood vessels.

🔑 In the first loop, blood travels from the heart to the lungs and then back to the heart. In the second loop, blood travels from the heart throughout the body and then back to the heart.

Vocabulary
- cardiovascular system • heart • atrium • ventricle
- pacemaker • valve • artery • aorta • capillary • vein

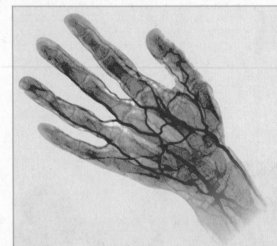

LESSON 2 A Closer Look at Blood Vessels

🔑 Arteries are thick-walled, muscular vessels that carry blood away from the heart to the body's cells. Capillaries are tiny, thin-walled vessels where materials and wastes are exchanged between the blood and the body's cells. Veins are large vessels with walls thinner than artery walls that carry blood from the body cells back to the heart.

🔑 The force with which ventricles contract causes blood pressure.

Vocabulary
- coronary artery • diffusion • blood pressure

LESSON 3 Composition of Blood

🔑 Blood has four components: plasma, red blood cells, white blood cells, and platelets.

🔑 The marker molecules on your red blood cells determine your blood type and the type of blood you can safely receive in transfusions.

Vocabulary
- plasma • red blood cell
- hemoglobin
- white blood cell • platelet
- lymphatic system • lymph
- lymph node

LESSON 4 Cardiovascular Health

🔑 Diseases of the cardiovascular system include atherosclerosis and hypertension.

🔑 To help maintain cardiovascular health, people should exercise regularly; eat a balanced diet that is low in saturated fats, trans fats, cholesterol, and sodium; and avoid smoking.

Vocabulary
- atherosclerosis
- heart attack • hypertension

Review and Assessment

LESSON 1 The Body's Transport System

1. What sends out signals that make the heart muscle contract?

   a. ventricle   **b.** pacemaker

   c. valve   **d.** artery

2. The heart, blood vessels, and _____ make up the cardiovascular system.

3. **Classify** Which chambers of the heart below are the ventricles? Through which chamber does oxygen-poor blood enter the heart?

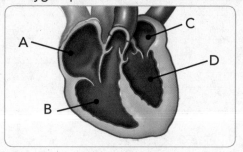

_____

_____

_____

_____

4. **Predict** Some babies are born with a hole between the left and right atria. How would this heart defect affect the ability of the cardiovascular system to deliver oxygen to body cells?

_____

_____

_____

_____

_____

5. **Write About It** Write a paragraph comparing the cardiovascular system to a system of roads. How are the systems alike and different?

LESSON 2 A Closer Look at Blood Vessels

6. Nutrients are exchanged between the blood and body cells in the

   a. capillaries.   **b.** veins.

   c. aorta.   **d.** arteries.

7. The _____ in your body carry blood back to the heart.

Use the graph below to answer Questions 8–10. The graph shows how average blood pressure changes as men and women grow older.

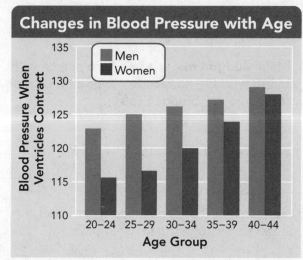

8. **Read Graphs** What is the difference in blood pressure for women from ages 24 to 44?

_____

_____

9. **Interpret Data** At age 20, are men or women more likely to have higher blood pressure?

_____

_____

10. **Draw Conclusions** In general, what happens to blood pressure as people age?

_____

_____

4 Review and Assessment

Composition of Blood

11. Blood components that help the body to control bleeding are

    a. hemoglobin.   **b.** red blood cells.

    c. white blood cells.   **d.** platelets.

12. _____ contain hemoglobin.

13. Summarize What is the role of plasma in the blood?

_____

_____

_____

14. Make Judgments Is it safe for a person with blood type O− to receive a blood transfusion from type A− blood? Explain.

_____

_____

_____

15. Sequence What happens to lymph after it travels through the lymphatic system?

_____

_____

16. Communicate How do platelets stop bleeding from a cut?

_____

_____

_____

_____

_____

17. Write About It People who do not have enough iron in their diets sometimes develop a condition called anemia in which their blood cannot carry a normal amount of oxygen. Write a paragraph to explain why this is so.

Cardiovascular Health

18. Cholesterol is a waxy substance that is associated with

    a. lymph nodes.   **b.** while blood cells.

    c. atherosclerosis.   **d.** plasma.

19. Elevated blood pressure is called

_____

20. Relate Cause and Effect Give two reasons why food choices are important to cardiovascular health.

_____

_____

_____

_____

_____

_____

APPLY THE BIG ? How does your body's transport system work?

21. A red blood cell is moving through an artery in your leg. Describe the path that the blood cell will follow back to your heart. Also, discuss one feature of the veins that helps move the cell through this path.

_____

_____

_____

_____

_____

_____

_____

_____

Standardized Test Prep

Multiple Choice

Circle the letter of the best answer.

1. Which statement below correctly describes the diagram?

    A Blood Vessel A carries blood to the heart.

    B Blood Vessel A is where a pulse can be measured.

    C Blood Vessel B is where diffusion takes place.

    D Blood Vessel B carries blood to the lungs.

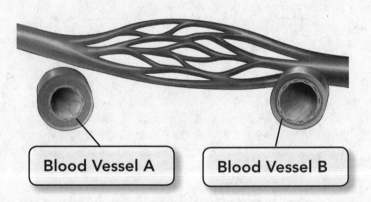

Blood Vessel A   **Blood Vessel B**

2. The most important function of the cardiovascular system is to

    A transport needed materials to body cells and remove wastes.

    B provide structural support for the lungs.

    C generate blood pressure so the arteries and veins do not collapse.

    D produce blood and lymph.

3. Which of the following is true about blood in the aorta?

    A The blood is going to the lungs.

    B The blood is dark red in color.

    C The blood is rich in oxygen.

    D The blood is going to the heart.

4. What will happen in the lymphatic system when a person gets an infection?

    A Lymph becomes thicker and moves slower.

    B Lymph nodes release more white blood cells to fight disease.

    C Lymph does not return to the bloodstream.

    D Lymph nodes filter out the bacteria in lymph.

5. The correct sequence for the path of blood through the body is

    A heart—lungs—other body parts

    B lungs—other body parts—heart

    C heart—lungs—heart—other body parts

    D heart—other body parts—lungs—heart

Constructed Response

Use the table below and your knowledge of science to help you answer Question 6. Write your answer on a separate sheet of paper.

Blood Types		
Blood Type	**Marker Molecules**	**Clumping Proteins**
A	A	anti-B
B	B	anti-A
AB	A and B	none
O	none	anti-A and anti-B

6. A blood bank stores donated blood for transfusions. Which blood type should a blood bank store the most of? People with which blood type will have the greatest chance of finding donated blood that will not cause clumping in a transfusion? Explain your answers.

Frontiers of Technology

Artificial Blood

Artist's drawing
of an artificial red
blood cell ▼

Blood is amazing. It carries oxygen, nutrients, and hormones throughout the body, and carries waste products away from cells. If you have a cut, blood cells called *platelets* quickly patch things up. Blood also carries cells that fight diseases and infections.

If patients lose a lot of blood, doctors must rely on donated blood supplies. This donated blood saves a lot of lives, but it is in short supply. So, scientists have been trying to develop compounds that make it possible to use less blood. One such compound is 50 times more effective at carrying oxygen than red blood cells are. This compound also delivers oxygen through blood vessels that are too damaged to allow red blood cells to pass.

Artificial blood compounds have been used to treat a small number of patients, but they can be expensive to make. Also, no compound can perform all the jobs that blood does. However, researchers hope to produce an artificial blood source that is as good as the real thing!

Write About It Scientists have been trying to find many ways to use less donated blood, including artificial blood. Research problems scientists have come across in developing blood replacements, and write an essay describing these problems.

Understanding Fitness Assessments

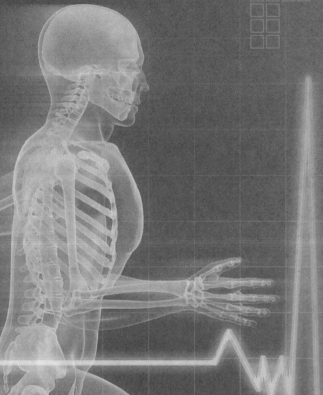

How hard does your heart work to pump blood? One tool for learning about a person's physical fitness is to measure how exercise affects his or her heart rate.

Cardiovascular appraisals measure the difference between a person's heart rate before exercise and during exercise. In simple cardiovascular fitness appraisals, participants check and record their resting heart rates. They then do some form of exercise for a set period of time. The exercises must be aerobic exercises—activities that increase the body's need for oxygen and raise the heart rates. Running, climbing stairs, or riding a bike are common aerobic exercise. After a period of time, participants stop their exercises and immediately check their heart rates again.

The graph below shows how exercise affects the heart rates of two people. Which person is more physically fit? Explain your reasoning.

Analyze It Just how much can you tell about the fitness and activity levels of the two people in the graph? List characteristics of Person A and Person B that might have affected the results of this fitness appraisal. Design a questionnaire that would allow you to find out more about the test subjects.

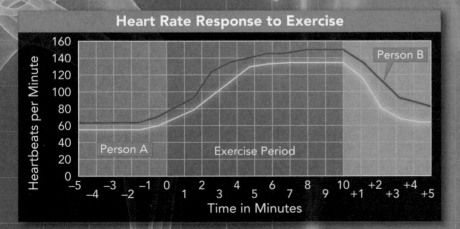

Heart Rate Response to Exercise

Person B

Person A

Exercise Period

Heartbeats per Minute

160 140 120 100 80 60 40 20 0

Time in Minutes

−5 −4 −3 −2 −1 0 1 2 3 4 5 6 7 8 9 10 +1 +2 +3 +4 +5

HOW DO MILLIONS OF "HAIRS" HELP YOU BREATHE?

How do you breathe?

Although this photo looks like a fuzzy pink scarf or a pink carpet with blue stains, it is actually a magnified view of the inside of your lungs. Tiny, hairlike structures called cilia move back and forth, acting like a broom to sweep trapped particles such as dust toward your throat. From there you can cough, spit out, or swallow the particles.

Infer How do cilia help you breathe freely?

> UNTAMED SCIENCE Watch the **Untamed Science** video to learn more about breathing.

_____

_____

_____

_____

_____

Respiration and Excretion

Check Your Understanding

1. Background Read the paragraph below and then answer the question.

> You have a cold and feel terrible. As your rib muscles **contract,** lifting your chest, you **inhale** air. As air fills your lungs, you hear a rattling sound. When you **exhale** air, you start to cough.

> To **contract** is to shrink or draw together.
>
> To **inhale** is to breathe or draw air into the lungs.
>
> To **exhale** is to breathe out.

• What happens to your ribs and chest when you inhale?

_____

_____

> **MY READING WEB** If you had trouble completing the question above, visit **My Reading Web** and type in *Respiration and Excretion.*

Vocabulary Skill

Identify Related Word Forms Learn related forms of words to increase your vocabulary. The table below lists forms of words related to key terms.

Verb	Noun	Adjective
respire, *v.* to obtain energy from the breakdown of food molecules	cellular respiration, *n.* the process by which cells obtain energy from the breakdown of food molecules	respiratory, *adj.* concerning respiration
excrete, *v.* to remove or eliminate as waste	excretion, *n.* the process by which wastes are removed from the body	excretory, *adj.* concerning excretion

2. Quick Check Fill in the blank with the correct form of *respire.*

• Obtaining energy from food is a _____ activity.

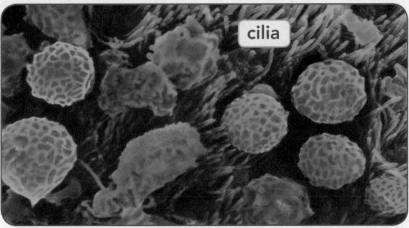

cilia

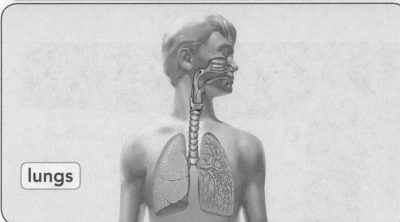

lungs

alveoli

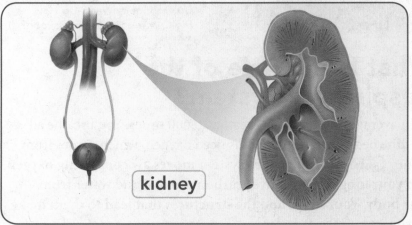

kidney

Chapter Preview

LESSON 1
- cellular respiration
- pharynx
- trachea
- cilia
- bronchi
- lungs
- alveoli
- diaphragm
- larynx
- vocal cords

⟳ **Sequence**
△ **Draw Conclusions**

LESSON 2
- tar
- carbon monoxide
- nicotine
- addiction
- bronchitis
- emphysema

⟳ **Identify Supporting Evidence**
△ **Communicate**

LESSON 3
- excretion
- urea
- urine
- kidney
- ureter
- urinary bladder
- urethra
- nephron

⟳ **Summarize**
△ **Infer**

> **VOCAB FLASH CARDS** For extra help with vocabulary, visit **Vocab Flash Cards** and type in *Respiration and Excretion.*

137

The Respiratory System

🔑 **What Is the Role of the Respiratory System?**

🔑 **How Do You Breathe?**

🔑 **What Happens During Gas Exchange?**

my planet diary

MISCONCEPTION

The Breath of Life

Misconception: The only gas you exhale is carbon dioxide.

Actually, about 16 percent of the air you exhale is oxygen. The air you inhale is made up of about 21 percent oxygen. Your body only uses a small portion of the oxygen in each breath, so the unused portion is exhaled.

Sometimes, this exhaled oxygen can mean the difference between life and death. If a person stops breathing, he or she needs to get more oxygen quickly. A rescuer can breathe into the person's mouth to give unused oxygen to the person. This process is called rescue breathing.

Read the following question. Then write your answer below.

Why would you want to learn to perform rescue breathing?

_____

_____

_____

_____

_____

_____

▷ PLANET DIARY Go to **Planet Diary** to learn more about the respiratory system.

 Do the Inquiry Warm-Up *How Big Can You Blow Up a Balloon?*

What Is the Role of the Respiratory System?

In an average day, you may breathe 20,000 times. You breathe all the time because your body cells need oxygen, which comes from the air. 🔑 **Your respiratory system moves air containing oxygen into your lungs and removes carbon dioxide and water from your body. Your lungs and the structures that lead to them make up your respiratory system.**

Vocabulary

- cellular respiration • pharynx • trachea • cilia • bronchi
- lungs • alveoli • diaphragm • larynx • vocal cords

Skills

↻ Reading: Sequence

△ Inquiry: Draw Conclusions

Respiration Your body needs the oxygen in air for cellular respiration. **Cellular respiration** is the process in which the body cells break down glucose, using oxygen and releasing the chemical energy in the glucose. During cellular respiration, carbon dioxide and water are produced. Carbon dioxide is a waste product. When you breathe out, you get rid of carbon dioxide.

Breathing gets oxygen needed for cellular respiration into your body. However, for oxygen to get to your cells, many body systems must work together, as you can see in **Figure 1.** Blood, part of the circulatory system, carries oxygen from the respiratory system and glucose from the digestive system to the body cells for respiration.

FIGURE 1 ·····················

Systems Working Together
Body systems work together to get body cells the materials they need for cellular respiration.

✎ **Describe** In the boxes, describe how each system provides cells with materials for cellular respiration. Then explain what happens during cellular respiration.

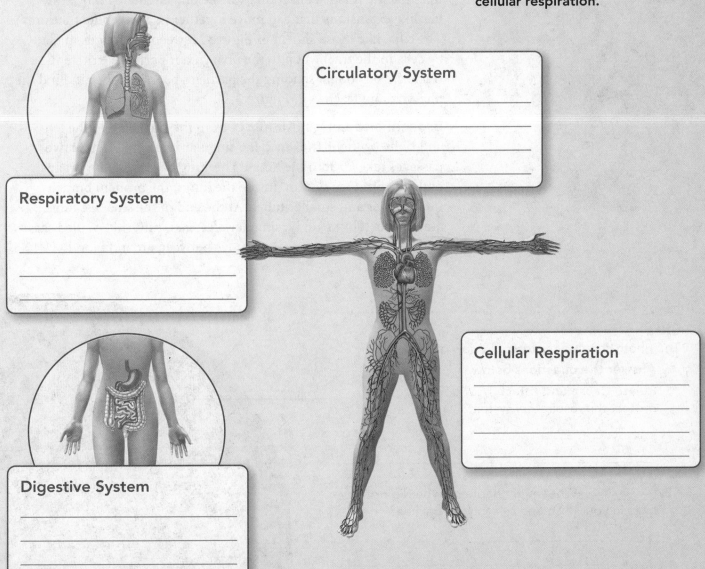

Circulatory System

_____

_____

_____

_____

Respiratory System

_____

_____

_____

_____

Cellular Respiration

_____

_____

_____

_____

Digestive System

_____

_____

_____

_____

139

Some particles can irritate the lining of your nose or throat, causing you to sneeze. This powerful force shoots the particles back into the air. The wet spray from a sneeze can travel up to 160 kilometers per hour and spread more than one meter away from the sneezer!

Breathing Structures When you breathe in air and the particles it contains such as pollen and dust, the air and particles move through a series of structures that you can see on the right—the nose, pharynx, trachea, and bronchi—and into the lungs. These structures also warm and moisten the air you breathe.

Nose Air enters the body through the nose or the mouth. Hairs in the nose trap large particles. The air passes into spaces called nasal cavities. Some cells lining the nasal cavities produce mucus, a sticky material that moistens the air and traps more particles.

Pharynx and Trachea From the nose, air enters the **pharynx** (FAR ingks), or throat. Both the nose and the mouth connect to the pharynx. So air and food enter the pharynx. From the pharynx, air moves into the **trachea** (TRAY kee uh), or windpipe. When you swallow, a thin flap of tissue called the epiglottis covers the opening of the trachea to keep food out. Cells that line the trachea have **cilia** (SIL ee uh; singular *cilium*), tiny hairlike extensions that can move together in a sweeping motion. The cilia, like those shown in **Figure 2,** sweep the mucus made by cells in the trachea up to the pharynx. If particles irritate the trachea, you cough, sending the particles back into the air. Find the pharynx and trachea in **Figure 3.**

Bronchi and Lungs Air moves from the trachea into the left and right **bronchi** (BRAHNG ky; singular *bronchus*). These two passages take air into the lungs. The **lungs** are the main organs of the respiratory system. Inside the lungs, the bronchi branch into smaller and smaller tubes. At the end of the smallest tubes are **alveoli** (al VEE uh ly; singular *alveolus*), tiny, thin-walled sacs of lung tissue where gases can move between air and blood.

FIGURE 2 ••
Cilia
The photo shows a microscopic view of cilia.

✎ **Answer the questions below.**

1. **Relate Cause and Effect** How does coughing protect the respiratory system?

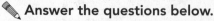

_____

_____

2. **CHALLENGE** What might happen if you did not have hairs in your nose and cilia in your trachea?

_____

_____

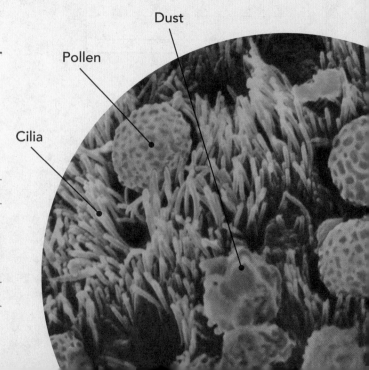

Dust

Pollen

Cilia

FIGURE 3 ·······················

Structures of the Respiratory System

Particles in air are filtered out as the air moves through your respiratory system.

✏️ **Summarize** In your own words, write what each part of the respiratory system does.

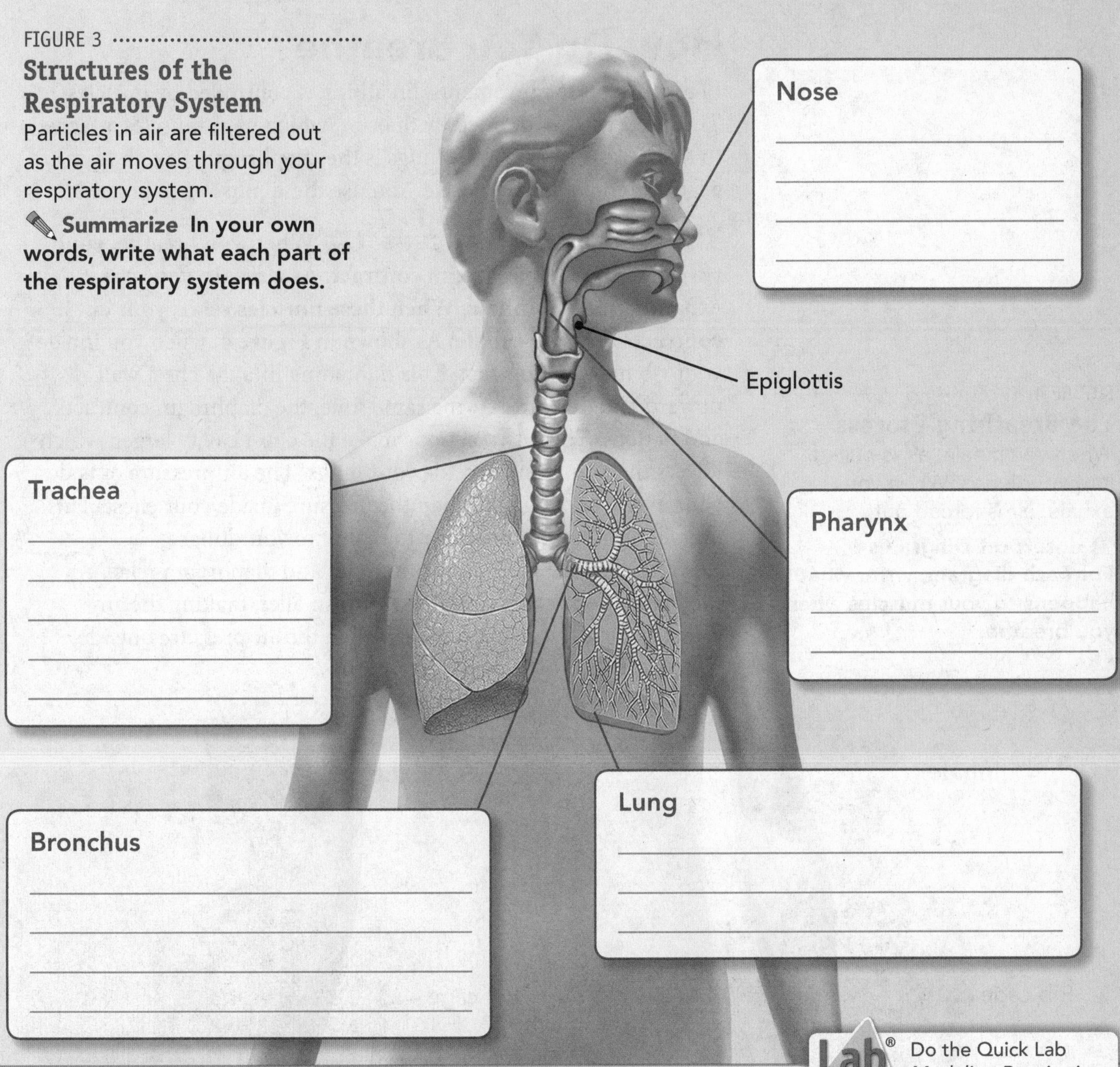

Nose
_____
_____
_____
_____

Epiglottis

Trachea
_____
_____
_____
_____

Pharynx
_____
_____
_____

Lung
_____
_____
_____

Bronchus
_____
_____
_____
_____

Lab ® Do the Quick Lab
zone *Modeling Respiration.*

🔑 Assess Your Understanding

1a. Define What is cellular respiration?

_____
_____
_____

b. Compare and Contrast How are breathing and cellular respiration different?

_____
_____
_____

got it?

○ **I get it!** Now I know that the respiratory

system _____
_____
_____
_____

○ **I need extra help with** _____

Go to **MY SCIENCE** 🔊 **COACH** *online for help with this subject.*

How Do You Breathe?

Like other body movements, breathing is controlled by muscles. The lungs are surrounded by the ribs, which have muscles attached to them. At the base of the lungs is the **diaphragm** (DY uh fram), a large, dome-shaped muscle. You use these muscles to breathe.

The Breathing Process 🔜 **When you breathe, your rib muscles and diaphragm contract. As a result, your chest expands and you inhale. When these muscles relax, your chest contracts and you exhale.** As shown in **Figure 4,** when you inhale your rib muscles contract. This tightening lifts the chest wall upward and outward. At the same time, the diaphragm contracts and flattens. These two actions make the chest cavity larger, which lowers the air pressure inside your lungs. The air pressure outside your body is now higher than the pressure inside your chest. This pressure difference causes air to rush into your lungs.

When you exhale, your rib muscles and diaphragm relax. As they relax, your chest cavity becomes smaller, making the air pressure inside your chest greater than the air pressure outside. As a result, air rushes out of your lungs.

FIGURE 4 ·····················

The Breathing Process
When you inhale, air is pulled into your lungs. When you exhale, air is forced out.

✏️ **Interpret Diagrams**
For each diagram, write what happens to your muscles when you breathe.

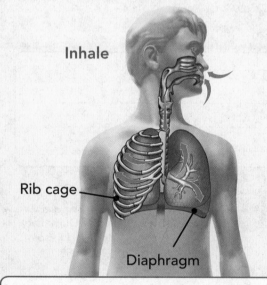

Inhale

Rib cage

Diaphragm

Rib Muscles
_____
_____
_____

Diaphragm
_____
_____
_____

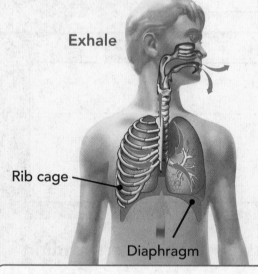

Exhale

Rib cage

Diaphragm

Rib Muscles
_____
_____
_____

Diaphragm
_____
_____
_____

Breathing and Speaking

Did you know that the air that moves out of your lungs when you breathe also helps you to speak? Your **larynx** (LAR ingks), or voice box, is located at the top of your trachea. Two **vocal cords,** which are folds of connective tissue, stretch across the opening of the larynx. When you speak, muscles make the vocal cords contract, narrowing the opening as air rushes through. Then the movement of the vocal cords makes air molecules vibrate, or move rapidly back and forth. This vibration causes a sound—your voice.

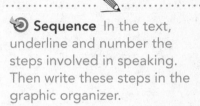

Sequence In the text, underline and number the steps involved in speaking. Then write these steps in the graphic organizer.

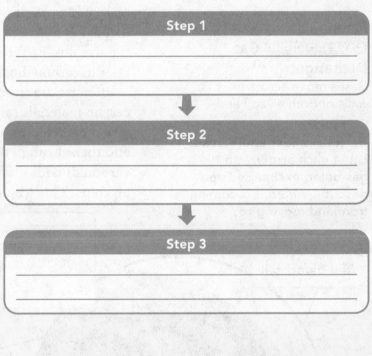

Step 1
_____
_____

Step 2
_____
_____

Step 3
_____
_____

 Do the Lab Investigation
A Breath of Fresh Air.

🔑 Assess Your Understanding

2a. Identify Where is the larynx located?

_____
_____
_____

b. Explain When you inhale, why does air rush into your lungs?

_____
_____
_____

got it?

○ **I get it!** Now I know that I breathe when my muscles _____

_____
_____
_____

○ **I need extra help with** _____

Go to **MY SCIENCE** ⓢ **COACH** *online for help with this subject.*

What Happens During Gas Exchange?

Take a closer look at the structure of the lungs. Air's final stop in its journey through the respiratory system is an alveolus in the lungs. An alveolus has thin walls and is surrounded by many thin-walled capillaries. **Figure 5** shows some alveoli.

How Gas Exchange Occurs Imagine that you are a drop of blood. You are traveling through a capillary that wraps around an alveolus. You have a lot of carbon dioxide and a little oxygen. As you move through the capillary, oxygen attaches to the hemoglobin in your red blood cells. Carbon dioxide moves into the alveolus. By the end of the alveolus, you are rich in oxygen and poor in carbon dioxide.

Because the alveoli and the capillaries have very thin walls, certain materials can pass through them easily. **After air enters an alveolus, oxygen passes through the wall of the alveolus and then through the capillary wall into the blood. Similarly, carbon dioxide and water pass from the blood into the air in the alveolus. This whole process is called gas exchange.**

FIGURE 5 ·······························
> ART IN MOTION **Gas Exchange**
Gases move across the thin walls of both alveoli and capillaries.

✎ **Relate Text and Visuals** Label each arrow with the gas being exchanged and describe where it is coming from and moving to.

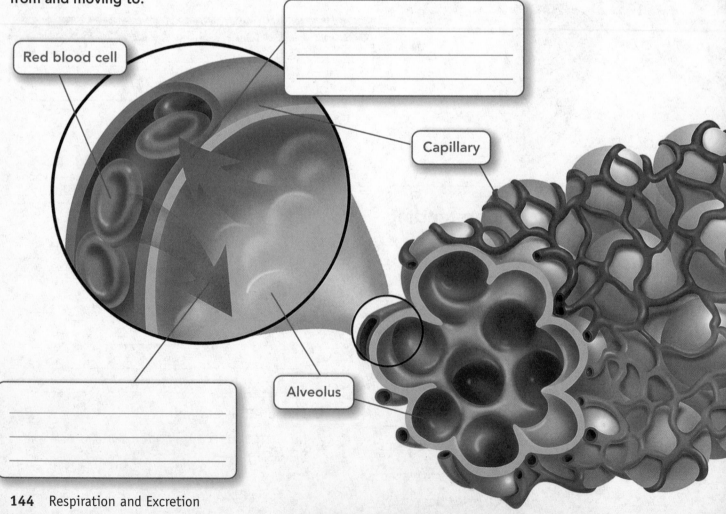

Red blood cell

Capillary

Alveolus

Surface Area for Gas Exchange

Your lungs can absorb a large amount of oxygen because of the surface area of the alveoli. An adult's lungs have about 300 million alveoli. As a result, the alveoli provide a huge amount of surface area for exchanging gases. Therefore, healthy lungs can supply all the oxygen that a person needs—even when the person is very active.

Vocabulary Identify Related Word Forms The verb *absorb* means "to take in." Use this meaning to write a sentence using the noun *absorption*.

_____

_____

_____

_____

Vessel with blood rich in oxygen from lungs

Branch of bronchus

Vessel with blood rich in carbon dioxide from body

do the math! Sample Problem

Surface area includes the area of all the surfaces of a three-dimensional object, such as a cube or a sphere. An alveolus is a sphere. The formula for finding the surface area of a sphere is $4\pi r^2$. The symbol π is pi (pie) and represents the number 3.14. In the formula, r stands for radius which is the distance from the center of the sphere to the edge. The steps below show you how to find the surface area of a sphere with a 2-cm radius.

$$\text{Surface area} = 4\pi r^2$$
$$= 4 \times \pi \times r \times r$$
$$= 4 \times 3.14 \times 2 \text{ cm} \times 2 \text{ cm}$$
$$= 50.24 \text{ cm}^2$$

The surface area of the sphere is 50.24 cm².

❶ Calculate Find the surface area of a baseball with a radius of 4 cm.

_____

❷ CHALLENGE The surface area of all the alveoli in an adult's lung is about the same as a sphere with a radius of 236 cm. Find the surface area of all the alveoli. Use a calculator if you have one.

_____

_____

A Breath of fresh Air

How do you breathe?

FIGURE 6 ···

▶ **INTERACTIVE ART** Many body parts work together to enable you to breathe.

✎ **Complete the tasks using what you've learned about breathing.**

1. **Summarize** In the boxes below, describe the function of each group of respiratory structures. Also, explain what changes occur in your chest cavity when you inhale and exhale.

2. **Compare and Contrast** In the Venn diagram on the next page, write how an alveolus and a capillary are alike and different.

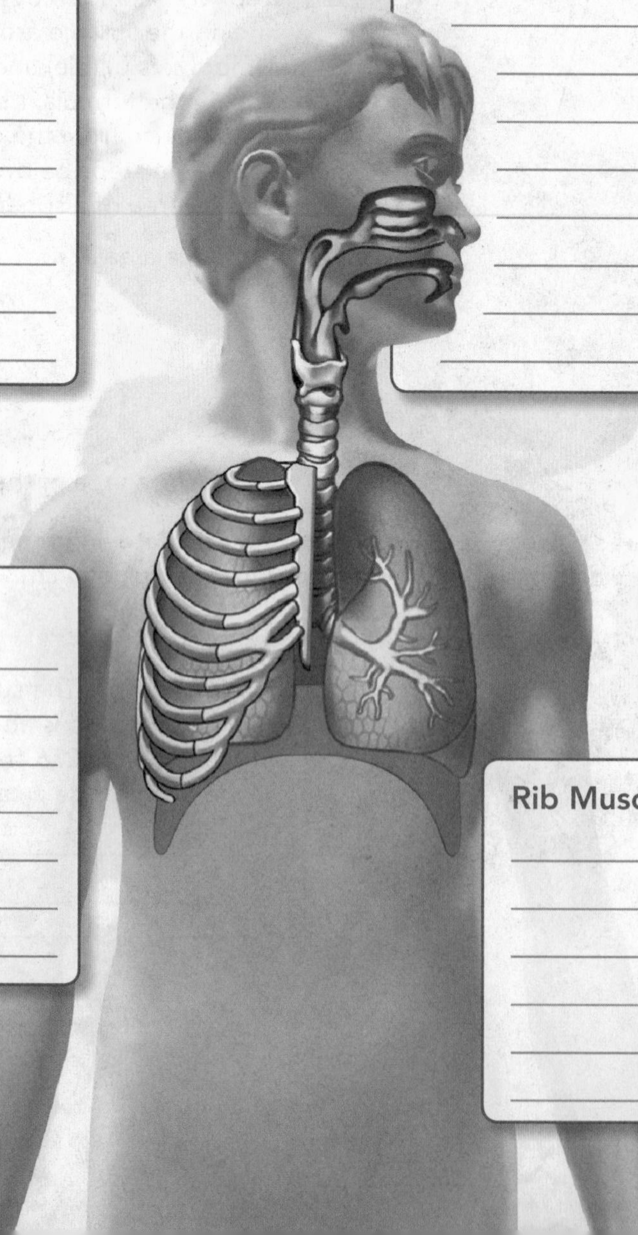

Inhale and Exhale

_____

_____

_____

_____

Nose, Pharynx, Trachea, and Bronchus

_____

_____

_____

_____

Alveoli

_____

_____

_____

_____

Rib Muscles and Diaphragm

_____

_____

_____

_____

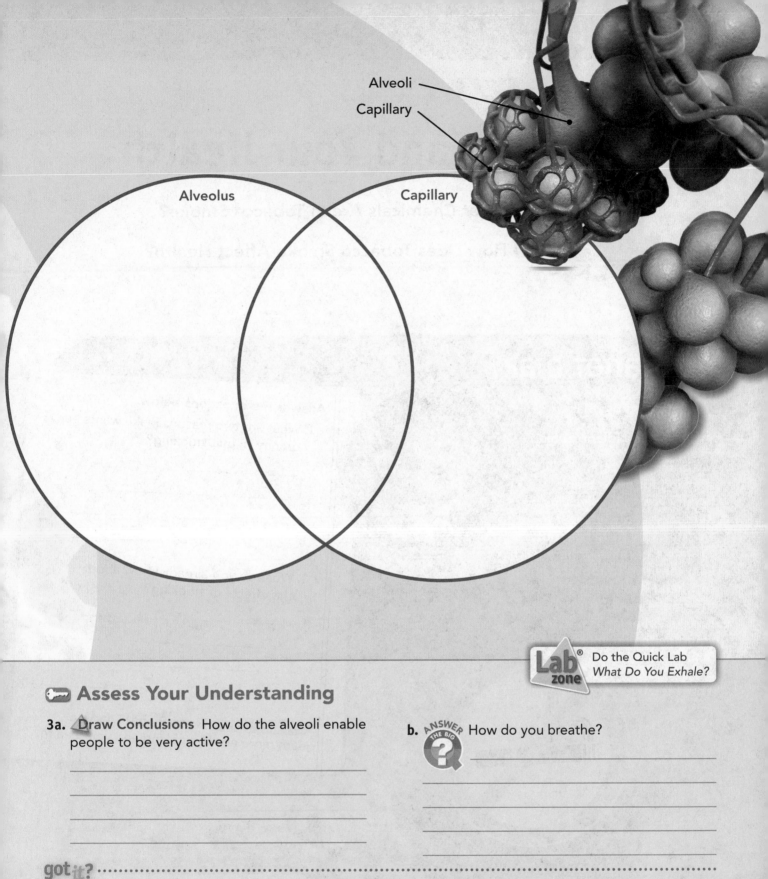

Alveoli

Capillary

Alveolus

Capillary

Lab zone® Do the Quick Lab *What Do You Exhale?*

🔑 Assess Your Understanding

3a. ⚠ Draw Conclusions How do the alveoli enable people to be very active?

_____

_____

_____

_____

b. ANSWER THE BIG ❓ How do you breathe?

_____

_____

_____

_____

got it? ....

○ **I get it!** Now I know that during gas exchange _____

_____

○ **I need extra help with** _____

Go to **MY SCIENCE ⓢ COACH** *online for help with this subject.*

Smoking and Your Health

🔑 **What Chemicals Are in Tobacco Smoke?**

🔑 **How Does Tobacco Smoke Affect Health?**

my planet diary

Posted by: Blake

Location: Toledo, Ohio

My granny has been smoking for more than twenty years. She lives in Kentucky, and whenever I visit her, I try to tell her not to smoke because of her health. I am sensitive to tobacco smoke, so when I was younger, the smoke would trigger asthma attacks. Smoking is bad for your health and your family's health.

Answer the questions below.

1. What are two reasons Blake wants her granny to quit smoking?

_____

_____

_____

2. What do you already know about the effects of smoking?

_____

_____

_____

_____

▷ PLANET DIARY Go to **Planet Diary** to learn more about smoking and your health.

Lab zone® Do the Inquiry Warm-Up
A Smoker's Lungs.

Vocabulary
- tar • carbon monoxide
- nicotine • addiction
- bronchitis • emphysema

Skills
- Reading: Identify Supporting Evidence
- Inquiry: Communicate

What Chemicals Are in Tobacco Smoke?

Whoosh! Millions of tiny but dangerous invaders are pulled into the mouth. Cilia trap some of these invaders, and others get stuck in mucus. Still, thousands of the invaders get past these defenses and enter the lungs. The invaders then arrive in the alveoli!

These invaders are the substances found in cigarette smoke, and they can damage the respiratory system. With each puff, a smoker inhales more than 4,000 chemicals. **Some of the most deadly chemicals in tobacco smoke are tar, carbon monoxide, and nicotine.**

Tar The dark, sticky substance that forms when tobacco burns is called **tar.** When someone inhales tobacco smoke, some tar sticks to cilia that line the trachea, bronchi, and smaller airways. Tar makes cilia clump together so they cannot function to keep harmful materials out of the lungs. Tar also contains chemicals that cause cancer. In **Figure 1,** you can see how the percentage of teen smokers has changed over time.

FIGURE 1 ···

> **REAL-WORLD INQUIRY** Teen Smoking
This graph shows the percentage of teens who smoked between 1991 and 2007.

✎ **Use the graph to answer the questions.**

1. **Read Graphs** What happened to the percentage of teen smokers between 1999 and 2007?

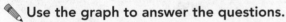
_____

_____

2. **Draw Conclusions** Why do you think there were fewer teen smokers in 2007?

_____

_____

_____

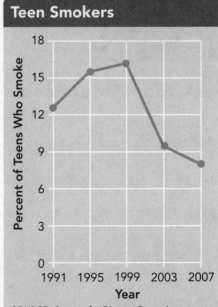

Teen Smokers

Percent of Teens Who Smoke (y-axis: 0, 3, 6, 9, 12, 15, 18)
Year (x-axis: 1991, 1995, 1999, 2003, 2007)

SOURCE: Centers for Disease Control and Prevention. *2007 Youth Risk Behavior Survey.* Available at: www.cdc.gov/yrbss.

Tobacco plant

Carbon Monoxide

When substances such as tobacco are burned, they produce a colorless, odorless gas called **carbon monoxide.** This gas is dangerous because it binds to hemoglobin in red blood cells. It takes the place of some oxygen that the blood usually carries. So the blood carries less oxygen to the body. To get more oxygen, a smoker's breathing and heart rates increase. The amount of carbon monoxide in the blood rises with the number of cigarettes a person smokes. The blood of heavy smokers may have too little oxygen to meet their bodies' needs.

Nicotine

Nicotine is a stimulant drug in tobacco that increases heart rate and blood pressure. Over time, nicotine causes an **addiction,** or physical dependence. Addiction to nicotine makes quitting difficult for smokers.

apply it!

The more cigarettes a person smokes, the more carbon monoxide he or she inhales.

❶ Predict Draw a bar on the graph to show how much carbon monoxide you think would be in the blood of a person who smoked three packs a day.

❷ CHALLENGE Why do you think people who do not smoke still have some carbon monoxide in their blood?

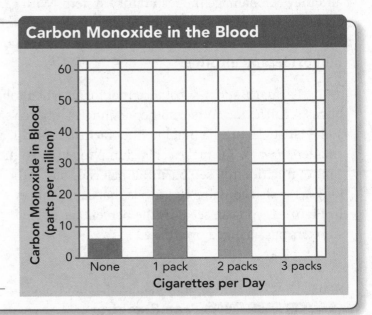

Carbon Monoxide in the Blood

Carbon Monoxide in Blood (parts per million)

Cigarettes per Day: None, 1 pack, 2 packs, 3 packs

Lab zone Do the Quick Lab *Chemicals in Tobacco Smoke.*

🔑 Assess Your Understanding

1a. Review How does tar affect the respiratory system?

_____

_____

b. Relate Cause and Effect What long-term effects does smoking have on your heart?

_____

_____

got it? ···

O **I get it!** Now I know that the chemicals in tobacco smoke include _____

_____

O **I need extra help with** _____

Go to MY SCIENCE ⓢ COACH online for help with this subject.

How Does Tobacco Smoke Affect Health?

Smokers face many health problems. For example, because the cilia cannot sweep away mucus, many smokers have a frequent cough. The mucus buildup also limits the space for airflow, which decreases oxygen intake. Because long-term or heavy smokers do not get enough oxygen, they are often short of breath. Smoking also strains the circulatory system. It increases blood pressure, damages artery walls, and can cause blood clots. If one system is damaged, the other one must work harder. ⟳ **Over time, smokers can develop diseases including chronic bronchitis, atherosclerosis, lung cancer, and emphysema.**

Chronic Bronchitis

Bronchitis (brahng KY tis) is an irritation of the breathing passages in which the small passages become narrower and may be clogged with mucus. People with bronchitis have difficulty breathing. If the bronchitis continues for a long time, it is called chronic bronchitis. Chronic bronchitis can cause permanent damage to the breathing passages. It is often accompanied by infection. Chronic bronchitis is five to ten times more common in heavy smokers than it is in nonsmokers.

⟳ **Identify Supporting Evidence** Read the statement below. Then write in the boxes evidence from the text that supports the statement.

Evidence
_____
_____
_____

Evidence
_____
_____
_____

Statement
Smokers face many health problems.

Evidence
_____
_____
_____

Evidence
_____
_____
_____

Atherosclerosis

Some of the chemicals in tobacco smoke move into the circulatory system. They can irritate the walls of the blood vessels. This irritation contributes to atherosclerosis, which is the buildup of fatty material in the blood vessel walls.

Lung Cancer

About 150,000 Americans die each year from lung cancer. Cigarette smoke has more than 50 chemicals that cause cancer. Cancerous growths, or tumors, take up space in the lungs that is needed for gas exchange. Unfortunately, lung cancer is rarely detected early, when treatment would be most effective.

Emphysema

Emphysema (em fuh SEE muh) occurs when lung tissue is damaged and breathing becomes difficult. People with emphysema cannot breathe in enough oxygen or breathe out enough carbon dioxide. So they are always short of breath. Unfortunately, the damage from emphysema is permanent, even if a person stops smoking. **Figure 2** shows some of this damage.

FIGURE 2 ···

Smoker's Lungs with Emphysema
Chemicals in tobacco smoke damage lung tissue.

✎ **Relate Text and Visuals** Use the photos and what you have read to fill in the table below.

	Healthy Lung	Damaged Lung from Emphysema
Appearance		
Breathing Function		

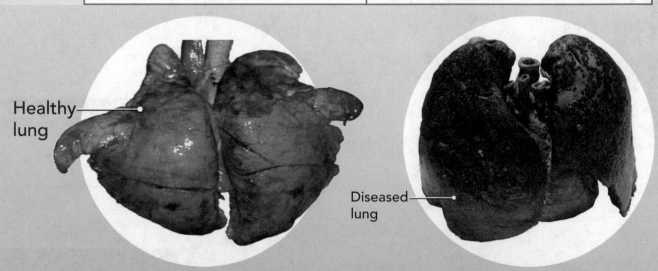

Healthy— lung

Diseased— lung

Passive Smoking Not only smokers suffer from the effects of tobacco smoke. In passive smoking, nonsmokers involuntarily inhale smoke from other people's cigarettes, cigars, or pipes. This smoke contains the same harmful chemicals that smokers inhale. Each year, passive smoking is linked to the development of bronchitis, asthma, and other respiratory problems in about 300,000 children in the United States. Billboards like the one shown in **Figure 3** can increase people's awareness about the harmful effects of passive smoking on nonsmokers.

FIGURE 3 ·······························
Passive Smoking
At least 3,000 nonsmokers in the United States die of lung cancer from passive smoke each year.

✎ Communicate **Work with a partner to write a message that might help people realize the dangers of passive smoking.**

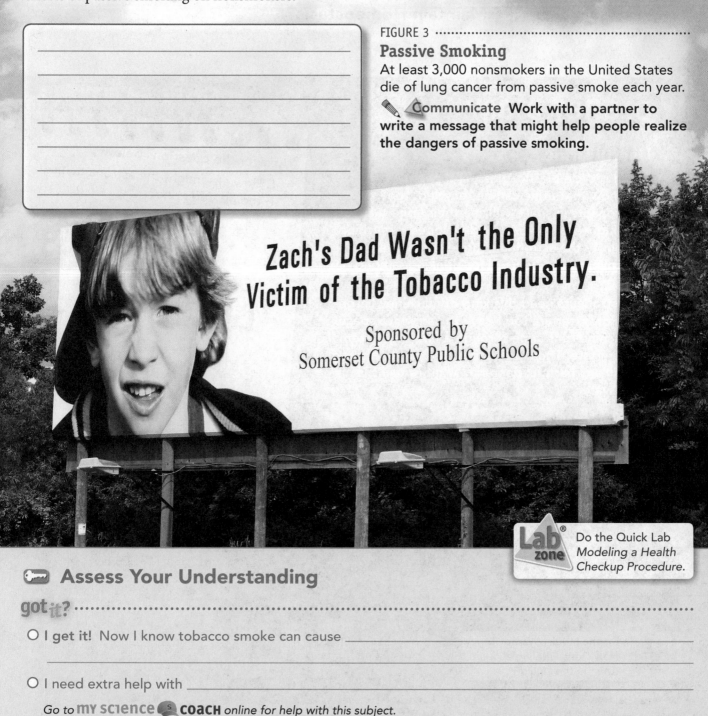

Zach's Dad Wasn't the Only Victim of the Tobacco Industry.

Sponsored by
Somerset County Public Schools

Lab zone® Do the Quick Lab
Modeling a Health Checkup Procedure.

⚷ Assess Your Understanding

got it? ···································

○ **I get it!** Now I know tobacco smoke can cause _____

_____

○ **I need extra help with** _____

Go to MY SCIENCE ⓢ COACH *online for help with this subject.*

The Excretory System

🔑 **What Is the Role of the Excretory System?**

🔑 **How Does Excretion Help Your Body Maintain Homeostasis?**

my planeT DiaRY

Useful Urine

You can recycle plastic, glass, and paper. Did you know that urine can be recycled, too? Some astronauts in space will see their urine turned into drinking water! NASA has developed a machine that will purify the astronauts' urine. The water that is recovered can be used for drinking, among other things.

Why do astronauts need this kind of machine? Large quantities of water are too heavy to carry into space. So the machine runs urine through a filtering system to remove waste. Then iodine is added to the filtered urine to kill any harmful bacteria. What remains is drinkable water.

Lab zone® Do the Inquiry Warm-Up *How Does Filtering a Liquid Change the Liquid?*

FUN FACTS

Answer the questions below.

1. How else might the astronauts use the filtered urine?

_____

_____

_____

2. Do you think this system would be useful on Earth? Why or why not?

_____

_____

_____

_____

_____

> **PLANET DIARY** Go to **Planet Diary** to learn more about excretion.

Vocabulary
- excretion • urea • urine • kidney • ureter
- urinary bladder • urethra • nephron

Skills
- Reading: Summarize
- Inquiry: Infer

What Is the Role of the Excretory System?

The human body faces a challenge similar to keeping your room clean. Just as you must clean up papers that pile up in your room, your body must remove wastes from cellular respiration and other processes. The process of removing waste is called **excretion.**

If wastes were not removed from your body, they would pile up and make you sick. 🔑 **The excretory system collects the wastes that cells produce and removes them from the body.** The system includes the kidneys, ureters, urinary bladder, urethra, lungs, skin, and liver. Two wastes that your body must eliminate are excess water and urea. **Urea** (yoo REE uh) is a chemical that comes from the breakdown of proteins. As you know, the lungs eliminate some water. Most remaining water is eliminated in a fluid called **urine,** which includes urea and other wastes.

do the math! Analyzing Data

Urine is made up of water, organic solids, and inorganic solids. The organic solids include urea and acids. The inorganic solids include salts and minerals. The solids are dissolved in the water.

1 Calculate Calculate and label on the *Normal Urine Content* graph the percentage of urine that is solids. Calculate and label on the *Solids in Normal Urine* graph the percentage of solids that is urea.

2 CHALLENGE What might a sharp decrease in the percentage of water in a person's urine indicate about the health of that person?

_____

_____

_____

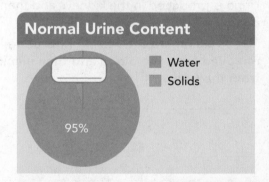

Normal Urine Content
- ■ Water
- ■ Solids

95%

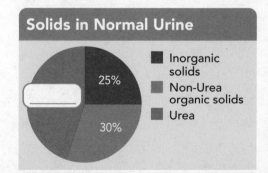

Solids in Normal Urine
- ■ Inorganic solids
- ■ Non-Urea organic solids
- ■ Urea

25%

30%

Structures That Remove Urine

Figure 1 shows the organs that remove urine from the body. Your two kidneys are the major organs of the excretory system. The **kidneys** act like filters. They remove urea and other wastes from the blood but keep materials that the body needs. These wastes are eliminated in the urine. Urine flows from the kidneys through two narrow tubes called **ureters** (yoo REE turz). The ureters carry urine to the **urinary bladder,** a muscular sac that stores urine. Urine leaves the body through a small tube called the **urethra** (yoo REE thruh).

Waste Filtration

Each kidney has about one million nephrons. A **nephron** is a tiny filtering factory that removes wastes from blood and produces urine. The nephrons filter wastes in two stages. First, both wastes and needed materials are filtered out of the blood. Next, much of the needed material is returned to the blood, and the wastes are eliminated from the body. Follow this process in **Figure 2.**

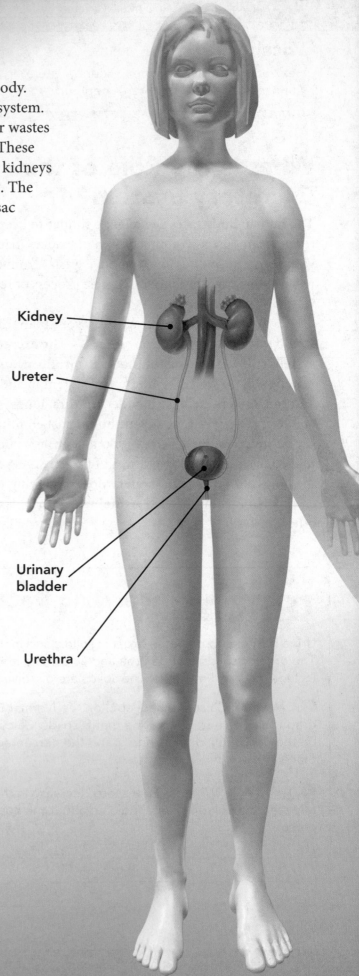

Kidney

Ureter

Urinary bladder

Urethra

FIGURE 1 ···

Removing Urine

Urine is produced in the kidneys and then removed from the body.

✎ ↻ **Summarize Describe how urine is removed from the blood and then eliminated from the body.**

_____

_____

_____

_____

_____

_____

_____

_____ .

FIGURE 2 ···

> **INTERACTIVE ART** **How the Kidneys Work**

Most of the work of the kidneys is done in the nephrons.

✏️ ⚠️ **Infer** In the key, write what each color represents in the diagram. Then explain why it is important for capillaries to surround the nephron tube.

_____
_____
_____
_____

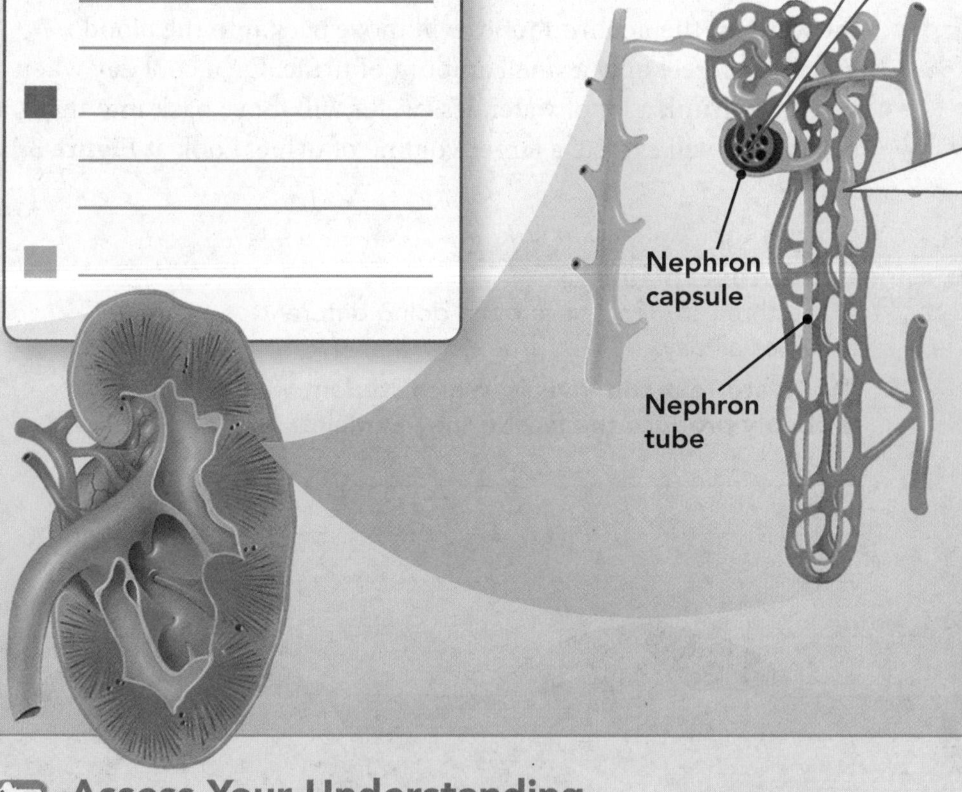

Stage 1
- Blood flows into the cluster of capillaries in the thin-walled, hollow nephron capsule.
- Urea, glucose, and some water are filtered out of the blood and into the capsule.
- These materials then pass into the nephron tube.

Key

■ _____
_____
_____
■ _____
_____
■ _____

Stage 2
- As the material flows through the nephron tube, most of the needed glucose and water move back into the blood through the capillaries.
- Most of the urea and some of the water stay in the nephron tube and become urine.

Nephron capsule

Nephron tube

Lab zone® Do the Quick Lab *Kidney Function.*

🔑 **Assess Your Understanding**

1a. Name The chemical _____ comes from the breakdown of proteins.

b. Draw Conclusions Why is it important for a kidney to have many nephrons?

_____
_____
_____

got it?

○ **I get it!** Now I know that the function of the excretory system is to _____
_____

○ **I need extra help with** _____

Go to **MY SCIENCE COACH** online for help with this subject.

How Does Excretion Help Your Body Maintain Homeostasis?

A buildup of wastes such as urea, excess water, and carbon dioxide can upset your body's balance. 🔑 **Excretion helps to maintain homeostasis by keeping the body's internal environment stable and free of harmful levels of chemicals.** The organs of excretion include the kidneys, lungs, skin, and liver.

Kidneys As the kidneys filter blood, they regulate the amount of water in your body to help maintain homeostasis, or internal stability. Remember that as urine is being formed, needed water passes from the nephron tubes into the blood. The amount of water that returns to the blood depends on conditions both outside and inside the body. For example, on a hot day when you have been sweating a lot and have not had much to drink, almost all the water in the nephron tubes will move back into the blood. You will excrete only a small amount of urine. On a cool day when you have drunk a lot of water, less water will move back into the blood. You will excrete a larger volume of urine. Look at **Figure 3.**

FIGURE 3

Fluid Absorption
These three students have been doing different activities all day.

✏️ **Relate Text and Visuals** Which student will probably produce the least urine? Explain.

_____

_____

_____

Vocabulary Identify Related Word Forms You know the noun *excretion* means "the process of removing wastes." Use this meaning to choose the correct meaning of the verb *excrete*.

○ relating to removing wastes

○ to remove wastes

○ the state of removing wastes

Maria has been in classes all morning. She has had nothing to eat or drink.

Kari has been running sprints. She forgot to bring her water bottle.

Mike has been sitting on the bench and drinking water.

Lungs, Skin, and Liver The organs in other systems in your body help you excrete waste and keep you healthy. For example, the kidneys remove many wastes. However, the lungs and skin remove some wastes from the body as well. For example, when you exhale, carbon dioxide and some water are removed from the body by the lungs. Sweat glands in the skin produce perspiration that contains water and a small amount of urea.

The liver makes urea from the breakdown of proteins in the body. In addition, the liver breaks down many wastes into forms that can be excreted. For example, the liver breaks down old red blood cells. It even recycles some of their parts. In this way, you can think of the liver as a recycling factory.

↻ **Summarize** In your own words, write each organ's role in excretion.

Lungs
_____
_____
_____

Skin
_____
_____
_____

Liver
_____
_____
_____

Kidneys
_____
_____
_____

Lab zone® Do the Quick Lab *Perspiration.*

⚷ **Assess Your Understanding**

got it? ....

○ **I get it!** Now I know that excretion helps _____
_____

○ **I need extra help with** _____

Go to **MY SCIENCE** ⬤ **COACH** *online for help with this subject.*

Study Guide

When I breathe, my _____ and _____ contract and relax, changing the size of my chest and letting air into and out of my _____.

LESSON 1 The Respiratory System

🔑 Your respiratory system moves air containing oxygen into your lungs and removes carbon dioxide and water from your body. Your lungs and the structures that lead to them make up your respiratory system.

🔑 When you breathe, your rib muscles and diaphragm contract. Your chest expands and you inhale. When these muscles relax, your chest contracts and you exhale.

🔑 After air enters an alveolus, oxygen passes through the wall of the alveolus and then through the capillary wall into the blood. Similarly, carbon dioxide and water pass from the blood into the air in the alveolus. This whole process is called gas exchange.

Vocabulary • diaphragm • larynx • vocal cords
• cellular respiration • pharynx • trachea • cilia • bronchi • lungs • alveoli

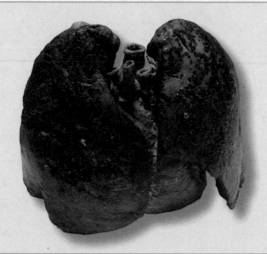

LESSON 2 Smoking and Your Health

🔑 Some of the most deadly chemicals in tobacco smoke are tar, carbon monoxide, and nicotine.

🔑 Over time, smokers can develop diseases including chronic bronchitis, atherosclerosis, lung cancer, and emphysema.

Vocabulary
• tar • carbon monoxide • nicotine
• addiction • bronchitis • emphysema

LESSON 3 The Excretory System

🔑 The excretory system collects the wastes that cells produce and removes them from the body.

🔑 Excretion helps maintain homeostasis by keeping the body's internal environment stable and free of harmful levels of chemicals.

Vocabulary
• excretion • urea • urine • kidney • ureter
• urinary bladder • urethra • nephron

Review and Assessment

LESSON 1 The Respiratory System

1. Your voice is produced by the

   a. pharynx.   **b.** larynx.

   c. trachea.   **d.** alveoli.

2. Clusters of air sacs in the lung are _____

3. Classify What part of the respiratory system connects the mouth and nose?

_____

4. Sequence What happens to the carbon dioxide in blood when it flows through the capillaries in the alveoli?

_____

_____

_____

_____

5. Compare and Contrast How do mucus and cilia work together to remove dust that enters your nose? How do they differ?

_____

_____

_____

_____

_____

_____

6. Write About It Suppose you are a doctor with patients who are mountain climbers. Write a letter to these patients that explains how gas exchange is affected at the top of a mountain, where air pressure is lower and there is less oxygen than at lower elevations.

LESSON 2 Smoking and Your Health

7. The disease caused by damaged lung tissue that results in breathing difficulties is

   a. emphysema.   **b.** bronchitis.

   c. atherosclerosis.   **d.** asthma.

8. _____ and

_____ are

chemicals in tobacco smoke that increase

heart rate.

Use the graph to answer Questions 9 and 10.

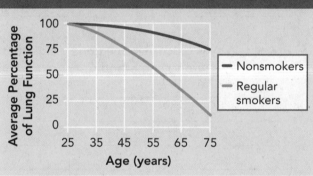

Comparing Lung Function in Nonsmokers and Smokers

9. Read Graphs At what age do the lungs of a smoker function at an average of 75 percent?

_____

10. Draw Conclusions How does smoking affect lung function?

_____

_____

_____

_____

11. Apply Concepts How can babies develop smoking-related respiratory problems?

_____

_____

_____

LESSON 3 **The Excretory System**

12. Urine leaves the body through the

a. ureters.   **b.** nephrons.

c. urinary bladder.   **d.** urethra.

13. Urine is stored in the _____

14. Relate Cause and Effect How do the kidneys help maintain homeostasis?

_____

_____

_____

_____

_____

15. Predict Why is glucose in the urine a sign that something is wrong in the body?

_____

_____

_____

_____

_____

_____

16. math! Suppose that on a Saturday Henry spent a quiet day at home. He drank 2,000 milliliters of water and produced 1,500 milliliters of urine. On Sunday, he played sports at the park. He drank 2,200 milliliters of water and produced 1,100 milliliters of urine. For each day, calculate the percent of water that became urine. Explain the difference in the results using your knowledge of the excretory system.

APPLY THE BIG ?

How do you breathe?

17. When paramedics rescue an unconscious person, they often loosen the person's clothing around the rib cage to ease the person's breathing. Explain how this action helps the breathing process.

_____

_____

_____

_____

_____

_____

_____

_____

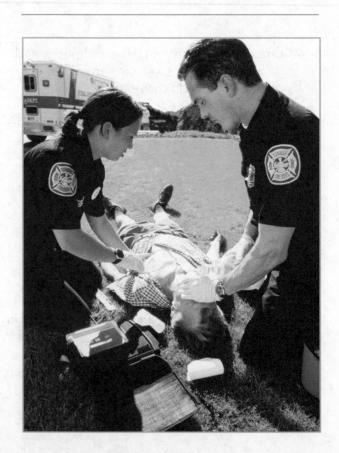

Standardized Test Prep

Multiple Choice

Circle the letter of the best answer.

1. What process is shown in the diagram below?

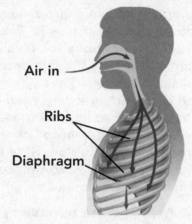

Air in

Ribs

Diaphragm

A the process of inhaling
B the process of exhaling
C the process of cellular respiration
D all of the above

2 On its way out of the body, urine passes *last* through the

A urinary bladder.
B kidney.
C ureters.
D urethra.

3 A colorless, odorless gas produced by burning tobacco is

A carbon monoxide.
B tar.
C nicotine.
D urea.

4. Which of the following organs functions as both a respiratory organ and an excretory organ?

A the liver
B the lungs
C the skin
D the kidneys

5. When a person inhales, air travels from

A the bronchi to the pharynx.
B the capillaries to the bronchi.
C the nose or mouth to the alveoli.
D the trachea to the pharynx.

Constructed Response

Use the table below and your knowledge of science to help you answer Question 6. Write your answer on a separate sheet of paper.

Average Daily Water Loss in Humans (mL)			
Source	Normal Weather	Hot Weather	Extended Heavy Exercise
Lungs	350	250	650
Urine	1,400	1,200	500
Sweat	450	1,750	5,350
Digestive Waste	200	200	200

6. What is the total amount of water lost on a hot-weather day? During heavy exercise?

Everyday Science

BREATHING THIN AIR

You're climbing a mountain. Suddenly you feel lightheaded and nauseous, and you've got a splitting headache. Chances are that you've got altitude sickness!

When people who live near sea level visit high-altitude places, such as La Paz, Bolivia (about 12,000 feet above sea level), they often experience the unpleasant symptoms of altitude sickness. The condition is caused by low oxygen content in the air. While air at high altitudes contains the same *percentage* of oxygen as air at sea level, the air pressure is lower. That means there are fewer molecules of oxygen in a given volume of air.

Fortunately, the human respiratory system quickly adjusts to the high altitude. You breathe more deeply. You take more breaths per minute. Over hours and days, your body begins to produce more red blood cells, and more hemoglobin, a substance that carries oxygen in the blood. After several days at high altitude, you start to feel better.

People who live at high altitudes seem to be unaffected by the "thin" air. Their respiratory systems and other body systems have adjusted to high-altitude conditions. For example, people who live at high elevations in the Andes Mountains in South America possess increased lung volume and take more breaths per minute compared to people living at sea level.

Infer It Research more about the effects of high altitude on the body. Make a pamphlet for people who are traveling to high-altitude locations. Include information on high-altitude locations, the effects of high altitude on the body, and tips on how to deal with altitude sickness. Include a map of places where people might experience altitude sickness.

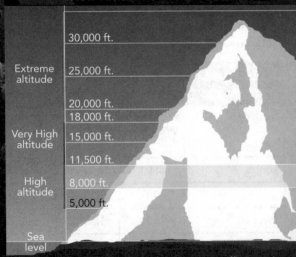

How Altitude Sickness Works

30,000 ft.

Extreme altitude — 25,000 ft.

20,000 ft.
18,000 ft.

Very High altitude — 15,000 ft.

11,500 ft.

High altitude — 8,000 ft.

5,000 ft.

Sea level

At 8,000 feet, altitude sickness can afflict travelers.

▲ High in the mountains, the air contains fewer molecules of oxygen per volume of air. Travelers climbing these peaks may develop altitude sickness.

An Olympic Experiment

Asthma is a respiratory disease that causes a person's air passages to narrow. People with asthma feel shortness of breath and have trouble getting enough oxygen. For a long time, scientists have known that a link exists between air pollution and asthma. Yet, it is difficult to determine how many cases of asthma are caused by or affected by air pollution. The 1996 Summer Olympics in Atlanta, Georgia, provided a rare chance to explore this question.

During the Olympics, city officials dramatically increased the number of public transportation vehicles in the city. They also limited the number of cars allowed on city roads. These policies reduced the levels of air pollutants that are suspected to trigger asthma attacks.

After the Olympics, researchers analyzed how many children received emergency treatment for asthma and other respiratory problems before, during, and after the Olympics. According to one source, the number of children who received emergency treatment for asthma dropped by 41 percent during the Olympics!

The Atlanta Olympics helped scientists develop a much better understanding of the links between air pollution and asthma. Studies such as these provide strong evidence that reducing air pollution can help us all breathe easier.

During the 1996 Summer Olympics, peak ozone levels in Atlanta declined as much as 28 percent. The levels of other pollutants also decreased by between 7 and 19 percent.

Design It Design a poster or public service announcement to communicate the results of this study.

WHAT CAN YOU DO TO PREVENT DISEASE?

> UNTAMED SCIENCE Watch the **Untamed Science** video to learn more about fighting disease.

Why do you sometimes get sick?

This three-year-old girl from Somalia is getting a polio vaccine. Polio is spread through contaminated water or food, or by contact with a person infected with the virus. It was a common disease in Somalia. In the United States, polio has been almost eliminated because most babies receive the polio vaccine. Vaccines prevent some viral diseases. Other viral diseases, such as the common cold, have no vaccine.

Infer What steps can you take to stop a virus such as a cold from spreading?

_____

_____

_____

_____

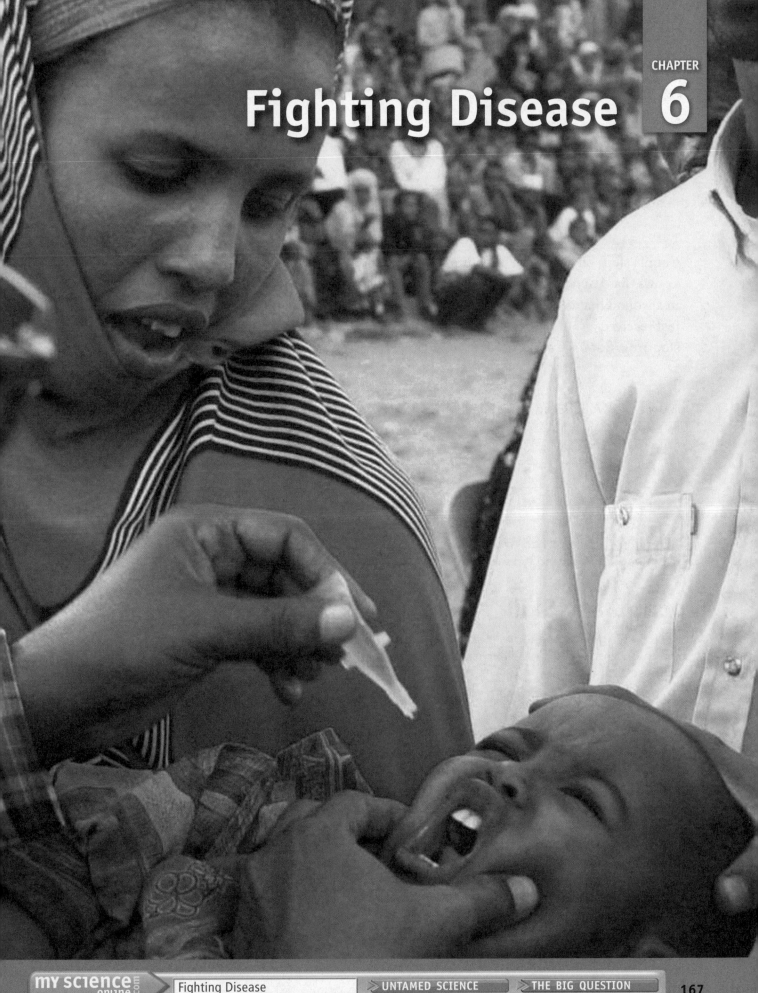

Fighting Disease

6 Getting Started

Check Your Understanding

1. Background Read the paragraph below and then answer the question.

> Camila steps on a nail that punctures her foot. She knows that **bacteria** can cause a disease called tetanus in a wound that is **contaminated**. Fortunately, Camila just received a shot to prevent tetanus. However, to help stop **infection**, she soaks her foot in warm soapy water.

Bacteria are single-celled organisms that lack a nucleus.

An object that is **contaminated** has become unclean and could possibly infect the body.

Infection is the process in which disease-causing microorganisms invade the body and then multiply.

- How can a wound lead to an infection?

_____

_____

_____

MY READING WEB If you had trouble completing the question above, visit **My Reading Web** and type in *Fighting Disease*.

Vocabulary Skill

Latin Word Origins Some terms in this chapter contain word parts with Latin origins. The table below lists some of the Latin words from which these terms come.

Latin Word	Meaning	Key Term
toxicum	poison	toxin, *n.* a poison produced by bacteria that damages cells
tumere	a swelling	tumor, *n.* an abnormal mass of tissue that results from uncontrolled division of cells

2. Quick Check In the table above, circle the meaning of the Latin word *toxicum*. The meaning may help you remember the term *toxin*.

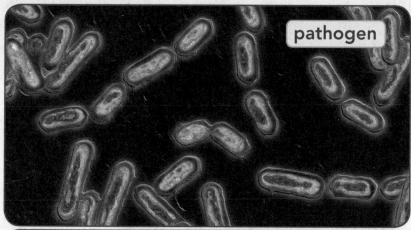

pathogen

Chapter Preview

LESSON 1

- microorganism • pathogen
- infectious disease • toxin

🔄 **Identify the Main Idea**
🔺 **Develop Hypotheses**

LESSON 2

- inflammatory response
- phagocyte • immune response
- lymphocyte • T cell • antigen
- B cell • antibody

🔄 **Compare and Contrast**
🔺 **Make Models**

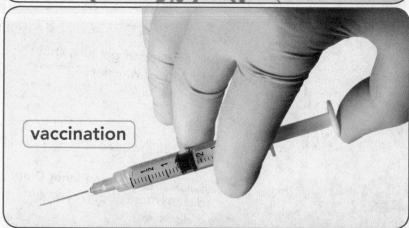

T cell

LESSON 3

- AIDS • HIV

🔄 **Sequence**
🔺 **Graph**

LESSON 4

- immunity • active immunity
- vaccination • vaccine
- passive immunity • antibiotic
- antibiotic resistance

🔄 **Relate Cause and Effect**
🔺 **Interpret Data**

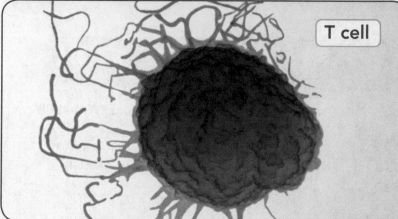

vaccination

LESSON 5

- noninfectious disease • allergy
- allergen • histamine • asthma
- insulin • diabetes • tumor
- carcinogen

🔄 **Summarize**
🔺 **Draw Conclusions**

> **VOCAB FLASH CARDS** For extra help with vocabulary, visit **Vocab Flash Cards** and type in *Fighting Disease.*

allergen

Infectious Disease

UNLOCK THE BIG ?

🔑 **How Do Pathogens Cause Disease?**

🔑 **What Pathogens Cause Infectious Disease and How Are They Spread?**

MY PLANET DiARY

Fight the Flu

Misconception: You cannot catch the flu if you have gotten a flu shot.

The flu vaccine decreases your chances of catching the flu, but it does not protect you 100 percent. However, if you get the shot and still end up catching the flu, your symptoms probably will be milder than if you had not gotten vaccinated.

There are many strains of the flu virus. Each year, scientists choose the strains that they think will appear in the United States. Then a vaccine is made that contains those strains. The vaccine is given to people across the country. However, getting a flu shot will not protect you against any strain that is not in the vaccine.

MISCONCEPTION

Read the following questions. Write your answers below.

1. What is one challenge that scientists face when making the flu vaccine?

_____

_____

2. Does a person need to get a flu shot every year? Why or why not?

_____

_____

_____

▷ PLANET DIARY Go to **Planet Diary** to learn more about infectious diseases.

Lab zone® Do the Inquiry Warm-Up *The Agents of Disease.*

Vocabulary
- microorganism • pathogen
- infectious disease • toxin

Skills
- ↻ Reading: Identify the Main Idea
- ▲ Inquiry: Develop Hypotheses

How Do Pathogens Cause Disease?

In ancient times, people had different ideas about what caused disease. They thought that things such as evil spirits or swamp air caused disease. In fact, they sometimes cut holes in the skulls of sick people to let the evil spirits out. The ancient Greeks thought that disease resulted from an imbalance of four body fluids: blood, phlegm (flem) or mucus, black bile, and yellow bile.

Louis Pasteur and Microorganisms It was not until the 1860s that a French scientist named Louis Pasteur discovered the cause of some diseases. After investigating what causes foods to spoil, Pasteur concluded that **microorganisms,** living things too small to see without a microscope, were the cause. Pasteur thought that microorganisms might be causing disease in animals and people, too. So he investigated a disease attacking silkworms at the time. Pasteur found microorganisms inside silkworms with the disease. He was able to show that these organisms caused the disease. Pasteur's work led to an understanding of what causes most infectious diseases—microorganisms.

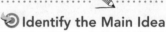

↻ **Identify the Main Idea**
In the graphic organizer, write the main idea of the first paragraph. Then write three details that support the main idea.

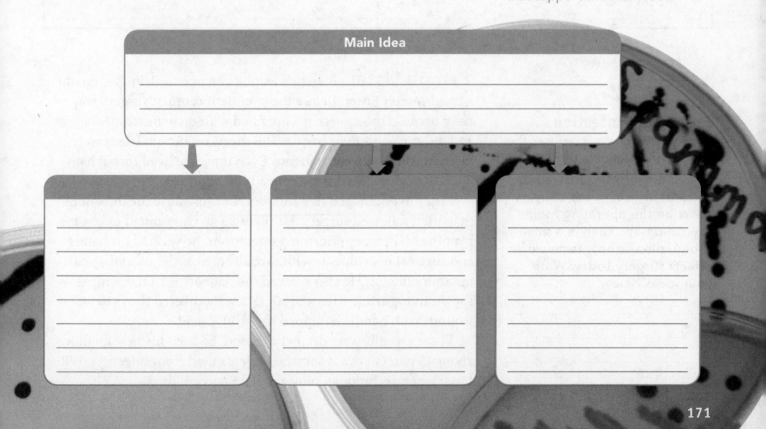

Main Idea

171

NOW

THEN

Then	Now

FIGURE 1 ·······································

Preventing Infection

A clean environment reduces the chance of infection after surgery.

✎ **Communicate** Observe the pictures above. In the table, describe the operating rooms then and now. Then in a small group, discuss how technology affects surgery today. Write your ideas below.

Joseph Lister Pasteur's work influenced a British surgeon named Joseph Lister. Before the twentieth century, surgery was risky because most surgeons operated with dirty instruments and did not wash their hands. The sheets on hospital beds were rarely washed between patients. Even if people lived through an operation, many died later from an infection.

Lister hypothesized that microorganisms cause the infections that often followed surgery. He planned an experiment to test his hypothesis. Before performing operations, he washed his hands and surgical instruments with carbolic acid, a chemical that kills microorganisms. He also sprayed the patients with the acid, as shown in **Figure 1**. After the surgeries, he covered the patients' wounds with bandages dipped in carbolic acid.

Lister's results were dramatic. Before he used his new methods, about 45 percent of his surgical patients died from infection. With Lister's new techniques, only about 15 percent died.

Robert Koch In the 1870s and 1880s, the German physician Robert Koch showed that a specific microorganism causes each disease. For example, the microorganism that causes strep throat cannot cause chickenpox or other diseases. Look at **Figure 2** to see how Koch identified the microorganism for a disease called anthrax.

Organisms that cause disease are called **pathogens.** A disease caused by a pathogen is an **infectious disease.** 🔑 **When you have an infectious disease, pathogens are in your body causing harm.** Pathogens damage large numbers of individual cells, which makes you sick.

FIGURE 2 ....

Koch's Experiment
Koch followed the scientific method in his research of pathogens.

✏️ **Draw Conclusions** How would Koch's conclusion have been different if Mouse B's blood had not contained the pathogen found in Mouse A's blood?

_____

_____

_____

_____

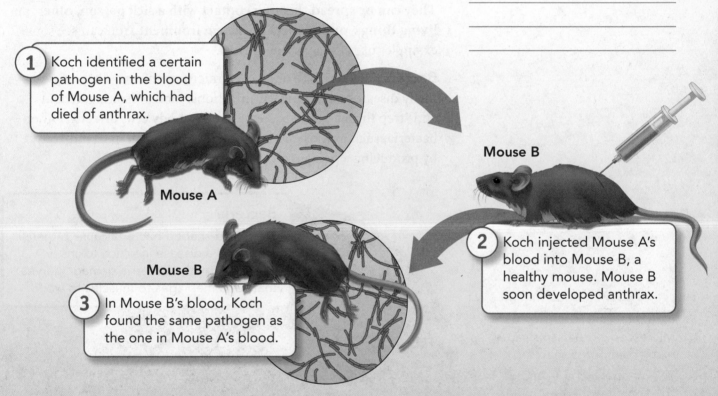

1. Koch identified a certain pathogen in the blood of Mouse A, which had died of anthrax.

Mouse A

Mouse B

2. Koch injected Mouse A's blood into Mouse B, a healthy mouse. Mouse B soon developed anthrax.

Mouse B

3. In Mouse B's blood, Koch found the same pathogen as the one in Mouse A's blood.

Lab zone® Do the Quick Lab *How Do Pathogens Cause Disease?*

🔑 **Assess Your Understanding**

1a. Define What is an infectious disease?

_____

_____

b. Make Generalizations How did Pasteur's work affect Lister's work?

_____

_____

_____

got it?

○ **I get it!** Now I know that pathogens cause

disease by _____

_____

_____

○ **I need extra help with** _____

Go to **MY SCIENCE** 🔍 **COACH** online for help with this subject.

What Pathogens Cause Infectious Disease and How Are They Spread?

You share Earth with many kinds of organisms. Most of these organisms are harmless, but some can make you sick. Some diseases are caused by multicelled animals, such as worms. However, most pathogens can be seen only with a microscope.

Types of Pathogens

The four major types of human pathogens are bacteria, viruses, fungi, and protists. They can be spread through contact with a sick person, other living things, or an object in the environment. You can see some examples of pathogens in **Figure 3.**

Bacteria Bacteria are one-celled microorganisms. They cause many diseases, including ear infections, food poisoning, tetanus, and strep throat. Some bacteria damage body cells directly. Other bacteria, such as those that cause tetanus, damage cells indirectly by producing a poison, or **toxin.**

FIGURE 3 ·······························

> **VIRTUAL LAB** **Pathogens**

Microscopic organisms cause many common diseases.

✎ **Compare and Contrast** In the table on the next page, use information in the text to write notes about pathogens. Then fill in the circle below to indicate which type of pathogen produces toxins.

- ○ viruses
- ○ bacteria
- ○ protists
- ○ fungi

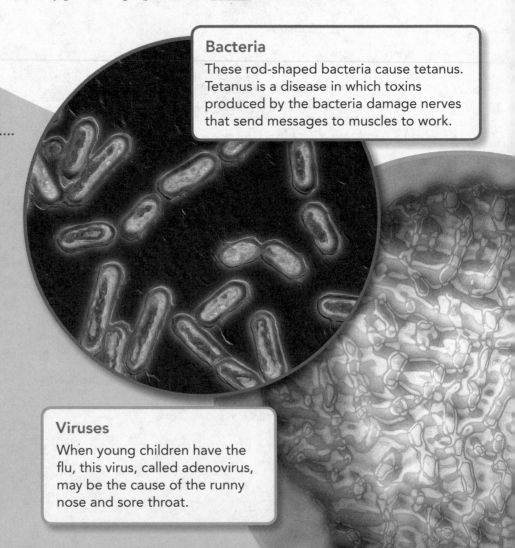

Bacteria

These rod-shaped bacteria cause tetanus. Tetanus is a disease in which toxins produced by the bacteria damage nerves that send messages to muscles to work.

Viruses

When young children have the flu, this virus, called adenovirus, may be the cause of the runny nose and sore throat.

Viruses Viruses are tiny nonliving particles much smaller than bacteria. They can reproduce only inside living cells. The cells are damaged or destroyed when the new virus particles are released. These new virus particles then infect other cells. Viruses cause many diseases including colds and the flu. There are more than 200 kinds of cold viruses alone.

Fungi Some fungi, such as molds and yeasts, also cause infectious diseases. Fungi that cause disease may be one-celled or multicelled living things. Fungi grow best in warm, dark, moist areas of the body. Athlete's foot and ringworm are two fungal diseases.

Protists Most protists are one-celled microorganisms and some can cause disease. They are larger than bacteria but still tiny. One type of protist causes the disease malaria, which is common in tropical areas. African sleeping sickness and hiker's disease are other diseases caused by protists.

Protists
This microorganism is called *Giardia* (jee AHR dee uh). People who drink from streams or lakes with this protist can get an intestinal disease called hiker's disease.

Fungi
This fungus causes a skin infection called athlete's foot.

Pathogen	Size	Characteristics	Type of Disease
Bacteria			
Viruses			
Fungi			
Protists			

Pathogens are spread through contaminated water.

Apply Concepts If you have a cold, what can you do to prevent spreading it?

_____

_____

_____

How Pathogens Are Spread Pathogens can infect you in several ways. They can spread through contact with an infected person; through soil, food, or water; and through a contaminated object or an infected animal.

Infected People Pathogens often pass from one person to another through direct physical contact, such as kissing and shaking hands. For example, if you kiss someone with an open cold sore, the virus that causes cold sores can get into your body. Pathogens spread indirectly, too. For example, when a person with a cold sneezes, pathogens shoot into the air. People who inhale these pathogens may catch the cold.

Soil, Food, and Water Some pathogens occur naturally in the environment. For example, the bacteria that cause botulism, a severe form of food poisoning, live in soil. These bacteria can produce toxins in foods that have been improperly canned. Other pathogens contaminate food and water and sicken people who eat the food or drink the water. Cholera and dysentery, deadly diseases that cause severe diarrhea, are spread through contaminated food or water.

apply it!

Cholera is a deadly disease caused by bacteria in drinking water. This map shows the locations of cholera cases in the 1854 cholera epidemic in London, England, and the city's water pumps.

1 **Develop Hypotheses** Which pump was probably the source of the contaminated water? What evidence do you have?

_____

_____

_____

_____

2 **Pose Questions** Suppose a doctor at the time learned that two more people had died of cholera. What two questions would the doctor most likely have asked?

_____

_____

Cholera Cases, London, 1854

• Cholera victims
○ Water pump

Contaminated Objects Some pathogens can survive for a time outside a person's body. People can contact pathogens by using objects, such as towels or keyboards, that an infected person touched. Colds and flu can be spread in this way. Tetanus bacteria can enter the body if a contaminated nail or other object punctures the skin.

Infected Animals If an animal that is infected with certain pathogens bites a person, the pathogens can pass to the person. For example, people get rabies, a serious disease of the nervous system, from the bite of an infected animal, such as a dog or raccoon. In tropical regions, mosquito bites transfer the malaria protist to people. Deer ticks, as shown in **Figure 4,** live mostly in the northeastern and upper mideastern United States. The bites of some deer ticks spread Lyme disease. If left untreated, Lyme disease can damage joints and cause many other health problems.

FIGURE 4 ·······················

Deer Ticks and Lyme Disease

To prevent Lyme disease, wear a long-sleeved shirt and tuck your pants into your socks if you plan to walk where ticks may live.

✎ **Infer** Explain how a deer tick could infect you without your realizing it.

_____

_____

_____

_____

Deer tick

Lab zone® Do the Quick Lab *How Does a Disease Spread?*

🔑 Assess Your Understanding

2a. Identify Name four types of pathogens that cause disease in humans.

_____

_____

b. [CHALLENGE] How could people make bacteria-contaminated water safe to drink in order to prevent illness?

_____

_____

_____

got it?

○ **I get it!** Now I know that disease-causing

pathogens include _____

_____ , and they are

spread by _____

_____

_____

○ I need extra help with _____

Go to **MY SCIENCE ⓢ COACH** online for help with this subject.

The Body's Defenses

🔑 **What Is the Body's First Line of Defense?**

🔑 **What Are the Inflammatory and Immune Responses?**

MY PLANET DIARY

The Kissing Disease

Have you ever heard of mononucleosis? Also known as mono, or the kissing disease, mononucleosis is most common among older teenagers and people in their twenties. It got its nickname because the disease can be spread through kissing. But, be careful. Because mono is passed through saliva, it can also be spread by sharing cups, forks, straws, and other utensils.

Some common symptoms of mono are fever, sore throat, swollen glands, and fatigue. If you display these symptoms, you might want to pay your doctor a visit, even if you haven't kissed anyone!

FUN FACTS

Read the following questions. Write your answers below.

1. How can mononucleosis be spread?

_____

_____

_____

_____

2. What can you do to lower your chances of catching mono?

_____

_____

_____

> **PLANET DIARY** Go to **Planet Diary** to learn more about the body's defenses.

Lab zone® Do the Inquiry Warm-Up *Which Pieces Fit Together?*

Vocabulary

- inflammatory response • phagocyte
- immune response • lymphocyte • T cell
- antigen • B cell • antibody

Skills

- Reading: Compare and Contrast
- Inquiry: Make Models

What Is the Body's First Line of Defense?

You have probably battled invaders in video games. Video games have fantasy battles, but on and in your body, real battles against invading pathogens happen all the time. You are hardly ever aware of these battles because the body's disease-fighting system has lines of defense that effectively eliminate pathogens before they can harm your cells. **In the first line of defense, the surface of your skin, breathing passages, mouth, and stomach function as barriers to pathogens. These barriers trap and kill most pathogens with which you come into contact.**

Skin Your skin is an effective barrier to pathogens, as you can see in **Figure 1.** Pathogens on the skin are exposed to destructive chemicals in oil and sweat. Even if these chemicals do not kill them, the pathogens may fall off with dead skin cells. Most pathogens get through the skin only when it is cut. However, blood clots at a cut. Then a scab forms over the cut. So pathogens have little time to enter the body this way.

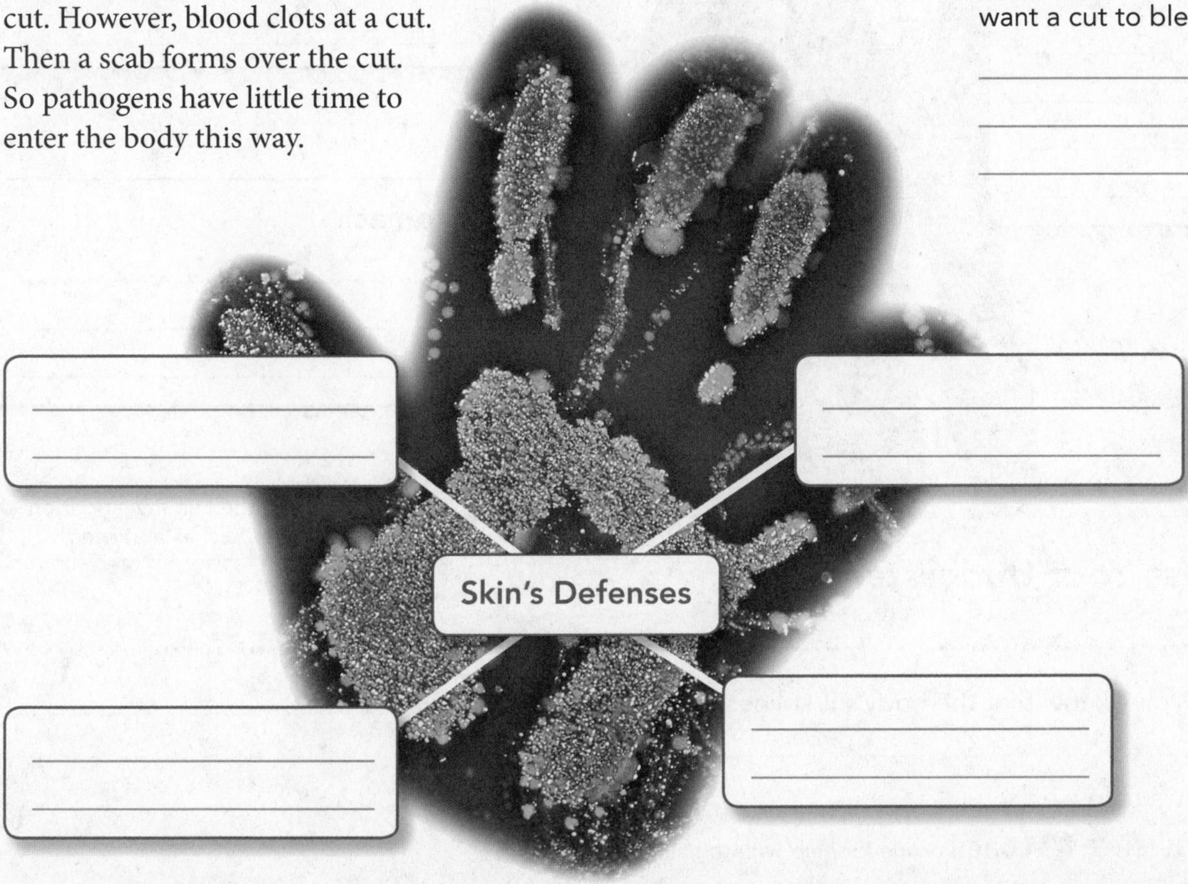

FIGURE 1 ·····························

Skin as a Barrier

The dots are groups of bacteria. The bacteria were on the skin of a person's hand.

✎ **Use the photo to complete the tasks.**

1. **Identify** In each box, write one of the skin's defenses against pathogens.

2. CHALLENGE Why would you want a cut to bleed some?

_____

_____

_____

Skin's Defenses

Breathing Passages Your breathing passages defend you from many pathogens you inhale. The nose, pharynx, trachea, and bronchi have hairs, mucus, and cilia, all of which trap pathogens from the air. In addition, you sneeze and cough when pathogens irritate your breathing passages. Sneezing and coughing force pathogens out of your body.

Mouth and Stomach Even if foods are handled safely, they still contain potential pathogens. Most of these pathogens are destroyed in your mouth or stomach. Saliva in your mouth contains destructive chemicals, and your stomach produces acid. **Figure 2** shows three of your body's barriers to pathogens.

FIGURE 2 ·····················

Barriers to Pathogens
Your breathing passages, mouth, and stomach are part of your first line of defense against pathogens.

✏ **Summarize** In each box, write how the barrier protects the body from pathogens.

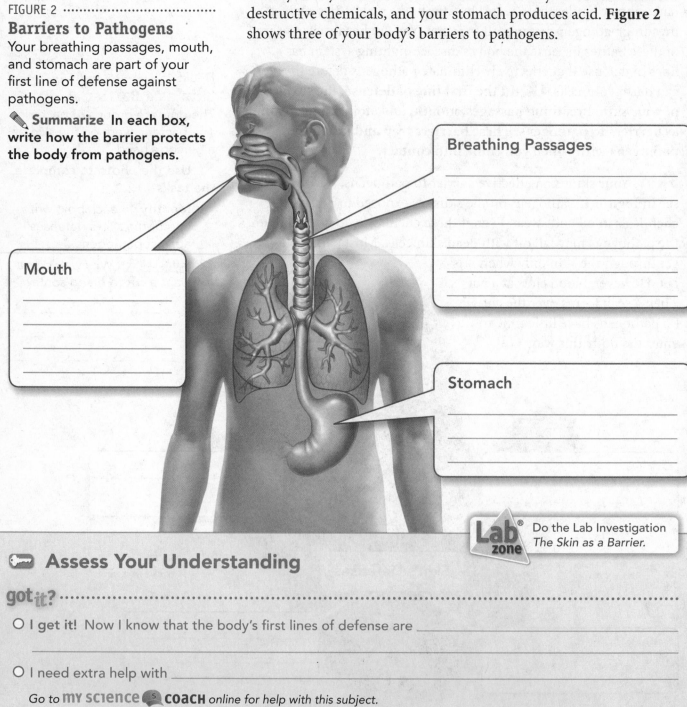

Breathing Passages
_____
_____
_____
_____
_____

Mouth
_____
_____
_____

Stomach
_____
_____
_____

Lab zone Do the Lab Investigation
The Skin as a Barrier.

🔑 **Assess Your Understanding**

got it? ···

O **I get it!** Now I know that the body's first lines of defense are _____

_____

O **I need extra help with** _____

Go to MY SCIENCE ⬤ COACH online for help with this subject.

What Are the Inflammatory and Immune Responses?

Sometimes the first line of defense fails, and pathogens get into your body. Fortunately, your body has a second and third line of defense—the inflammatory response and the immune response. **🗝 In the inflammatory response, fluid and white blood cells leak from blood vessels and fight pathogens in nearby tissues. In the immune response, certain immune cells in the blood and tissues react to each kind of pathogen with a defense targeted specifically at the pathogen.**

Inflammatory Response Have you ever scraped your knee? When body cells are damaged, they release chemicals that trigger the **inflammatory response,** which is your body's second line of defense. The inflammatory response is the same regardless of the pathogen, so it is a general defense. This response involves white blood cells, inflammation, and sometimes fever.

Vocabulary Latin Word Origins The Latin word *inflammare* means "to set on fire." How does the Latin meaning relate to the word *inflammation*?

_____

_____

_____

⟳ Compare and Contrast Use the first paragraph of the text to list how the inflammatory and immune responses are alike and different in the Venn diagram.

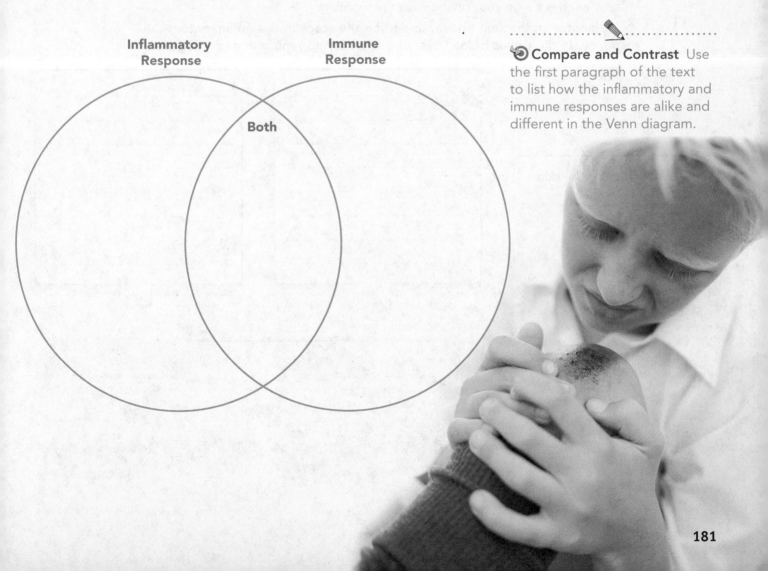

Inflammatory Response   Immune Response

Both

181

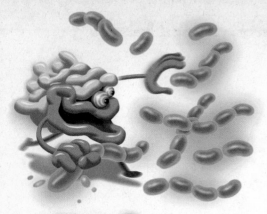

White Blood Cells Most white blood cells are disease fighters. However, each type of white blood cell has a particular function. The type of white blood cell involved in the inflammatory response is the phagocyte. A **phagocyte** (FAG uh syt) is a white blood cell that engulfs pathogens and destroys them by breaking them down.

Inflammation The inflammatory response is shown in **Figure 3**. During this response, capillaries widen in the area with pathogens. This enlargement increases blood flow to the area. Fluid and phagocytes leak out of the enlarged capillaries, and the affected area becomes red and swollen. In fact, if you touch the area, it will feel slightly warmer than usual. The phagocytes engulf the pathogens and destroy them.

Fever Chemicals produced during the inflammatory response sometimes cause a fever. Although a fever makes you feel bad, it helps your body fight the infection. Some pathogens do not grow or reproduce well at higher temperatures.

FIGURE 3 ···

The Inflammatory Response
Inflammation is a sign your phagocytes are working.

✎ **Sequence In the text above, underline the steps in the inflammatory response. In the boxes below, describe what is happening in each diagram.**

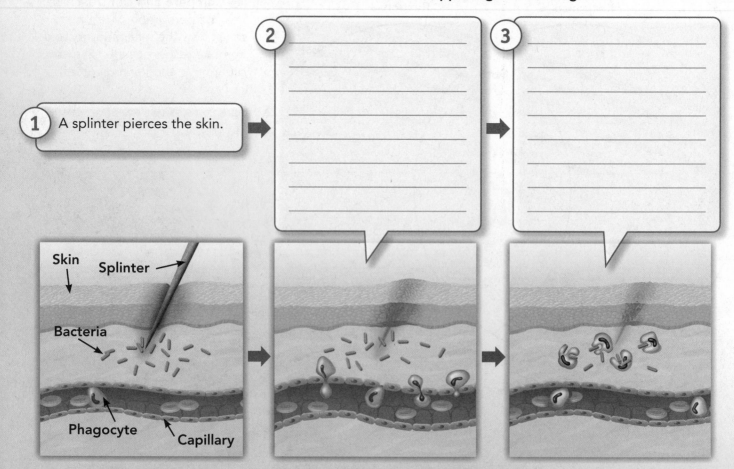

Immune Response If an infection from a pathogen is severe enough, it triggers the body's third line of defense—the **immune response.** The immune response is controlled by the immune system. The cells of the immune system can distinguish between different kinds of pathogens. They react to invaders with a defense targeted against that pathogen.

The white blood cells that distinguish between different kinds of pathogens are called **lymphocytes** (LIM fuh syts). Your body has two major kinds of lymphocytes: T cells and B cells.

T Cells A **T cell** is a lymphocyte that identifies pathogens and distinguishes one pathogen from another. Each kind of T cell recognizes a different kind of pathogen. What T cells actually recognize are a pathogen's marker molecules, which are called antigens. **Antigens** are molecules that the immune system recognizes either as part of your body or as coming from outside your body. Each different pathogen has its own antigen, with its own chemical structure. Look at **Figure 4** to see how T cells function.

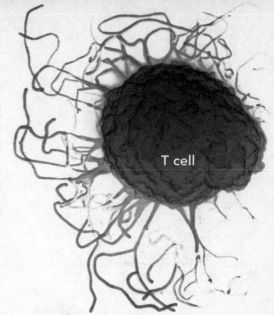

T cell

FIGURE 4 ···

T Cell Function
Healthy people have tens of millions of T cells in their blood.

✏ **Describe** What two roles does a T cell play after it divides?

_____

_____

_____

_____

_____

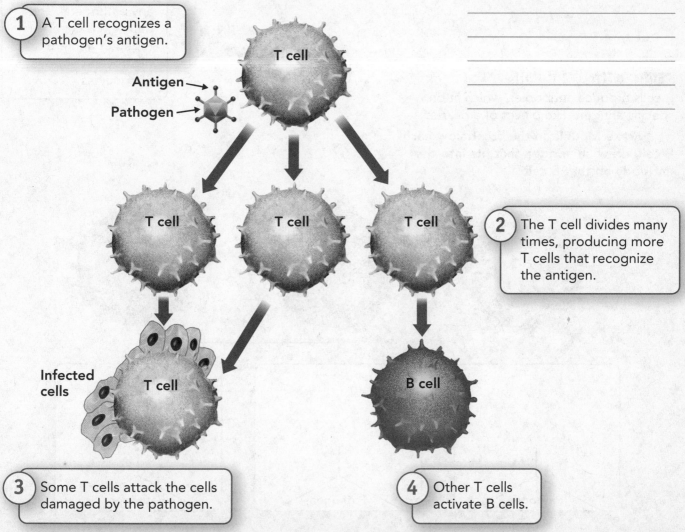

1 A T cell recognizes a pathogen's antigen.

Antigen →

Pathogen →

T cell

T cell   T cell   T cell

2 The T cell divides many times, producing more T cells that recognize the antigen.

Infected cells

T cell

B cell

3 Some T cells attack the cells damaged by the pathogen.

4 Other T cells activate B cells.

B Cells The lymphocytes called **B cells** produce proteins that help destroy pathogens. These proteins are called **antibodies.** Each kind of B cell produces only one kind of antibody, and each kind of antibody has a different structure. Antigen and antibody molecules fit together like pieces of a puzzle. When antibodies bind to the antigens on a pathogen, they mark the pathogen for destruction. Some antibodies make pathogens clump together like those shown in **Figure 5.** Others keep pathogens from attaching to the body cells they might harm. Still other antibodies make it easier for phagocytes to destroy the pathogens.

T cells activate B cells to make antibodies against a pathogen's antigens.

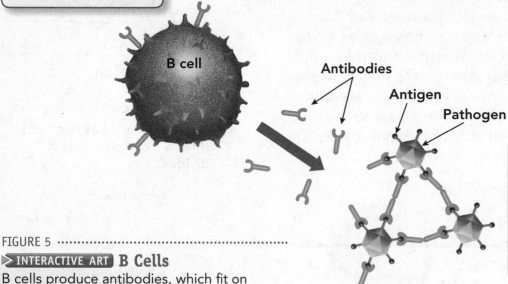

The antibodies then bind to antigens on any pathogens. The pathogens clump together and are destroyed by the phagocytes.

FIGURE 5 ·······························

> **INTERACTIVE ART** **B Cells**
B cells produce antibodies, which fit on specific antigens like pieces of a puzzle.

✎ **Make Models In the box below each B cell, draw an antigen that fits into the antibody on that B cell.**

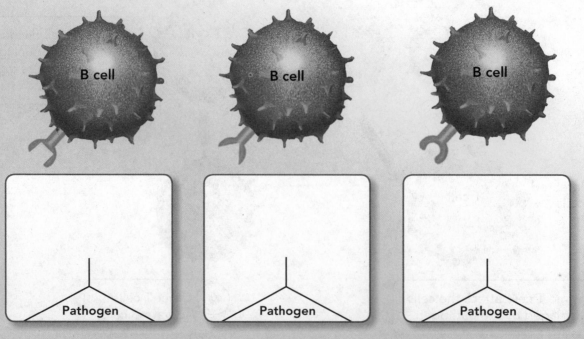

apply it!

Certain bacteria cause strep throat. Your T cells and B cells work together to combat the infection.

1 Identify Number each step in the immune response.

2 Sequence Describe each step of the immune response against the bacteria that causes strep throat.

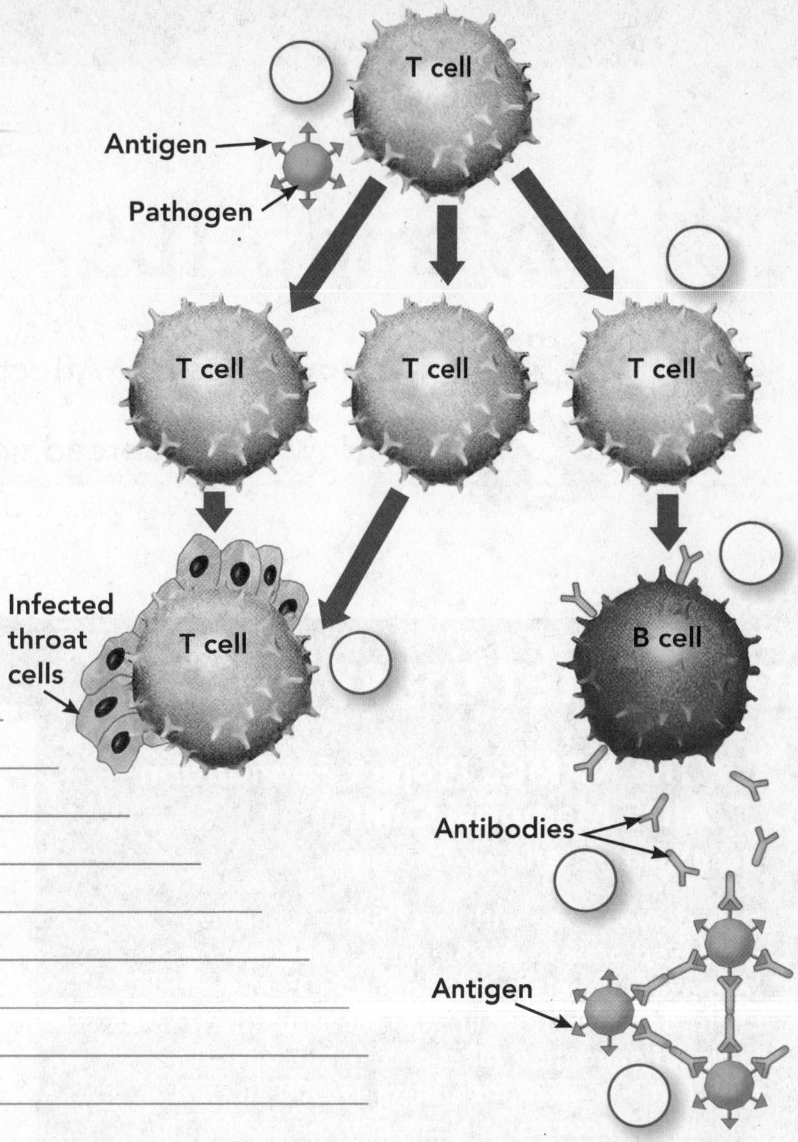

_____
_____
_____
_____
_____
_____
_____
_____
_____
_____
_____
_____
_____

T cell

Antigen →
Pathogen →

T cell   T cell   T cell

Infected throat cells →   T cell

B cell

Antibodies →

Antigen →

Lab zone® Do the Quick Lab *Stuck Together.*

🔑 Assess Your Understanding

1a. Name Identify the key cells that are part of the immune response.

_____
_____

b. Explain How does the inflammatory response defend against pathogens?

_____
_____
_____
_____

got it?

○ **I get it!** Now I know the inflammatory and immune responses are the body's _____
_____
_____
_____

○ **I need extra help with** _____

Go to **MY SCIENCE** ⒮ **COACH** online for help with this subject.

HIV and AIDS

🔑 How Does HIV Affect the Body?

🔑 How Is HIV Spread and Treated?

UNLOCK THE BIG ?

my planet diary

PROFILE

The NAMES Project Foundation—AIDS Memorial Quilt

Headquarters: Atlanta, Georgia

How do you cope with loss? Some who have lost loved ones to AIDS express their feelings by making panels to add to the AIDS Memorial Quilt. Begun in 1987 in San Francisco, the NAMES Project Foundation takes care of the quilt. The quilt is made up of more than 47,000 individual panels from countries all around the world. The panels help people honor those whom they have lost to the tragic disease. The large number of panels sadly illustrates that AIDS has taken so many lives. Yet, the quilt is a symbol of unity that supports continuing research to find a cure for this devastating disease.

Communicate Discuss the following questions with a partner. Write your answers below.

1. The quilt is made up of panels from around the world. What does this tell you about AIDS?

_____

_____

2. Why do you think scientists are important in the fight against AIDS?

_____

_____

_____

> PLANET DIARY Go to **Planet Diary** to learn more about HIV and AIDS.

Lab zone® Do the Inquiry Warm-Up *How Does HIV Spread?*

Vocabulary
- AIDS
- HIV

Skills
- Reading: Sequence
- Inquiry: Graph

How Does HIV Affect the Body?

Our immune system protects us well. So we usually do not even realize that our body has been attacked by a pathogen. But what happens when our immune system itself is sick?

Acquired immunodeficiency syndrome, or **AIDS,** is a disease caused by a virus that attacks the immune system. The virus that causes AIDS is called the human immunodeficiency virus, or **HIV.** 🔑 **HIV is the only kind of virus known to attack the human immune system directly and destroy T cells.** Once inside the body, HIV enters T cells and reproduces. People can be infected with HIV—that is, have the virus living in their T cells—for many years before they become sick.

In 1981, the first case of AIDS was reported in the United States. Nearly one million Americans may now be infected with HIV. Many of these people—one in four—do not realize yet that they are infected. However, the disease is not found only in the United States. It is a worldwide epidemic.

do the math!

The table shows the number of men, women, and children under age 15 worldwide living with HIV in 2007.

1 ◢ **Graph** Use the data in the table to make a bar graph. Then write a title for the graph.

2 **Interpret Data** What do you notice about the number of men and women living with HIV in 2007?

_____

_____

_____

3 **Draw Conclusions** What conclusion can you make about the populations the virus affects?

_____

_____

_____

Populations Living With HIV in 2007	
Population	Number of People
Men	15.3 million
Women	15.5 million
Children under age 15	2 million

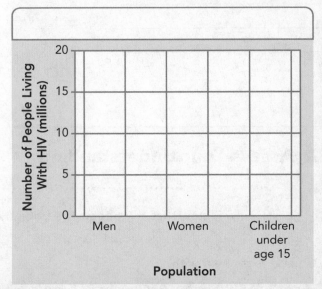

HIV and AIDS
When people first become infected with HIV, they often have no symptoms. A month or so later, they may seem to have the flu, but it goes away. Although they may not have symptoms at first, people can still spread the virus.

It may take ten years or more for severe symptoms to appear. However, in time, HIV begins to destroy the T cells it has infected. As the virus destroys T cells like the one shown in **Figure 1,** the body begins to lose its ability to fight disease. This is a symptom of the disease called AIDS.

Infections
People with AIDS start to get diseases that healthy people do not get normally. Development of these infections is one symptom of the disease AIDS. Most people infected with HIV eventually develop the symptoms of AIDS. Many survive attack after attack of infections. Yet, in time, their immune systems fail, and they die.

Sequence Complete the steps that happen after a person is infected with HIV and develops AIDS.

Step 1 A person is infected.

Step 2

_____
_____
_____

Step 3

_____
_____
_____

Step 4

_____
_____
_____

Step 5

_____
_____
_____

FIGURE 1 ···
HIV
HIV reproduces inside T cells. It then bursts out to attack other T cells.

CHALLENGE **Use what you see in the photo to explain why HIV destroys an immune system.**

_____
_____
_____
_____
_____

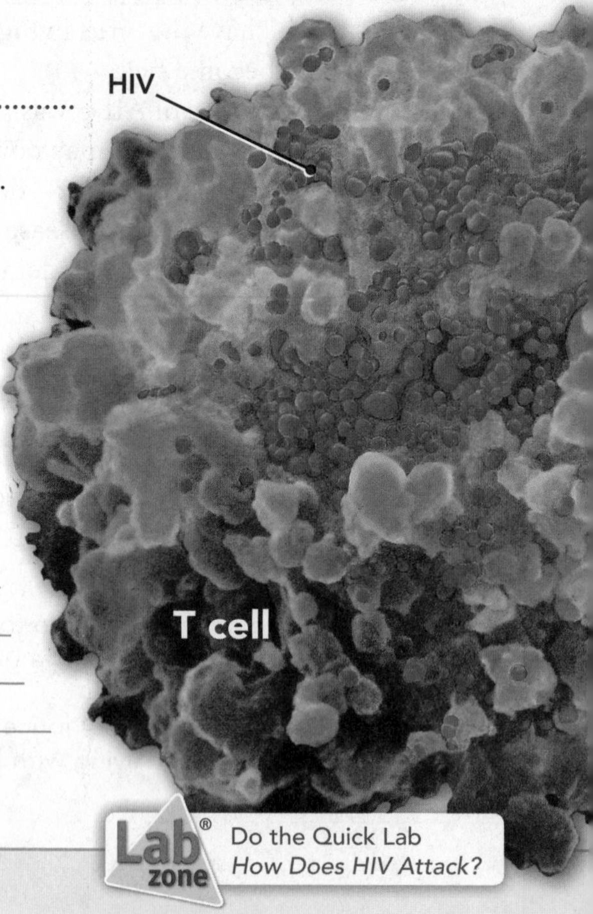

HIV

T cell

Lab zone® Do the Quick Lab
How Does HIV Attack?

Assess Your Understanding
got it? ···

O **I get it!** Now I know that HIV affects the body by _____
_____

O **I need extra help with** _____

Go to MY SCIENCE COACH online for help with this subject.

How Is HIV Spread and Treated?

Like all other viruses, HIV can reproduce only inside cells. However, the virus can survive for a short time outside the human body in fluids. These fluids include blood and the fluids that the male and female reproductive systems produce.

HIV can spread from one person to another if body fluids from an infected person come in contact with body fluids of an uninfected person. Sexual contact is one way this transfer happens. HIV may also pass from an infected woman to her baby during pregnancy or childbirth, or through breast milk. Infected blood can also spread HIV. For example, drug users who share needles can pass HIV. Since 1985, all donated blood in the United States has been tested for HIV.

At this time, there is no cure for AIDS. However, combinations of drugs that fight the virus in different ways can delay the development of AIDS and extend life expectancy. See **Figure 2** for information about young people living with AIDS.

FIGURE 2 ·····················

Young People and AIDS

The graph shows how advances in HIV treatments enabled more people to live with AIDS.

✎ **Read Graphs** Using the graph, estimate how many 13- to 24-year-olds were living with AIDS in 2007.

_____

_____

_____

_____

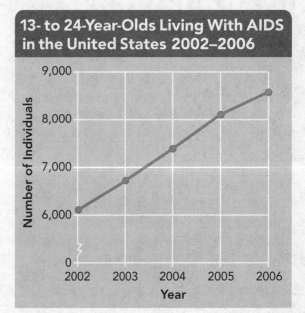

13- to 24-Year-Olds Living With AIDS in the United States 2002–2006

Number of Individuals vs. Year

Lab zone ® Do the Quick Lab
What Will Spread HIV?

Assess Your Understanding

1a. Review Where does HIV reproduce in people?

_____

_____

b. Summarize How is AIDS treated?

_____

_____

got it? ··

○ **I get it!** Now I know that HIV can spread _____

_____

○ **I need extra help with** _____

Go to MY SCIENCE ⬤ COACH online for help with this subject.

Infectious Disease and Your Health

UNLOCK THE BIG ?

🗝 **How Can You Become Immune?**

🗝 **How Can Infectious Diseases Be Treated and Prevented?**

my planet diary

Chickenpox Vaccine

Before the chickenpox vaccine was developed, more than 4 million Americans were infected with the chickenpox virus every year. Parents planned chickenpox parties to spread the disease. Parents wanted to expose their children to chickenpox early in life because children are less likely to get seriously ill from chickenpox than adults.

The development of a chickenpox vaccine in 1995 has made chickenpox parties mostly a thing of the past. Now, anyone over one year old can get the vaccine. The vaccine has reduced the likelihood of getting chickenpox to just 10 to 30 percent. Since the vaccine is somewhat new, more research is being done to determine if the vaccine can last through adulthood.

Write your answers to the questions below.

1. What was the purpose of chickenpox parties?

_____

_____

_____

_____

2. Why do you think there is a 10 to 30 percent chance of chickenpox with the vaccine?

_____

_____

_____

> PLANET DIARY Go to **Planet Diary** to learn more about how infectious diseases affect your health.

 Do the Inquiry Warm-Up *Types of Immunity.*

Vocabulary
- immunity - active immunity - vaccination - vaccine
- passive immunity - antibiotic - antibiotic resistance

Skills
- Reading: Relate Cause and Effect
- Inquiry: Interpret Data

How Can You Become Immune?

People get diseases. However, they get some diseases only once. This is because people develop immunity to some diseases once they recover from them. **Immunity** is the body's ability to destroy pathogens before they can cause disease. Immunity can be active or passive. **You acquire active immunity when your own immune system produces antibodies against a pathogen in your body. You acquire passive immunity when the antibodies come from a source outside your body.**

Active Immunity People who have had chickenpox were once invaded by the chickenpox virus. In response, their immune systems produced antibodies. The next time the chickenpox virus invades their bodies, their immune systems will produce antibodies quickly. So they will not become sick with chickenpox again. This reaction is called **active immunity** because the body has produced the antibodies that fight pathogens. Active immunity can result from either getting the disease or being vaccinated. It often lasts for many years. Sometimes it lasts for life.

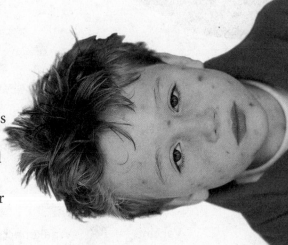

Cause	Effect
Contract chickenpox virus the first time.	_____

Relate Cause and Effect
Complete the graphic organizer with the effects of contracting the chickenpox virus.

Cause	Effect
Contract chickenpox virus the second time.	_____

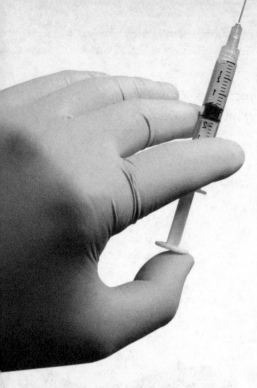

The Immune Response The immune system produces active immunity as part of the immune response. Recall that during the immune response, T cells and B cells help destroy pathogens. After the person recovers, some T cells and B cells keep the "memory" of the pathogen's antigen. If that kind of pathogen invades again, these memory cells recognize the antigen. They start the immune response so quickly that the person often does not get sick.

Vaccination Vaccination is another way of gaining immunity, as shown in **Figure 1.** **Vaccination** (vac suh NAY shun), or immunization, is the process by which harmless antigens are put into a person's body to produce active immunity. Vaccinations are given by injection, by mouth, or through a nasal spray.

The substance used in a vaccination is a vaccine. A **vaccine** (vak SEEN) usually consists of weakened or killed pathogens that trigger the immune response into action. The T cells and B cells still recognize and respond to the antigens of these weakened or killed pathogens and destroy them. So when you receive a vaccination, you usually do not get sick. However, after destroying these pathogens, your immune system responds by producing memory cells and active immunity to the disease.

FIGURE 1 ··································

▶ ART IN MOTION **Vaccination**
A vaccine activates
the immune response.

✎ **Interpret Diagrams** In the
empty boxes, describe what is
happening in each diagram.

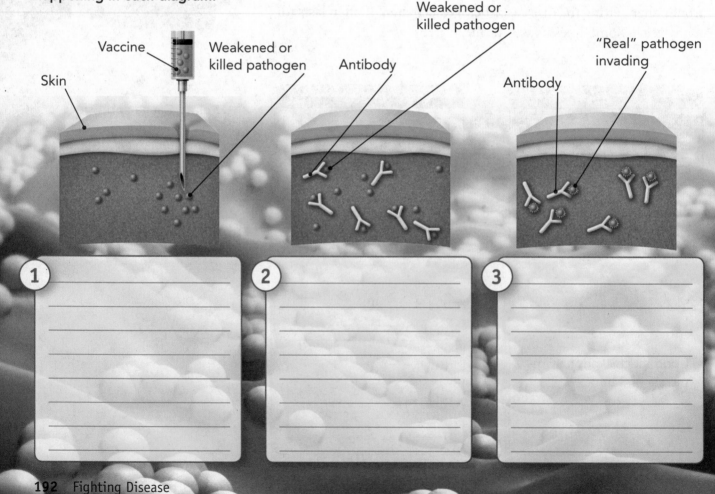

Passive Immunity Some diseases, such as rabies, are uncommon. So people rarely receive vaccinations against them. However, someone who is bitten by an animal with rabies is usually given injections containing antibodies to the rabies antigen. This type of protection is called passive immunity. **Passive immunity** results when antibodies are given to a person. Unlike active immunity, passive immunity usually lasts no more than a few months.

A baby acquires passive immunity to some diseases before birth. This immunity results from antibodies that are passed from the mother's blood into the baby's blood during pregnancy. After birth, these antibodies protect the baby for about six months.

FIGURE 2 ···

Immune Responses
Your body can destroy pathogens in two different ways.

✎ **Compare and Contrast**
Use the Venn diagram to compare and contrast active immunity and passive immunity.

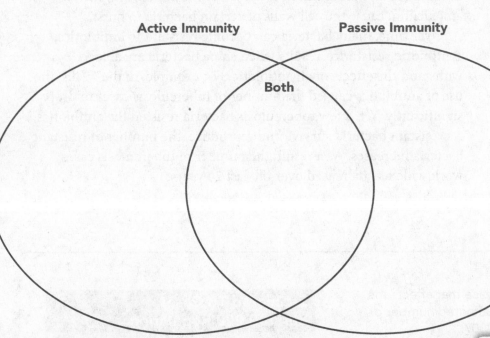

Active Immunity   Passive Immunity

Both

Do the Quick Lab *Modeling Active and Passive Immunity.*

🔑 **Assess Your Understanding**

1a. Explain What are two ways that you could acquire active immunity?

_____

_____

_____

b. Develop Hypotheses Why does passive immunity usually not last for long?

_____

_____

_____

got it? ··

○ **I get it!** Now I know that I can become immune by _____

_____

○ I need extra help with _____

    Go to MY SCIENCE ⓢ COACH online for help with this subject.

How Can Infectious Diseases Be Treated and Prevented?

Bacteria and viruses can cause infectious diseases that require treatment. 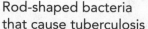 **Bacterial diseases can be treated with specific medications. Viral diseases have no known cure. Both types of diseases can be prevented.**

Bacterial Diseases If you get a bacterial disease, you may be given an antibiotic. An **antibiotic** (an tih by AHT ik) is a chemical that kills bacteria or slows their growth without harming body cells. Antibiotics are made naturally by some bacteria and fungi. They also are made in factories. Some antibiotics, such as amoxicillin, cause the cell walls of certain bacteria to burst.

Over time, many bacteria can become resistant to antibiotics. **Antibiotic resistance** results when some bacteria are able to withstand the effects of an antibiotic. For example, in the 1940s, the use of antibiotics caused the number of tuberculosis cases to drop significantly. Yet, a few tuberculosis bacteria resisted the antibiotics. As resistant bacteria survive and reproduce, the number of resistant bacteria increases. As a result, the number of tuberculosis cases worldwide has increased over the last 20 years.

Rod-shaped bacteria that cause tuberculosis

apply it!

Tuberculosis (TB) is a bacterial disease that affects the lungs. The data table shows the estimated number of new TB cases in 1997, 2002, and 2007.

1 Interpret Data Which country has the greatest problem with TB? Explain how you know.

_____

_____

_____

_____

2 CHALLENGE Why are the data presented as the number of new cases per 100,000 people?

_____

_____

_____

Estimated TB Cases per 100,000 Population			
Country	1997	2002	2007
Brazil	67	57	48
China	109	103	98
India	168	168	168
Mexico	39	28	20
Russia	94	108	110
South Africa	360	780	948
United States	7	5	4

Viral Diseases Medicines you take when you have a cold or the flu do not kill the viruses because the viruses are nonliving. But, medicines can reduce your symptoms so you feel better. Always follow the medicine's directions. Medicine can sometimes hide symptoms that should send you to see a doctor.

To recover from a bacterial or viral disease, get plenty of rest and drink fluids. If you do not feel better in a short time, see a doctor.

Prevention There are ways to prevent getting sick from microorganisms. You can avoid contact with infected people and wash your hands often. You can also eat a balanced diet and exercise to stay healthy. To prevent some diseases, such as the flu, you can get a vaccine. However, you cannot get a vaccine for cold viruses.

FIGURE 3 ·······························
Colds and the Flu
✏ **Describe** Complete the common cold card. Use the flu card as a guide.

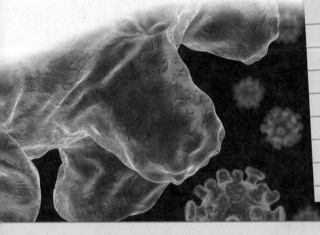

INFLUENZA (Flu)

Symptoms: High fever; sore throat; headache; cough

How It Spreads: Contact with contaminated people or objects; inhaling droplets

Treatment: Bed rest; fluids

Prevention: Vaccine (mainly for the high-risk ill, elderly, and young)

COMMON COLD

Symptoms:

How It Spreads:

Treatment:

Prevention:

Lab zone® Do the Quick Lab *What Substances Can Kill Pathogens?*

🔑 **Assess Your Understanding**

2a. Review What is the best treatment for viral diseases?

_____

_____

b. Infer Explain why antibiotics are ineffective against viral diseases.

_____

_____

got it? ·······························

○ **I get it!** Now I know that if I get sick, I can treat _____

and prevent _____

○ **I need extra help with** _____

Go to MY SCIENCE 💬 COACH *online for help with this subject.*

Noninfectious Disease

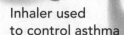

UNLOCK
THE BIG
?

🔑 **How Do Allergies, Asthma, and Diabetes Affect the Body?**

🔑 **What Is Cancer and How Can It Be Treated?**

Inhaler used
to control asthma

my planet Diary

Athletes With Asthma

Asthma is a disease that causes shortness of breath and wheezing or coughing. You may think people who have asthma cannot excel in sports. But asthma does not have to stop anyone from succeeding. Here are some facts about asthma and athletics.

• One out of six athletes in the 1996 Summer Olympics had a history of asthma. Thirty percent of them won a medal.

• 22 percent of the athletes in the 1998 Winter Olympics suffered from asthma.

• Jerome Bettis (NFL football player), Jackie Joyner-Kersee (Olympic track and field medalist), Hakeem Olajuwon (NBA basketball player), and Amy VanDyken (Olympic swimmer) all live with asthma.

SCIENCE STATS

Answer the following questions.

1. Why might people think that someone with asthma cannot play sports?

_____

_____

_____

_____

2. What would you tell a friend who has asthma and wants to join the swim team?

_____

_____

_____

> PLANET DIARY Go to **Planet Diary** to learn more about noninfectious disease.

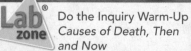

Lab® zone Do the Inquiry Warm-Up *Causes of Death, Then and Now*

Vocabulary

- noninfectious disease
- allergy
- allergen
- histamine
- asthma
- insulin
- diabetes
- tumor
- carcinogen

Skills

- Reading: Summarize
- Inquiry: Draw Conclusions

How Do Allergies, Asthma, and Diabetes Affect the Body?

Americans are living longer than ever before. A person who was born in 2000 can expect to live about 77 years. In contrast, a person who was born in 1950 could expect to live only about 68 years, and a person born in 1900 only about 50 years.

Progress against infectious disease is one reason why life spans have increased. However, as most infectious diseases have become less common, noninfectious diseases have grown more common. **Noninfectious diseases** are diseases that are not caused by pathogens. Unlike infectious diseases, noninfectious diseases cannot be transmitted from person to person. Two noninfectious diseases, cardiovascular disease and cancer, are the first and second leading causes of death from disease in the United States. Allergies, asthma, and diabetes are other noninfectious diseases. While not often fatal, these diseases are chronic. That is, they reappear frequently over time. **Allergies cause an inflammatory response by the body. Asthma affects breathing, while diabetes affects how body cells take up glucose.**

Summarize Use your own words to summarize the information about diseases on this page.

197

Observe Name two foods that many people are allergic to.

_____

_____

_____

_____

_____

Allergies People who sneeze a lot in the spring may not have a cold. Instead, they may be showing a symptom of an allergy. An **allergy** is a reaction caused when the immune system is overly sensitive to a foreign substance—something not normally found in the body.

Any substance that causes an allergy is an **allergen.** Allergens include pollen, dust, molds, some foods, pet dander (dandruff), and even some medicines. Unfortunately, the bodies of many people react to one or more allergens.

Allergens may get into your body when you inhale them, eat them in food, or touch them. Allergens signal cells in the body to release a substance called histamine. **Histamine** (HIS tuh meen) is a chemical that is responsible for the symptoms of an allergy, such as a rash, sneezing, and watery eyes. Drugs that interfere with the action of histamine, called antihistamines, may lessen this reaction. However, if you have an allergy, the best way to prevent allergy symptoms is to try to avoid the substance to which you are allergic.

apply it!

Suzy ate some strawberries. A short time later, she broke out in a rash.

❶ Identify What might have caused Suzy's rash?

_____

❷ Sequence Explain how eating strawberries can cause a rash.

_____

_____

_____

❸ Predict What might a doctor prescribe to relieve Suzy's rash?

_____

_____

Asthma Some allergic reactions can cause a condition called asthma. **Asthma** (AZ muh) is a disease in which the airways in the lungs narrow significantly. This narrowing causes wheezing, coughing, and shortness of breath. Other factors that may trigger asthma attacks include stress and heavy exercise. Tobacco smoke, air pollution, strong odors, and respiratory infections can also trigger an attack. More than 20 million Americans have asthma.

Figure 1 shows a normal airway and an airway affected by asthma. During an asthma attack, the muscles around the airways tighten, narrowing the airways. At the same time, the inner walls of the airways become irritated, red, swollen, and warm. They produce mucus. The mucus clogs the airways and makes breathing even more difficult.

Someone who is having an asthma attack needs medicines, such as an inhaler, to open the airways and reduce swelling. A severe attack may require emergency care. An asthma attack can be fatal.

FIGURE 1 ·······································

Airways With and Without Asthma
Asthma is a common condition among young people.

✎ **Relate Text and Visuals** Look at the diagram of a normal airway. Then in each box of the second diagram, describe what happens in an airway affected by asthma.

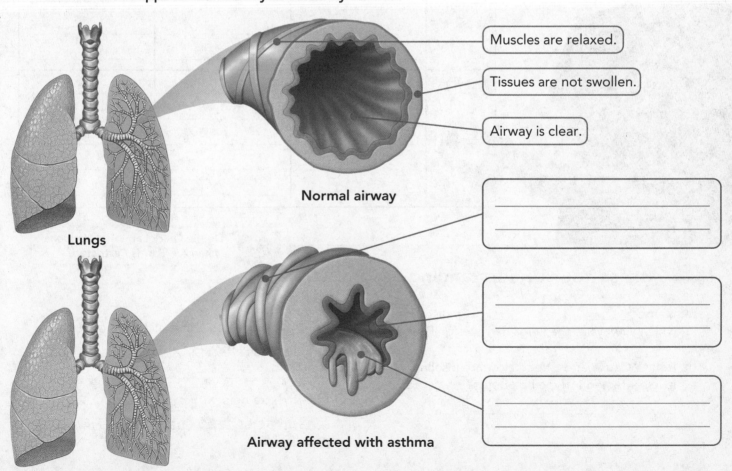

Muscles are relaxed.

Tissues are not swollen.

Airway is clear.

Normal airway

Lungs

Airway affected with asthma

FIGURE 2 ··························

Glucose Testing

The student is using a device called a glucometer to measure the amount of glucose in his blood.

✏️ 🔄 **Summarize** Write notes in the table about Type I and Type II diabetes.

Diabetes One function of the pancreas is to produce insulin. **Insulin** (IN suh lin) is a substance that enables body cells to take glucose from the blood and use it for energy. In the condition called **diabetes** (dy uh BEE teez), either the pancreas produces too little insulin or body cells do not use insulin properly. People with diabetes, or diabetics, have high levels of glucose in their blood but not enough of it in their body cells. If untreated, diabetics may lose weight and feel weak and hungry. They also may urinate often and feel thirsty.

Diabetes has two main forms. Type I diabetes often begins in childhood. The pancreas produces little or no insulin. People with this condition need insulin injections. Type II diabetes usually develops in adults. Either body cells stop responding normally to insulin or the pancreas stops making enough insulin. Some Type II diabetics can control their symptoms through diet, weight control, and exercise instead of insulin injections. All diabetics must check their blood frequently, as shown in **Figure 2**.

Type of Diabetes	Cause	Symptoms	Treatment
Type I			
Type II			

Lab zone Do the Quick Lab *What Happens When Air Flow Is Restricted?*

🔑 Assess Your Understanding

1a. Name _____ is a disorder in which airways of the lungs narrow significantly.

b. Relate Cause and Effect How are insulin levels affected in Type I diabetes?

_____

_____

got it?

○ **I get it!** Now I know that allergies, asthma, and diabetes affect _____

_____

○ **I need extra help with** _____

Go to MY SCIENCE 🔊 COACH *online for help with this subject.*

What Is Cancer and How Can It Be Treated?

Usually, the body produces new cells at about the same rate that other cells die. **However, cancer is a disease in which cells multiply uncontrollably, over and over, destroying healthy tissue. Treatments include surgery, radiation, and drugs.**

How Cancer Develops As cells divide over and over, they often form abnormal masses of cells called **tumors.** Not all tumors are cancerous. Cancerous tumors invade and destroy the healthy tissue around them. Eventually, cells from a tumor may break away from the tumor and enter the blood or lymph vessels. The blood or lymph carries the cancer cells to other parts of the body, where they may form new tumors. Unless stopped by treatment, cancer progresses through the body.

Causes of Cancer Different factors may work together to cause cancer. Inherited characteristics make some people more likely to develop certain cancers. For example, daughters of mothers who had breast cancer have an increased chance of developing breast cancer themselves. Factors in the environment, called **carcinogens** (kahr SIN uh junz), can also cause cancer. The tar in cigarette smoke is a carcinogen.

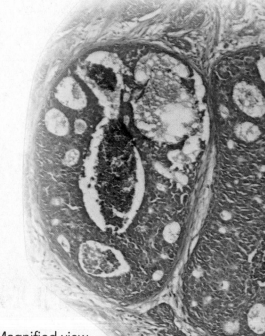

Magnified view of cancerous cells

do the math!

This data table shows the estimated number of new cases of different cancers in the United States in 1981 and 2007.

1 Interpret Tables Which type of cancer has increased the most from 1981 to 2007 in men? In women?

Men _____

Women _____

2 Draw Conclusions Explain why the number of new cancer cases might increase as tests to detect cancer improve.

_____

_____

_____

_____

Estimated New Cancer Cases

Type of Cancer	New Cases (1981)	New Cases (2007)
Men		
Prostate	70,000	218,890
Lung	88,000	114,760
Colon and Rectum	58,000	79,130
Oral Cavity and Pharynx	18,400	24,180
Women		
Breast	110,000	178,480
Lung	34,000	98,620
Colon and Rectum	62,000	74,630
Uterus	54,000	50,230

201

Cancer Treatment

Surgery, radiation, and drugs are used to treat cancer. If cancer is detected before it has spread, doctors may remove tumors with surgery. After surgery, radiation or drugs may be used to kill remaining cancer cells.

Radiation treatment uses high-energy waves to kill cancer cells. When these waves are aimed at tumors, the intense energy damages and kills cancer cells. Drug therapy is the use of chemicals to destroy cancer cells. It is often called chemotherapy. However, many of these chemicals can destroy some normal cells, too. Both radiation and chemotherapy can have side effects, such as nausea and hair loss.

Cancer Prevention

People can reduce their risk of cancer by avoiding carcinogens, such as those in tobacco and sunlight. A low-fat diet that includes plenty of fruits and vegetables can help prevent cancers of the digestive system.

Also, people can get regular checkups to increase their chance of surviving cancer. The earlier cancer is detected, the more likely it can be treated successfully. In **Figure 3,** you can see a blackened spot on skin. This spot is a skin cancer called melanoma. Exposing unprotected skin to sunlight too often contributes to the development of skin cancer. It is especially important to avoid sunburns, which damage skin cells.

FIGURE 3 ·····································

Melanoma

Melanoma is the most serious skin cancer. It can affect many other organs in your body if not treated quickly.

✎ **On the notebook paper, write answers to the questions below.**

1. **Explain** What can you do to prevent skin cancer?
2. **CHALLENGE** What steps might a doctor take to treat melanoma?

Melanoma

EXPLORE THE BIG ? INVISIBLE INVADERS

Why do you sometimes get sick?

FIGURE 4 ··

> REAL-WORLD INQUIRY This boy's sneeze
might be a symptom of a cold or an allergy.

✎ Apply Concepts Answer the questions
in the boxes.

If this boy has a cold, what made him sick? Explain how you know.

How might he spread his sickness if it is a cold?

What might cause him to sneeze if he has an allergy?

 Do the Quick Lab *What Does Sunlight Do to the Beads?*

🔑 Assess Your Understanding

2a. Review What is a tumor?

_____

_____

b. Relate Cause and Effect How do cancerous
tumors harm the body?

_____

_____

c. ANSWER THE BIG ? Why do you sometimes get sick?

_____

_____

_____

_____

_____

_____

got it? ··

○ I get it! Now I know that cancer is _____

_____

○ I need extra help with _____

Go to MY SCIENCE ⓢ COACH online for help with this subject.

REVIEW THE BIG ?

A _____ in my body may cause an _____ disease.
I can also get sick from a _____ disease.

LESSON 1 Infectious Disease

🗝 When you have an infectious disease, pathogens are in your body causing harm.

🗝 The four major types of human pathogens are bacteria, viruses, fungi, and protists. They can be spread through contact with a sick person, other living things, or an object in the environment.

Vocabulary
- microorganism
- pathogen
- infectious disease
- toxin

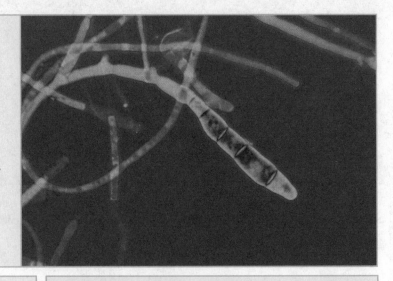

LESSON 2 The Body's Defenses

🗝 The first line of defense is your outer coverings, which trap and kill most pathogens.

🗝 In the inflammatory response, fluid and white blood cells fight pathogens in nearby tissues. In the immune response, cells in the blood and tissues target each kind of pathogen.

Vocabulary
- inflammatory response
- phagocyte
- immune response
- lymphocyte
- T cell
- antigen
- B cell
- antibody

LESSON 3 HIV and AIDS

🗝 HIV is the only kind of virus known to attack the human immune system directly and destroy T cells.

🗝 HIV can spread from one person to another if body fluids from an infected person come in contact with body fluids of an uninfected person.

Vocabulary
- AIDS
- HIV

LESSON 4 Infectious Disease and Your Health

🗝 You acquire active immunity when your own immune system produces antibodies. You acquire passive immunity when the antibodies come from a source outside your body.

🗝 Bacterial diseases can be treated with medications. Viral diseases have no known cure.

Vocabulary
- immunity
- active immunity
- vaccination
- vaccine
- passive immunity
- antibiotic
- antibiotic resistance

LESSON 5 Noninfectious Disease

🗝 Allergies cause an inflammatory response by the body. Asthma affects breathing, while diabetes affects how body cells take up glucose.

🗝 Cancer is a disease in which cells multiply uncontrollably, destroying healthy tissue. Treatments include surgery, radiation, and drugs.

Vocabulary
- noninfectious disease
- allergy
- allergen
- histamine
- asthma
- insulin
- diabetes
- tumor
- carcinogen

Review and Assessment

Infectious Disease

1. Organisms that cause disease are called

   a. histamines.   **b.** pathogens.

   c. phagocytes.   **d.** toxins.

2. _____ are living things too small to see with a microscope that cause most infectious diseases.

3. Classify What are the four ways in which a person can become infected with a pathogen?

_____

_____

_____

_____

_____

4. Compare and Contrast Describe how bacteria and viruses are alike and different in terms of how they cause disease.

_____

_____

_____

_____

_____

5. Apply Concepts Can you catch a cold by sitting in a chilly draft? Explain.

_____

_____

_____

6. Write About It Write a short speech that Joseph Lister might have delivered to other surgeons to convince them to use his surgical techniques. In the speech, Lister should explain why his techniques were so successful.

The Body's Defenses

7. Proteins produced by B cells are called

   a. phagocytes.   **b.** T cells.

   c. antibodies.   **d.** pathogens.

8. _____ engulf pathogens and destroy them.

9. Communicate How does the body make it difficult for a pathogen to reach a part of the body where it can cause disease?

_____

_____

_____

_____

_____

10. Interpret Diagrams In the diagram below, identify each labeled structure and its role in the immune response.

_____

_____

_____

_____

_____

_____

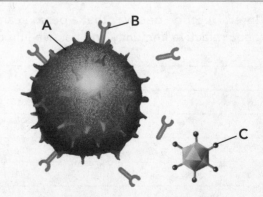

6 Review and Assessment

LESSON 3 HIV and AIDS

11. HIV attacks the human immune system and destroys

    a. B cells.   **b.** antigens.

    c. antibodies.   **d.** T cells.

12. HIV spreads from an infected person to an uninfected person through the contact of

_____

13. Relate Cause and Effect How does the destruction of T cells interfere with the body's ability to fight disease?

_____

_____

_____

_____

LESSON 4 Infectious Disease and Your Health

14. Which of the following produce active immunity without causing illness?

    a. vaccines   **b.** antibody injections

    c. antibiotics   **d.** phagocytes

15. _____ are chemicals that can kill bacteria without harming body cells.

16. Infer Describe one way that a person can acquire active immunity and passive immunity.

_____

_____

_____

_____

_____

LESSON 5 Noninfectious Disease

17. Abnormal tissue masses are called

    a. allergies.   **b.** cancer.

    c. diabetes.   **d.** tumors.

18. An _____ is any substance that causes an allergy.

19. Write About It For some people, dander of a cat causes an allergic reaction. On a separate paper, describe how a person's body responds when exposed to this allergen. How can they lessen the reaction?

APPLY THE BIG ? Why do you sometimes get sick?

20. Strep throat is an example of an infectious disease, while asthma is an example of a noninfectious disease. Compare and contrast what causes these diseases and how your body protects you from them.

_____

_____

_____

_____

_____

_____

_____

_____

_____

Standardized Test Prep

Multiple Choice

Circle the letter of the best answer.

1. SARS is a respiratory disease caused by a virus. Use the data table to decide which statement below is true.

SARS Cases (Nov. 2002–July 2003)		
Country	No. of Cases	No. of Deaths
Canada	251	43
China, mainland	5,327	349
China, Taiwan	346	37
Singapore	238	33
United States	29	0

  A Most of the people who got SARS died.
  B Most SARS cases were in mainland China.
  C Most SARS cases were in North America.
  D Most SARS cases were in Singapore.

2. All of the following are the body's defenses against pathogens *except*

  A a physical barrier such as the skin.
  B the inflammatory response.
  C the immune response.
  D attacks by red blood cells.

3. A chemical that can kill disease-causing bacteria is called

  A a vaccine.
  B a phagocyte.
  C an antibiotic.
  D an active immunity.

4. Which of these diseases occurs when the airways in the lungs narrow significantly during an allergic reaction?

  A asthma
  B diabetes
  C AIDS
  D melanoma

5. Which of the following is paired correctly?

  A rabies: infectious disease
  B diabetes: infectious disease
  C AIDS: noninfectious disease
  D allergy: infectious disease

Constructed Response

Use the graph below and your knowledge of science to help you answer Question 6. Write your answer on a separate sheet of paper.

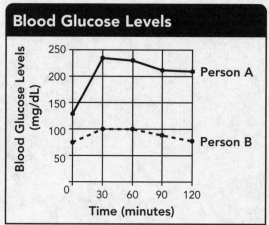

6. In a glucose tolerance test, a doctor gives a patient a sugar drink and measures the blood glucose level over time. The graph above shows two people's test results. Which person may have diabetes? Explain your answer.

Making H2O A-OK

What runs, but never walks? *Water!* Even though water is all around us, over 1 billion people across the world can only dream of having clean drinking water. Every day, about 4,000 children die from water-related diseases because they drink unsafe water. But now, a packet of powder the size of a ketchup packet at a cafeteria can stop this from happening.

Scientists have created a powder that can purify dirty, polluted water in 30 minutes. Just one small packet of the stuff can clean 2.5 gallons of water! The powder is made up of bleach and iron sulfate. The bleach kills bacteria and viruses. The iron sulfate causes solids in the water, such as metals like lead, to bind together in clumps. These clumps can be filtered out using a cotton cloth.

With helpful technology like this, more kids will be able to have safe and clean drinking water.

Write About It Natural disaster victims, such as those who survive a hurricane or a flood, often have a hard time getting clean drinking water. Write a letter to a rescue agency, such as the Red Cross, explaining the importance of having clean drinking water and what they can do to purify the water.

Museum of Science

Colwell's Gift

Cholera is an infection of the intestines that is spread by drinking water or eating food contaminated with cholera bacteria. It causes diarrhea, vomiting, and cramps. When cholera strikes, approximately one victim in 20 can become seriously ill, and may die within hours. Because most places in the United States have safe drinking water, we don't see a lot of cholera here. But in many developing countries, cholera is still common.

For a long time, scientists could not predict cholera epidemics. Outbreaks happened suddenly, with no warning. And after the epidemic, scientists could not detect the cholera bacteria in the water. So, where did the bacteria go, and how did they reappear so suddenly?

Rita Colwell suspected that the cholera bacteria were present in the water in an inactive state between outbreaks. She thought that the bacteria became active when the water temperature rose.

After many years, Colwell proved her hypothesis. Using new methods, scientists were able to detect the inactive cholera bacteria in water where they had not previously been able to detect cholera. Satellite data also confirmed that cholera outbreaks occur when ocean temperatures rise. Warmer water causes cholera bacteria to multiply. Now, scientists use this information to help prevent future cholera outbreaks.

Illustrate It Rita Colwell developed a simple cloth filter to help prevent the spread of cholera. Research the life cycle of cholera bacteria. Prepare an information card that uses diagrams to explain how Colwell's filter helps to stop the spread of bacteria.

HOW
DO THESE
ATHLETES
REACT?

How does your body sense and react to your surroundings?

Soccer, known as football in most of the world, can be an exciting game. But these athletes don't look like they're having fun. The Brazilian player in yellow is trying to advance the ball past the U.S. goalie in red and the U.S. defender in white. Not only are both U.S. players trying to prevent a goal, they are trying hard not to collide.

△Infer **When you are about to collide with someone, how do you react?**

_____

_____

_____

_____

▷ UNTAMED SCIENCE Watch the **Untamed Science** video to learn more about the nervous system.

The Nervous System

CHAPTER

7

Check Your Understanding

1. Background Read the paragraph below and then answer the question.

Rajev wakes up gasping. Smoke enters his nose and stings his eyes. He feels the **involuntary** pounding of his heart. His **sense organs** send signals to his brain—alarms, shouts, smoke, heat, and sirens. Instantly, Rajev interprets the signals and takes **voluntary** action. He crawls to the window as the fire ladder rises below him.

> **Involuntary** action is not under a person's conscious control.
>
> **Sense organs,** such as eyes and ears, are body structures that gather information from your surroundings.
>
> **Voluntary** action is under a person's conscious control.

- Why is Rajev's crawling to the window a voluntary rather than an involuntary action?

_____

_____

> **MY READING WEB** If you had trouble completing the question above, visit **My Reading Web** and type in *The Nervous System.*

Vocabulary Skill

Prefixes A prefix is a word part that is added to the beginning of a word to change its meaning. The table below lists prefixes that will help you learn terms in this chapter.

Prefix	Meaning	Term
inter-	between, among	interneuron, *n.* a neuron, or nerve cell, that is between other neurons
semi-	half, partly	semicircular canal, *n.* structures in the ear shaped like half-circles.

2. Quick Check The prefix *inter-* has more than one meaning. In the table above, circle the meaning of *inter-* that relates to the word *interneuron.*

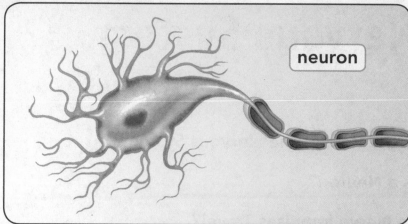

neuron

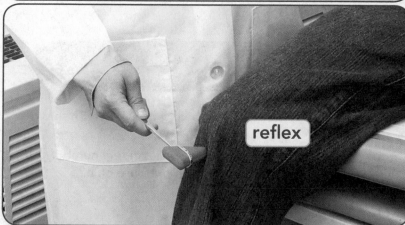

reflex

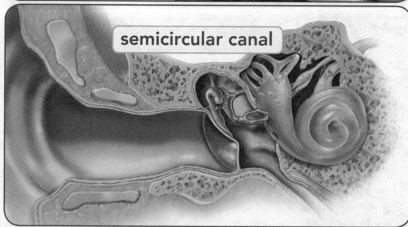

semicircular canal

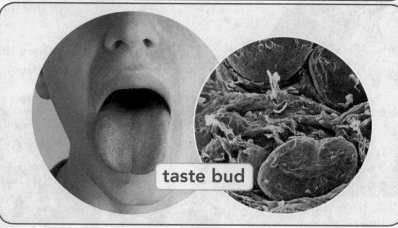

taste bud

Chapter Preview

LESSON 1

- stimulus • response • neuron
- nerve impulse • dendrite
- axon • nerve • sensory neuron
- interneuron • motor neuron
- synapse

↻ **Compare and Contrast**
△ **Infer**

LESSON 2

- central nervous system
- peripheral nervous system
- brain • spinal cord • cerebrum
- cerebellum • brain stem
- somatic nervous system
- autonomic nervous system
- reflex • concussion

↻ **Sequence**
△ **Draw Conclusions**

LESSON 3

- cornea • pupil • iris • lens
- retina • nearsightedness
- farsightedness • eardrum
- cochlea • semicircular canal

↻ **Relate Cause and Effect**
△ **Observe**

LESSON 4

- taste bud

↻ **Identify the Main Idea**
△ **Classify**

LESSON 5

- drug • drug abuse • tolerance
- addiction • withdrawal
- depressant • stimulant
- anabolic steroid • alcoholism

↻ **Summarize**
△ **Communicate**

› **VOCAB FLASH CARDS** For extra help with vocabulary, visit **Vocab Flash Cards** and type in *The Nervous System.*

How the Nervous System Works

UNLOCK THE BIG ?

🔑 **What Is the Role of the Nervous System?**

🔑 **What Is a Neuron?**

🔑 **How Do Nerve Impulses Travel?**

MY PLANET DiARY

Wake Up!

Did you ever wake from a nap, only to find that your arm is "asleep"? What causes this "pins-and-needles" sensation? If you lie on your arm for a long period of time, too much pressure is placed on the nerves. The communication between your arm and brain no longer flows smoothly. A decrease in normal signals makes your arm feel odd. The pins-and-needles feeling actually happens when you remove the pressure from the nerves. They begin to send a normal flow of messages from your arm to your brain again. You slowly regain normal feeling in your arm. Remember to change your position often when you sit or lie down. If you don't, you'll end up having to wake up your arms and legs!

FUN FACTS

Read the following questions. Then write your answers below.

1. Why would your arm feel numb if you put too much pressure on it?

_____

_____

_____

2. Describe a time when one of your limbs fell asleep. How did it feel?

_____

_____

_____

_____

_____

> PLANET DIARY Go to **Planet Diary** to learn more about the nervous system.

 Do the Inquiry Warm-Up
How Simple Is a Simple Task?

Vocabulary

- stimulus • response • neuron • nerve impulse
- dendrite • axon • nerve • sensory neuron
- interneuron • motor neuron • synapse

Skills

↻ Reading: Compare and Contrast

△ Inquiry: Infer

What Is the Role of the Nervous System?

You can use the Internet to chat with a friend hundreds of miles away. You can also use it to gather information from anywhere in the world. Like the Internet, your nervous system is a communications network. It includes the brain, the spinal cord, and the nerves that run throughout the body. It also includes the eyes, ears, and other sense organs. **Your nervous system receives information about what is happening both inside and outside your body. It directs how your body responds to this information. In addition, your nervous system helps maintain homeostasis.** Without your nervous system, you could not move, think, or sense the world around you.

Receiving Information Your nervous system makes you aware of what is happening around you. For example, if you were at a cookout like the one shown in **Figure 1,** you would know when the wind was blowing or a fly was buzzing around your head. Your nervous system also checks conditions inside your body, such as the level of glucose in your blood and your internal body temperature.

FIGURE 1 ....
Gathering Information
The nervous system allows people to react to their environment.

✎ **Describe** List four things that your nervous system would help you notice if you were enjoying a meal with these people.

_____

_____

_____

_____

_____

_____

Responding to Information

Any change or signal in the environment that an organism can recognize and react to is called a **stimulus** (STIM yoo lus; plural *stimuli*). For example, a buzzing fly is a stimulus. After your nervous system analyzes a stimulus, it causes a response. A **response** is a reaction to a stimulus. Some nervous system responses, such as swatting a fly, are voluntary, or under your control. But heart rate, breathing, sweating, and other necessary processes are involuntary responses to stimuli inside your body.

Maintaining Homeostasis

The nervous system helps maintain homeostasis by directing your body to respond properly to information it receives. For example, when your blood's glucose level drops, your nervous system signals that you are hungry. So, you eat. This action maintains homeostasis by supplying your body with needed nutrients and energy.

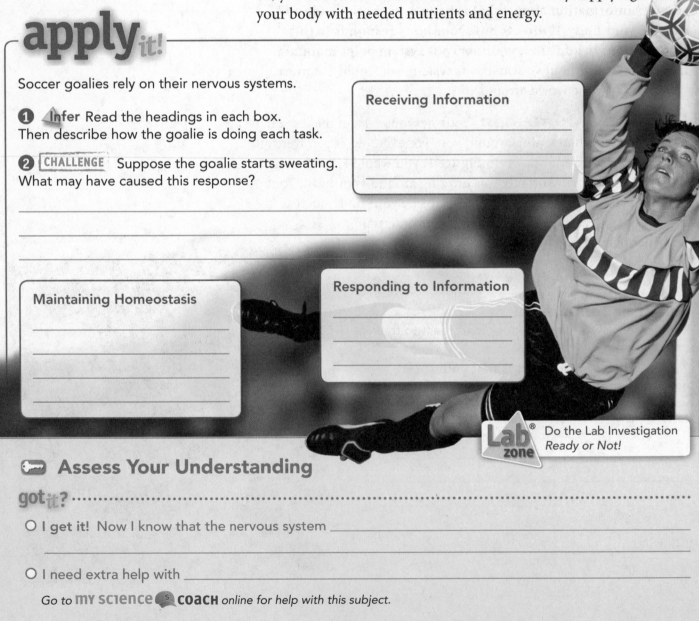

apply it!

Soccer goalies rely on their nervous systems.

❶ **Infer** Read the headings in each box. Then describe how the goalie is doing each task.

❷ CHALLENGE Suppose the goalie starts sweating. What may have caused this response?

_____
_____

Receiving Information

_____
_____
_____

Responding to Information

_____
_____
_____

Maintaining Homeostasis

_____
_____
_____

Lab zone Do the Lab Investigation *Ready or Not!*

🔑 Assess Your Understanding

got it?

○ **I get it!** Now I know that the nervous system _____
_____

○ **I need extra help with** _____

Go to **MY SCIENCE** ⓢ **COACH** online for help with this subject.

What Is a Neuron?

Your nervous system includes various organs, tissues, and cells. For example, your brain is an organ, and the nerves running throughout your body are tissues. **Cells that carry information through your nervous system are called neurons (NOO rahnz), or nerve cells.** The message that a neuron carries is called a **nerve impulse.**

The Structure of a Neuron A neuron's structure enables the neuron to carry nerve impulses. A neuron has a large cell body that contains the nucleus, threadlike extensions called dendrites, and an axon. Nerve impulses begin in a **dendrite,** a branchlike structure that picks up the impulses. Next, the impulses move through the neuron's cell body. They then travel to the **axon,** the long structure leading away from the cell body. The axon sends the impulses away from the cell body to the axon tips at the end of the neuron. A neuron can have many dendrites, but it has only one axon, as you can see in **Figure 2.** However, the axon can have more than one tip. Therefore, the impulse can go to more than one cell.

Axons and their tissue covering make up nerve fibers. Nerve fibers are often arranged in parallel bundles covered with more connective tissue. They look like uncooked spaghetti wrapped in thin plastic. A bundle of nerve fibers is called a **nerve.**

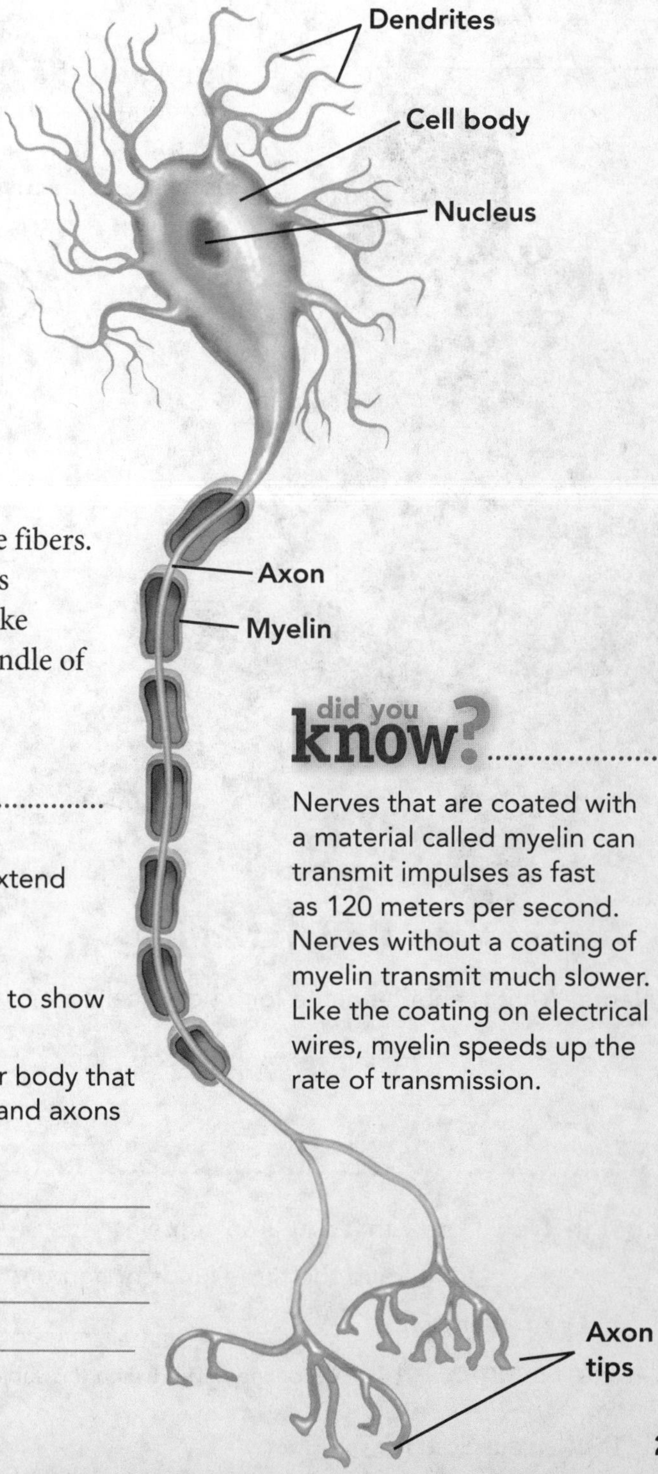

Dendrites

Cell body

Nucleus

Axon

Myelin

FIGURE 2 ·······································

Structure of a Neuron

A neuron has one axon and many dendrites that extend from the cell body.

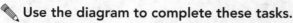 **Use the diagram to complete these tasks.**

1. **Interpret Diagrams** Draw a line with an arrow to show the path of a nerve impulse in the neuron.

2. **Draw Conclusions** What does it mean for your body that dendrites carry impulses toward the cell body and axons carry impulses away from the cell body?

_____

_____

_____

did you know?

Nerves that are coated with a material called myelin can transmit impulses as fast as 120 meters per second. Nerves without a coating of myelin transmit much slower. Like the coating on electrical wires, myelin speeds up the rate of transmission.

Axon tips

217

Compare and Contrast

How is a sensory neuron similar to a motor neuron? How is it different?

_____

_____

_____

_____

_____

Kinds of Neurons

Your nervous system includes three kinds of neurons: sensory neurons, interneurons, and motor neurons. A **sensory neuron** picks up a stimulus and converts it into a nerve impulse. The impulse travels along sensory neurons until it reaches an interneuron, usually in the brain or spinal cord. An **interneuron** carries a nerve impulse to another interneuron or to a motor neuron. A **motor neuron** sends an impulse to a muscle or gland, enabling it to respond. Look at **Figure 3**.

FIGURE 3 ··

The Path of a Nerve Impulse

To answer the phone, you use three kinds of neurons.

✏️ **Relate Text and Visuals Write the kind of neuron used in each activity described in the boxes below.**

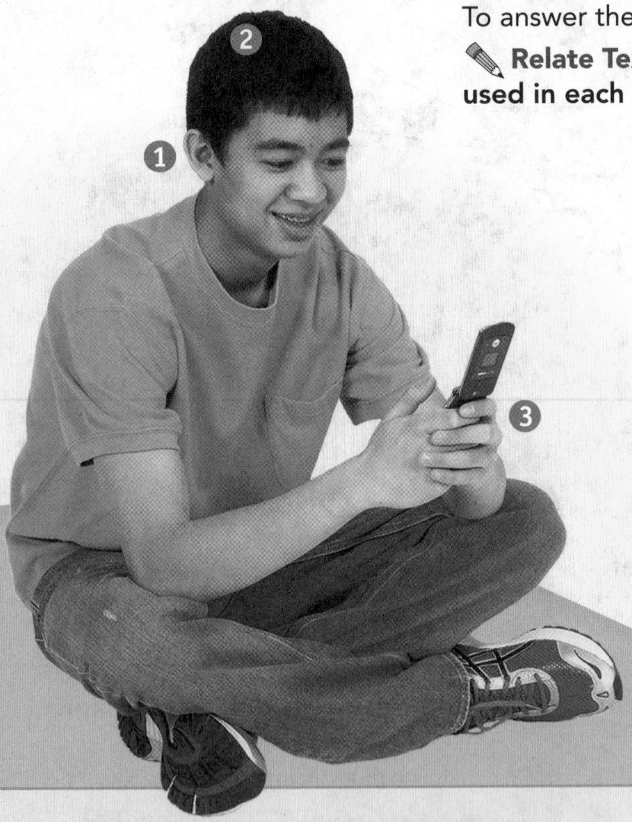

1 _____ Receptors in your ear pick up the sound of the phone ringing and trigger nerve impulses.

2 _____ The nerve impulses move to your brain. Your brain interprets them as a ringing phone.

3 _____ Your brain sends impulses to the muscles that you use to pick up the phone.

Lab zone ® Do the Quick Lab *Modeling a Neuron.*

🔑 Assess Your Understanding

1a. Name What is another name for a nerve cell?

_____

_____

b. Classify What kind of neuron senses a mosquito on your arm?

_____

_____

got it? ··

○ **I get it!** Now I know that a neuron contains _____

_____, and the three kinds of neurons are _____

○ **I need extra help with** _____

Go to **MY SCIENCE** ⓢ **COACH** *online for help with this subject.*

How Do Nerve Impulses Travel?

Every day, billions of nerve impulses travel through your nervous system. Each nerve impulse begins in the dendrites of a neuron. The impulse moves rapidly toward the neuron's body and then down the axon until it reaches the axon tip. A nerve impulse travels in the form of electrical and chemical signals.

The place where a neuron transfers an impulse to another structure is called a **synapse** (SIN aps). **Figure 4** shows a gap in a synapse between the axon tip of one neuron and the dendrite of another neuron. A nerve impulse must cross the gap to continue. ⚲ **At the axon tips, electrical signals change to a chemical form, allowing the message to cross the gap in the synapse.** This change is like answering a phone and then writing down the information you learn. The change from hearing information to writing it is like the change from electrical to chemical form.

FIGURE 4 ••••••••••••••••••••••••

> ART IN MOTION **The Synapse**

A synapse transfers a nerve impulse from one neuron to another.

✎ **Sequence** Write the steps that describe how the nerve impulse crosses the gap between the axon tip of one neuron and the dendrite of the other neuron.

Step 1:

_____

_____

_____

Step 2:

_____

_____

_____

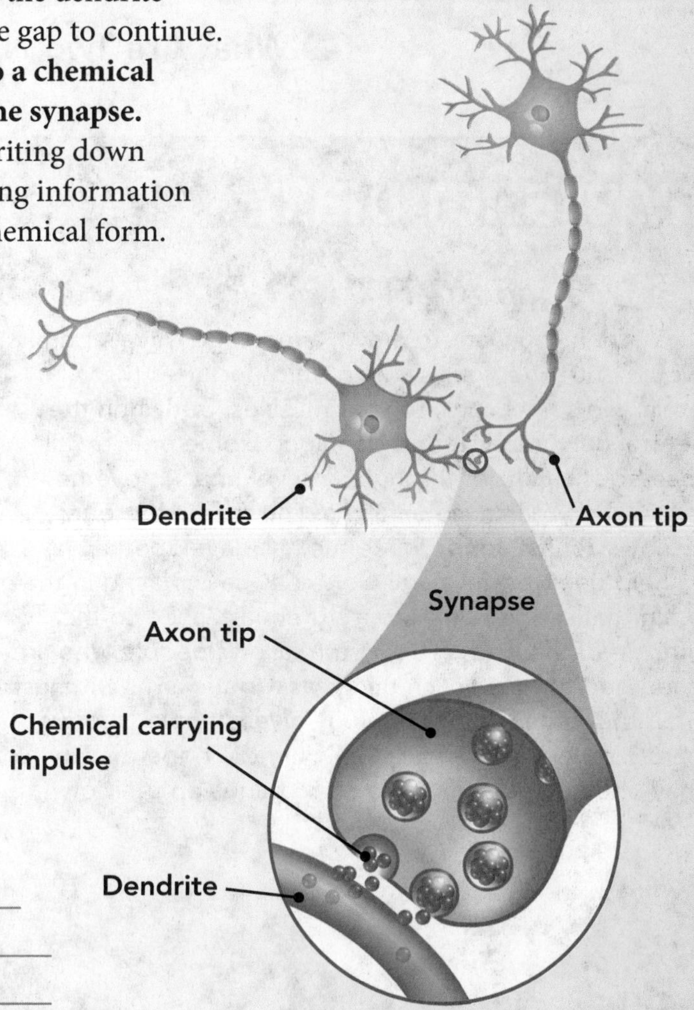

Dendrite   Axon tip

Synapse

Axon tip

Chemical carrying impulse

Dendrite

Lab zone® Do the Quick Lab *Getting the Message Across.*

⚲ Assess Your Understanding

got it? ••

○ **I get it!** Now I know that a nerve impulse travels from one neuron to another structure by _____

_____

○ **I need extra help with** _____

Go to **my science** 🔵 **coach** *online for help with this subject.*

Divisions of the Nervous System

UNLOCK THE BIG Q

🔑 **What Is the Role of the Central Nervous System?**

🔑 **What Is the Role of the Peripheral Nervous System?**

🔑 **What Are Two Nervous System Injuries?**

my planet diary

Moving Again

When you want to move, a message travels from your central nervous system, which includes the brain and spinal cord, to your muscles. But when the central nervous system is damaged, some or even all messages can't get through, and voluntary movement is lost. This can cause paralysis. The research group led by scientist John Donoghue has developed a way to help people with paralysis. A device is placed in the brain that sends signals to a system attached to the outside of the body. This system allows people who are paralyzed to move such things as robotic arms with just their thoughts. This technology gives people who are paralyzed because of a spine injury the hope that they may one day be able to do more things on their own.

DISCOVERY

Communicate Discuss the following questions with a partner. Then write your answers below.

1. What happens in the nervous system when a person becomes paralyzed?

_____

_____

_____

_____

2. What other technology do you know of that helps people who are paralyzed? Explain how it helps them.

_____

_____

_____

_____

_____

_____

> **PLANET DIARY** Go to **Planet Diary** to learn more about divisions of the nervous system.

 Lab zone® Do the Inquiry Warm-Up *What Are the Parts of the Nervous System?*

Vocabulary

- central nervous system • peripheral nervous system
- brain • spinal cord • cerebrum • cerebellum
- brain stem • somatic nervous system
- autonomic nervous system • reflex • concussion

Skills

↻ Reading: Sequence

△ Inquiry: Draw Conclusions

What Is the Role of the Central Nervous System?

Like a traffic cop directing car drivers through a busy intersection, your nervous system directs your movements. It has two divisions that work together: the central nervous system and the peripheral nervous system. The **central nervous system** includes the brain and spinal cord and acts like the traffic cop. The **peripheral nervous system** includes all the nerves outside of the central nervous system, which are like the car drivers. **Figure 1** shows both systems.

How the Central Nervous System Works

🗝 **The central nervous system controls the functions of the body.** The **brain** is its control center. The **spinal cord** is a thick column of nervous tissue that links the brain to the peripheral nervous system. Most impulses from the peripheral nerves travel through the spinal cord to get to the brain. The brain then directs a response, which usually travels through the spinal cord and back to peripheral nerves.

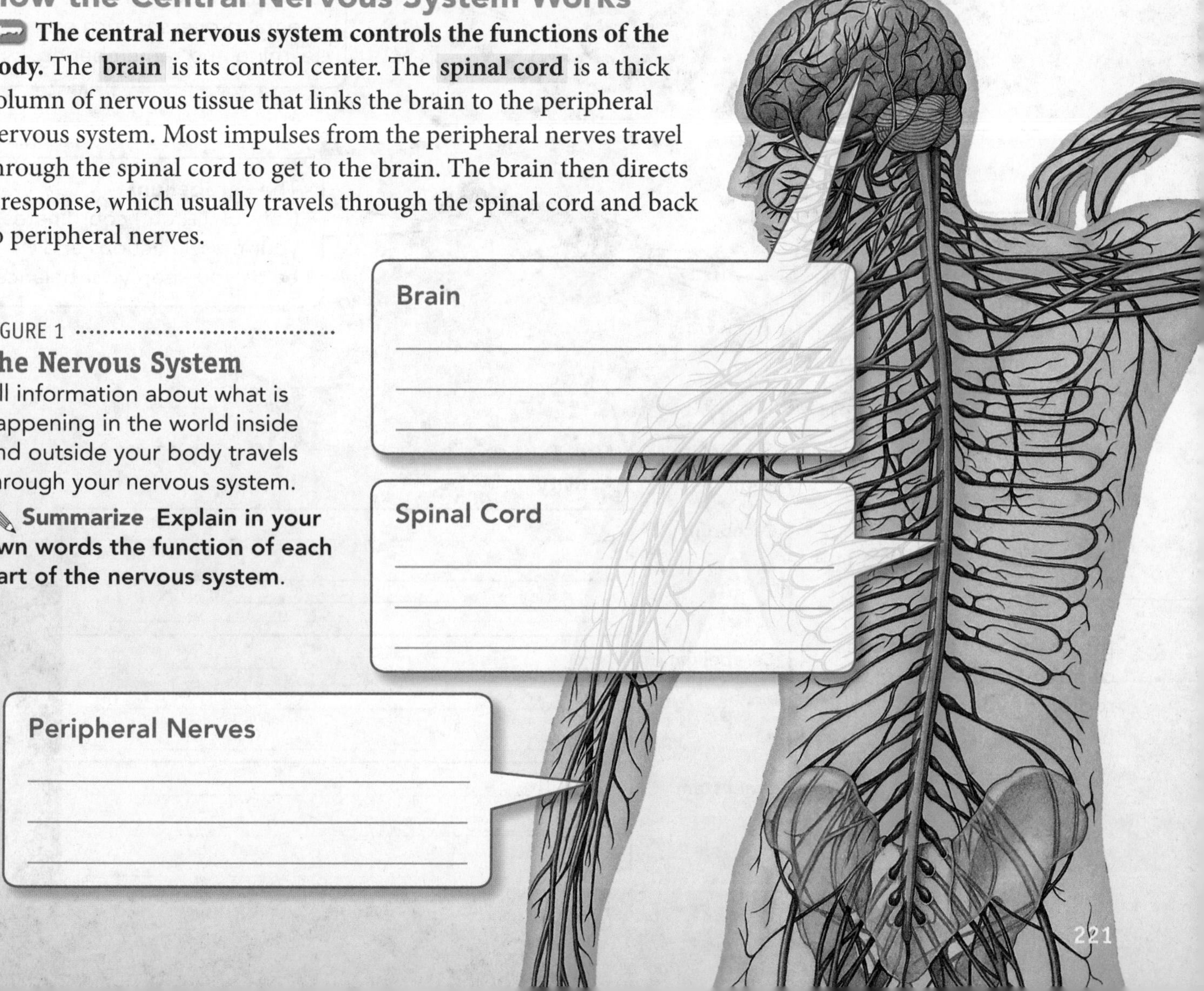

FIGURE 1 ·······················

The Nervous System
All information about what is happening in the world inside and outside your body travels through your nervous system.

✎ **Summarize** Explain in your own words the function of each part of the nervous system.

Brain
_____
_____
_____

Spinal Cord
_____
_____
_____

Peripheral Nerves
_____
_____
_____

Infer How can fluid protect the brain from injury?

____

____

____

____

____

The Brain Your brain has about 100 billion neurons, all of which are interneurons. Each of those neurons may receive up to 10,000 messages from other neurons and may send messages to about 1,000 more! Three layers of connective tissue under the skull cover the brain. Fluid fills the space between the middle layer and the innermost layer of connective tissue. The skull, the connective tissue, and the fluid all help protect the brain from injury. Three main regions of the brain are the brain stem, the cerebellum, and the cerebrum, as shown in **Figure 2.**

The Brain Stem and Cerebellum The brain stem connects the brain and spinal cord. It controls the flow of information between the brain and the rest of the body. The cerebellum, found at the back of the skull, is the second largest region of the brain.

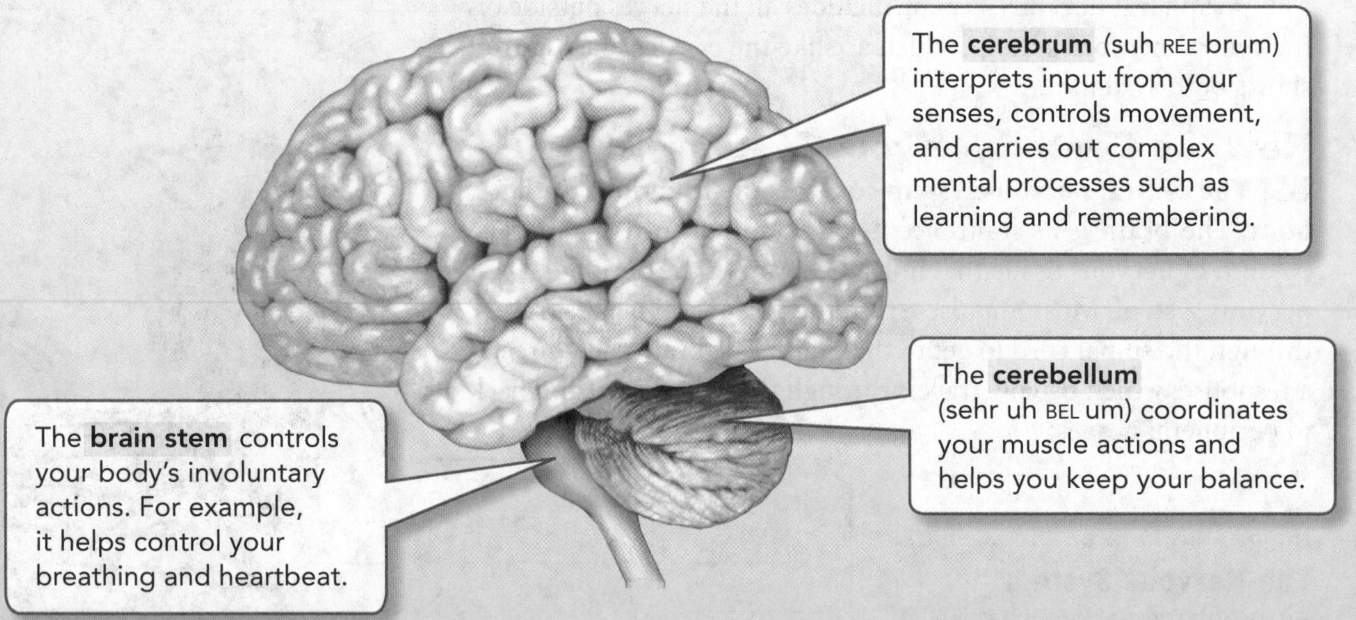
The **cerebrum** (suh REE brum) interprets input from your senses, controls movement, and carries out complex mental processes such as learning and remembering.
The **cerebellum** (sehr uh BEL um) coordinates your muscle actions and helps you keep your balance.
The **brain stem** controls your body's involuntary actions. For example, it helps control your breathing and heartbeat.

FIGURE 2
The Brain
Different regions of the brain receive and process different information.

Apply Concepts In the chart, write examples of how you use each region of your brain.

Region	Activity
Cerebrum	
Cerebellum	
Brain stem	

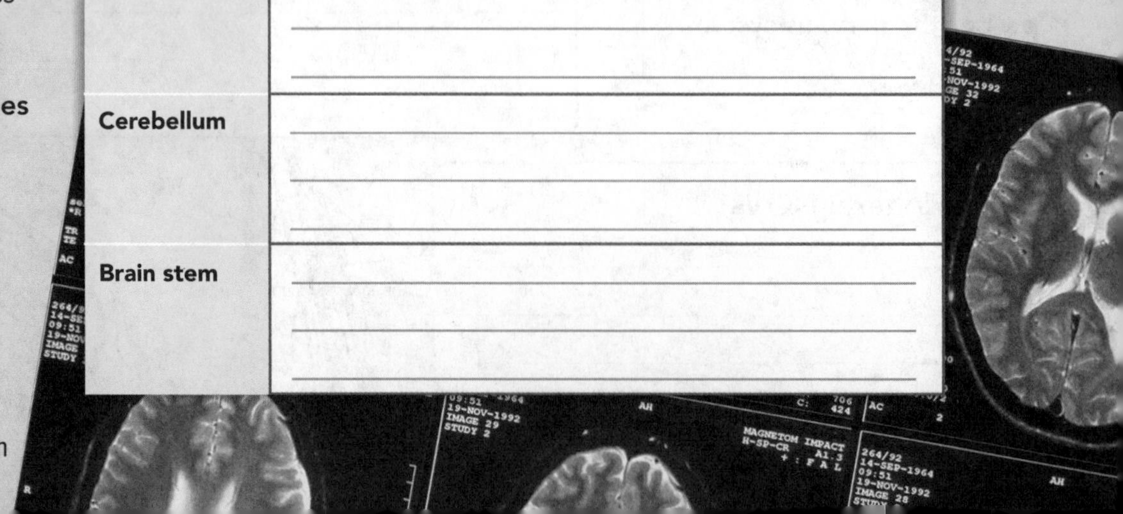

The Cerebrum The cerebrum is the largest region of the brain. It is divided into a right and a left half, as shown in **Figure 3.** The right half controls the left side of the body. The left half controls the right side of the body. Different areas control functions such as movement, sight, hearing, speech, and abstract thought.

The Spinal Cord
Run your fingers down the center of your back to feel the bones of the vertebral column. The vertebral column surrounds and protects your spinal cord. Like the brain, layers of connective tissue cover the spinal cord. Also like the brain, fluid protects the spinal cord.

FIGURE 3 ··································

The Cerebrum
The cerebrum is divided into a right and a left half.

✎ **Classify** Write *L* or *R* to indicate which half of the brain is involved in each of the activities below.

_____ Reading the manual to help you fix your digital camera

_____ Making a scrapbook to display your photos

_____ Comparing the prices of new digital cameras

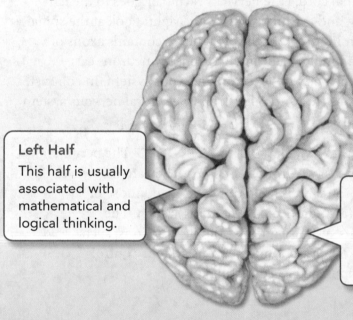

Left Half
This half is usually associated with mathematical and logical thinking.

Right Half
This half is usually associated with creativity and artistic skills.

 Do the Quick Lab *Making Models of the Brain.*

🔑 Assess Your Understanding

1a. Review Which region of your brain helps you keep from falling when you walk?

_____

b. CHALLENGE What symptoms might indicate that a person's cerebellum has been injured?

_____

_____

c. Draw Conclusions Why is it important for the brain to be so well protected?

_____

_____

_____

_____

got**it?** ··

○ **I get it!** Now I know that the role of the central nervous system is _____

_____

○ I need extra help with _____

Go to **MY SCIENCE COACH** *online for help with this subject.*

223

What Is the Role of the Peripheral Nervous System?

The second division of the nervous system is the peripheral nervous system. 🔑 **The peripheral nervous system is a network of nerves that branches out from the central nervous system and connects it to the rest of the body. The peripheral nervous system is involved in both involuntary and voluntary actions.**

The peripheral nervous system has 43 pairs of nerves. Twelve pairs begin in the brain. The other 31 pairs—the spinal nerves—begin in the spinal cord. One nerve in each pair goes to the left side of the body, and the other goes to the right. Look at the spinal nerves shown in **Figure 4.** Each spinal nerve contains axons of both sensory and motor neurons. The sensory neurons carry impulses from the body to the central nervous system. In contrast, the motor neurons carry impulses from the central nervous system to the body.

Somatic and Autonomic Systems

The peripheral nervous system has two groups of nerves. They are the nerves of the somatic (soh MAT ik) nervous system and those of the autonomic (awt uh NAHM ik) nervous system. The **somatic nervous system** controls voluntary actions, such as using a fork. The **autonomic nervous system** controls involuntary actions, such as digesting food.

Vocabulary Prefixes The prefix *auto-* comes from the Greek word for "self." How can this prefix help you to remember the function of the autonomic nervous system?

_____

_____

_____

FIGURE 4 ·····················

The Spinal Nerves
The spinal nerves leave the spinal cord through spaces between the vertebrae.

✎ **Infer** Circle on the diagram the two spinal nerves that are a pair. Then explain how a spinal nerve is like a two-lane highway.

_____

_____

_____

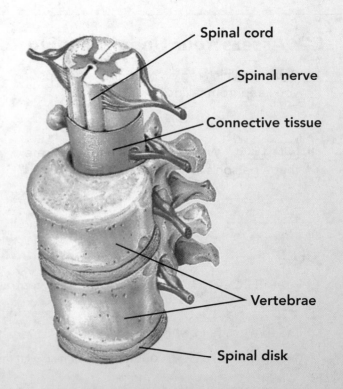

Spinal cord

Spinal nerve

Connective tissue

Vertebrae

Spinal disk

Reflexes When a fly zooms in front of your eyes, your eyelids blink shut. This blinking action is a **reflex,** an automatic response that occurs rapidly without conscious control.

The brain usually controls the contraction of skeletal muscles. Sometimes, however, skeletal muscles contract without involving the brain. For example, when your finger touches a sharp object, sensory neurons detect a pain stimulus. They send impulses to the spinal cord. Interneurons there pass those impulses directly to motor neurons. The motor neurons cause your arm muscles to contract, pulling your finger away from the sharp object. **Figure 5** shows the steps in this reflex action.

As the reflex action happens, other nerve impulses travel to your brain. As your brain interprets them, you feel a pain in your finger. It takes longer for the pain impulses to reach the brain and be interpreted than it does for the reflex action to occur. By the time you feel the pain, you have already jerked your hand away.

Sequence In the second paragraph, underline the steps involved in the reflex action. Then number each step.

FIGURE 5 ....

> INTERACTIVE ART **A Reflex Action**
Reflexes help protect your body.

Relate Text and Visuals On the diagram, number the steps in a reflex action. Then describe each step on the notebook paper.

apply *it!*

When you go to the doctor for a checkup, your doctor probably tests your reflex action using the knee-jerk test. The doctor uses a small hammer to provide a stimulus to sensory neurons just under your kneecap.

1 ⟳ **Sequence** List the sequence of steps that happens when the doctor strikes sensory neurons below the boy's kneecap.

_____

_____

_____

_____

_____

_____

2 ◢ **Draw Conclusions** Why does it benefit you that some reflexes occur without involving neurons in the brain?

_____

_____

_____

_____

_____

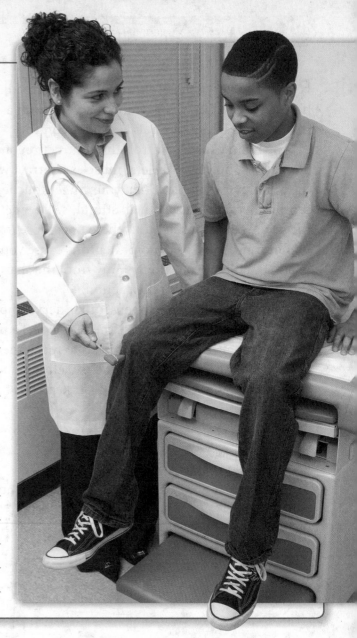

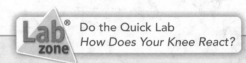

Lab ® Do the Quick Lab
zone *How Does Your Knee React?*

🔑 **Assess Your Understanding**

2a. Identify The two groups of nerves in the peripheral nervous system are the

_____

_____

b. Compare and Contrast How do the two groups of peripheral nerves differ?

_____

_____

_____

got *it?*

○ **I get it!** Now I know that the role of the peripheral nervous system is _____

_____

_____

_____

○ **I need extra help with** _____

Go to **MY SCIENCE** 🗨 **COACH** *online for help with this subject.*

What Are Two Nervous System Injuries?

The nervous system can suffer injuries that interfere with its functioning. 🔑 **Concussions and spinal cord injuries are two ways in which the central nervous system can be damaged.**

A **concussion** occurs when the soft tissue of the brain is bruised as it collides against the skull. Concussions can happen when you bump your head in a hard fall, a car crash, or a contact sport such as football. Most concussions cause a headache, but the injured tissue heals by itself. More serious concussions may cause you to feel drowsy, become confused, or lose consciousness. To protect your brain, wear a helmet when you risk bumping your head.

If the spinal cord is cut or crushed, axons in that region are damaged, so impulses cannot pass through them. This injury often results in paralysis, the loss of movement in part of the body. Car crashes are the most common cause of spinal cord injuries. Wear a seat belt, as the young woman is doing in **Figure 6.**

FIGURE 6 ·····················

Protecting the Nervous System
Cars have seat belts to protect you from injury.

✏️ **Relate Cause and Effect** In the graphic organizer, write how wearing a seat belt can help prevent a concussion and a spinal cord injury in a car crash.

Cause
Wearing a seat belt

Effect	Effect
Prevents a concussion by	Prevents a spinal cord injury by

Lab zone ® Do the Quick Lab
When Things Go Wrong.

🔑 Assess Your Understanding

got it? ··

○ **I get it!** Now I know that the nervous system can be injured by _____

_____

○ **I need extra help with** _____

Go to **MY SCIENCE** 🅢 **COACH** *online for help with this subject.*

🔑 **How Do You See?**

🔑 **How Do Your Ears Work?**

my planeT DiaRY

BLOG

Posted by: Kelly

Location: Old Tappan, New Jersey

If I just hear something, I don't understand it as well as when I read it a few times. Since I know this, I always make sure I read over everything. Whenever I have to study for a test or quiz, it helps to visualize things as I read the chapter and notes.

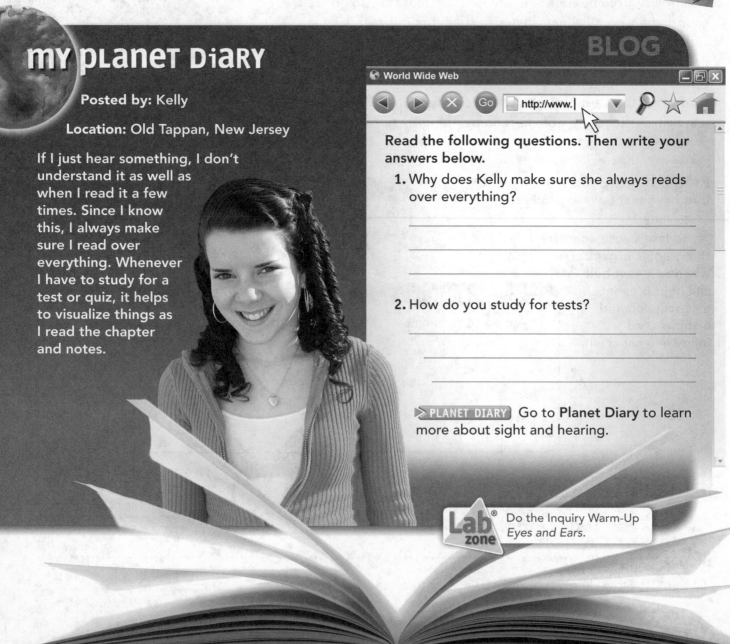

🌐 World Wide Web

http://www.

Read the following questions. Then write your answers below.

1. Why does Kelly make sure she always reads over everything?

_____

_____

_____

2. How do you study for tests?

_____

_____

▷ **PLANET DIARY** Go to **Planet Diary** to learn more about sight and hearing.

Lab zone Do the Inquiry Warm-Up *Eyes and Ears.*

Vocabulary
- cornea • pupil • iris • lens • retina
- nearsightedness • farsightedness • eardrum
- cochlea • semicircular canal

Skills
- Reading: Relate Cause and Effect
- Inquiry: Observe

How Do You See?

Going to the movie theater, like the one shown in **Figure 1**, can be a treat for your senses. Show times and titles flash on displays. Moviegoers chatter excitedly in line. As you walk into the theater, it takes time for your eyes to adjust to the dim light. But once they do, you find a seat. The theater gets even darker, but then the screen brightens. You slide on your 3-D glasses. You are ready for an exciting experience.

You would not be able to enjoy the visual experience of the movie without your sight. Your eyes are one of your specialized sense organs. They enable you to see the objects in your environment. For example, they let you see this page, the window across the room, and the world outside the window. 🔑 Your eyes respond to the stimulus of light. They convert that stimulus into impulses that your brain interprets, enabling you to see.

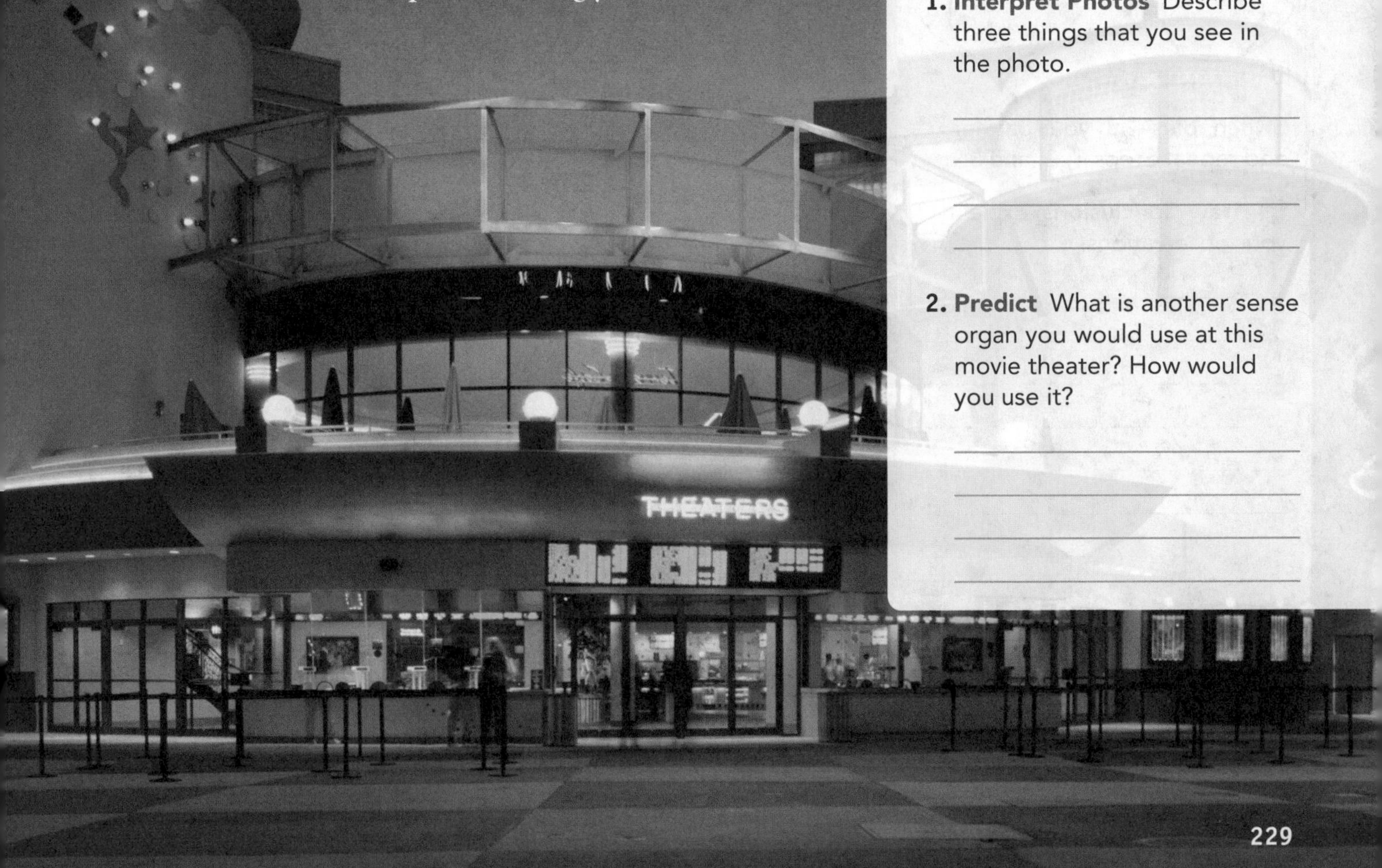

FIGURE 1 ·······················

Sense of Sight

Your sense of sight and your brain allow you to gather information about your environment.

✏️ **Use the photo to answer the questions.**

1. **Interpret Photos** Describe three things that you see in the photo.

   _____
   _____
   _____
   _____

2. **Predict** What is another sense organ you would use at this movie theater? How would you use it?

   _____
   _____
   _____
   _____

229

apply it!

Do the following activity to see what happens to a partner's pupils in different amounts of light.

1 **Observe** Look at your partner's pupils in normal light. Below, draw what you see.

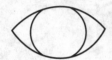

2 Measure With your partner's eyes closed and covered tightly, time your partner for two minutes.

3 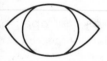**Observe** Look at your partner's pupils. Below, draw them again.

Switch roles with your partner and repeat Steps 1, 2, and 3.

4 Draw Conclusions Explain your observations.

_____
_____
_____
_____
_____
_____
_____

How Light Enters Your Eye When rays of light strike the eye, they pass through the structures shown in **Figure 2**. First, the light strikes the **cornea** (KAWR nee uh), the clear tissue that covers the front of the eye. The light then passes through a fluid-filled chamber behind the cornea and reaches the pupil. The **pupil** is the opening through which light enters the eye. The size of the pupil is adjusted by muscles in the iris. The **iris** is a circular structure that surrounds the pupil and regulates how much light enters the eye. The iris also gives the eye its color.

Light that passes through the pupil strikes the lens. The **lens** is a flexible structure that focuses light. After passing through the lens, the focused light rays pass through a transparent, jellylike fluid. Then the light rays strike the **retina** (RET in uh), which lines the back of the eye and contains light-sensitive cells.

FIGURE 2 ···

Parts of the Eye
The eye is a complex structure that enables you to sense light.

✎ **Relate Text and Visuals** Using the text, label the parts of the eye on the diagram.

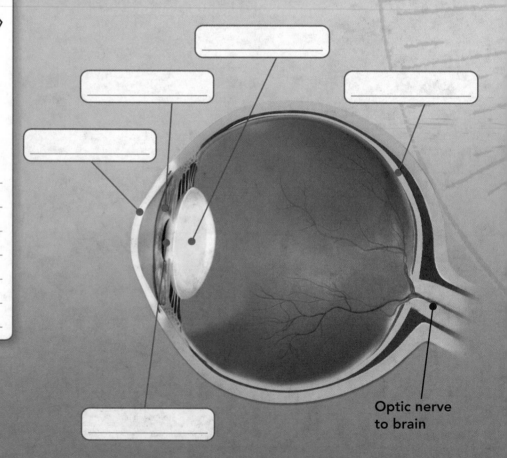

Optic nerve to brain

How You See an Image Muscles attached to the lens adjust its shape and focus light rays on the retina. Because the lens bends light rays, it produces an image that is upside down and reversed, as you can see in **Figure 3.**

Each retina contains about 130 million receptor cells that respond to light. There are two types of receptor cells: rods and cones. Rods work best in dim light and enable you to see black, white, and shades of gray. In contrast, cones work best in bright light and enable you to see colors. That is why you see colors best in bright light, but see only shadowy gray images in dim light.

When light strikes the rods and cones, nerve impulses travel to the cerebrum through the optic nerves. The cerebrum turns the reversed image right-side up and combines the images from both eyes to produce a single image.

FIGURE 3 ·······································

How You See an Image
Light from an object produces an upside-down image on the retina.

✎ **Sequence In each numbered box, describe how light travels from the object.**

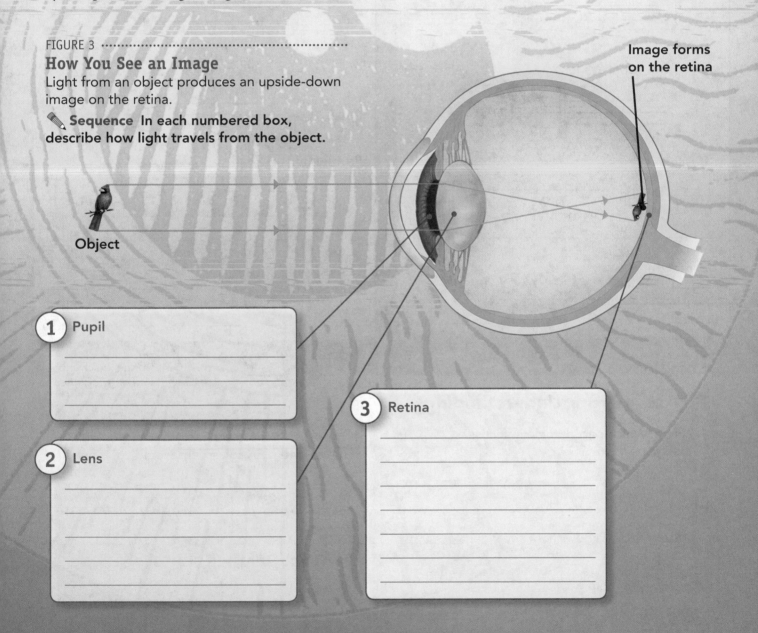

Image forms on the retina

Object

1 Pupil

2 Lens

3 Retina

FIGURE 4 ················

Correcting Vision Problems

✎ **Complete these tasks.**

1. **Interpret Diagrams** Identify and explain the vision problem shown in each diagram.

2. **CHALLENGE** Explain how each lens corrects the problem.

Correcting Vision Any transparent object that bends light rays as they pass through it is a lens. Eyeglass lenses can correct vision problems in an eye, as shown in **Figure 4.**

People with **nearsightedness** see nearby objects clearly but not distant objects. Their eyeball is too long, so the image comes into focus in front of the retina. Eyeglasses with concave lenses can correct this problem. People with **farsightedness** see distant objects clearly, but not nearby objects. Their eyeball is too short, so the image does not come into focus before light strikes the retina. Convex lenses can correct this problem.

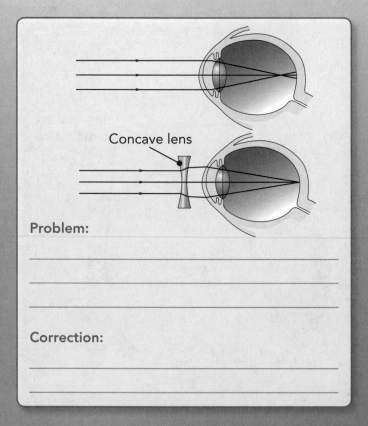

Problem:

_____

_____

_____

Correction:

_____

_____

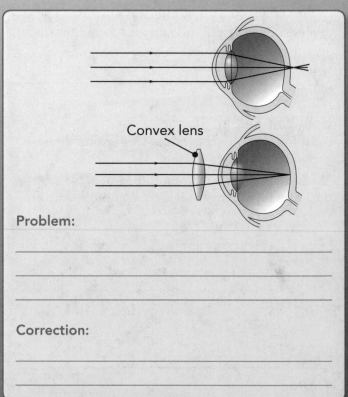

Problem:

_____

_____

_____

Correction:

_____

_____

Lab **zone®** Do the Quick Lab
Working Together.

🔑 Assess Your Understanding

1a. Name Which part of the eye focuses the image?

_____

b. Apply Concepts If nearby objects look blurry, what kind of eyeglass lens would you need?

_____

got it? ··

○ **I get it!** Now I know that I see when _____

_____

○ I need extra help with _____

Go to **MY SCIENCE** 💬 **COACH** online for help with this subject.

How Do Your Ears Work?

What wakes you up in the morning? Maybe an alarm clock rings, or a family member calls you. When you hear this sound, your brain tells you it is time to get up. 🔑 **Ears are the sense organs that respond to the stimulus of sound. An ear converts sound into nerve impulses that your brain interprets. Also, structures in your inner ear help to control your balance.**

How Sound Is Produced Most sounds you hear are caused by vibrations of air particles. The material that causes air particles to vibrate, or move rapidly back and forth, can be almost anything—for example, an insect's beating wings, guitar strings, or construction sounds. The air particle vibrations move outward from the source of the sound, like waves moving out from a stone dropped in water. In this way, sound is carried as waves. For example, when you hear a friend's voice, sound waves have traveled from your friend's larynx to your ears. In addition to passing through gases such as air, sound waves can also pass through liquids, such as water, and solids, such as wood. You feel the sound waves passing through wood as a vibration.

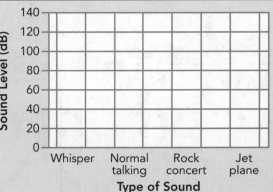

do the math!

Sound intensity, or loudness, is measured in units called decibels (dB). The pain threshold, the maximum level of sound you can tolerate without pain, is about 120 decibels. For every 10-decibel increase, the sound intensity increases ten times. The data table shows sound levels for different types of sounds.

Type of Sound	Sound Level (dB)
Whisper	20
Normal talking	60
Rock concert	120
Jet plane	130

1 Graph Use the data about sound types to draw a bar graph. Then write a title for the graph.

2 Read Graphs Draw a line on the graph that represents the pain threshold. What sounds could be painful for you?

_____

_____

_____

The Outer Ear The three parts of the ear—outer, middle, and inner—are shown in **Figure 5.** The outer ear is funnel-shaped and gathers sound waves. Then the waves travel down the ear canal, which is also part of the outer ear.

The Middle Ear At the end of the ear canal, sound waves reach the eardrum, which separates the outer ear from the middle ear. The **eardrum** is a membrane that vibrates when sound waves strike it. These vibrations pass to the hammer, anvil, and stirrup, small bones named for their shapes. The hammer passes vibrations to the anvil, and the anvil passes them to the stirrup.

The Inner Ear The stirrup vibrates against a thin membrane that covers the opening of the inner ear. The membrane transfers the vibrations into fluid in the cochlea. The **cochlea** (KAHK lee uh) is a snail-shaped tube lined with sound receptor cells. When the fluid in the cochlea vibrates, it stimulates these receptors. Sensory neurons then send nerve impulses to the cerebrum through the auditory nerve. The cerebrum interprets these impulses as sounds.

✎ Relate Cause and Effect
What might happen if the anvil could no longer transmit vibrations?

_____

_____

_____

_____

_____

_____

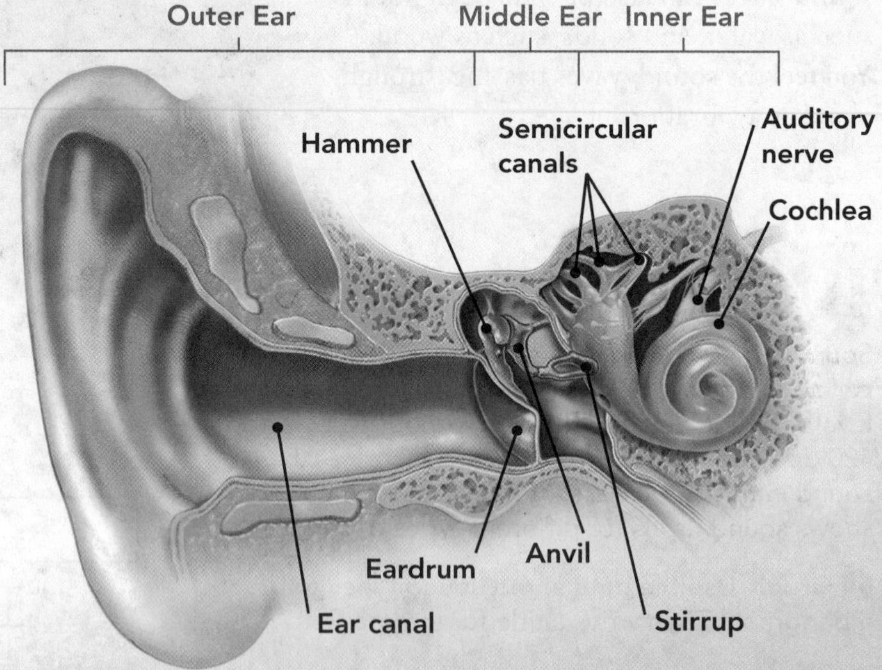

FIGURE 5 ·······················
The Ear
Sound waves pass through the structures of the ear and are carried by nerve impulses to the brain.

✎ Summarize In the boxes below, write in your own words how sound waves travel in each part of the ear.

Outer Ear · · · Middle Ear · Inner Ear

Hammer · Semicircular canals · Auditory nerve · Cochlea

Eardrum · Anvil · Ear canal · Stirrup

Outer Ear	Middle Ear	Inner Ear

The Inner Ear and Balance

Above the cochlea in your inner ear are the **semicircular canals,** which help your central nervous system maintain your balance. You can see how these structures got their name by looking at **Figure 5.** These canals, as well as the two tiny sacs behind them, are full of fluid. The canals and sacs are lined with tiny cells that have hairlike extensions. When your head moves, the fluid in the semicircular canals moves, causing the hairlike extensions to bend. The bending produces nerve impulses in sensory neurons. The impulses contain information about your body motion and position. The impulses travel to the cerebrum, where they are analyzed. The cerebrum can send information to the cerebellum if you are in danger of losing your balance. In **Figure 6,** the surfer's semicircular canals are helping him balance on a surfboard.

FIGURE 6 ·······························

Balancing Act

The surfer's semicircular canals help him keep good balance.

✎ **Communicate Work with a partner to do the activity.**

Step 1 Stand on both feet. Bend one leg up and hold your ankle behind you. Your partner should record how long you keep your balance. Then switch roles and repeat the step.

Time: _____

Step 2 Balance on one foot again. This time, close your eyes. Your partner should record how long you keep your balance. Then switch roles and repeat the step.

Time: _____

Step 3 Use your data to explain what other structure plays a role in keeping your balance.

_____

_____

_____

_____

Lab zone® Do the Quick Lab
Making Models of the Ear.

🔑 Assess Your Understanding

2a. List What are the three regions of the ear?

_____

_____

b. Describe Describe the eardrum's function.

_____

_____

_____

_____

got it?

○ **I get it!** Now I know that my ears _____

_____

_____

_____

○ **I need extra help with** _____

Go to **MY SCIENCE** Ⓢ **COACH** *online for help with this subject.*

Smell, Taste, and Touch

UNLOCK
THE BIG
?

🔑 **How Do Smell and Taste Work Together?**

🔑 **How Do You Sense Touch?**

my planeT DiaRY

CAREER

An Odd Job

Who decides how products such as perfumes, deodorants, and mouthwashes will smell? Believe it or not, companies hire professional odor testers to help.

The tasks of odor testers include smelling people's armpits and breath for product effectiveness. They also may smell thousands of possible scents for new products to find the one they like best. Companies use the information that their odor testers gather to develop products. If you have a keen sense of smell, you might want to consider becoming an odor tester!

Answer the questions below.

1. Why are odor testers important to companies that make scented products?

_____

_____

_____

_____

_____

2. What are two other types of companies that you think might use odor testers?

_____

_____

_____

▶ **PLANET DIARY** Go to **Planet Diary** to learn more about smell, taste, and touch.

Lab zone® Do the Inquiry Warm-Up *Can You Feel It?*

Vocabulary
- taste bud

Skills
- Reading: Identify the Main Idea
- Inquiry: Classify

How Do Smell and Taste Work Together?

You smell cookies. Receptors in your nose are reacting to chemicals that the air carries from the cookies to your nose. You bite into a cookie and taste its flavor. **Taste buds,** which are sensory receptors on your tongue, are responding to chemicals from the cookie that has dissolved in your saliva. Look at the taste buds in **Figure 1.**

The senses of smell and taste work together. Both depend on chemicals in the air or in food. The chemicals trigger responses in receptors in the nose and mouth. Nerve impulses then travel to the brain and are interpreted as smells or tastes.

The nose can distinguish at least 50 basic odors. In contrast, there are only five main taste sensations—sweet, sour, salty, bitter, and a meatlike taste called *umami*. When you eat, however, you experience a wider variety of flavors, since both smell and taste affect the flavor of food.

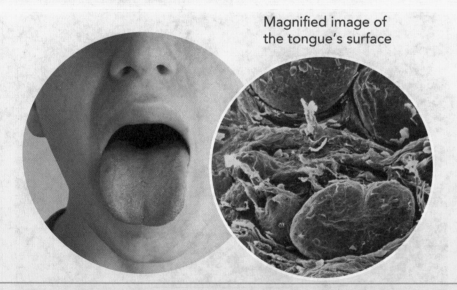

Magnified image of the tongue's surface

FIGURE 1 ....

Taste Buds
The bumps on your tongue contain taste buds.

✎ **Sequence** Write the steps involved in tasting a food.

Step 1

_____

_____

Step 2

_____

_____

Step 3

_____

_____

Lab zone® Do the Quick Lab *Taste and Smell.*

Assess Your Understanding

got it? ....

○ I get it! Now I know that my senses of smell and taste _____

_____

○ I need extra help with _____

Go to **my science** ⓢ **coach** online for help with this subject.

How Do You Sense Touch?

Unlike your other senses, the sense of touch is not found in one place. It is in all areas of your skin. **Your skin has different kinds of touch receptors that respond to different stimuli.** Some receptors respond to delicate or light touch and others to heavy pressure. Still other receptors pick up sensations of pain and temperature change.

The receptors that respond to light touch are in the upper part of the dermis. These receptors also let you feel textures, such as smooth glass and rough sandpaper. Receptors deep in the dermis pick up the feeling of heavy pressure. For example, if you press down hard on your desk, you will feel pressure in your fingertips.

The dermis also contains receptors that respond to temperature and pain. Pain can be one of your most important sensations because it alerts you to possible danger.

✎ **Identify the Main Idea**
Underline the main idea in these paragraphs. Then circle details that support the main idea.

apply it!

Your skin lets you feel the world around you.

1 **Classify** Look at each photo. In the boxes, describe the kind of touch receptors each person is using.

2 CHALLENGE What do you think happens when you accidentally touch a hot stove?

_____

_____

_____

_____

_____

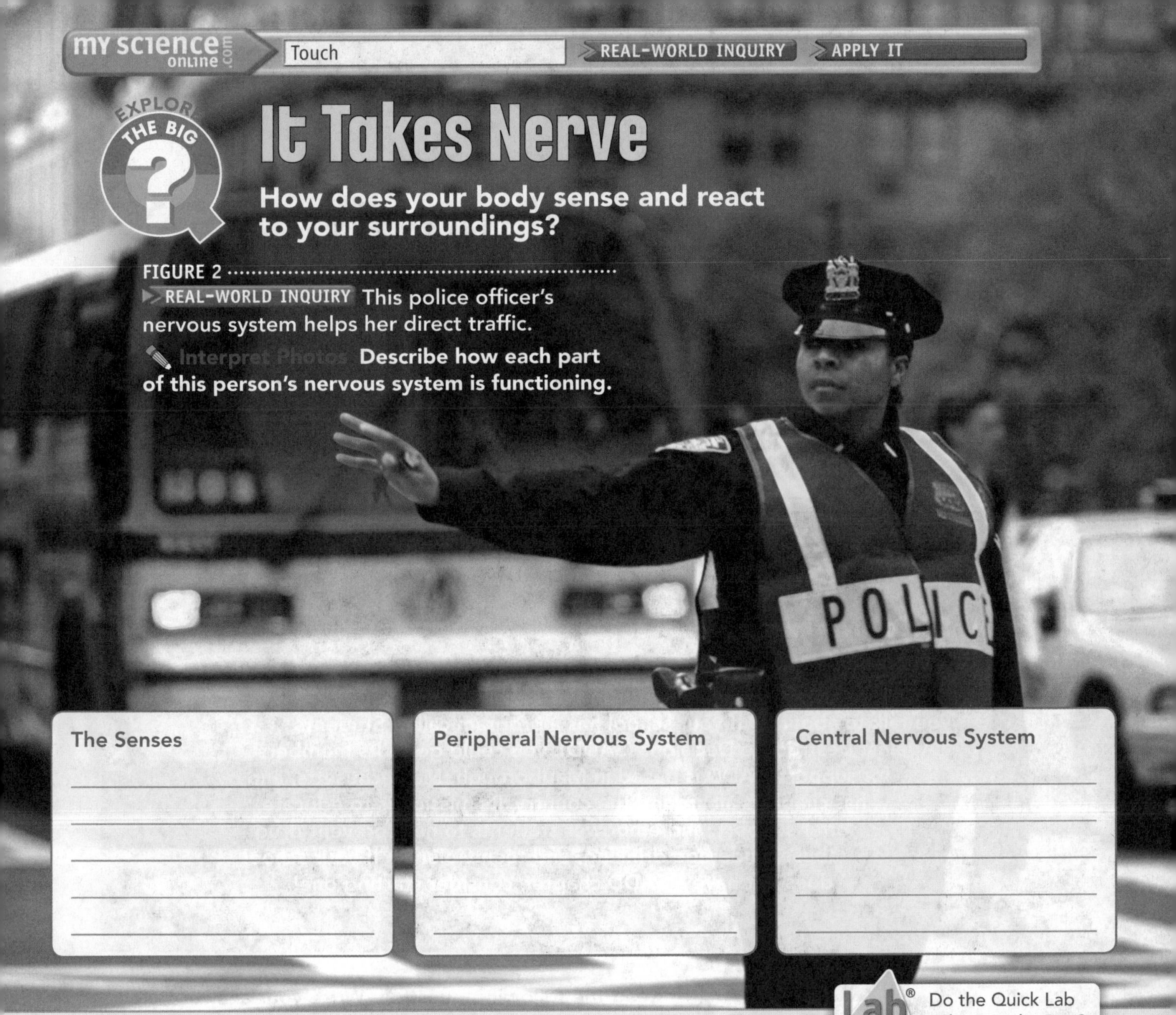

It Takes Nerve

How does your body sense and react to your surroundings?

FIGURE 2 ···

▷ **REAL-WORLD INQUIRY** This police officer's nervous system helps her direct traffic.

✏ **Interpret Photos** **Describe how each part of this person's nervous system is functioning.**

The Senses	Peripheral Nervous System	Central Nervous System
_____	_____	_____
_____	_____	_____
_____	_____	_____
_____	_____	_____
_____	_____	_____

 Lab zone® Do the Quick Lab *What's in the Bag?*

Assess Your Understanding

1a. Review What kinds of touch receptors are found in the skin?

_____

_____

_____

_____

b. ANSWER THE BIG ? How does your body sense and react to your surroundings?

_____

_____

_____

_____

got it? ··

○ **I get it!** Now I know that my skin _____

_____

○ **I need extra help with** _____

Go to **my science** Ⓢ **COACH** online for help with this subject.

Alcohol and Other Drugs

UNLOCK THE BIG ?

🔑 How Does Drug Abuse Affect the Body?

🔑 What Are Some Commonly Abused Drugs?

🔑 How Does Alcohol Abuse Harm the Body?

my PLaNeT DiaRY

PROFILE

SADD National

Marlborough, Massachusetts

If you knew that a friend was abusing drugs or alcohol, whom would you talk to about it? If your school has a program called Students Against Destructive Decisions (SADD), you could go to its members for support. SADD is based in Marlborough, Massachusetts, and has chapters all around the country. Its mission is to educate, offer support, and empower students to help prevent drug abuse, underage drinking, and teen violence. If your school does not have a SADD chapter, consider starting one!

Read the following question. Write your answer below.

SADD uses scientific data to support its mission. Why do you think the data are important?

_____

_____

_____

_____

▷ PLANET DIARY Go to **Planet Diary** to learn more about alcohol and other drugs.

Lab zone® Do the Inquiry Warm-Up
How Can You Best Say No?

Vocabulary

- drug • drug abuse • tolerance • addiction
- withdrawal • depressant • stimulant
- anabolic steroid • alcoholism

Skills

- Reading: Summarize
- Inquiry: Communicate

How Does Drug Abuse Affect the Body?

Alcohol and marijuana are commonly known as drugs. But drugstores also sell drugs to relieve headaches, soothe upset stomachs, and stop coughs. Your school probably has a program to educate you about drugs. But when people talk about drugs, what do they mean? To a scientist, a **drug** is any chemical taken into the body that causes changes in a person's body or behavior. For example, medicines you take when you have a cold are drugs. Use **Figure 1** to list information about a drug you take when you are sick.

Drug Abuse The deliberate use of a drug for nonmedical purposes or the use of an illegal drug is called **drug abuse.** Medicines can be abused drugs if they are used in a nonmedical, unintended way. In addition, many abused drugs, such as cocaine and heroin, are illegal. Using these drugs is against the law because their effects on the body are almost always dangerous.

Abused drugs start to affect the body soon after they are taken. **Drug abuse is dangerous because of its immediate effects on the brain and other parts of the nervous system. In addition, long-term drug abuse can lead to addiction and other health and social problems.**

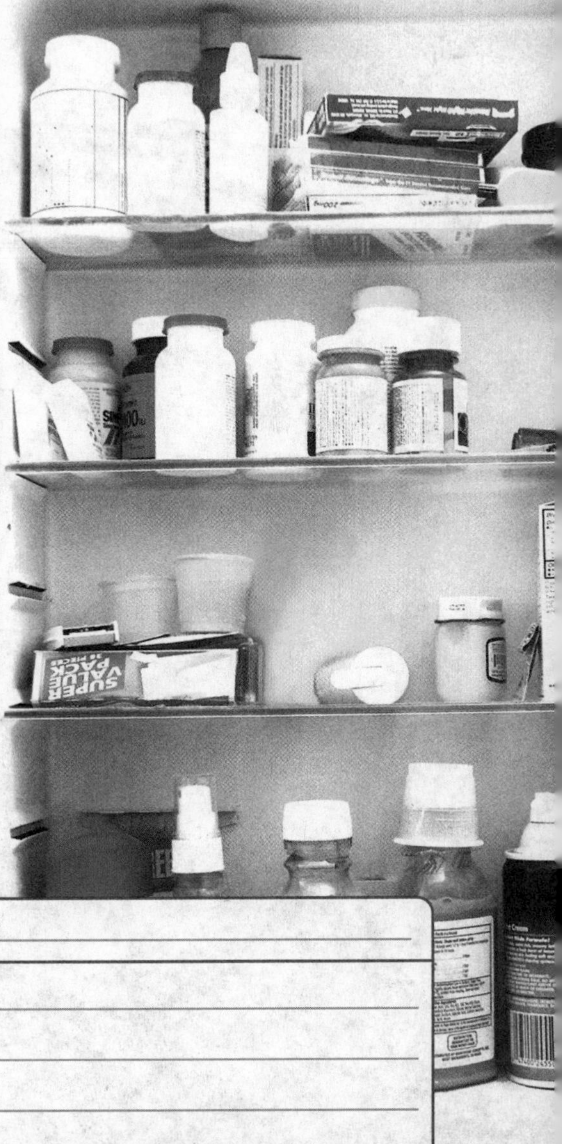

FIGURE 1 ....

Over-the-Counter Medicine

Medicine that can be bought without a prescription is called over-the-counter (OTC) medicine.

✎ **Observe** When you go home, read with an adult the label for an OTC medicine that you take when you are sick. Write the medicine's name, the dosage, and any warnings that are on the label.

Medicine: _____

Dosage: _____

Warnings: _____

_____

_____

Effects of Abused Drugs

Abused drugs have a variety of effects. Some cause nausea and a fast, irregular heartbeat. Others cause sleepiness, headaches, dizziness, or trembling. Alcohol can cause confusion, poor muscle coordination, and blurred vision. These effects are particularly dangerous when someone drives a car.

Most abused drugs can alter, or change, a person's mood and feelings. For example, alcohol can sometimes make a person angry and even violent. Mood-altering drugs also affect the way in which the brain interprets information from the senses. Look at **Figure 2.**

Tolerance

People taking a drug regularly may develop a tolerance to the drug. **Tolerance** is a state in which a drug user needs more of a drug to produce the same effect on the body. Tolerance can cause people to take a large amount of a drug, called an overdose. An overdose can cause unconsciousness or even death.

FIGURE 2 ·······························
Drug Abuse

Drugs can affect a person shortly after they are taken and have serious consequences.

✎ **Communicate** In a small group, discuss signs of drug abuse and ways that you can help someone who is abusing drugs. List them on the clipboards.

Signs of Drug Abuse

How to Help if Someone Is Abusing Drugs

Addiction For many abused drugs, repeated drug use can result in addiction. In **addiction,** the body becomes physically dependent on the drug. If an addict misses a few doses, the body may react with a headache, dizziness, fever, vomiting, or body aches. This person is experiencing **withdrawal,** an adjustment period that occurs when a person stops taking a drug on which the body is dependent. In addition to physical dependence, most drugs can also cause emotional dependence, so the person strongly desires to continue using them.

Other Effects of Drug Abuse Drugs can affect a person's health indirectly. Sometimes drug users share needles. When people inject a drug, some of their blood remains in the needle after it is withdrawn. If the drug user has HIV or another blood disease, the next person to use the needle may become infected.

Drug abusers also face serious legal and social effects. Someone caught using or selling an illegal drug may go to jail. In addition, drug abusers may have difficulty getting along with others, doing well in school, or holding a job.

✎ **Summarize** In the boxes, write in your own words about the physical, behavioral, legal, and social effects that drugs have on people's lives.

Physical Effects	Behavioral Effects	Legal and Social Effects

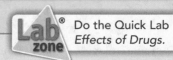 Do the Quick Lab *Effects of Drugs.*

⚷ Assess Your Understanding

1a. Define What is drug abuse?

_____

_____

_____

b. Explain How can the repeated use of drugs lead to addiction?

_____

_____

got it?

○ **I get it!** Now I know that drug abuse has

_____

_____

_____

_____

○ I need extra help with _____

Go to **MY SCIENCE** ⬢ **COACH** *online for help with this subject.*

What Are Some Commonly Abused Drugs?

🔑 **Some commonly abused drugs are marijuana, depressants, stimulants, inhalants, hallucinogens, and steroids.** Depressants such as alcohol and narcotics are drugs that slow down the activity of the central nervous system. In contrast, **stimulants,** such as caffeine, are drugs that speed up body processes. Some substances, called inhalants, have mood-altering effects. Others, called hallucinogens, can make people see or hear things that do not really exist. Steroids are drugs some athletes take to improve their performance. **Anabolic steroids** (an uh BAH lik) are synthetic chemicals that are similar to some hormones naturally produced in the body. **Figure 3** lists some commonly abused drugs and their effects.

FIGURE 3 ·····················

▶ INTERACTIVE ART **Abused Drugs**

Drugs can affect the central nervous system or the body's overall chemical balance. Most drugs can cause emotional dependence.

✎ **Apply Concepts** Circle the names of the depressants. Underline the names of the stimulants.

Some Effects of Commonly Abused Drugs

Drug Name	Short-Term Effects	Long-Term Effects	Addiction
Marijuana	Unclear and slowed thinking, loss of coordination, increased heart rate	Difficulty with concentration and memory; respiratory disease and lung cancer	Probably not
Nicotine	Increased heart and breathing rates, nausea	Heart and lung disease, difficulty breathing	Yes, strongly so
Alcohol	Decreased alertness, poor reflexes, nausea, emotional depression	Liver and brain damage, inadequate nutrition	Yes
Cocaine (crack)	Nervousness, increased heart and breathing rates, disturbed sleep, loss of appetite	Mental illness, irregular heartbeat, heart or breathing failure, liver damage	Yes
Amphetamines (crystal meth, ecstasy)	Restlessness, increased heart and breathing rates, rapid speech	Restlessness, irritability, irregular heartbeat, liver damage	Possible
Inhalants (glue, spray paint)	Sleepiness, nausea, headaches, depression	Liver, kidney, and brain damage; hallucinations	No
Hallucinogens (LSD, mescaline, PCP)	Hallucinations, anxiety, panic; thoughts and actions not connected to reality	Mental illness; fearfulness; behavioral changes, including violence	No
Narcotics (opium, codeine, morphine, heroin)	Depression, sleepiness, nausea, hallucinations	Convulsion, coma, death	Yes, strongly so
Anabolic steroids	Mood swings, increased muscle size	Heart, liver, and kidney damage; hypertension; overgrowth of skull and facial bones	No

apply it!

This teen is active in an anti-drug campaign.

1 △ **Communicate** After reading **Figure 3** with a partner, discuss how you could make a sign to educate others about drug abuse.

2 **Make Models** Sketch your sign in the poster at the left.

 Do the Quick Lab *Over-the-Counter Medication Labels.*

⚷ Assess Your Understanding

2a. List Name two abused stimulants.

_____

_____

b. CHALLENGE Why might a person's risk of a heart attack increase with the use of stimulants?

_____

_____

_____

got it?

○ **I get it!** Now I know that some commonly abused drugs are _____

_____

_____

_____

○ I need extra help with _____

Go to **my science** **coach** *online for help with this subject.*

How Does Alcohol Abuse Harm the Body?

Alcohol, a drug found in beer, wine, cocktails, and hard liquor, is a powerful depressant. In all states, it is illegal for people under the age of 21 to buy or possess alcohol. Yet alcohol is the most commonly abused legal drug for people aged 12 to 17.

How Alcohol Affects the Body Alcohol is quickly absorbed into the blood from the digestive system, especially if the person has an empty stomach. Effects can include blurred vision and changes in heart rate and blood pressure. The more alcohol in the blood, the more serious the effects. The amount of alcohol in the blood is called the blood alcohol concentration, or BAC. In some states, drivers with a BAC of 0.08 percent are legally drunk. In other states, a BAC of 0.1 percent is legally drunk.

Alcohol can produce serious negative effects, including loss of judgment, at a BAC of less than 0.08 percent. People who have been drinking may not realize that they cannot drive a car safely, as shown in **Figure 4.** About every two minutes, a person in the United States is injured in a car crash related to alcohol.

FIGURE 4 ···

Alcohol and Peer Pressure
A police officer tests the blood alcohol concentration of a driver suspected of drinking.

✎ Communicate **In a small group, discuss the situations described on each clipboard. Record your ideas.**

A neighbor's older brother arrives to take you and your neighbor home from school. You can tell he has been drinking. What do you do?

_____

_____

_____

_____

_____

_____

_____

_____

A group of friends are drinking alcohol at a school dance. List the choices you have. Then describe which you would choose and why.

_____

_____

_____

_____

_____

_____

_____

_____

Long-Term Alcohol Abuse Many adults drink in moderation without serious health problems. However, heavy drinking, especially over a long period, can result in significant health problems. 🔑 **Alcohol abuse can destroy brain cells and liver cells. It can also lead to addiction and emotional dependence.** Damage to the brain can cause mental disturbances, such as hallucinations and loss of consciousness. The liver breaks down alcohol for elimination from the body. It can become so scarred that it does not function properly.

Alcohol abuse can result in **alcoholism,** a disease in which a person is physically addicted to and emotionally dependent on alcohol. To give up alcohol, alcoholics must go through withdrawal. Medical professionals, psychologists, and groups such as Alcoholics Anonymous can help a person stop drinking.

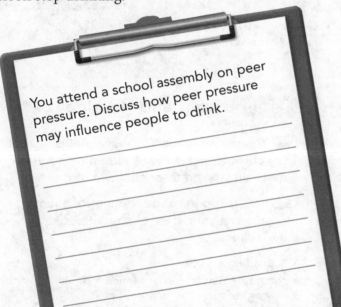

You attend a school assembly on peer pressure. Discuss how peer pressure may influence people to drink.

Suppose you find out that your friend has started to drink alcohol often. Discuss what you could do in this situation. What would you do?

Do the Quick Lab
Demonstrating BAC.

🔑 Assess Your Understanding

3a. Describe Why is alcohol a depressant?

_____

_____

b. Make Judgments Is it fair that drivers can be arrested for having a BAC above a certain level? Explain your answer.

_____

_____

_____

_____

got it?

○ **I get it!** Now I know that alcohol abuse can

_____

_____

_____

_____

○ I need extra help with _____

Go to my science s **coach** *online for help with this subject.*

7 Study Guide

My _____ gather information about my surroundings. My _____ and _____ nervous systems enable me to process and react to what is happening.

LESSON 1 How the Nervous System Works

🔑 Your nervous system receives information about what is happening both inside and outside your body. It directs how your body responds to this information and helps maintain homeostasis.

🔑 Cells that carry information through your nervous system are called neurons, or nerve cells.

🔑 At the axon tips, electrical signals change to a chemical form, allowing the message to cross the gap in the synapse.

Vocabulary
- stimulus • response • neuron • nerve impulse • dendrite • axon
- nerve • sensory neuron • interneuron • motor neuron • synapse

LESSON 2 Divisions of the Nervous System

🔑 The central nervous system controls the functions of the body.

🔑 The peripheral nervous system connects the brain to the rest of the body.

Vocabulary
- central nervous system • peripheral nervous system
- brain • spinal cord • cerebrum • cerebellum
- brain stem • somatic nervous system
- autonomic nervous system • reflex • concussion

LESSON 3 Sight and Hearing

🔑 Your eyes respond to the stimulus of light. They convert that stimulus into impulses that your brain interprets, enabling you to see.

🔑 Ears respond to the stimulus of sound. Structures in your inner ear help to control your balance.

Vocabulary
- cornea • pupil • iris • lens • retina
- nearsightedness • farsightedness
- eardrum • cochlea • semicircular canal

LESSON 4 Smell, Taste, and Touch

🔑 The senses of smell and taste work together. Both depend on chemicals in the air or in food. The chemicals trigger responses in receptors in the nose and mouth.

🔑 Your skin has different kinds of touch receptors that respond to different stimuli.

Vocabulary
- taste bud

LESSON 5 Alcohol and Other Drugs

🔑 Drug abuse is dangerous because of its immediate and long-term effects.

🔑 Some commonly abused drugs are marijuana, depressants, stimulants, inhalants, hallucinogens, and steroids.

🔑 Alcohol abuse can harm the body and lead to addiction and dependence.

Vocabulary
- drug • drug abuse • tolerance • addiction
- withdrawal • depressant • stimulant
- anabolic steroid • alcoholism

Review and Assessment

LESSON 1 How the Nervous System Works

1. A change or signal in the environment that can make the nervous system react is called a

  a. stimulus.   **b.** response.

  c. nerve impulse.   **d.** synapse.

2. A _____ sends an impulse to a muscle or gland.

3. **Compare and Contrast** Compare and contrast the functions of axons and dendrites.

_____

_____

_____

_____

_____

4. **Interpret Diagrams** Use the diagram below to explain how a nerve impulse travels between neurons.

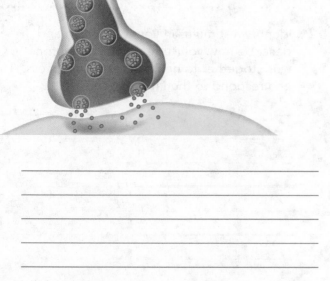

_____

_____

_____

_____

_____

_____

LESSON 2 Divisions of the Nervous System

5. Which structure links the brain and the peripheral nervous system?

  a. the cerebrum   **b.** the cerebellum

  c. the cochlea   **d.** the spinal cord

6. The _____ is the region of the brain that controls involuntary actions.

7. **Make Generalizations** What is the function of the autonomic nervous system?

_____

_____

8. **Draw Conclusions** What is the result if the spinal cord is cut?

_____

_____

_____

_____

9. **Apply Concepts** As a man walks barefoot along a beach, he steps on a sharp shell. His foot automatically jerks upward, even before he feels pain. What process is this an example of? How does it help protect the man?

_____

_____

_____

_____

_____

10. Write About It The cerebrum, the cerebellum, and the brain stem are regions of the brain that carry out specific functions. Write a brief job description for each of these regions of the brain.

249

Sight and Hearing

11. Which structure adjusts the size of the pupil?

a. the cornea   **b.** the iris

c. the lens   **d.** the retina

12. A person with _____ can see nearby objects clearly, but not distant objects.

13. Sequence List in order the ear structures that must vibrate before you hear a sound.

_____

_____

_____

14. **Write About It** Sometimes when people get off an amusement park ride, they feel dizzy. Based on what you know about balance, write a paragraph explaining why they might feel this way.

Smell, Taste, and Touch

15. Which organ works closely with your mouth to help the brain interpret taste?

a. the eyes   **b.** the ears

c. the nose   **d.** the skin

16. The _____ on your tongue respond to chemicals in food.

17. Apply Concepts The greatest numbers of touch receptors are located in the fingers, toes, and face. What do you think is the advantage of this placement?

_____

_____

_____

_____

Alcohol and Other Drugs

18. Physical dependence on a drug is called

a. a withdrawal.   **b.** a response.

c. an addiction.   **d.** a tolerance.

19. Alcohol is a _____ because it slows down the central nervous system.

20. Make Judgments If someone tried to persuade you to take drugs, what arguments would you use as a way of refusing? Why do you think these arguments would be effective?

_____

_____

_____

_____

_____

_____

APPLY THE BIG ?

How does your body sense and react to your surroundings?

21. Identify a stimulus in your classroom and describe how your three types of neurons work together to help you gather, process, and respond to the information.

_____

_____

_____

_____

_____

_____

_____

_____

Standardized Test Prep

Multiple Choice

Circle the letter of the best answer.

1. What is the function of the part labeled A on the neuron shown below?

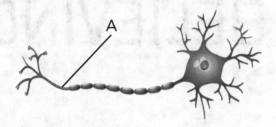

   A It carries the nerve impulse toward the cell body.

   B It protects the neuron from damage.

   C It carries the nerve impulse away from the cell body.

   D It picks up stimuli from the environment.

2. A scientist studying the brain is studying part of the

   A peripheral nervous system.

   B somatic nervous system.

   C autonomic nervous system.

   D central nervous system.

3. The brain stem is involved in controlling

   A breathing.

   B the ability to learn.

   C movement of skeletal muscles.

   D balance.

4. You can infer that a person who has lost his or her sense of smell is also likely to have a poor

   A sense of balance.

   B sense of taste.

   C sense of touch.

   D sense of hearing.

5. Which structure in the ear is responsible for helping a person balance on one leg?

   A the eardrum

   B the cochlea

   C the hammer

   D the semicircular canals

Constructed Response

Use the diagram below and your knowledge of science to help you answer Question 6. Write your answer on a separate sheet of paper.

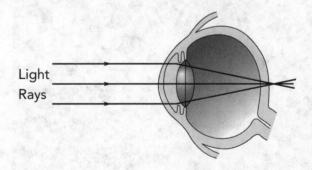

Light Rays

6. Identify the vision problem shown in the eye above. What type of corrective lens should be used? Explain your answer.

SEEING IS BELIEVING ... SOMETIMES

▲ What do you see? What does someone else see? Can you see the faces and the vase at the same time?

Your eyes are constantly checking out the world around you and sending visual information to your brain. Signals from the optic nerves take about one tenth of a second to become a visual image in the brain. Researchers think this lag causes the brain to predict images that will occur one tenth of a second in the future, filling in the gaps. This lag may explain why you see certain types of optical illusions.

Many optical illusions rely on the fact that the brain easily perceives patterns. Scientists think that when there is a gap in a pattern, the brain tries to predict what fills the gap. When these predictions don't match reality, you may end up seeing a false image. You probably experience an optical illusion every day without even noticing it. Television and movies are actually a series of images that are played rapidly, creating the illusion of motion.

Is the figure above an image of a vase or of two people facing each other? You can't see both images at the same time, because your brain gets fooled by thinking there's only one possible background. You can see both images at different times by shifting your attention.

Research It Research more about optical illusions. Then present three of your favorite optical illusions to your class and explain how each one works.

SEEING WITH YOUR TONGUE?

It's sensitive. Very, very sensitive. The human tongue has some of the highest concentrations of nerve endings of any body part. It can sense stimulation from two points that are less than a millimeter apart. Now scientists are taking advantage of this amazing sensitivity to help blind people "see." Cutting-edge technology is helping blind people see with their tongues! And they don't even have to lick anything!

The technology uses a video camera mounted on the person's forehead, like a headlamp. The video camera records images of the environment. These images are translated into electrical impulses that are sent to a small pad placed on the tongue. The pad transmits the electrical impulses to all those nerve endings in the tongue. The nervous system then relays this information to the brain.

The device works because the brain is very adaptable. The nervous system carries impulses from the tongue to the part of the brain that processes touch. However, the brain can learn to interpret these electrical impulses as images. This effect, called sense substitution, is central to how the device works.

Research It Learn more about another device that helps people use their senses. Describe how the device uses video or audio input and output to transmit sensory information. Write a short magazine-style article that describes the device and how it is used.

WHAT WILL YOUR BODY BE LIKE AT 80?

THE BIG ?

What changes happen in your body over your lifetime?

Getting older can be a challenge. As you grow and change, your shoes might get too small and your pants too short. You might even feel uncomfortable in your own body. During the teen years, your hands and feet grow larger and your legs get longer. Your spine lengthens and your skin might become oily. By your 20s you will be fully mature, but then your body will begin to age.

Predict How might your body change by the time you are 80 years old?

_____

_____

_____

▷ UNTAMED SCIENCE Watch the **Untamed Science** video to learn more about aging.

The Endocrine System and Reproduction

8 Getting Started

Check Your Understanding

1. Background Read the paragraph below and then answer the question.

> Mia's parents celebrate the birth of their baby girl. Mia **inherited** thin lips from her mother and dimples from her father. These **traits** were passed to Mia from her parents during **sexual reproduction.**

To **inherit** is to receive physical characteristics from parents.

A **trait** is a specific characteristic that a parent can pass to its offspring through its genes.

Sexual reproduction involves two parents and combines their genetic material to produce an offspring that is different from each parent.

- How does sexual reproduction cause the baby's inherited traits?

_____

_____

_____

> **MY READING WEB** If you had trouble completing the question above, visit **My Reading Web** and type in *The Endocrine System and Reproduction.*

Vocabulary Skill

Identify Related Word Forms Increase your vocabulary by learning related forms of words. The table below lists word forms and their definitions.

Verb	Noun	Adjective
fertilize, *v.* to join an egg cell and a sperm cell	fertilization, *n.* the process in sexual reproduction in which an egg cell and a sperm cell join	fertilized, *adj.* describes an egg cell that has joined with a sperm cell in sexual reproduction
ovulate, *v.* to release an egg from an ovary	ovulation, *n.* the process in which an egg is released from an ovary	ovulating, *adj.* describes the process of releasing an egg from an ovary

2. Quick Check Fill in the blanks with the correct form of the words.

- When a woman _____ and releases an egg, _____ can occur.

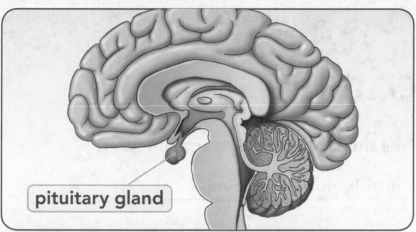

pituitary gland

fertilization

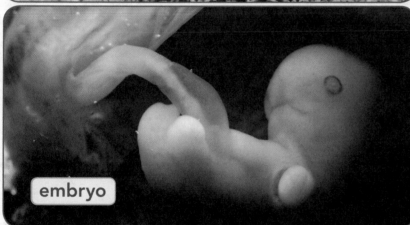

embryo

adolescence

Chapter Preview

LESSON 1
- gland • duct • hormone
- target cell • hypothalamus
- pituitary gland
- negative feedback

↻ **Identify the Main Idea**
△ **Make Models**

LESSON 2
- fertilization • egg • sperm
- zygote • testes • testosterone
- scrotum • semen
- penis • ovary • estrogen
- Fallopian tube • uterus • vagina
- menstrual cycle • menstruation
- ovulation

↻ **Sequence**
△ **Develop Hypotheses**

LESSON 3
- embryo • fetus • amniotic sac
- placenta • umbilical cord

↻ **Compare and Contrast**
△ **Calculate**

LESSON 4
- adolescence
- puberty

↻ **Relate Cause and Effect**
△ **Graph**

> **VOCAB FLASH CARDS** For extra help with vocabulary, visit **Vocab Flash Cards** and type in *The Endocrine System and Reproduction.*

257

UNLOCK THE BIG ?

🔑 **How Does the Endocrine System Function?**

🔑 **What Controls Hormone Levels?**

my planet DiaRY

MISCONCEPTION

The Cause of Acne

Misconception: Eating oily foods can cause acne.

Scientists have not found a link between eating certain foods and acne. So, what does cause acne? Much of the blame falls on certain hormones. Your body starts to produce these hormones when you enter adolescence. They stimulate your body to produce an oily substance called sebum. When your body produces too much sebum, some hair follicles in your skin may become blocked. This blockage causes bacteria to get trapped. Because the sebum and bacteria have nowhere to go, your skin becomes inflamed. The result is acne.

Communicate Discuss the following question with a partner. Write your answer below.

How would you explain to a friend what causes acne?

_____

_____

_____

_____

_____

_____

_____

_____

_____

_____

_____

> **PLANET DIARY** Go to **Planet Diary** to learn more about the endocrine system.

 Lab zone® Do the Inquiry Warm-Up *What's the Signal?*

Vocabulary

- gland • duct • hormone • target cell • hypothalamus
- pituitary gland • negative feedback

Skills

↻ Reading: Identify the Main Idea

△ Inquiry: Make Models

How Does the Endocrine System Function?

Have you ever been so afraid that you heard your heart thump rapidly in your chest? When something frightens you, your body's endocrine system (EN duh krin) reacts.

Your body has two systems that regulate its activities: the nervous system and the endocrine system. The nervous system regulates most activities by sending nerve impulses throughout the body. ⊙━ **The endocrine system regulates short-term and long-term activities by sending chemicals throughout the body. Long-term changes include growth and development.**

The endocrine system is made up of glands. A **gland** is an organ that produces or releases a chemical. Some glands, such as those producing saliva and sweat, release their chemicals into tiny tubes, or **ducts.** The ducts deliver the chemicals to specific places in the body or to the skin's surface. However, the glands of the endocrine system do not have delivery ducts. The endocrine glands produce and release chemicals directly into the blood. Then the blood carries those chemicals throughout the body.

Main Idea
_____
_____

↻ **Identify the Main Idea**
In the graphic organizer, write the main idea of the third paragraph. Then write two details that support the main idea.

Detail
_____
_____
_____

Detail
_____
_____
_____

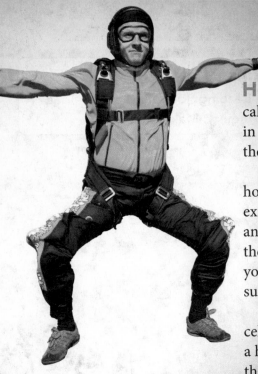

Hormones The chemical produced by an endocrine gland is called a **hormone.** Hormones are chemical messengers that travel in the blood. Hormones turn on, turn off, speed up, or slow down the activities of organs and tissues.

Nerve impulses from the brain act quickly. In contrast, hormones usually cause a slower, longer-lasting response. For example, if you see danger, your brain interprets the information and sends an impulse to an endocrine gland. The gland releases the hormone adrenaline into your blood. Adrenaline speeds up your heart rate and breathing rate. Even a quick hormonal response such as releasing adrenaline is much slower than a nerve response.

Each hormone affects specific target cells. **Target cells** are cells that are specialized in a way that enables them to recognize a hormone's chemical structure. Hormones travel in the blood until they find their target cells. Read about the endocrine glands and the hormones they produce in **Figure 1** on the next page.

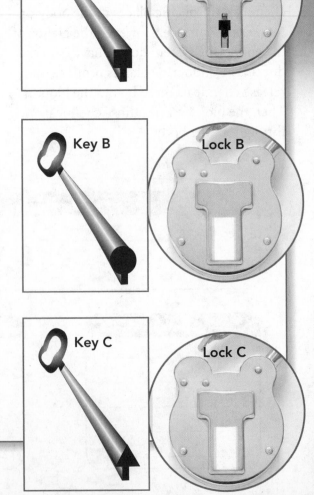

apply it!

Hormones interact with target cells much like keys interact with locks.

1 **Make Models** Look at Key A and Lock A. Then draw the shapes of the keyholes for the locks that Key B and Key C will unlock.

2 **Draw Conclusions** How do a hormone and a target cell function like a key and a lock?

_____

_____

_____

_____

3 [CHALLENGE] What body system does the endocrine system depend on to function? Explain.

_____

_____

_____

_____

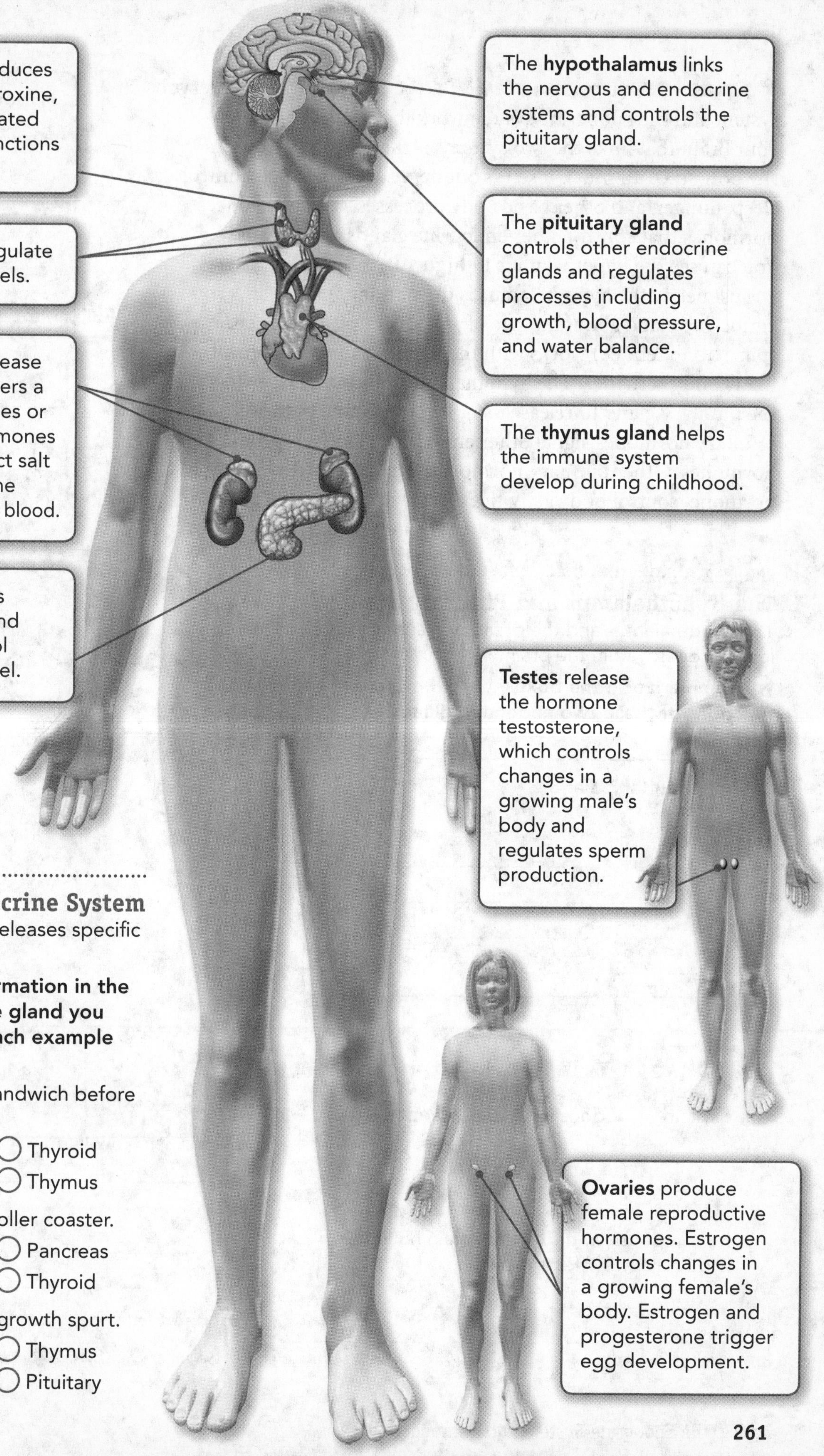

The **thyroid gland** produces hormones, such as thyroxine, that control energy-related reactions and other functions in cells.

Parathyroid glands regulate the blood's calcium levels.

The **adrenal glands** release adrenaline, which triggers a response to emergencies or excitement. Other hormones from these glands affect salt and water balance in the kidneys and sugar in the blood.

The **pancreas** produces the hormones insulin and glucagon, which control the blood's glucose level.

The **hypothalamus** links the nervous and endocrine systems and controls the pituitary gland.

The **pituitary gland** controls other endocrine glands and regulates processes including growth, blood pressure, and water balance.

The **thymus gland** helps the immune system develop during childhood.

Testes release the hormone testosterone, which controls changes in a growing male's body and regulates sperm production.

Ovaries produce female reproductive hormones. Estrogen controls changes in a growing female's body. Estrogen and progesterone trigger egg development.

FIGURE 1 ···

Glands of the Endocrine System

Each endocrine gland releases specific hormones.

✎ **Infer** Use the information in the diagram to choose the gland you think is involved for each example below.

Example 1: You eat a sandwich before your soccer game.

○ Adrenal   ○ Thyroid
○ Testes   ○ Thymus

Example 2: You ride a roller coaster.

○ Pituitary ○ Pancreas
○ Adrenal   ○ Thyroid

Example 3: You have a growth spurt.

○ Ovaries   ○ Thymus
○ Parathyroid ○ Pituitary

Regulators of the Endocrine System The nervous system and the endocrine system work together. The part of your brain that links the two systems is the **hypothalamus** (hy poh THAL uh mus). It sends out nerve messages that control sleep, hunger, and other basic body processes. It also produces hormones that control other endocrine glands and organs. You can see the hypothalamus in **Figure 2**.

Just below the hypothalamus is the pituitary gland, an endocrine gland about the size of a pea. The **pituitary gland** (pih TOO ih tehr ee) works with the hypothalamus to control many body activities. The hypothalamus sends messages to the pituitary gland to release its hormones. Some of those pituitary hormones signal other endocrine glands to produce hormones. Other pituitary hormones, such as growth hormone, control body activities directly.

FIGURE 2 ·······························

The Hypothalamus and Pituitary Gland
The hypothalamus and the pituitary gland are located deep within the brain.

✎ **Summarize** In the boxes, describe the functions of these two endocrine glands.

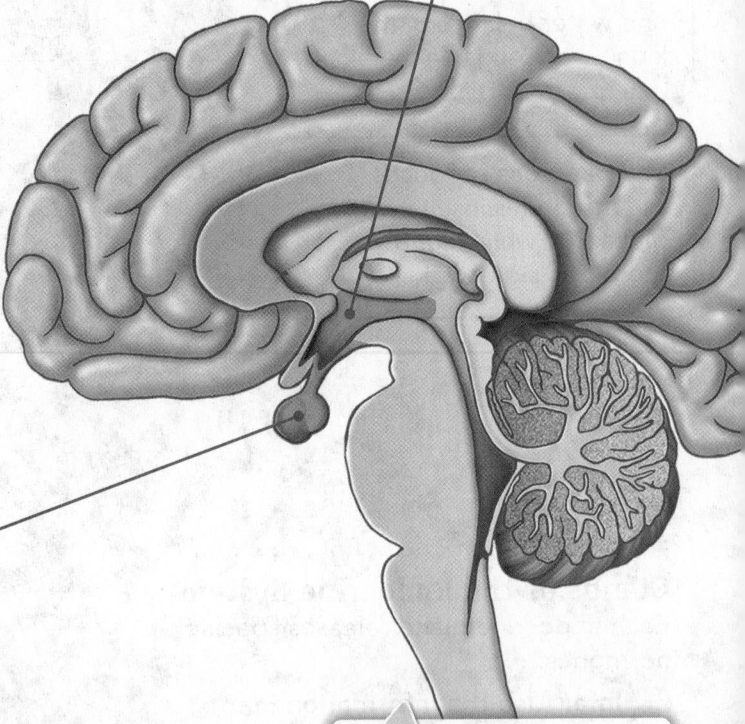

Hypothalamus
_____
_____
_____
_____
_____
_____
_____

Pituitary Gland
_____
_____
_____
_____
_____

Lab ® Do the Quick Lab
zone Making Models.

🔑 **Assess Your Understanding**

1a. Explain How does adrenaline affect the heart?

_____
_____

b. Relate Cause and Effect Explain how the hypothalamus affects growth.

_____
_____
_____

got it?

○ I get it! Now I know that my endocrine system
_____
_____
_____

○ I need extra help with _____

Go to MY SCIENCE ⓢ COACH online for help with this subject.

What Controls Hormone Levels?

Suppose you set a thermostat at 20°C. If the room temperature falls below 20°C, the thermostat signals the furnace to turn on. When heat from the furnace warms the room to 20°C, the thermostat shuts off the furnace. In certain ways, the endocrine system works like a thermostat. It uses a process called **negative feedback** in which a system is turned off by the condition it produces. **When the amount of a hormone in the blood reaches a certain level, the endocrine system sends signals that stop the release of that hormone.** In **Figure 3,** you can see how negative feedback regulates the level of the hormone thyroxine in the blood.

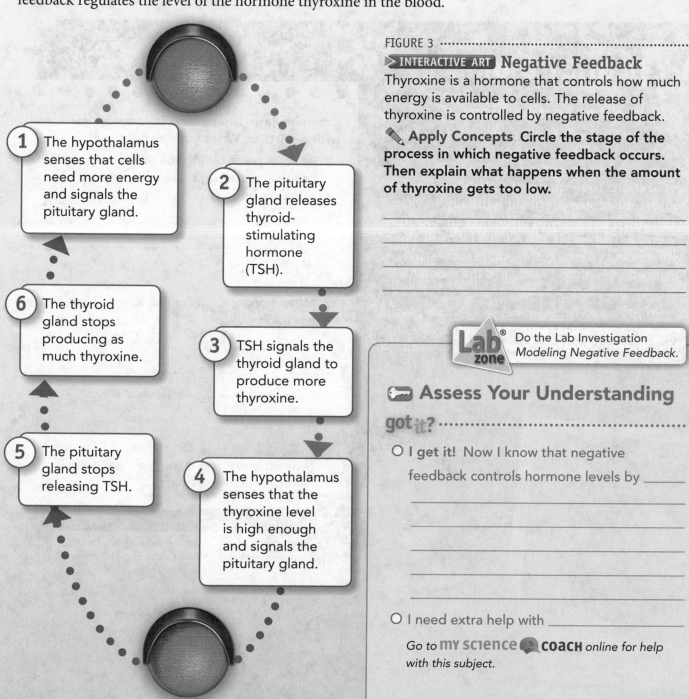

1 The hypothalamus senses that cells need more energy and signals the pituitary gland.

2 The pituitary gland releases thyroid-stimulating hormone (TSH).

3 TSH signals the thyroid gland to produce more thyroxine.

4 The hypothalamus senses that the thyroxine level is high enough and signals the pituitary gland.

5 The pituitary gland stops releasing TSH.

6 The thyroid gland stops producing as much thyroxine.

FIGURE 3

> **INTERACTIVE ART** **Negative Feedback**
Thyroxine is a hormone that controls how much energy is available to cells. The release of thyroxine is controlled by negative feedback.

Apply Concepts Circle the stage of the process in which negative feedback occurs. Then explain what happens when the amount of thyroxine gets too low.

_____

_____

_____

_____

Lab zone Do the Lab Investigation *Modeling Negative Feedback.*

Assess Your Understanding

got it?

○ **I get it!** Now I know that negative feedback controls hormone levels by _____

_____

_____

_____

○ **I need extra help with** _____

Go to **my science** **coach** *online for help with this subject.*

The Male and Female Reproductive Systems

🔑 **What Are the Functions of the Reproductive Systems?**

🔑 **What Happens During the Menstrual Cycle?**

my planet diary

DISCOVERY

In Vitro Fertilization

In 1977, Dr. Patrick Steptoe and Dr. Robert Edwards had been working for years on an experimental procedure called in vitro fertilization. Their goal was to help women who could not become pregnant naturally. In vitro fertilization begins with retrieving an egg from a woman. The egg is placed in a lab dish along with a man's sperm. If the egg is successfully fertilized, it is placed back into the woman's body to grow into a baby.

Dr. Steptoe and Dr. Edwards were unsuccessful time and time again, until they met Lesley and John Brown. The doctors implanted a fertilized egg in Lesley. Nine months later, on July 25, 1978, the world's first in vitro baby was born. Her parents named her Louise Joy Brown.

Communicate Discuss the following questions with a partner. Write your answers below.

1. At what point during the in vitro fertilization process is the egg placed back into the woman's body?

_____

_____

_____

2. What impact do you think in vitro fertilization has had?

_____

_____

_____

_____

▶ PLANET DIARY Go to **Planet Diary** to learn more about the male and female reproductive systems.

Louise Joy Brown
at birth

Lab zone Do the Inquiry Warm-Up *What's the Big Difference?*

Louise Joy Brown
as an adult

Vocabulary

- fertilization • egg • sperm • zygote • testes
- testosterone • scrotum • semen • penis • ovary
- estrogen • Fallopian tube • uterus • vagina
- menstrual cycle • menstruation • ovulation

Skills

⟳ Reading: Sequence

△ Inquiry: Develop Hypotheses

What Are the Functions of the Reproductive Systems?

Have you noticed how a child's body changes as the child grows? Two different endocrine glands—the ovaries and the testes—release hormones that control many of these changes. They also produce the sex cells that are part of sexual reproduction.

Sexual Reproduction You were once a single cell. That cell resulted from the joining of an egg cell and a sperm cell, which is a process called **fertilization.** An **egg** is the female sex cell. The male sex cell is a **sperm.** Both cells are shown in **Figure 1.** Fertilization is part of sexual reproduction, the process by which males and females produce new individuals. Sexual reproduction involves the production of eggs by the female and sperm by the male. The egg and sperm join together during fertilization. When fertilization occurs, a fertilized egg, or **zygote,** is produced. The zygote contains all the information needed to produce a new human being.

FIGURE 1 ·····························

Egg and Sperm

An egg is one of the largest cells in the body. A sperm cell is much smaller than an egg and can move.

✎ **Describe** In the table, describe each of the cells involved in fertilization.

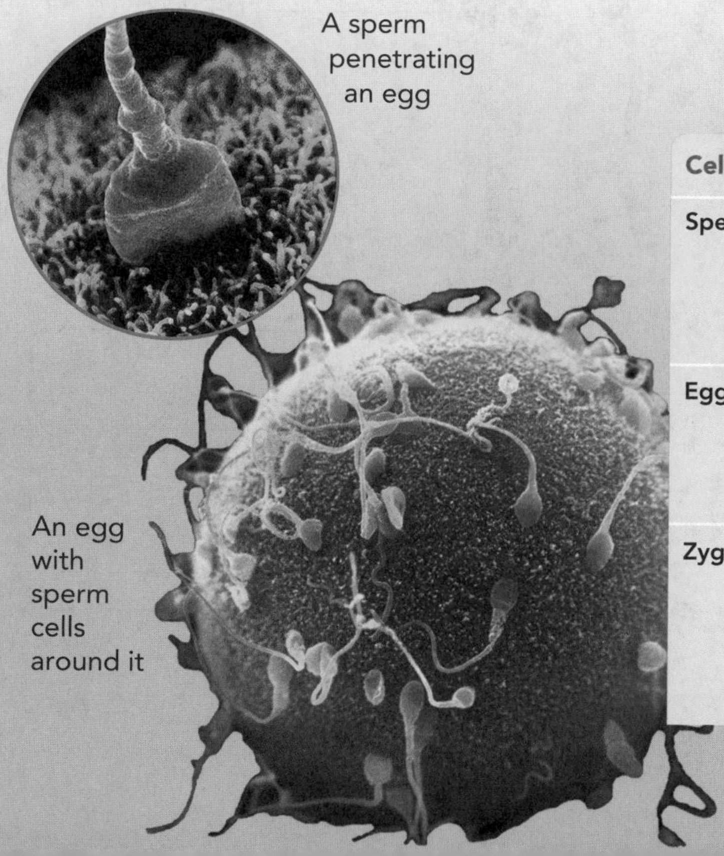

A sperm penetrating an egg

An egg with sperm cells around it

Cell	Description
Sperm	
Egg	
Zygote	

Sperm cells

Male Reproductive System
Look at the organs of the male reproductive system shown in **Figure 2**. 🔑 **The male reproductive system is specialized to produce sperm cells and the hormone testosterone.** The structures of this system include the testes, scrotum, and penis.

The Testes The **testes** (TES teez; singular *testis*) are the organs in which sperm are produced. The testes consist of clusters of tiny, coiled tubes where sperm are formed. In addition to sperm, the testes produce testosterone. The hormone **testosterone** (tes TAHS tuh rohn) controls the development of adult male characteristics. These include facial hair, deepening of the voice, broadening of the shoulders, and the ability to produce sperm.

The testes are located in a pouch of skin called the **scrotum** (SKROH tum). The scrotum holds the testes away from the rest of the body. This distance keeps the testes about 2°C to 3°C below normal body temperature, which is 37°C. The cooler temperature is important because sperm cannot develop properly at 37°C.

FIGURE 2 ·····························
▶ **INTERACTIVE ART** **Structures of the Male Reproductive System**

✎ **Complete the tasks.**

1. **Summarize** In the boxes, describe the structure and function of each organ.

2. **Calculate** Find the temperatures at which sperm develop properly.

_____

_____

_____

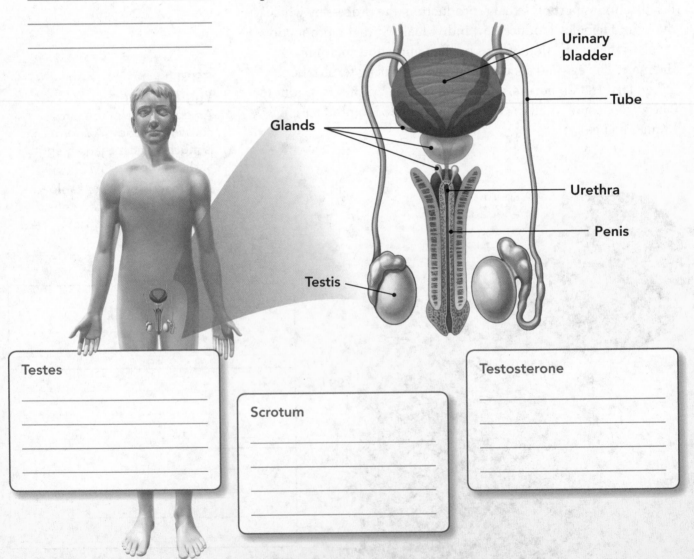

Urinary bladder

Tube

Glands

Urethra

Penis

Testis

Testes

_____

_____

_____

_____

Scrotum

_____

_____

_____

_____

Testosterone

_____

_____

_____

_____

Sperm The production of sperm cells begins during the teenage years. Each sperm cell has a head that contains chromosomes, and a long, whiplike tail. The chromosomes carry the information that controls inherited characteristics, such as blood type. The tail helps the sperm swim in fluid.

After forming in the testes, sperm travel through tubes in the male reproductive system. As they travel, sperm mix with fluids produced by nearby glands, as shown in **Figure 3.** This mixture of sperm cells and fluids is called **semen** (SEE mun). The fluids in semen provide an environment where sperm can swim. Semen also contains nutrients that the sperm use for energy.

Semen leaves the body through an organ called the **penis.** The semen travels through the tube in the penis called the urethra. Urine also leaves the body through the urethra. When semen passes through the urethra, however, muscles near the bladder contract. Those muscles prevent urine and semen from mixing.

> ↻ **Sequence** Underline in the paragraphs the path that sperm take to leave the body. Then write the steps on the notepaper below.

FIGURE 3 ································

Sperm Production and Passage From the Body

Sperm are produced in the testes and leave the body through the urethra.

✎ **Use the diagram to complete the tasks.**

1. **Relate Text and Visuals** On the diagram, draw arrows to trace the path that sperm travel through the male reproductive system.

2. **CHALLENGE** Why do sperm need to swim?

   _____

   _____

   _____

   _____

   _____

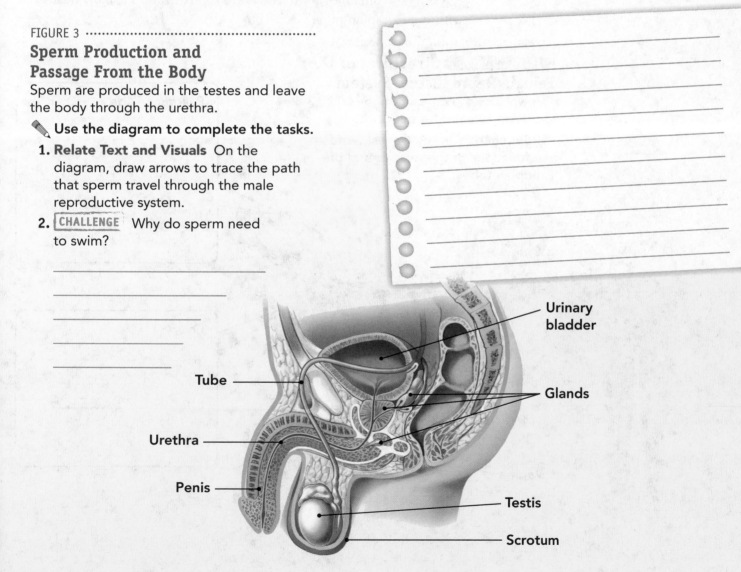

Urinary bladder

Tube

Glands

Urethra

Penis

Testis

Scrotum

know? ....

When the female reproductive system becomes mature, the ovaries contain about 400,000 undeveloped eggs. However, only about 450 of those eggs will actually leave the ovaries and reach the uterus during a typical woman's life.

Female Reproductive System 🖾 **The female reproductive system is specialized to produce eggs and nourish a developing baby until birth. It also produces estrogen and other hormones.** The organs of this system include the ovaries, Fallopian tubes, uterus, and vagina.

The Ovaries The **ovaries** (OH vuh reez) are the female reproductive structures that produce eggs. They are located slightly below the waist, one on each side of the body, as shown in **Figure 4.** Like the testes in males, the ovaries are also endocrine glands that produce hormones. One hormone, **estrogen** (ES truh jun), triggers the development of some adult female characteristics. For example, estrogen causes the hips to widen and the breasts to develop. Estrogen is also involved in the development of egg cells. Each month, one of the ovaries releases a mature egg into the nearest oviduct, or Fallopian tube. A **Fallopian tube** is the passageway an egg travels from an ovary to the uterus. Fertilization usually occurs within a Fallopian tube.

FIGURE 4 ···

> INTERACTIVE ART **Structures of the Female Reproductive System**
The word *ovary* comes from the Latin word *ova* meaning "eggs."

✎ **Summarize** In the boxes, write the functions of the ovaries and the Fallopian tubes.

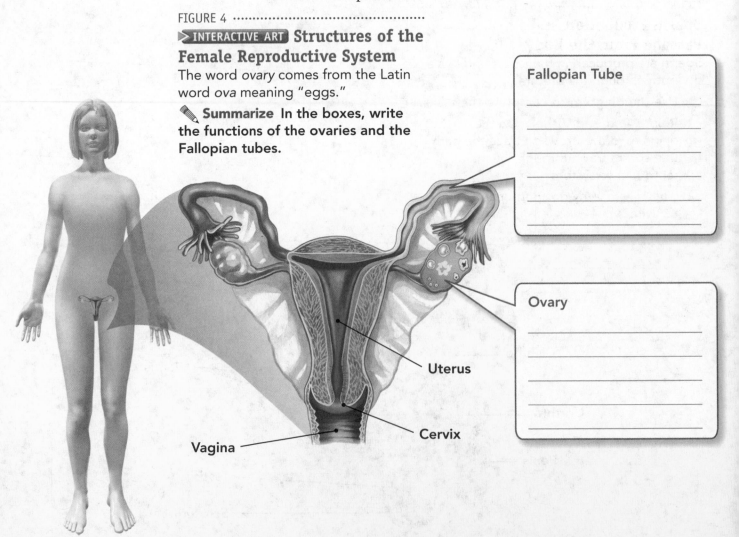

Fallopian Tube

_____
_____
_____
_____
_____

Ovary

_____
_____
_____
_____

Uterus

Cervix

Vagina

Egg Cells From an ovary, an egg travels through the Fallopian tube to the uterus. The **uterus** (YOO tur us) is a hollow, muscular organ. If an egg has been fertilized in the Fallopian tube, it attaches to the wall of the uterus. An unfertilized egg breaks down in the uterus. It leaves through the cervix, an opening at the base of the uterus. The egg then enters the vagina. The **vagina** (vuh JY nuh) is a muscular passageway leading to the outside of the body. The vagina, or birth canal, is the passageway through which a baby leaves its mother's body during childbirth. **Figure 5** shows the female reproductive system.

🖉

Vocabulary Identify Related Word Forms When you know the meaning of a word, you can often identify and understand related words. How are the meanings of *fertilized* and *fertilization* related?

_____

_____

_____

FIGURE 5 ·····················

Egg Production and Passage From the Body

Each month, an ovary produces an egg that leaves the body if it is not fertilized.

✏ **Describe** In the boxes, write the functions of the uterus and the vagina.

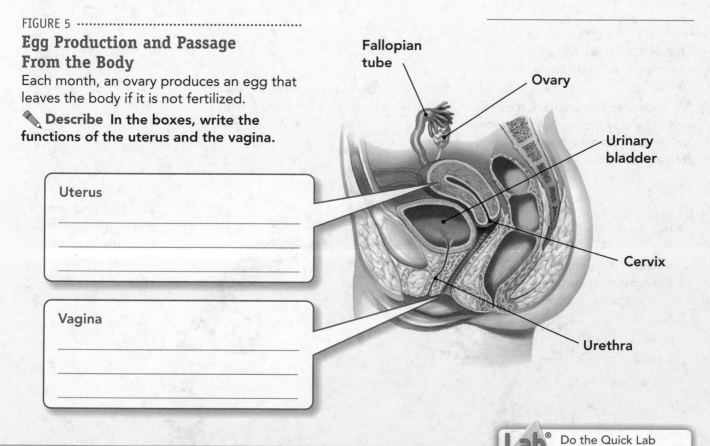

Fallopian tube

Ovary

Urinary bladder

Cervix

Urethra

Uterus

_____

_____

Vagina

_____

_____

Lab® zone Do the Quick Lab *Reproductive Systems.*

🔑 **Assess Your Understanding**

1a. Review What is fertilization?

_____

_____

b. Relate Cause and Effect What changes does estrogen cause in a female's body?

_____

_____

got it?

○ **I get it!** Now I know that the male and female reproductive systems _____

_____

_____

○ **I need extra help with** _____

Go to MY SCIENCE ⓢ COACH online for help with this subject.

What Happens During the Menstrual Cycle?

Usually starting sometime during a girl's teenage years, an egg develops and is released about once a month. This event is part of the **menstrual cycle** (MEN stroo ul), or the monthly cycle of changes that occurs in females. 🗝 **During the menstrual cycle, an egg develops in an ovary. At the same time, the lining of the uterus thickens in a way that prepares the uterus for a fertilized egg.** Follow the stages of the menstrual cycle in **Figure 6.**

FIGURE 6 ··

The Menstrual Cycle
The menstrual cycle takes about 28 days.

✎ **Interpret Diagrams** On the lines, write the day or days of the cycle in which each stage occurs. The first stage is done for you.

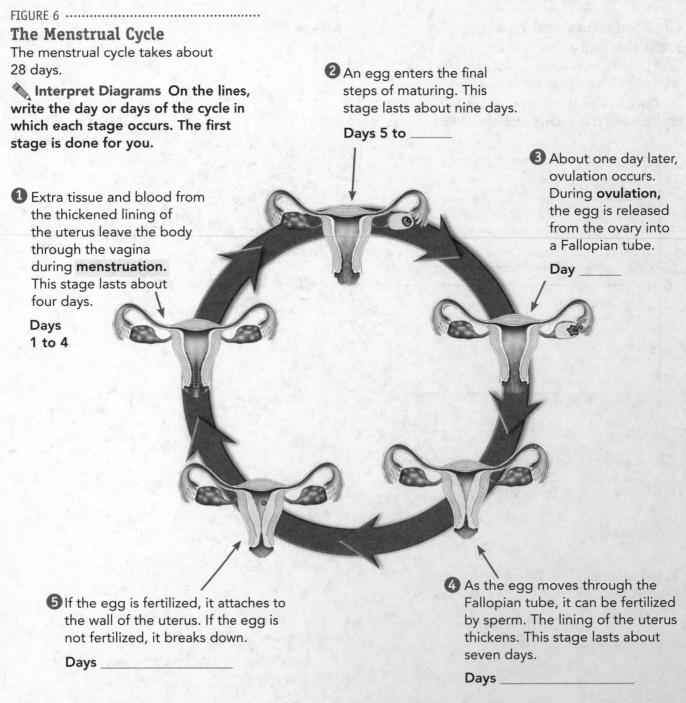

❶ Extra tissue and blood from the thickened lining of the uterus leave the body through the vagina during **menstruation.** This stage lasts about four days.

Days 1 to 4

❷ An egg enters the final steps of maturing. This stage lasts about nine days.

Days 5 to _____

❸ About one day later, ovulation occurs. During **ovulation,** the egg is released from the ovary into a Fallopian tube.

Day _____

❹ As the egg moves through the Fallopian tube, it can be fertilized by sperm. The lining of the uterus thickens. This stage lasts about seven days.

Days _____

❺ If the egg is fertilized, it attaches to the wall of the uterus. If the egg is not fertilized, it breaks down.

Days _____

do the math!

A woman's hormone levels change throughout her menstrual cycle. One such hormone is called LH.

1 Graph Use the data in the table to draw a line graph. Label the axes and write a title for the graph.

Day	1	5	9	13	17	22	25	28
Level of LH	12	13	13	70	12	12	8	10

2 Read Graphs On what day was the LH level the lowest? The highest?

_____

_____

3 Develop Hypotheses How might LH level and ovulation be related?

_____

_____

_____

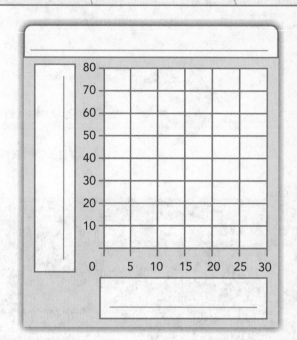

Lab zone® Do the Quick Lab *Looking at Hormone Levels.*

Assess Your Understanding

2a. Identify In the menstrual cycle, what happens after ovulation occurs?

_____

_____

_____

b. Infer What happens in the menstrual cycle if an egg is fertilized?

_____

_____

_____

got it? ....

○ **I get it!** Now I know that during the menstrual cycle _____

_____

○ **I need extra help with** _____

Go to **my science coach** online for help with this subject.

Pregnancy and Birth

- 🔑 **What Happens Before Birth?**
- 🔑 **How Is the Embryo Protected and Nourished?**
- 🔑 **What Happens During Childbirth?**

my planeT DiaRY

CAREER

Obstetrician

Some doctors specialize in caring for women during pregnancy. These doctors are called obstetricians. Obstetricians care for pregnant women, deliver babies, and make sure the mothers and new babies are healthy in the days that follow childbirth.

If you are interested in becoming an obstetrician, plan on spending at least ten years in school and training after you graduate high school. During this time you will learn how to care for mothers during pregnancy, childbirth, and after delivery. You will also learn about the serious conditions that babies may be born with. This career can be rewarding, even though it takes a lot of time and effort to get there.

Answer the questions below.

1. What are two responsibilities of an obstetrician?

_____

_____

_____

2. Why do you think a woman should see an obstetrician when she is pregnant?

_____

_____

_____

> PLANET DIARY Go to **Planet Diary** to learn more about pregnancy and birth.

Do the Inquiry Warm-Up *Prenatal Growth.*

What Happens Before Birth?

When sperm are deposited into the vagina, they swim into and through the uterus and enter the Fallopian tubes. An egg can be fertilized in the Fallopian tubes during the first few days after ovulation. If a sperm fertilizes an egg, pregnancy can occur. The fertilized egg is called a zygote. 🔑 **Before birth, the zygote develops first into an embryo and then into a fetus.**

Vocabulary
- embryo • fetus • amniotic sac
- placenta • umbilical cord

Skills
- 🔄 Reading: Compare and Contrast
- 🔺 Inquiry: Calculate

Zygote and Embryo After fertilization, the zygote divides into two cells. These cells continue to divide as they travel toward the uterus. They form a hollow ball of more than one hundred cells by the time they reach the uterus. The ball attaches to the lining of the uterus. From the two-cell stage through the eighth week, a developing human is called an **embryo** (EM bree oh).

Fetus From the end of the eighth week until birth, a developing human is called a **fetus** (FEE tus). The internal organs that began to form in the embryo, such as the brain, continue to develop and start to function. The eyes, ears, and nose also develop, as you can see in **Figure 1**. The heart becomes large enough that a doctor can use a tool to hear it beat. The fetus begins to move and kick.

FIGURE 1 ···
❯ **ART IN MOTION** Development of the Fetus
An embryo develops into a fetus. Note: These photos do not show the actual sizes.

✏️ **Interpret Photos** In each box, describe the body parts of the embryo and fetus that you can see.

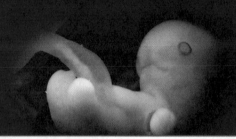

6-Week Embryo

_____

_____

_____

_____

24-Week Fetus

_____

_____

_____

_____

 Do the Quick Lab
Way to Grow!

🔑 Assess Your Understanding

got it? ···

⭕ **I get it!** Now I know that before birth _____

_____

⭕ **I need extra help with** _____

Go to **my science** 💬 **COACH** *online for help with this subject.*

How Is the Embryo Protected and Nourished?

Soon after the embryo attaches to the uterus, new membranes and structures form. 🔑 **The membranes and structures that form in the uterus during pregnancy protect and nourish the developing baby.**

Membranes **Figure 2** shows the two membranes that form during development. The **amniotic sac** (am NEE aht ik) surrounds the embryo and is filled with fluid. The fluid cushions and protects the embryo and later the fetus.

Another membrane helps form the **placenta** (pluh SEN tuh), which links the embryo and the mother. In the placenta, the embryo's blood vessels are next to the mother's blood vessels. Their blood does not mix, but substances are exchanged from one bloodstream to the other. The embryo's carbon dioxide and other wastes diffuse to the mother. Nutrients and oxygen diffuse from the mother to the embryo. In addition, drugs, alcohol, and chemicals in tobacco can diffuse from the mother to the embryo and cause it harm. However, most pathogens are prevented from reaching the embryo.

⟲ **Compare and Contrast**
In the paragraphs, underline how the amniotic sac and placenta are different. Then write how they are alike below.

_____

_____

_____

FIGURE 2 ·····························

The Amniotic Sac and the Placenta
A fetus needs nourishment and protection to develop properly.

✎ **Complete the tasks.**

1. **Describe** In the boxes, describe the functions of the amniotic sac and the placenta.

2. **CHALLENGE** How do you think it is possible for a baby to be born addicted to drugs?

_____

_____

_____

_____

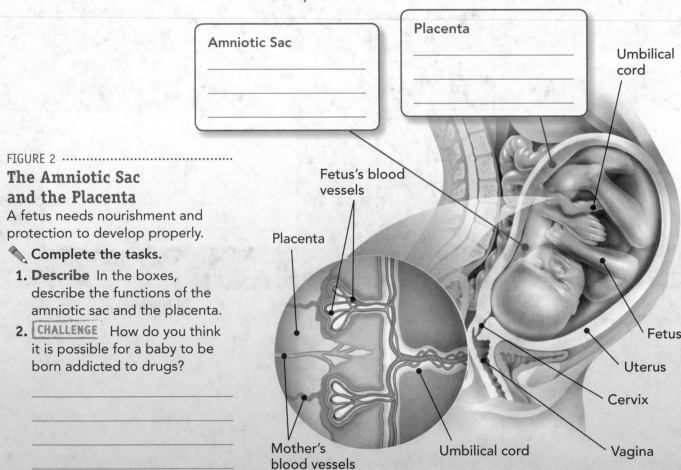

Amniotic Sac
_____
_____
_____

Placenta
_____
_____
_____

Umbilical cord

Fetus's blood vessels

Placenta

Mother's blood vessels

Umbilical cord

Fetus

Uterus

Cervix

Vagina

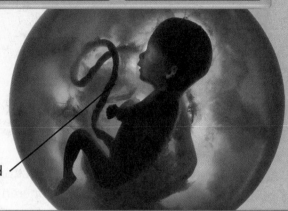

Umbilical cord

Structures

A ropelike structure, called the **umbilical cord,** begins to form between the embryo and the placenta. It contains blood vessels from the embryo that link the embryo to the placenta.

do the math!

A pregnancy is often divided into three stages called trimesters. Each trimester is three months.

1 Interpret Tables How much mass does a developing fetus gain during each trimester?

First Trimester _____

Second Trimester _____

Third Trimester _____

2 Calculate To find the percentage mass increase in a trimester, divide the mass gained in the trimester by the mass at the start of the trimester. Then multiply by 100. The percentage mass increase for the second trimester is as follows: (614 ÷ 26) x 100 = about 2,361 percent.

Find the percentage mass increase for the third trimester.

_____

_____

Change in Mass of a Developing Baby	
Month of Pregnancy	Mass (grams)
1	0.02
2	2
3	26
4	150
5	460
6	640
7	1,500
8	2,300
9	3,200

Lab zone Do the Quick Lab
Egg-cellent Protection.

🔑 Assess Your Understanding

1a. Explain What substances pass from the embryo or fetus to the mother?

_____

_____

_____

b. Relate Cause and Effect Why is it dangerous for a pregnant woman to drink alcohol?

_____

_____

_____

got it? ....

○ **I get it!** Now I know that an embryo or fetus is protected and nourished by _____

_____

○ **I need extra help with** _____

Go to **my science** **coach** *online for help with this subject.*

What Happens During Childbirth?

After about nine months of development inside a uterus, a baby is ready to be born. 🔑 **The birth of a baby takes place in three stages: labor, delivery, and afterbirth.**

Labor Labor is the first stage of birth. Strong muscle contractions of the uterus cause the cervix to open. Eventually, the opening is large enough for the baby to fit through. Labor may last from about two hours to more than 20 hours.

Delivery and Afterbirth The second stage of birth is called delivery. During a normal delivery the baby is pushed out of the uterus through the vagina. The head usually comes out first. Delivery can last several minutes to an hour or so. Shortly after delivery, the umbilical cord is cut about five centimeters from the baby's abdomen, as you can see in **Figure 3.** Seven to ten days later, the rest of the umbilical cord, which is now dried, falls off. It leaves a scar called the navel, or bellybutton.

Soon after delivery, muscles in the uterus contract, pushing the placenta and empty amniotic sac out through the vagina. This last stage, called afterbirth, usually takes less than an hour.

FIGURE 3 ·······························

Birth
Contractions in the uterus signal the start of labor.

✎ **Sequence** In the boxes below, describe the events in each stage of birth.

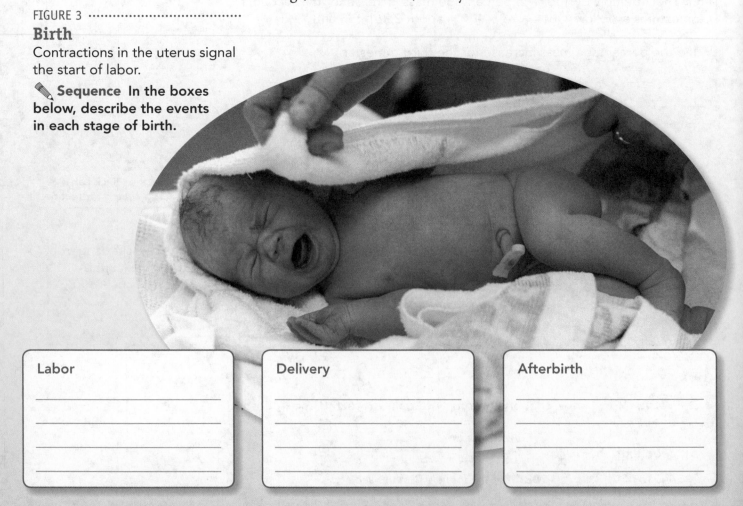

Labor	Delivery	Afterbirth
_____	_____	_____
_____	_____	_____
_____	_____	_____

Birth and the Baby During birth, pressure caused by the muscle contractions briefly decreases the baby's oxygen supply. In response, the baby's endocrine system releases adrenaline, which increases the baby's heart rate. Seconds after delivery, the baby cries and begins breathing. The newborn's heart rate then slows down.

Multiple Births The delivery of more than one baby from a single pregnancy is called a multiple birth. Twin births are the most common multiple births. There are two types of twins: identical and fraternal. **Figure 4** shows how both types develop.

FIGURE 4 ······································

Multiple Births

Other multiple births, such as triplets, can also be fraternal or identical.

✎ **Interpret Diagrams** Explain on the notebook paper why fraternal twins can be different sexes and identical twins cannot.

Identical Twins

A sperm fertilizes a single egg.

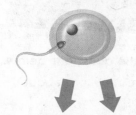

The zygote splits and forms two embryos.

Fraternal Twins

Two sperm fertilize two eggs.

Each zygote forms an embryo.

 Do the Quick Lab
Labor and Delivery.

🔑 Assess Your Understanding

2a. Name During labor, contractions cause the _____ to open.

b. Apply Concepts Why must a baby start breathing right after birth?

_____

got it?

○ **I get it!** Now I know that childbirth involves

_____

○ **I need extra help with** _____

Go to **my science** coach online for help with this subject.

UNLOCK
THE BIG

?

🔑 **What Changes Occur From Infancy to Adulthood?**

my planet Diary

BLOG

Posted by: Mackenzye

Location: Redlands, California

As I look back at baby pictures, I realize how much I have changed. I was born with black hair. Now I have blondish-colored hair. My hair used to be straight and dark but it has started to curl and become wavy. I have noticed my face is beginning to break out. When I was younger my face was clear and smooth.

I used to not mind my freckles but now that I have matured, I do not like that I have more freckles than most people. I know I have become more self-conscious. When I was younger, my appearance didn't really matter to me. As I get older, I know I will continue to change.

Write your answers to the questions below.

1. How have Mackenzye's feelings about her appearance changed?

_____

_____

_____

2. How have you changed since you were younger?

_____

_____

_____

▶ PLANET DIARY Go to **Planet Diary** to learn more about the human life cycle.

 Lab zone® Do the Inquiry Warm-Up *A Precious Bundle.*

What Changes Occur From Infancy to Adulthood?

A newborn baby cannot do much on its own. But you can do many things, from playing sports to solving math problems. 🔑 **The changes that take place between infancy and adulthood include physical changes, such as an increase in size. They also include mental changes, such as the ability to communicate.**

Vocabulary
• adolescence
• puberty

Skills
↻ Reading: Relate Cause and Effect
△ Inquiry: Graph

Infancy During the first year to two years of life, or infancy, a baby's shape and size change greatly. Its weight may double within just the first year. At birth, a baby's head is about one fourth of its body length. As the infant develops, its head grows more slowly, and the rest of its body catches up. As its nervous and muscular systems develop, the baby is able to hold up its head, crawl, and then walk. By the end of infancy, babies learn to speak and follow simple instructions. They can do many things for themselves, such as feed themselves and play with toys.

Childhood By two years of age, childhood usually begins. Children grow taller and heavier. They become more coordinated as they practice skills such as running and coloring pictures.

If you have ever spent time with children, then you know that they show a growing curiosity and increasing mental abilities. In addition, their language skills improve rapidly. For example, most four-year-olds can carry on conversations. With help, children learn to read, play games, and solve problems.

do the math!

Age (years)	0	1	2	3	4	5
Average Height (cm)	50	75	87	95	103	110

These data show a person's average height from birth to age five.

❶ △ **Graph** Use the data table to draw a line graph. Then write a title for the graph.

❷ **Read Graphs** Between which two years does a person's height increase the most?

_____

_____

❸ [CHALLENGE] At what age would an average person be 80 centimeters tall? Use the graph to explain your answer.

_____

_____

_____

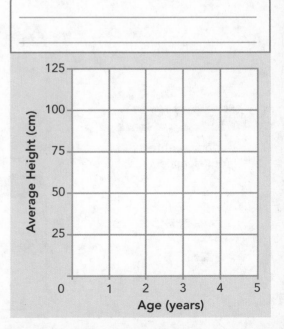

Adolescence The stage during which children start to become adults physically and mentally is called **adolescence** (ad ul ES uns). Adolescents gradually become able to think like adults and take on adult responsibilities. Their bodies also undergo specific physical changes.

Sometime between the ages of about 9 and 15 years, girls and boys enter puberty. **Puberty** (PYOO bur tee) is the period of physical sexual development that usually leads to the ability to reproduce. Hormones produced by the pituitary gland and the ovaries in girls or the testes in boys control changes in their bodies. As a result, girls and boys begin to look more like adults. In girls, ovulation and menstruation begin. In boys, sperm production starts.

Adulthood After puberty, mental, emotional, and physical growth continue into adulthood. After about the age of 30, some signs of aging become visible. Skin may show wrinkles and muscle strength decreases. At some point in their forties or fifties, women stop menstruating and ovulating. As men age, they produce smaller quantities of sperm. By practicing healthy behaviors, adults can remain active throughout their lives.

⟳ Relate Cause and Effect
Write in the graphic organizer three effects of entering adolescence.

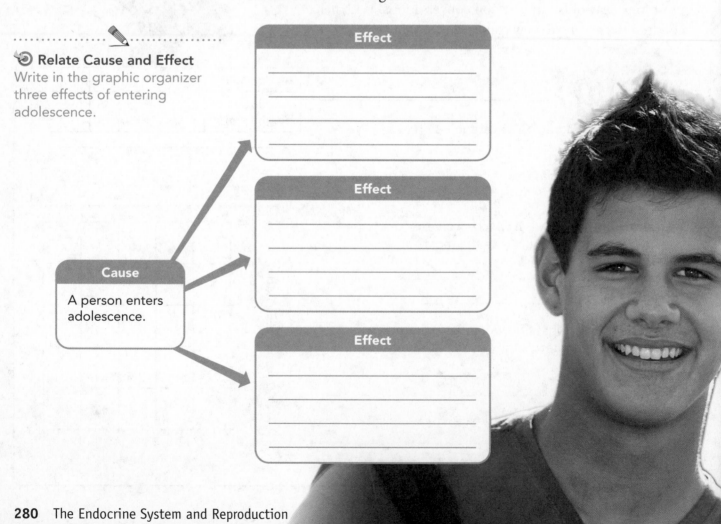

Effect

Effect

Cause

A person enters adolescence.

Effect

March Through Time

What changes happen in your body over your lifetime?

FIGURE 1 ·······································

> REAL-WORLD INQUIRY Mental and physical changes occur in your body over your lifetime.

✎ Review In the boxes, describe the changes that occur during each stage of a person's life.

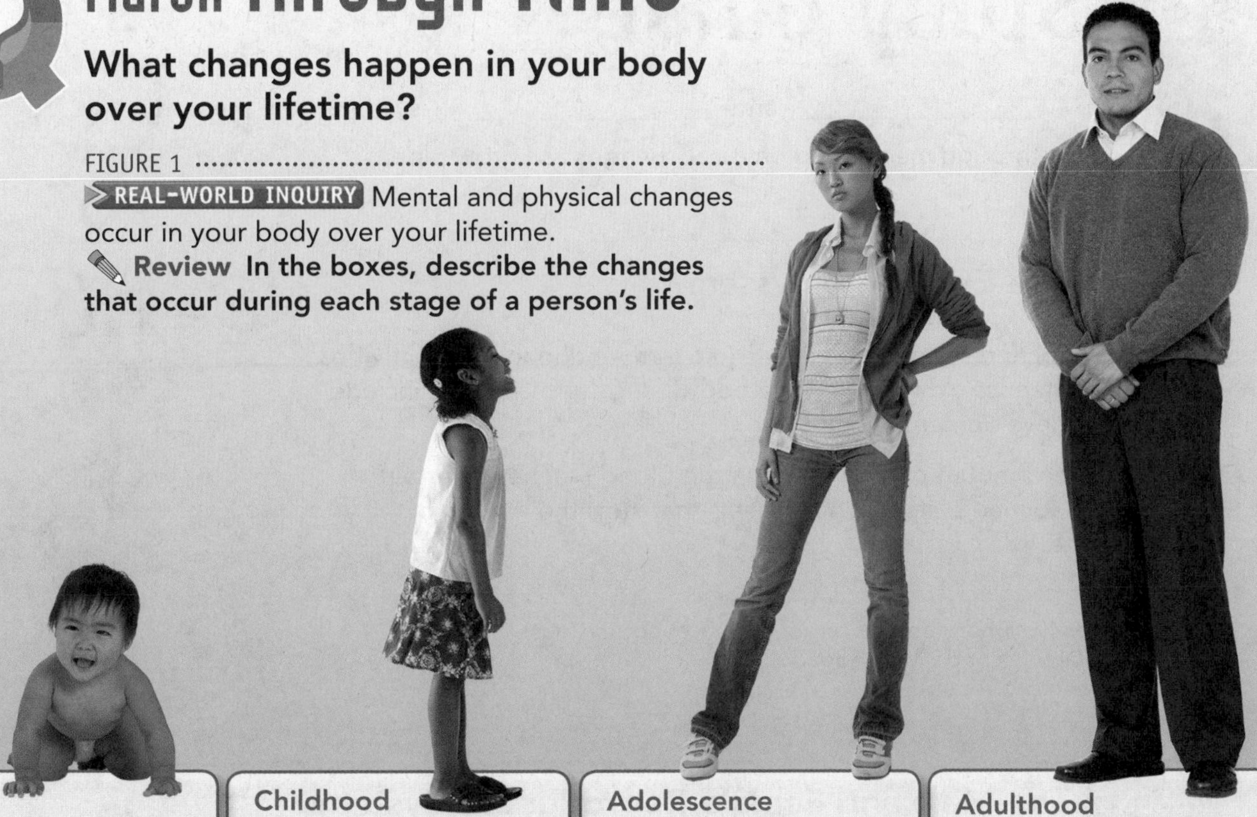

Infancy
_____
_____
_____
_____
_____

Childhood
_____
_____
_____
_____
_____

Adolescence
_____
_____
_____
_____
_____

Adulthood
_____
_____
_____
_____
_____

Lab zone ® Do the Quick Lab *Growing Up.*

🔑 Assess Your Understanding

1a. Draw Conclusions Why is adolescence such an important part of the human life cycle?

_____
_____
_____
_____

b. ANSWER THE BIG ? What changes happen in your body over your lifetime?

_____
_____
_____
_____

got it? ·······································

○ **I get it!** Now I know that the changes that occur from infancy to adulthood are _____
_____

○ **I need extra help with** _____

Go to **MY SCIENCE** 💬 **COACH** online for help with this subject.

8 Study Guide

My _____ and _____ systems help my body go through mental and physical changes as I grow older.

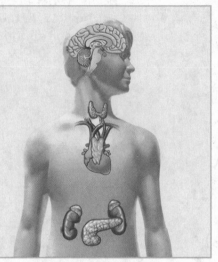

LESSON 1 The Endocrine System

🔑 The endocrine system regulates short-term and long-term activities by sending chemicals throughout the body. Long-term changes include growth and development.

🔑 When the amount of a hormone in the blood reaches a certain level, the endocrine system sends signals that stop the release of that hormone.

Vocabulary
• gland • duct • hormone • target cell • hypothalamus
• pituitary gland • negative feedback

LESSON 2 The Male and Female Reproductive Systems

🔑 The male reproductive system is specialized to produce sperm and the hormone testosterone.

🔑 The female reproductive system is specialized to produce eggs and nourish a developing baby until birth. It also produces estrogen and other hormones.

🔑 During the menstrual cycle, an egg develops in an ovary and the lining of the uterus thickens in a way that prepares the uterus for a fertilized egg.

Vocabulary
• fertilization • egg • sperm • zygote • testes • testosterone
• scrotum • semen • penis • ovary • estrogen • Fallopian tube
• uterus • vagina • menstrual cycle • menstruation • ovulation

LESSON 3 Pregnancy and Birth

🔑 Before birth, the zygote develops first into an embryo and then into a fetus.

🔑 The membranes and structures that form in the uterus during pregnancy protect and nourish the developing baby.

🔑 The birth of a baby takes place in three stages: labor, delivery, and afterbirth.

Vocabulary
• embryo • fetus • amniotic sac
• placenta • umbilical cord

LESSON 4 The Human Life Cycle

🔑 The changes that take place between infancy and adulthood include physical changes, such as an increase in size. They also include mental changes, such as the ability to communicate.

Vocabulary
• adolescence
• puberty

Review and Assessment

LESSON 1 The Endocrine System

1. The structure that links the nervous system and the endocrine system is the

  a. thyroid gland.   **b.** umbilical cord.

  c. target cell.   **d.** hypothalamus.

2. _____ recognize

a hormone's chemical structure.

3. Make Generalizations What is the endocrine system's role?

_____

_____

_____

_____

4. Infer Study the diagram below. Then suggest how the hormones glucagon and insulin might work together to maintain homeostasis in a healthy person.

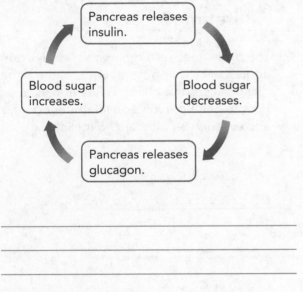

_____

_____

_____

_____

_____

LESSON 2 The Male and Female Reproductive Systems

5. The release of an egg from an ovary is called

  a. ovulation.   **b.** menstruation.

  c. fertilization.   **d.** negative feedback.

6. A mixture of sperm and fluids is called

_____

7. Draw Conclusions What is the role of the fluids in semen?

_____

_____

8. Relate Cause and Effect What changes occur in the uterus during the menstrual cycle?

_____

_____

_____

_____

_____

_____

9. Compare and Contrast In what ways are the functions of the ovaries and the testes similar? How do their functions differ?

_____

_____

_____

_____

_____

10. math! The average menstrual cycle is 28 days in length. But it can vary from 21 to 35 days. Ovulation usually occurs 14 days before the end of the cycle. On what day will ovulation occur after the start of a 21-day cycle? A 35-day cycle?

LESSON 3 Pregnancy and Birth

11. The membrane that protects and cushions the embryo is called the

a. umbilical cord.   b. scrotum.

c. amniotic sac.   d. ovary.

12. The _____ contains blood vessels from the embryo that link the embryo and the placenta.

13. Sequence What three steps of development does a fertilized egg go through before birth?

_____

_____

14. Interpret Diagrams Which of the diagrams below shows how fraternal twins develop? Which shows how identical twins develop? Explain.

A   B

_____

_____

_____

_____

_____

_____

_____

15. Write About It Imagine you just found out that you have an identical twin who was raised in another country. Write a description of what you think your twin would be like. Include information about what your twin looks like, his or her possible interests, and your twin's unique characteristics.

LESSON 4 The Human Life Cycle

16. Sex organs develop rapidly during

a. fertilization.   b. puberty.

c. childhood.   d. adulthood.

17. Children physically and mentally become adults during _____

18. Apply Concepts Name five physical and mental changes that a ten-year-old boy will go through during the next five years.

_____

_____

_____

_____

_____

_____

_____

APPLY THE BIG **What changes happen in your body over your lifetime?**

19. The body goes through many changes during adolescence. Suppose a tumor in the pituitary gland causes the gland to function incorrectly. How might a person's development during adolescence be affected? Explain.

_____

_____

_____

_____

_____

_____

_____

_____

_____

Standardized Test Prep

Multiple Choice

Circle the letter of the best answer.

1. Look at the table below. At the twelfth week, a developing baby measures about 75 mm. By which week has the fetus grown to four times this length?

Length of Fetus			
Week of Pregnancy	Average Length (mm)	Week of Pregnancy	Average Length (mm)
4	4	24	300
8	30	28	350
12	75	32	410
16	180	36	450
20	250	38	500

A week 4   B week 12
C week 24   D week 32

2. You are riding your bike when a small child suddenly darts out in front of you. Which of your endocrine glands is most likely to release a hormone in response to this situation?

A pituitary gland
B adrenal gland
C thyroid gland
D parathyroid gland

3. A change that occurs in girls during puberty is

A their skin wrinkles.
B egg production begins.
C muscle strength decreases.
D ovulation and menstruation begins.

4. A woman gives birth to twins who developed from a single fertilized egg that split early in development. Which of the following is a reasonable prediction that you can make about the twins?

A They will be the same sex.
B They will have similar interests.
C They will not look alike.
D They will have different inherited traits.

5. For sperm to develop properly, which structure must be slightly cooler than the normal body temperature?

A penis
B scrotum
C uterus
D Fallopian tubes

Constructed Response

Use the diagram below and your knowledge of science to help you answer Question 6. Write your answer on a separate sheet of paper.

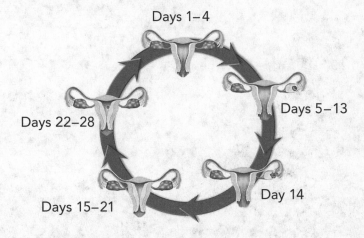

6. Describe what happens during each of the five stages of the menstrual cycle.

THE SCIENCE OF JET LAG

When baseball teams fly across the country to play a game, they may be at risk of losing more than their luggage! A new study found that when baseball teams fly across three time zones to play a game, they have up to a 60 percent chance of losing. Scientists think that the reason for this may be jet lag—the fatigue that comes when people cross several time zones quickly.

Jet lag affects the endocrine system in many ways. For example, the endocrine system produces a hormone called melatonin. Your body releases melatonin when your nervous system detects periods of darkness. The melatonin in your system makes you feel sleepy. When your nervous system detects light, melatonin production is reduced, and you feel alert. It takes a while for melatonin production to adjust to new cycles.

So, when that baseball team arrives for the game, their internal clocks may think it's time to go to bed even though it is light outside.

Design It Find out more about how jet lag affects the endocrine system and other body systems. Then, create a guide that helps travelers reduce the effects of jet lag. Include information about the body systems in your guide.

FETAL SURGERY

Michael Skinner had surgery at a very young age. How young? He was the first patient ever to undergo fetal surgery—an operation on a developing fetus.

In 1981, Michael's mother was pregnant with twins. Although one twin was developing normally, doctors noticed that Michael had a serious condition that affected his development. After consulting with medical ethicists who helped them consider the risks, Michael's parents and doctors decided to risk surgery on the fetus. Surgeons used a long needle to reach the fetus inside the mother's uterus and to deliver the treatment Michael needed. The risk paid off, and the surgery was a success!

Hospitals in the United States now perform two types of fetal surgery. In some cases, surgeons use a needle, as they did with Michael Skinner's mother, to deliver treatment. Sometimes, surgeons are able to insert tiny cameras and surgical instruments through a small incision in the uterus. The cameras allow doctors to view the fetus on a computer monitor. These procedures are much less invasive than surgeries in which the uterus is opened. Therefore, they greatly reduce the risks to the mother and the developing fetus.

For other problems, surgeons may need to open the mother's uterus and operate on the fetus directly. At the end of surgery, the surgeon closes the uterus. The fetus is allowed to develop normally inside the mother.

Think About It List three questions you have about fetal surgery. Research to find the answers, and write one or two paragraphs to answer each question.

APPENDIX

Using a Microscope

The microscope is an essential tool in the study of life science. It allows you to see things that are too small to be seen with the unaided eye.

You will probably use a compound microscope like the one you see here. The compound microscope has more than one lens that magnifies the object you view.

Typically, a compound microscope has one lens in the eyepiece, the part you look through. The eyepiece lens usually magnifies 10×. Any object you view through this lens would appear 10 times larger than it is.

A compound microscope may contain one or two other lenses called objective lenses. If there are two, they are called the low-power and high-power objective lenses. The low-power objective lens usually magnifies 10×. The high-power objective lens usually magnifies 40×.

To calculate the total magnification with which you are viewing an object, multiply the magnification of the eyepiece lens by the magnification of the objective lens you are using. For example, the eyepiece's magnification of 10× multiplied by the low-power objective's magnification of 10× equals a total magnification of 100×.

Use the photo of the compound microscope to become familiar with the parts of the microscope and their functions.

The Parts of a Microscope

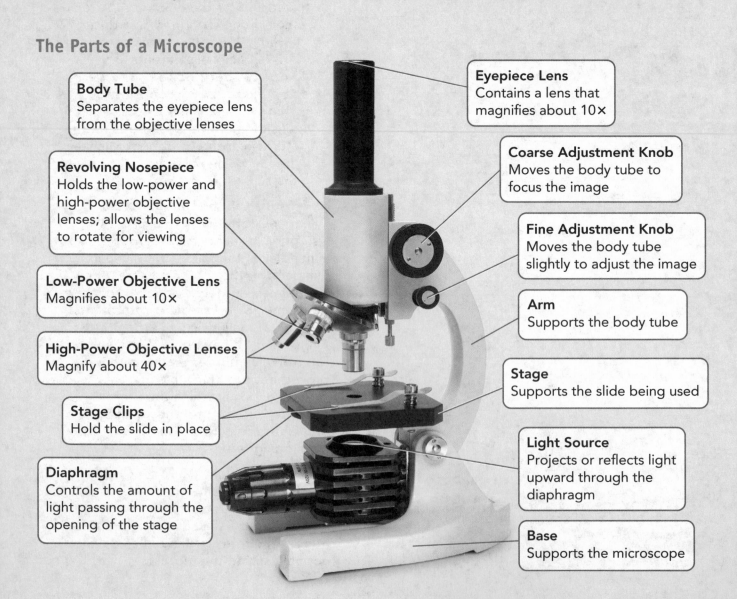

Body Tube
Separates the eyepiece lens from the objective lenses

Revolving Nosepiece
Holds the low-power and high-power objective lenses; allows the lenses to rotate for viewing

Low-Power Objective Lens
Magnifies about 10×

High-Power Objective Lenses
Magnify about 40×

Stage Clips
Hold the slide in place

Diaphragm
Controls the amount of light passing through the opening of the stage

Eyepiece Lens
Contains a lens that magnifies about 10×

Coarse Adjustment Knob
Moves the body tube to focus the image

Fine Adjustment Knob
Moves the body tube slightly to adjust the image

Arm
Supports the body tube

Stage
Supports the slide being used

Light Source
Projects or reflects light upward through the diaphragm

Base
Supports the microscope

Using the Microscope

Use the following procedures when you are working with a microscope.

1. To carry the microscope, grasp the microscope's arm with one hand. Place your other hand under the base.
2. Place the microscope on a table with the arm toward you.
3. Turn the coarse adjustment knob to raise the body tube.
4. Revolve the nosepiece until the low-power objective lens clicks into place.
5. Adjust the diaphragm. While looking through the eyepiece, also adjust the mirror until you see a bright white circle of light. **CAUTION:** *Never use direct sunlight as a light source.*
6. Place a slide on the stage. Center the specimen over the opening on the stage. Use the stage clips to hold the slide in place. **CAUTION:** *Glass slides are fragile.*
7. Look at the stage from the side. Carefully turn the coarse adjustment knob to lower the body tube until the low-power objective almost touches the slide.
8. Looking through the eyepiece, very slowly turn the coarse adjustment knob until the specimen comes into focus.
9. To switch to the high-power objective lens, look at the microscope from the side. Carefully revolve the nosepiece until the high-power objective lens clicks into place. Make sure the lens does not hit the slide.
10. Looking through the eyepiece, turn the fine adjustment knob until the specimen comes into focus.

Making a Wet-Mount Slide

Use the following procedures to make a wet-mount slide of a specimen.

1. Obtain a clean microscope slide and a coverslip. **CAUTION:** *Glass slides and coverslips are fragile.*
2. Place the specimen on the center of the slide. The specimen must be thin enough for light to pass through it.
3. Using a plastic dropper, place a drop of water on the specimen.
4. Gently place one edge of the coverslip against the slide so that it touches the edge of the water drop at a 45° angle. Slowly lower the coverslip over the specimen. If you see air bubbles trapped beneath the coverslip, tap the coverslip gently with the eraser end of a pencil.
5. Remove any excess water at the edge of the coverslip with a paper towel.

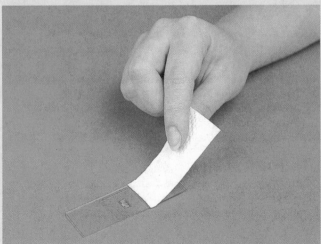

GLOSSARY

A

absorption 1. The process by which nutrient molecules pass through the wall of the digestive system into the blood. (15, 81) **2.** The process by which an object takes in, or absorbs, light.
absorción 1. Proceso en el cual las moléculas de nutrientes pasan a la sangre a través de las paredes del sistema digestivo. **2.** Proceso en el cual un objeto recibe, o absorbe, luz.

active immunity Immunity that occurs when a person's own immune system produces antibodies in response to the presence of a pathogen. (191)
inmunidad activa Inmunidad que ocurre cuando el sistema inmunológico de una persona produce anticuerpos en respuesta a la presencia de un patógeno.

addiction A physical dependence on a substance. (150, 243)
adicción Dependencia física de una sustancia.

adolescence The stage of development between childhood and adulthood when children become adults physically and mentally. (280)
adolescencia Etapa de desarrollo entre la niñez y la adultez en la que los niños comienzan a convertirse en adultos física y mentalmente.

AIDS (acquired immunodeficiency syndrome) A disease caused by a virus that attacks the immune system. (187)
SIDA (síndrome de inmunodeficiencia adquirida) Enfermedad causada por un virus que ataca el sistema inmunológico.

alcoholism A disease in which a person is both physically addicted to and emotionally dependent on alcohol. (247)
alcoholismo Enfermedad en la que una persona es adicta físicamente y depende emocionalmente del alcohol.

allergen A substance that causes an allergy. (198)
alérgeno Sustancia que causa la alergia.

allergy A reaction caused when the immune system is overly sensitive to a foreign substance. (198)
alergia Reacción que ocurre cuando el sistema inmunológico es extremadamente sensible a sustancias externas.

alveoli Tiny sacs of lung tissue specialized for the movement of gases between air and blood. (140)
alvéolos Sacos diminutos de tejido pulmonar que se especializan en el intercambio de gases entre el aire y la sangre.

amino acid One of 20 kinds of organic compounds that are linked chemically to one another, forming proteins. (71)
aminoácido Uno de los 20 compuestos orgánicos relacionados químicamente que forman proteínas.

amniotic sac A fluid-filled sac that cushions and protects a developing embryo or fetus in the uterus. (274)
saco amniótico Saco lleno de líquido que acojina y protege al embrión o feto dentro del útero.

anabolic steroids Synthetic chemicals that are similar to hormones produced in the body. (244)
esteroides anabólicos Sustancias químicas sintéticas semejantes a las hormonas producidas por el cuerpo.

antibiotic A chemical that kills bacteria or slows their growth without harming body cells. (194)
antibiótico Sustancia química que mata las bacterias o disminuye la velocidad de su crecimiento sin dañar las células del cuerpo humano.

antibiotic resistance The ability of bacteria to withstand the effects of an antibiotic. (194)
resistencia a los antibióticos Capacidad de la bacteria de resistir los efectos de los antibióticos.

antibody A protein produced by a B cell of the immune system that destroys pathogens. (184)
anticuerpo Proteína producida por una célula B del sistema inmunológico que destruye patógenos.

antigen A molecule that the immune system recognizes either as part of the body or as coming from outside the body. (183)
antígeno Molécula que el sistema inmunológico puede reconocer como parte del cuerpo o como un agente extraño.

anus The opening at the end of an organism's digestive system (in humans, the rectum) through which waste material is eliminated from the body. (90)
ano Abertura al final del sistema digestivo de un organismo (el recto, en los humanos) por la que se elimina del cuerpo el material de desecho.

aorta The largest artery in the body; receives blood from the left ventricle. (106)
aorta La arteria más grande del cuerpo; recibe sangre del ventrículo izquierdo.

artery A blood vessel that carries blood away from the heart. (106)
arteria Vaso sanguíneo que transporta la sangre que sale del corazón.

asthma A disease in which the airways in the lungs narrow significantly. (199)
asma Enfermedad en la que las vías respiratorias de los pulmones se estrechan considerablemente.

atherosclerosis A condition in which an artery wall thickens as a result of the buildup of fatty materials. (125)
aterosclerosis Condición en la que la pared de una arteria se hace más gruesa debido a la acumulación de materia grasa.

atrium An upper chamber of the heart that receives blood. (104)
atrio Cámara superior del corazón que recibe sangre.

autonomic nervous system The group of nerves in the peripheral nervous system that controls involuntary actions. (224)
sistema nervioso autónomo Grupo de nervios del sistema nervioso periférico que controla las acciones involuntarias.

axon A threadlike extension of a neuron that carries nerve impulses away from the cell body. (217)
axón Extensión con forma de hilo de una neurona que transmite los impulsos nerviosos del cuerpo de la célula.

B

B cell A lymphocyte that produces proteins that help destroy pathogens. (184)
célula B Linfocito que produce proteínas que ayudan a destruir patógenos.

bile A substance produced by the liver that breaks up fat particles. (88)
bilis Sustancia producida por el hígado que descompone partículas grasas.

blood pressure The force that is exerted by the blood against the walls of blood vessels. (113)
presión arterial Fuerza que ejerce la sangre contra las paredes de los vasos sanguíneos.

brain 1. An organized grouping of neurons in the head of an animal with bilateral symmetry. **2.** The part of the central nervous system that is located in the skull and controls most functions in the body. (221)
encéfalo 1. Agrupación organizada de neuronas situada en la cabeza de animales que tienen simetría bilateral. **2.** Parte del sistema nervioso central situada en el cráneo y que controla la mayoría de las funciones del cuerpo.

brain stem The part of the brain that lies between the cerebellum and spinal cord and controls the body's involuntary actions. (222)
tronco encefálico Parte del encéfalo que se encuentra entre el cerebelo y la médula espinal, y que controla las acciones involuntarias del cuerpo.

bronchi The passages that direct air into the lungs. (140)
bronquios Conductos que dirigen el aire hacia los pulmones.

bronchitis An irritation of the breathing passages in which the small passages become narrower than normal and may be clogged with mucus. (151)
bronquitis Irritación de los conductos respiratorios en la que los conductos pequeños se estrechan más de lo normal y se pueden obstruir con mucosidad.

C

calorie The amount of energy needed to raise the temperature of one gram of water by 1°C. (67)
caloría Cantidad de energía que se necesita para elevar en 1°C la temperatura de un gramo de agua.

cancer A disease in which some body cells grow and divide uncontrollably, damaging the parts of the body around them. (55)
cáncer Enfermedad en la que algunas células del cuerpo crecen y se dividen sin control, y causan daño a las partes del cuerpo que las rodean.

capillary A tiny blood vessel where substances are exchanged between the blood and the body cells. (106)
capilar Vaso sanguíneo diminuto donde se intercambian sustancias entre la sangre y las células del cuerpo.

carbohydrate An energy-rich organic compound, such as sugar or a starch, that is made of the elements carbon, hydrogen, and oxygen. (68)
carbohidrato Compuesto orgánico rico en energía, como el azúcar o el almidón, formado por los elementos carbono, hidrógeno y oxígeno.

carbon monoxide A colorless, odorless gas produced when substances—including tobacco—are burned. (150)
monóxido de carbono Gas incoloro e inodoro producido cuando se queman algunas sustancias, entre ellas el tabaco.

GLOSSARY

carcinogen A substance or a factor in the environment that can cause cancer. (201)
carcinógeno Sustancia o factor ambiental que puede causar cáncer.

cardiac muscle Involuntary muscle tissue found only in the heart. (46)
músculo cardiaco Tejido de músculo involuntario, que sólo se encuentra en el corazón.

cardiovascular system The body system that consists of the heart, blood vessels, and blood; also called the circulatory system. (102)
sistema cardiovascular Sistema corporal formado por el corazón, los vasos sanguíneos y la sangre; se conoce también como sistema circulatorio.

cartilage A connective tissue that is more flexible than bone and that protects the ends of bones and keeps them from rubbing together. (42)
cartílago Tejido conector más flexible que el hueso, que protege los extremos de los huesos y evita que se rocen.

cell The basic unit of structure and function in living things. (5)
célula Unidad básica de estructura y función de los seres vivos.

cell membrane A thin, flexible barrier that surrounds a cell and controls which substances pass into and out of a cell. (5)
membrana celular Barrera delgada y flexible alrededor de la célula, que regula lo que entra y sale de la célula.

cellular respiration The process in which oxygen and glucose undergo a complex series of chemical reactions inside cells, releasing energy. (139)
respiración celular Proceso en el cual el oxígeno y la glucosa pasan por una serie compleja de reacciones químicas dentro de las células y así liberan energía.

central nervous system The division of the nervous system consisting of the brain and spinal cord. (221)
sistema nervioso central División del sistema nervioso formada por el cerebro y la médula espinal.

cerebellum The part of the brain that coordinates the actions of the muscles and helps maintain balance. (222)
cerebelo Parte del encéfalo que coordina las acciones de los músculos y ayuda a mantener el equilibrio.

cerebrum The part of the brain that interprets input from the senses, controls movement, and carries out complex mental processes. (222)
cerebro Parte del encéfalo que interpreta los estímulos de los sentidos, controla el movimiento y realiza procesos mentales complejos.

cilia Tiny, hairlike projections on the outside of cells that move in a wavelike manner. (140)
cilio Estructuras diminutas parecidas a pelos, ubicadas en el exterior de las células y que ondulan.

cochlea A fluid-filled cavity in the inner ear that is shaped like a snail shell and lined with receptor cells that respond to sound. (234)
cóclea Cavidad llena de fluido situada en el oído interno, con forma de caracol, forrada de células receptoras que responden a los sonidos.

compact bone Hard and dense, but not solid, bone tissue that is beneath the outer membrane of a bone. (41)
hueso compacto Tejido de hueso denso y duro, pero no sólido, que se encuentra debajo de la membrana externa de un hueso.

concussion A bruiselike injury of the brain that occurs when the soft tissue of the brain collides against the skull. (227)
contusión Magulladura del encéfalo que ocurre cuando el tejido suave del encéfalo choca con el cráneo.

connective tissue A body tissue that provides support for the body and connects all its parts. (6)
tejido conector Tejido del cuerpo que mantiene la estructura del cuerpo y une todas sus partes.

cornea The transparent tissue that covers the front of the eye. (230)
córnea Tejido transparente que cubre la parte delantera del ojo.

coronary artery An artery that supplies blood to the heart muscle itself. (110)
arteria coronaria Arteria que lleva sangre directamente al músculo cardiaco.

cytoplasm The thick fluid region of a cell located inside the cell membrane (in prokaryotes) or between the cell membrane and nucleus (in eukaryotes). (5)
citoplasma Región de la célula de fluido espeso que se encuentra dentro de la membrana celular (en los procariotas) o entre la membrana celular y el núcleo (en los eucariotas).

D

dendrite A threadlike extension of a neuron that carries nerve impulses toward the cell body. (217)
dendrita Extensión en forma de hilo de una neurona que lleva los impulsos nerviosos hacia el cuerpo de las células.

depressant A drug that slows down the activity of the central nervous system. (244)
depresora Droga que disminuye la velocidad de la actividad del sistema nervioso central.

dermis The inner layer of the skin. (53)
dermis Capa más interna de la piel.

diabetes A condition in which the pancreas fails to produce enough insulin or the body's cells cannot use it properly. (200)
diabetes Condición en la que el páncreas no puede producir suficiente insulina o las células del cuerpo no la pueden usar correctamente.

diaphragm A large, dome-shaped muscle located at the base of the lungs that helps with breathing. (142)
diafragma Músculo grande y redondo situado en la base de los pulmones que ayuda a la respiración.

Dietary Reference Intakes (DRIs) Guidelines that show the amounts of nutrients humans need every day. (79)
Ingestas Dietéticas de Referencia Recomendaciones sobre la cantidad de nutrientes que los humanos necesitan diariamente.

diffusion The process by which molecules move from an area of higher concentration to an area of lower concentration. (111)
difusión Proceso por el cual las moléculas se mueven de una área de concentración mayor a una área de concentración menor.

digestion The process that breaks down complex molecules of food into smaller nutrient molecules. (81)
digestión Proceso que descompone las moléculas complejas de los alimentos en moléculas de nutrientes menos complejas.

drug abuse The deliberate misuse of drugs for purposes other than medical. (241)
abuso de drogas Uso indebido deliberado de drogas sin fines medicinales.

drug Any chemical taken into the body that causes changes in a person's body or behavior. (241)
droga Cualquier sustancia química que se introduce en el cuerpo y que causa cambios en el cuerpo o el comportamiento de una persona.

duct A tiny tube through which chemicals are released from a gland. (259)
ducto Conducto diminuto por el cual se liberan sustancias químicas de una glándula.

E

eardrum The small, tightly stretched drumlike membrane that separates the outer ear from the middle ear that vibrates when sound waves strike it. (234)
tímpano Membrana pequeña, extendida y tensa como la de un tambor que separa el oído externo del oído medio y que vibra cuando la golpean las ondas sonoras.

egg A female sex cell. (265)
óvulo Célula sexual femenina.

embryo 1. The young organism that develops from a zygote. **2.** A developing human during the first eight weeks following fertilization. (273)
embrión 1. Organismo inmaduro que se desarrolla de un cigoto. **2.** Ser humano en desarrollo durante las primeras ocho semanas posteriores a la fecundación.

emphysema A serious disease that destroys lung tissue and causes breathing difficulties. (152)
enfisema Enfermedad grave que destruye el tejido pulmonar y causa dificultades respiratorias.

enzyme 1. A type of protein that speeds up a chemical reaction in a living thing. (83) **2.** A biological catalyst that lowers the activation energy of reactions in cells.
enzima 1. Tipo de proteína que acelera una reacción química de un ser vivo. **2.** Catalizador biológico que reduce la energía de activación de las reacciones celulares.

epidermis The outer layer of the skin. (53)
epidermis Capa externa de la piel.

epiglottis A flap of tissue that seals off the windpipe and prevents food from entering the lungs. (84)
epiglotis Lámina de tejido que sella la tráquea y evita que los alimentos entren en los pulmones.

epithelial tissue A body tissue that covers the interior and exterior surfaces of the body. (6)
tejido epitelial Tejido del cuerpo que cubre las superficies interiores y exteriores.

esophagus A muscular tube that connects the mouth to the stomach. (84)
esófago Tubo muscular que conecta la boca con el estómago.

GLOSSARY

estrogen A hormone produced by the ovaries that controls the development of eggs and adult female characteristics. (268)
estrógeno Hormona producida por los ovarios que controla el desarrollo de los óvulos y de las características femeninas adultas.

excretion The process by which wastes are removed from the body. (155)
excreción Proceso por el cual se eliminan los desechos del cuerpo.

F

Fallopian tube A passageway for eggs from an ovary to the uterus. (268)
trompa de falopio Pasaje por el que pasan los óvulos de un ovario al útero.

farsightedness The condition in which a person can see distant objects clearly and nearby objects as blurry. (232)
hipermetropía Condición en la que una persona ve con claridad los objetos lejanos y ve borrosos los objetos cercanos.

fat Energy-containing nutrients that are composed of carbon, oxygen, and hydrogen. (70)
grasas Nutrientes que contienen energía y están compuestos de carbono, oxígeno e hidrógeno.

fertilization The process in sexual reproduction in which an egg cell and a sperm cell join, forming a new cell. (265)
fecundación Proceso de la reproducción sexual en el que se unen un óvulo y un espermatozoide, formando así una célula nueva.

fetus A developing human from the ninth week of development until birth. (273)
feto Humano en desarrollo desde la novena semana de desarrollo hasta el nacimiento.

follicle Structure in the dermis of the skin from which a strand of hair grows. (53)
folículo Estructura en la dermis de la piel de donde crece un pelo.

G

gallbladder The organ that stores bile after it is produced by the liver. (88)
vesícula biliar Órgano que almacena la bilis producida por el hígado.

gland An organ that produces and releases chemicals either through ducts or into the bloodstream. (16, 259)
glándula Órgano que produce y libera sustancias químicas por los ductos o al torrente sanguíneo.

glucose 1. A sugar that is the major source of energy for the body's cells. (68) **2.** A simple carbohydrate; the monomer of many complex carbohydrates.
glucosa 1. Azúcar que es la fuente principal de energía para las células corporales. **2.** Carbohidrato simple; monómero de muchos carbohidratos complejos.

H

heart A hollow, muscular organ that pumps blood throughout an organism's body. (104)
corazón Órgano hueco y muscular que bombea la sangre por todas partes del cuerpo de un organismo.

heart attack A sudden instance in which blood flow to part of the heart muscle is blocked, causing heart cells to die. (125)
infarto cardiaco Suceso repentino en la que se obstruye el flujo de sangre a una parte del músculo cardiaco, lo que causa la muerte de las células cardiacas.

hemoglobin An iron-containing protein that binds chemically to oxygen molecules; makes up most of red blood cells. (116)
hemoglobina Proteína que contiene hierro, y que se enlaza químicamente las moléculas de oxígeno; forma la mayoría de los glóbulos rojos.

histamine A chemical that is responsible for the symptoms of an allergy. (198)
histamina Sustancia química responsable de los síntomas de una alergia.

HIV (human immunodeficiency virus) The virus that causes AIDS. (187)
VIH (virus de la inmunodeficiencia humana) Virus que causa el SIDA.

homeostasis The condition in which an organism's internal environment is kept stable in spite of changes in the external environment. (19)
homeostasis Condición en la que el medio ambiente interno de un organismo se mantiene estable a pesar de cambios en el medio ambiente externo.

hormone 1. A chemical that affects growth and development. **2.** The chemical produced by an endocrine gland. (17, 260)
hormona 1. Sustancia química que afecta el crecimiento y el desarrollo. **2.** Sustancia química producida por una glándula endocrina.

hypertension A disease in which a person's blood pressure is consistently higher than normal; also called high blood pressure. (126)
hipertensión Enfermedad en la que la presión arterial de una persona es constantemente más alta de lo normal; se llama también presión sanguínea alta.

hypothalamus A part of the brain that links the nervous system and the endocrine system. (262)
hipotálamo Parte del encéfalo que une el sistema nervioso con el sistema endocrino.

I

immune response Part of the body's defense against pathogens in which cells of the immune system react to each kind of pathogen with a defense targeted specifically at that pathogen. (183)
reacción inmunológica Parte de la defensa del cuerpo contra los patógenos, en la que las células del sistema inmunológico reaccionan a cada tipo de patógeno con una defensa específica.

immunity The body's ability to destroy pathogens before they can cause disease. (191)
inmunidad Capacidad del cuerpo para destruir los patógenos antes de que causen enfermedades.

infectious disease A disease caused by the presence of a living thing in the body that can pass from one organism to another. (173)
enfermedad infecciosa Enfermedad causada por la presencia de un ser vivo en el cuerpo y que puede pasar de un organismo a otro.

inflammatory response Part of the body's defense against pathogens, in which fluid and white blood cells leak from blood vessels into tissues and destroy pathogens by breaking them down. (181)
reacción inflamatoria Parte de la defensa del cuerpo contra los patógenos en la cual los fluidos y los glóbulos blancos salen de los vasos sanguíneos hacia los tejidos y destruyen los patógenos descomponiéndolos.

insulin A hormone produced in the pancreas that enables the body's cells to take in glucose from the blood and use it for energy. (200)
insulina Hormona producida por el páncreas, que permite que las células del cuerpo absorban glucosa de la sangre y la usen como energía.

interneuron A neuron that carries nerve impulses from one neuron to another. (218)
interneurona Neurona que lleva los impulsos nerviosos de una neurona a otra.

involuntary muscle A muscle that is not under conscious control. (45)
músculo involuntario Músculo que no se puede controlar conscientemente.

iris The ring of muscle that surrounds the pupil and regulates the amount of light entering the eye; gives the eye its color. (230)
iris Disco de músculo que rodea la pupila y regula la cantidad de luz que entra al ojo; da color al ojo.

J

joint A place in the body where two bones come together. (12, 39)
articulación Parte del cuerpo donde se unen dos huesos.

K

kidney A major organ of the excretory system; removes urea and other wastes from the blood. (156)
riñón Órgano principal del sistema excretor que elimina la urea, el exceso de agua y otros materiales de desecho del cuerpo.

L

large intestine The last section of the digestive system, where water is absorbed into the bloodstream and the remaining material is eliminated from the body. (90)
intestino grueso Última sección del sistema digestivo, donde se absorbe agua dirigida al torrente sanguíneo y se eliminan del cuerpo los materiales restantes.

GLOSSARY

larynx The voice box; located in the top part of the trachea, underneath the epiglottis. (143)
laringe Caja de la voz; está ubicada en la parte superior de la tráquea debajo de la epiglotis.

lens 1. The flexible structure that focuses light that has entered the eye. (230) **2.** A curved piece of glass or other transparent material that is used to refract light.
lente 1. Estructura flexible que enfoca la luz que entra al ojo. **2.** Trozo curvo de vidrio u otro material transparente que se usa para refractar la luz.

ligament Strong connective tissue that holds bones together in movable joints. (39)
ligamentos Tejido conector resistente que une dos huesos en las articulaciones móviles.

liver The largest organ inside the body; it plays a role in many body processes, such as producing bile for the digestive system. (88)
hígado El órgano más grande dentro del cuerpo; interviene en muchos procesos corporales, como la producción de bilis para el sistema digestivo.

lung 1. An organ found in air-breathing vertebrates that exchanges oxygen and carbon dioxide with the blood. **2.** In humans, one of two main organs of the respiratory system. (140)
pulmón 1. Órgano que tienen los vertebrados que respiran aire, que intercambia oxígeno y dióxido de carbono en la sangre. **2.** En los humanos, uno de los dos órganos principales del sistema respiratorio.

lymph node A small knob of tissue in the lymphatic system that filters lymph, trapping bacteria and other microorganisms that cause disease. (121)
ganglio linfático Pequeña prominencia de tejido en el sistema linfático que filtra la linfa, atrapando las bacterias y otros microorganismos que causan enfermedades.

lymph The fluid consisting of water and other dissolved materials that the lymphatic system collects and returns to the bloodstream. (121)
linfa Fluido formado por agua y otros materiales disueltos que el sistema linfático recoge y devuelve al torrente sanguíneo.

lymphatic system A network of veinlike vessels that returns the fluid that leaks out of blood vessels to the bloodstream. (120)
sistema linfático Red de vasos que parecen venas que devuelve al torrente sanguíneo el fluido que sale de los vasos sanguíneos.

lymphocyte A white blood cell that distinguishes between each kind of pathogen. (183)
linfocito Glóbulo blanco que distingue cada tipo de patógeno.

M

marrow The soft connective tissue that fills the internal spaces in bone. (41)
médula ósea Tejido conector suave que llena los espacios internos de un hueso.

melanin A pigment that gives the skin its color. (53)
melanina Pigmento que da color a la piel.

menstrual cycle The monthly cycle of changes that occurs in the female reproductive system, during which an egg develops and the uterus prepares for the arrival of a fertilized egg. (270)
ciclo menstrual Ciclo mensual de cambios del sistema reproductor femenino, durante el cual se desarrolla un óvulo y el útero se prepara para la llegada del óvulo fecundado.

menstruation The process in which the thickened lining of the uterus breaks down and blood and tissue then pass out of the female body through the vagina. (270)
menstruación Proceso en el cual el recubrimiento grueso del útero se rompe, y sangre y tejido salen del cuerpo femenino a través de la vagina.

microorganism A living thing too small to see without a microscope. (171)
microorganismo Ser vivo que es tan pequeño que sólo es visible a través de un microscopio.

mineral 1. A naturally occurring solid that can form by inorganic processes and that has a crystal structure and a definite chemical composition. **2.** A nutrient that is needed by the body in small amounts and is not made by living things. (73)
mineral 1. Sólido natural que puede formarse por procesos inorgánicos, con estructura cristalina y composición química específica. **2.** Nutriente inorgánico que el cuerpo necesita en pequeñas cantidades y que no es producido por los seres vivos.

motor neuron A neuron that sends an impulse to a muscle or gland, causing the muscle or gland to react. (218)
neurona motora Neurona que envía un impulso a un músculo o glándula y hace que el músculo o la glándula reaccione.

mucus A thick, slippery substance produced by the body. (84)
mucosidad Sustancia espesa y lubricante que produce el cuerpo.

muscle tissue A body tissue that contracts, or shortens, making body parts move. (6)
tejido muscular Tejido del cuerpo que se contrae o encoge, y permite que se muevan las partes del cuerpo.

N

nearsightedness The condition in which a person can see nearby objects clearly and distant objects as blurry. (232)
miopía Condición en la que una persona ve con claridad los objetos cercanos y ve borrosos los objetos lejanos.

negative feedback A process in which a system is turned off by the condition it produces. (263)
reacción negativa Proceso en el cual un sistema cesa de funcionar debido a la condición que produce.

nephron Small filtering structure found in the kidneys that removes wastes from blood and produces urine. (156)
nefrona Estructura diminuta de filtración ubicada en los riñones, que elimina los desechos de la sangre y produce la orina.

nerve A bundle of nerve fibers. (217)
nervio Conjunto de fibras nerviosas.

nerve impulse The message carried by a neuron. (217)
impulso nervioso Mensaje que una neurona transporta.

nervous tissue A body tissue that carries electrical messages back and forth between the brain and other parts of the body. (6)
tejido nervioso Tejido del cuerpo que transporta impulsos eléctricos entre el cerebro y otras partes del cuerpo.

neuron A cell that carries information through the nervous system. (217)
neurona Célula que transporta información a través del sistema nervioso.

nicotine A stimulant drug in tobacco that increases the activities of the nervous system, heart, and other organs. (150)
nicotina Droga estimulante del tabaco que acelera la actividad del sistema nervioso, el corazón y otros órganos.

noninfectious disease A disease that is not caused by a pathogen. (197)
enfermedad no infecciosa Enfermedad que no es causada por un patógeno.

nucleus 1. In cells, a large oval organelle that contains the cell's genetic material in the form of DNA and controls many of the cell's activities. (5) **2.** The central core of an atom which contains protons and neutrons. **3.** The solid inner core of a comet.
núcleo 1. En las células, orgánulo grande y ovalado que contiene el material genético de la célula en forma de ADN y que controla muchas de las actividades celulares. **2.** Centro de un átomo que contiene los protones y neutrones. **3.** Centro sólido de un cometa.

nutrient 1. A substance such as nitrogen or phosphorus that enables plants and algae to grow. **2.** Substances in food that provide the raw materials and energy needed for an organism to carry out its essential processes. (15, 68)
nutriente 1. Sustancia como el nitrógeno o el fósforo que hace posible que las plantas y algas crezcan. **2.** Sustancias de los alimentos que dan el material y la energía que un organismo necesita para sus funciones vitales.

O

organ A body structure that is composed of different kinds of tissues that work together. (7)
órgano Estructura del cuerpo compuesta de distintos tipos de tejidos que trabajan conjuntamente.

organ system A group of organs that work together, performing major functions. (8)
sistema de órganos Grupo de órganos que trabajan conjuntamente y realizan funciones importantes.

osteoporosis A condition resulting from a loss of minerals in which the body's bones become weak and break easily. (43)
osteoporosis Condición producida por la pérdida de minerales en la que los huesos del cuerpo se vuelven frágiles y se quiebran fácilmente.

ovary 1. A flower structure that encloses and protects ovules and seeds as they develop. **2.** Organ of the female reproductive system in which eggs and estrogen are produced. (268)
ovario 1. Estructura de la flor que encierra y protege a los óvulos y las semillas durante su desarrollo. **2.** Órgano del sistema reproductivo femenino en el que se producen los óvulos y el estrógeno.

ovulation The process in which a mature egg is released from the ovary into a Fallopian tube. (270)
ovulación Proceso en el cual el óvulo maduro sale del ovario y pasa a las trompas de falopio.

GLOSSARY

P

pacemaker A group of cells located in the right atrium that sends out signals that make the heart muscle contract and that regulates heart rate. (104)
marcapasos Grupo de células ubicado en la aurícula derecha que envía señales para que el músculo cardiaco se contraiga, y que regula el ritmo cardiaco.

pancreas A triangular organ that lies between the stomach and first part of the small intestine; it produces digestive enzymes that break down nutrients. (88)
páncreas Órgano triangular ubicado entre el estómago y la parte superior del intestino delgado; produce enzimas digestivas que descomponen los nutrientes.

passive immunity Immunity in which antibodies are given to a person rather than produced within the person's own body. (193)
inmunidad pasiva Inmunidad en la que una persona recibe anticuerpos en vez de producirlos en su propio cuerpo.

pathogen An organism that causes disease. (173)
patógeno Organismo que causa enfermedades.

penis The organ through which both semen and urine leave the male body. (267)
pene Órgano por el cual salen del cuerpo masculino tanto el semen como la orina.

Percent Daily Value A value that shows how the nutritional content of one serving of food fits into the diet of a person who consumes 2,000 Calories a day. (78)
porcentaje del valor diario Valor que muestra cómo el contenido nutricional de una porción de alimento se corresponde con la dieta de una persona que consume 2,000 calorías al día.

peripheral nervous system The division of the nervous system consisting of all of the nerves located outside the central nervous system. (221)
sistema nervioso periférico División del sistema nervioso formada por todos los nervios ubicados fuera del sistema central nervioso.

peristalsis Waves of smooth muscle contractions that move food through the esophagus toward the stomach. (84)
peristalsis Contracciones progresivas de músculo liso que mueven el alimento por el esófago hacia el estómago.

phagocyte A white blood cell that destroys pathogens by engulfing them and breaking them down. (182)
fagocito Glóbulo blanco que destruye los patógenos envolviéndolos y descomponiéndolos.

pharynx The throat; part of both the respiratory and digestive systems. (140)
faringe Garganta; parte de los sistemas respiratorio y digestivo.

pituitary gland An endocrine gland that regulates many body activities and controls the actions of several other endocrine glands. (262)
glándula pituitaria Glándula endocrina que regula muchas actividades corporales y controla las acciones de varias otras glándulas endocrinas.

placenta An organ in most pregnant mammals, including humans, that links the mother and the developing embryo and allows for the passage of materials between them. (274)
placenta Órgano de la mayoría de los mamíferos en estado de gravidez, incluidos los humanos, que conecta a la madre con el embrión en desarrollo y que permite el intercambio de materiales.

plasma **1.** The liquid part of blood. (115) **2.** A gaslike state of matter consisting of a mixture of free electrons and atoms that are stripped of their electrons.
plasma **1.** Parte líquida de la sangre. **2.** Materia gaseosa compuesta de la mezcla de electrones libres y átomos que han perdido sus electrones.

platelet A cell fragment that plays an important part in forming blood clots. (117)
plaqueta Fragmento de la célula que juega un papel muy importante en la formación de coágulos sanguíneos.

pore An opening through which sweat reaches the surface of the skin. (53)
poros Aberturas a través de las cuales sale el sudor a la superficie de la piel.

protein Large organic molecule made of carbon, hydrogen, oxygen, nitrogen, and sometimes sulfur. (71)
proteína Molécula orgánica grande compuesta de carbono, hidrógeno, oxígeno, nitrógeno y, a veces, azufre.

puberty The period of sexual development in which the human body becomes able to reproduce. (280)
pubertad Período del desarrollo sexual en el que el cuerpo humano se vuelve capaz de reproducirse.

pupil The opening in the center of the iris through which light enters the inside of the eye. (230)
pupila Apertura en el centro del iris por donde entra la luz al ojo.

R

rectum A short tube at the end of the large intestine where waste material is compressed into a solid form before being eliminated. (90)
recto Conducto corto al final del intestino grueso, donde el material de desecho se comprime hasta formar un sólido que será eliminado.

red blood cell A cell in the blood that takes up oxygen in the lungs and delivers it to cells throughout the body. (116)
glóbulo rojo Célula sanguínea que capta el oxígeno de los pulmones y lo lleva a las células de todo el cuerpo.

reflex An automatic response that occurs rapidly and without conscious control. (225)
reflejo Respuesta automática que ocurre rápida e involuntariamente.

response An action or change in behavior that occurs as a result of a stimulus. (16, 216)
respuesta Acción o cambio de comportamiento que ocurre como consecuencia de un estímulo.

retina The layer of receptor cells at the back of the eye on which an image is focused. (230)
retina Capa de células receptoras de la parte posterior del ojo donde se enfoca una imagen.

S

saliva The fluid released from glands in the mouth that plays an important role in both mechanical and chemical digestion. (82)
saliva Líquido secretado por glándulas en la boca que juega un papel muy importante en la digestión química y mecánica.

scrotum An external pouch of skin in which the testes are located. (266)
escroto Bolsa de piel externa en donde se encuentran los testículos.

semen A mixture of sperm and fluids. (267)
semen Mezcla de espermatozoides y fluidos.

semicircular canals Structures in the inner ear that are responsible for the sense of balance. (235)
canales semicirculares Estructuras del oído interno responsables por el sentido del equilibrio.

sensory neuron A neuron that picks up stimuli from the internal or external environment and converts each stimulus into a nerve impulse. (218)
neurona sensorial Neurona que recoge los estímulos del medio ambiente interno o externo y convierte a cada estímulo en un impulso nervioso.

skeletal muscle A muscle that is attached to the bones of the skeleton and provides the force that moves the bones; also called striated muscle. (11, 46)
músculo esquelético Músculo que está conectado a los huesos del esqueleto y que proporciona la fuerza que mueve los huesos; llamado también músculo estriado.

skeleton 1. The inner framework made up of all the bones of the body. (11, 37) 2. A framework that shapes and supports an animal, protects its internal organs, and allows it to move in its environment.
esqueleto 1. Estructura interna compuesta de todos los huesos del cuerpo. 2. Estructura que da forma y soporte a un animal, protege sus órganos internos y le permite moverse en su medio ambiente.

small intestine The part of the digestive system in which most chemical digestion takes place. (87)
intestino delgado Parte del sistema digestivo en la que ocurre la mayoría de la digestión química.

smooth muscle Involuntary muscle found inside many internal organs of the body. (46)
músculo liso Músculo involuntario que se halla dentro de muchos órganos internos del cuerpo.

somatic nervous system The group of nerves in the peripheral nervous system that controls voluntary actions. (224)
sistema nervioso somático Grupo de nervios del sistema nervioso periférico que controla las acciones voluntarias.

sperm A male sex cell. (265)
espermatozoide Célula sexual masculina.

spinal cord The thick column of nervous tissue that links the brain to most of the nerves in the peripheral nervous system. (221)
médula espinal Columna gruesa de tejido nervioso que une al encéfalo con la mayoría de los nervios del sistema nervioso periférico.

GLOSSARY

spongy bone Layer of bone tissue that has many small spaces and is found just inside the layer of compact bone. (41)
hueso esponjoso Capa de tejido óseo que tiene muchos orificios pequeños y que se encuentra próxima a la capa de hueso compacto.

stimulant A drug that speeds up body processes. (244)
estimulante Droga que acelera los procesos del cuerpo.

stimulus Any change or signal in the environment that can make an organism react in some way. (16, 216)
estímulo Cualquier cambio o señal del medio ambiente que puede causar una reacción en un organismo.

stomach An organ in the form of a muscular pouch where food is broken down; located in the abdomen. (84)
estómago Órgano con forma de bolsa muscular donde se descompone el alimento; ubicado en el abdomen.

stress 1. A force that acts on rock to change its shape or volume. 2. The reaction of a person's body to potentially threatening, challenging, or disturbing events. (22)
1. presión Fuerza que actúa sobre las rocas y que cambia su forma o volumen. **2. estrés** Reacción del cuerpo de un individuo a sucesos como posibles amenazas, desafíos o trastornos.

striated muscle A muscle that appears banded; also called skeletal muscle. (46)
músculo estriado Músculo con forma de franjas; también se llama músculo esquelético.

synapse The junction where one neuron can transfer an impulse to the next structure. (219)
sinapsis Confluencia donde una neurona puede transferir un impulso a la siguiente estructura.

T

T cell A lymphocyte that identifies pathogens and distinguishes one pathogen from another. (183)
célula T Linfocito que identifica a los patógenos y distingue un patógeno de otro.

tar A dark, sticky substance that forms when tobacco burns. (149)
alquitrán Sustancia oscura y pegajosa producida cuando se quema tabaco.

target cell A cell in the body that recognizes a hormone's chemical structure. (260)
célula destinataria Célula del cuerpo que reconoce la estructura química de una hormona.

taste buds Sensory receptors on the tongue that respond to chemicals in food. (237)
papila gustativa Receptores sensoriales de la lengua que responden a las sustancias químicas de los alimentos.

tendon Strong connective tissue that attaches muscle to bone. (46)
tendón Tejido conectivo resistente que une un músculo a un hueso.

testis Organ of the male reproductive system in which sperm and testosterone are produced. (266)
testículo Órgano del sistema reproductor masculino en el que se producen los espermatozoides y la testosterona.

testosterone A hormone produced by the testes that controls the development of sperm and adult male characteristics. (266)
testosterona Hormona producida por los testículos que controla el desarrollo de los espermatozoides y las características del hombre adulto.

tissue A group of similar cells that perform the same function. (6)
tejido Grupo de células similares que realizan la misma función.

tolerance A state in which a drug user needs larger amounts of the drug to produce the same effect on the body. (242)
tolerancia Estado en el que un drogadicto necesita mayores cantidades de la droga para que su cuerpo experimente un efecto previsto.

toxin A poison that can harm an organism. (174)
toxina Veneno que puede dañar un organismo.

trachea The windpipe; a passage through which air moves in the respiratory system. (140)
tráquea Conducto por el cual circula el aire en el sistema respiratorio.

tumor A mass of rapidly dividing cells that can damage surrounding tissue. (201)
tumor Masa de células que se dividen rápidamente y que pueden dañar los tejidos que la rodean.

U

umbilical cord A ropelike structure that forms between the embryo or fetus and the placenta. (275)
cordón umbilical Estructura con forma de cuerda que se forma en el útero entre el embrión o feto y la placenta.

urea A chemical that comes from the breakdown of proteins. (155)
urea Sustancia química que resulta de la descomposición de proteínas.

ureter A narrow tube that carries urine from one of the kidneys to the urinary bladder. (156)
uretra Conducto estrecho que lleva la orina desde uno de los riñones a la vejiga urinaria.

urethra A small tube through which urine leaves the body. (156)
uretra Conducto pequeño a través del cual la orina sale del cuerpo.

urinary bladder A sacklike muscular organ that stores urine until it is eliminated from the body. (156)
vejiga urinaria Órgano muscular con forma de saco que almacena la orina hasta que se elimine del cuerpo.

urine A watery fluid produced by the kidneys that contains urea and other wastes. (155)
orina Fluido acuoso producido por los riñones que contiene urea y otros materiales de desecho.

uterus The hollow muscular organ of the female reproductive system in which a fertilized egg develops. (269)
útero Órgano muscular hueco del sistema reproductor femenino en el que se desarrolla un óvulo fertilizado.

V

vaccination The process by which harmless antigens are deliberately introduced into a person's body to produce active immunity; also called immunization. (192)
vacunación Proceso por el cual antígenos inocuos se introducen deliberadamente en el cuerpo de una persona para producir una inmunidad activa; también se le llama inmunización.

vaccine A substance used in a vaccination that consists of pathogens that have been weakened or killed but can still trigger the body to produce chemicals that destroy the pathogens. (192)
vacuna Sustancia que se inyecta en la vacunación; consiste de patógenos débiles o muertos que pueden estimular al cuerpo a producir sustancias químicas que destruyan esos patógenos.

vagina A muscular passageway leading to the outside of a female's body; also called the birth canal. (269)
vagina Pasaje muscular que se extiende hasta una abertura del cuerpo de una mujer; también llamada canal de nacimiento.

valve A flap of tissue in the heart or a vein that prevents blood from flowing backward. (105)
válvula Lámina de tejido del corazón o de una vena que impide que la sangre fluya hacia atrás.

vein 1. A narrow deposit of a mineral that is sharply different from the surrounding rock. 2. A blood vessel that carries blood back to the heart. (106)
vena 1. Placa delgada de un mineral que es marcadamente distinto a la roca que lo rodea. 2. Vaso sanguíneo que transporta la sangre al corazón.

ventricle A lower chamber of the heart that pumps blood out to the lungs or body. (104)
ventrículo Cámara inferior del corazón que transporta la sangre a los pulmones o al cuerpo.

vertebrae The bones that make up the backbone of an organism. In humans, the 26 bones that make up the backbone. (37)
vértebras Huesos que componen la columna vertebral de un organismo. En los humanos, los 26 huesos que componen la columna vertebral.

villi Tiny finger-shaped structures that cover the inner surface of the small intestine and provide a large surface area through which digested food is absorbed. (89)
vellosidades Pequeñas estructuras con forma de dedo que cubren la superficie interna del intestino delgado y proporcionan una superficie amplia a través de la cual se absorbe el alimento digerido.

vitamin One of many organic molecules needed in small amounts in a variety of chemical reactions within the body. (72)
vitaminas Moléculas orgánicas que se necesitan, en cantidades pequeñas, para una gran variedad de reacciones químicas del cuerpo.

GLOSSARY

vocal cords Folds of connective tissue that stretch across the opening of the larynx and produce a person's voice. (143)
cuerdas vocales Pliegues de tejido conector que se extienden a lo largo de la abertura de la laringe y que producen la voz de una persona.

voluntary muscle A muscle that is under conscious control. (45)
músculo voluntario Músculo que se puede controlar conscientemente.

W

white blood cell A blood cell that fights disease. (117)
glóbulo blanco Célula sanguínea que protege al organismo de las enfermedades.

withdrawal An adjustment period that occurs when a person stops taking a drug on which their body is dependent. (243)
síndrome de abstinencia Período de ajuste que ocurre cuando una persona con una dependencia a una droga deja de consumirla.

Z

zygote A fertilized egg, produced by the joining of a sperm and an egg. (265)
cigoto Óvulo fertilizado, producido por la unión de un espermatozoide y un óvulo.

INDEX

Page numbers for key terms are printed in **boldface** type.

INDEX

Page numbers for key terms are printed in **boldface** type.

INDEX

Page numbers for key terms are printed in **boldface** type.

Pituitary gland, 261, **262**
Placenta, **274**
Plasma, **115**, 123
Platelets, **117**, 123
Pores, **53**
Pregnancy, **272–275**, 287
Process Skills. *See* Science Inquiry
    Skills; Science Literacy Skills
Proteins, **71**
Protists, 175
Puberty, **280**
Pupil, **230**

R

Reading Skills
    graphic organizers
        Venn diagram, 147, 181, 193
    reading/thinking support
    strategies
        apply concepts, 8, 17, 24, 27,
            40, 43, 48, 54, 57, 93, 113,
            117, 127, 161, 176, 185, 203,
            205, 222, 232, 244, 249, 250,
            263, 277, 284
        define, 25, 47, 79, 113, 117,
            126, 141, 173, 243
        describe, 19, 51, 90, 112,
            139, 183, 195, 206, 215, 235,
            247, 265, 269, 274
        explain, 15, 16, 17, 40, 43,
            71, 88, 89, 90, 121, 127, 143,
            185, 193, 202, 205, 243, 262,
            275
        identify, 13, 38, 72, 77, 78,
            83, 107, 110, 143, 177, 179,
            185, 198, 226, 271
        interpret diagrams, 12, 27,
            48, 82, 83, 94, 106, 110, 142,
            192, 205, 217, 232, 249, 270,
            277, 284
        interpret photos, 22, 37, 52,
            78, 112, 125, 229, 239, 273
        interpret tables, 201, 275
        list, 15, 25, 71, 115, 205, 235,
            245
        make generalizations, 49, 58,
            77, 117, 173, 249, 283
        make judgments, 9, 130,
            247, 250
        mark text, 15, 105, 110, 111,
            125, 143, 182, 225, 238, 267,
            274
        name, 5, 21, 76, 78, 82, 83,
            105, 157, 185, 200, 218, 232,
            277
        read graphs, 18, 28, 55, 107,
            120, 126, 129, 149, 161, 189,
            233, 271, 279

    review, 9, 49, 81, 85, 91, 123,
        127, 150, 189, 195, 203, 223,
        239, 269, 281
    target reading skills
        ask questions, 76
        compare and contrast, 12,
            17, 27, 43, 47, 57, 67, 79, 85,
            112, 141, 146, 161, 174, 181,
            193, 205, 218, 226, 249, 274,
            283
        identify supporting evidence,
            151
        identify the main idea, 6, 87,
            116, 171, 238, 259
        outline, 71
        relate cause and effect, 21,
            25, 40, 52, 57, 89, 94, 113,
            125, 126, 130, 140, 150, 162,
            191, 200, 203, 206, 227, 234,
            262, 269, 275, 280, 283
        relate text and visuals, 6, 41,
            45, 53, 104, 115, 116, 144,
            152, 158, 199, 218, 225, 230,
            267
        sequence, 14, 16, 20, 27, 73,
            84, 105, 130, 143, 161, 182,
            185, 188, 198, 219, 225, 226,
            231, 237, 250, 267, 276, 284
        summarize, 12, 42, 54, 73,
            79, 83, 109, 119, 122, 130,
            141, 146, 156, 159, 180, 189,
            197, 200, 221, 234, 243, 262,
            266, 268
Rectum, **90**
Red blood cells, **116,** 123
    and breathing, 144–145
Reflex, **225**
Reproductive system, 9, **264–271**
    birth, 276–277
    female, 268–270
    male, 266–267
    pregnancy, 272–275, 287
Resistance to antibiotics, **194**
Respiration, **139**
Respiratory system, 8, **138–147**
    and asthma, 196, **199**
    breathing process, 142–147
    as defense against disease, 180
    function of, 138–139
    gas exchange, 144–145
    and health, 148–153, 164, 165
    and smoking, 148–153
    speaking process, 143
    structure of, 140–141
Response to stimulus, **16, 216**
Retina, **230**
Rh factor, 120

S

Saliva, **82**–83
Science Inquiry Skills
    basic process skills
        calculate, 55, 78, 89, 93, 107,
            120, 145, 155, 266, 275
        classify, 39, 40, 46, 71, 75,
            77, 93, 129, 161, 218, 223,
            238
        communicate, 4, 10, 23, 36,
            50, 66, 69, 74, 86, 98, 124,
            126, 130, 153, 172, 186, 220,
            235, 242, 245, 246, 258, 264
        create data tables, 118
        estimate, 78
        graph, 76, 187, 233, 271, 279
        infer, xxii, 9, 17, 27, 32, 39,
            42, 47, 48, 55, 57, 84, 85, 93,
            103, 107, 111, 121, 134, 152,
            157, 166, 177, 195, 210, 216,
            222, 224, 261, 271, 283
        make models, 7, 184, 245,
            260
        measure, 230
        observe, 7, 40, 52, 83, 110,
            198, 230, 241
        predict, 13, 38, 57, 94, 105,
            123, 129, 150, 162, 198, 254
Science Literacy Skills
    integrated process skills
        develop hypotheses, 11, 88,
            176, 193, 271
        draw conclusions, 15, 57,
            62, 73, 77, 107, 120, 129,
            147–149, 157, 161, 173, 187,
            201, 217, 223, 226, 230, 249,
            260, 281, 283
        interpret data, 58, 70, 93,
            129, 187, 194
        pose questions, 176
Science Matters. *See* Application
    of skills
Scrotum, **266**
Semen, **267**
Semicircular canals, 234, **235**
Sensory neurons, **218**
Sexual reproduction. *See*
    Reproductive system
Sight, **229–232**
    correcting, 232
    optical illusions, 252
    process of, 230–231, 253
Simple carbohydrates, 68
Skeletal muscles, **11, 46**
Skeletal system, 8, **11–12, 36–43**
    function of, 37–38
    X-rays and bone scans, 61
    See also Bones

INDEX

Page numbers for key terms are printed in **boldface** type.

ACKNOWLEDGMENTS

Staff Credits

The people who made up the *Interactive Science* team—representing composition services, core design digital and multimedia production services, digital product development, editorial, editorial services, manufacturing, and production—are listed below.

Jan Van Aarsen, Samah Abadir, Ernie Albanese, Zareh MacPherson Artinian, Bridget Binstock, Suzanne Biron, MJ Black, Nancy Bolsover, Stacy Boyd, Jim Brady, Katherine Bryant, Michael Burstein, Pradeep Byram, Jessica Chase, Jonathan Cheney, Arthur Ciccone, Allison Cook-Bellistri, Rebecca Cottingham, AnnMarie Coyne, Bob Craton, Chris Deliee, Paul Delsignore, Michael Di Maria, Diane Dougherty, Kristen Ellis, Theresa Eugenio, Amanda Ferguson, Jorgensen Fernandez, Kathryn Fobert, Julia Gecha, Mark Geyer, Steve Gobbell, Paula Gogan-Porter, Jeffrey Gong, Sandra Graff, Adam Groffman, Lynette Haggard, Christian Henry, Karen Holtzman, Susan Hutchinson, Sharon Inglis, Marian Jones, Sumy Joy, Sheila Kanitsch, Courtenay Kelley, Chris Kennedy, Toby Klang, Greg Lam, Russ Lappa, Margaret LaRaia, Ben Leveillee, Thea Limpus, Dotti Marshall, Kathy Martin, Robyn Matzke, John McClure, Mary Beth McDaniel, Krista McDonald, Tim McDonald, Rich McMahon, Cara McNally, Melinda Medina, Angelina Mendez, Maria Milczarek, Claudi Mimo, Mike Napieralski, Deborah Nicholls, Dave Nichols, William Oppenheimer, Jodi O'Rourke, Ameer Padshah, Lorie Park, Celio Pedrosa, Jonathan Penyack, Linda Zust Reddy, Jennifer Reichlin, Stephen Rider, Charlene Rimsa, Stephanie Rogers, Marcy Rose, Rashid Ross, Anne Rowsey, Logan Schmidt, Amanda Seldera, Laurel Smith, Nancy Smith, Ted Smykal, Emily Soltanoff, Cindy Strowman, Dee Sunday, Barry Tomack, Patricia Valencia, Ana Sofia Villaveces, Stephanie Wallace, Christine Whitney, Brad Wiatr, Heidi Wilson, Heather Wright, Rachel Youdelman

Photography

All uncredited photos copyright © 2011 Pearson Education.

Cover

Alfred Pasieka/Science Photo Library/Photo Researchers, Inc.

Front Matter

Page vii, Rob Carr/AP Images; **x,** Pete Saloutos/Corbis; **xi,** AP Photo/Sayyid Azim; **xiii,** Don Farrall/Photodisc/Getty Images; **xv laptop,** iStockphoto.com; **xvii girl,** JupiterImages/Getty Images; **xx laptop,** iStockphoto.com; **xxii climber,** ArtmannWitte/Fotolia; **xxiii l,** Mike Powell/Allsport Concepts/Getty Images; **xxiii r,** iStockphoto.com.

Chapter 1

Page 4, iStockphoto.com; **5,** Dr. Gopal Murti/Photo Researchers, Inc.; **6 bl,** P&R Fotos/age fotostock/Alamy; **6 br,** Biophoto Associates/Photo Researchers, Inc.; **6 tl,** Michael Abbey/Science Source; **6 tr,** Innerspace Imaging/Photo Researchers, Inc.; **6–7 heart,** Dorling Kindersley; **17,** iStockphoto.com; **10,** Lebedinski Vladislav/Shutterstock; **11 l,** Claro Cortes IV/Reuters/Corbis; **11 r,** Jeff Rotman/Nature Picture Library; **12,** Juice Images/Photolibrary New York; **14–15,** Photodisc/Photolibrary New York; **16,** Dorling Kindersley; **18,** O. Burriel/Photo Researchers, Inc.; **20–21,** Duomo TIPS/Photolibrary New York; **21,** Mike Chew/Corbis; **22–23 bkgrnd,** ArtmannWitte/Fotolia; **22 inset,** Mike Kemp/age Fotostock; **23 tl,** John Henley/Corbis; **23 tr,** Doable/Amana Images/Corbis; **24,** Michael Wong/Photolibrary New York; **28,** Martin Lee/Mediablitz Images Limited (UK)/Alamy; **3 t,** Dr. Gopal Murti/Photo Researchers, Inc.; **3 b,** Mike Kemp/age Fotostock; **3 m1,** Innerspace Imaging/Photo Researchers, Inc.; **26 t,** Dorling Kindersley; **26 b,** Claro Cortes IV/Reuters/Corbis.

Interchapter Feature

Page 31 inset, J. Pat Carter/AP Images; **31 bkgrnd,** iStockphoto.com.

Chapter 2

Pages 32–33 spread, Rob Carr/AP Images; **35 t,** Corbis/age Fotostock; **35 m2,** Ed Reschke/Peter Arnold, Inc.; **35 b,** Comstock Select/Corbis; **36 m,** Nick Caloyanis/National Geographic Stock; **36 r,** Copyright © 2008 Bone Clones; **36 l,** Thinkstock/PunchStock; **37,** Steve Gorton/Dorling Kindersley; **39,** Corbis/age Fotostock; **42 t,** JGI/Blend Images/Getty Images; **42 b,** Moodboard/Corbis; **43 l,** Steve Gschmeissner/Photo Researchers, Inc.; **43 r,** Professor Pietro M. Motta/Science Source; **44 bkgrnd,** Dan Galic/Alamy; **46 t,** Astrid & Hans-Frieder/Photo Researchers, Inc.; **46 bl,** Eric Grave/Photo Researchers, Inc.; **46 br,** Ed Reschke/Peter Arnold, Inc.; **47,** Image Source/age Fotostock; **49,** NASA/Corbis; **50 b,** Custom Medical Stock Photo; **50 t,** Mauritius/SuperStock; **51,** Tom Carter/Alamy; **52 l,** Alloy Photography/Veer; **52 m,** David Vintiner/zefa/Corbis; **52 r,** Comstock Select/Corbis; **53,** Dave and Les Jacobs/Blend/IPN Stock; **54 bkgrnd,** Image100/Corbis; **54 m,** Andy Crawford/Dorling Kindersley/Getty Images; **55,** Photodisc/SuperStock; **56 t,** Steve Gorton/Dorling Kindersley; **57,** Hans Neleman/Taxi/Getty Images; **58,** Andy Crawford/Dorling Kindersley/Getty Images.

Interchapter Feature

Page 60 t, Kyle Robertson/Columbus Dispatch/AP Images; **60,** iStockphoto.com; **61,** Phanie/Photo Researchers, Inc.

Chapter 3

Pages 62–63 bkgrnd, Chris Crafter/iStockphoto.com; **65 t,** Angelo Cavalli/zefa/Corbis; **65 b,** CNRI/Photo Researchers, Inc.; **66 b,** BlueMoon Stock/Alamy; **68 m,** Frances Janisch/Corbis; **69 r,** Westend61 GmbH/Alamy; **70 bl,** Dorling Kindersley; **70 bm,** Dorling Kindersley; **71 t,** Angelo Cavalli/zefa/Corbis; **73 r,** Emma Firth/Dorling Kindersley; **74 l,** Mike Kemp/Rubberball/Getty Images; **76,** JupiterImages/Polka Dot/Alamy; **80,** David Musher/Science Source; **82,** Richard Haynes; **83,** Burke/Triolo Productions/Brand X/Corbis; **84,** CNRI/SPL/Photo Researchers, Inc.; **86,** Don Farrall/Digital Vision/Getty Images; **86–87,** Scimat/Photo Researchers, Inc.; **92 b,** Scimat/Photo Researchers, Inc.

Interchapter Feature

Page 96, Michelangelo Gratton/Stone/Getty Images; **97 t,** Cordelia Molloy/Photo Researchers, Inc.; **97 b,** Robot/Alamy.

Chapter 4

Pages 98–99 spread, Raga Jose Fuste/age Fotostock; **101 m2,** Odilon Dimier/PhotoAlto/age Fotostock; **102 m,** Sheila Terry/Photo Researchers, Inc.; **102–103 spread,** Zephyr Photo Researchers, Inc.; **104–105 spread,**

ACKNOWLEDGMENTS

3D Clinic/Getty; **106 bkgrnd,** CMC Images/Brand X Pictures/JupiterImages; **107 girl,** Carson Ganci/Design Pics, Inc./Alamy; **107 bkgrnd,** Image Source/Getty Images; **108 bkgrnd,** Stockbyte/Getty Images; **108,** BSIP/Science Source; **110,** Tim Ridley/Dorling Kindersley; **112 b,** Biophoto Associates/Photo Researchers, Inc.; **112–113 hose,** Brian Hagiwara/Brand X/Corbis; **113 r,** Odilon Dimier/PhotoAlto/age Fotostock; **114 b,** Arthur Turner/Alamy; **114 t,** Sean Gladwell/Alamy; **115,** Masterfile; **118,** Photodisc/Alamy; **119,** Digital Vision Photography/Veer; **122 tl,** Carlos Davila/Alamy; **122 bkgrnd,** Powered by Light/Alamy; **124,** Goodshoot/Corbis; **124 bkgrnd,** Photodisc; **125 t,** Custom Medical Stock Photo; **125 b,** Custom Medical Stock Photo; **126 tl,** Dorling Kindersley; **127 t,** Chris Collins/Corbis; **128 m,** BSIP/Science Source; **128 bl,** Masterfile; **128 br,** Dorling Kindersley; **128 t,** Sheila Terry/Photo Researchers, Inc.

Interchapter Feature
Page 132 m, Laguna Designs/Photo Researchers, Inc.; **133,** iStockphoto.com.

Chapter 5
Pages 134–135 spread, Eye of Science/Photo Researchers, Inc.; **137 t,** Eddy Gray/Photo Researchers, Inc.; **137 b,** Masterfile; **140 t,** BananaStock/JupiterImages; **140 b,** Eddy Gray/Photo Researchers, Inc.; **143,** Anne Ackermann/Digital Vision/Getty Images; **146 bkgrnd,** Masterfile; **147,** Masterfile; **148 b inset,** Image Source Black/Alamy; **148 bkgrnd,** UK Alan King/Alamy; **149 t,** Peter Hatter/Alamy; **150,** Joseph Sohm/Visions of America/Digital Vision/Getty Images; **151 woman,** Nic Cleave/Alamy; **151 bkgrnd,** James Cavallini/Photo Researchers, Inc.; **152 l,** Biophoto Associates/Science Source; **152 r,** Nancy Kaszerman/Zuma/Corbis; **153 sky,** PhotoLink/Getty Images; **153 billboard,** Sonda Dawes/The Image Works; **154 b,** Science Source; **155,** JGI/Jamie Grill/Corbis; **158 l,** Polka Dot Images/JupiterImages; **158 m,** Steve Skjold/Alamy; **158 r,** Anderson Ross/Digital Vision/Getty Images; **159,** Pete Saloutos/Corbis; **160 t,** Nancy Kaszerman/Zuma/Corbis; **160 b,** Pete Saloutos/Corbis; **162,** UpperCut Images/Masterfile.

Interchapter Feature
Page 164 bkgrnd, Galyna Andrushko/Shutterstock; **165 inset,** Tannen Muary/AP Images; **165 bkgrnd,** Simon Meeds/Alamy.

Chapter 6
Pages 166–167, AP Photo/Sayyid Azim; **169 t,** J. Cavallini/Custom Medical Stock Photo, Inc.; **169 tm,** Stem Jems/Photo Researchers, Inc.; **169 bm,** D. Hurst/Alamy; **169 b,** Frank Krahmer/Corbis; **170,** David Grossman/Alamy; **171,** Andrew Brookes/Corbis; **172 l,** Bettmann/Corbis; **172 r,** Jochen Sands/Digital Vision/Getty Images; **174 l,** J. Cavallini/Custom Medical Stock Photo, Inc.; **174 r,** BSIP/Corbis; **175 b,** Joaquin Carrillo-Farga/Science Source; **175 t,** SPL/Photo Researchers, Inc.; **176,** Jose Pedro Fernandes/Alamy; **177 r,** Karen Kasmauski/Corbis; **177 l,** Peter Arnold, Inc./Alamy; **177 bkgrnd,** Bruce Heinemann/Getty Images; **178 t,** Viktor Fischer/Alamy; **179,** Science Pictures Ltd./Photo Researchers, Inc.; **181,** Stockbyte/Getty Images; **183,** Stem Jems/Photo Researchers, Inc.; **186 t,** Digital Vision/Alamy; **186 b,** Hisham Ibrahim/Photov.com/Alamy; **187,** Alex Segre/Alamy; **188,** NIBSC/Photo Researchers, Inc.; **190 l,** Justin Leighton/Alamy; **190 r,** VEM/Photo Researchers, Inc.; **191,** Digital Vision/Getty Images; **192 t,** D. Hurst/Alamy; **192 b,** MedicalRF.com/Alamy; **193,** Stockbyte/Getty Images; **195,** Stephen Sweet/Alamy; **196 t,** Judith Collins/Alamy; **197 b,** Santokh Kochar/Photodisc/Getty Images; **197 t,** Altrendo Images/Getty Images; **197 bkgrnd,** Frank Krahmer/Corbis; **198 l,** Crystal Cartier Photography/Brand X Pictures/JupiterImages; **198 r,** Chris Rout/Alamy; **200,** David Kelly Crow/PhotoEdit; **201,** Eye of Science/Photo Researchers, Inc.; **202 l,** Scott Camazine/Alamy; **202 r,** Michael Keller/Corbis; **203,** leungchopan/Fotolia; **204 t,** Joaquin Carrillo-Farga/Science Source; **204 b,** MedicalRF.com/Getty Images.

Interchapter Feature
Page 208, Tom Merton/OJO Images/Getty Images; **209,** Adrian Arbib/Alamy.

Chapter 7
Pages 210–211 spread, AFP/Getty Images; **213 bl,** Richard Haynes; **213 bl,** SPL/Photo Researchers, Inc.; **214 r,** Science Photo Library/Alamy; **215,** Larry Dale Gordon/Getty Images; **216 t,** Cre8tive Studios/Alamy; **216 b,** Mike Powell/Allsport Concepts/Getty Images; **220 l,** John Donoghue et al/Nature/dpa/Corbis; **220 bkgrnd,** Science Photo Library/Alamy; **221,** Dorling Kindersley; **222,** Gregor Schuster/Getty Images; **225 girl,** Richard Haynes; **225 cactus,** Image Source/Corbis; **227,** Dylan Ellis/Corbis; **228 t,** Wingnutdesigns/Dreamstime.com; **228 b,** Andrew Brookes/Corbis; **229,** Dan Forer/Beateworks/Corbis; **230–231 bkgrnd,** Simone End/Dorling Kindersley; **233,** Mark English/Alamy; **235,** Dirk v. Mallinckrodt/Alamy; **236,** JP Amet/The Image Bank; **236 t inset,** Hemera Technologies/JupiterUnlimited; **237 l,** Richard Haynes; **237 r,** SPL/Photo Researchers, Inc.; **238 t,** Comstock/Corbis; **238 m,** Michael Nemeth/Getty Images; **238 b,** Chris Knorr/Design Pics/Corbis; **239,** David R. Frazier Photolibrary, Inc./Alamy; **240,** Anthony Redpath/Corbis; **241,** Carol & Mike Werner/SuperStock; **242,** Flying Colours Ltd./Photodisc/Getty Images; **243,** JupiterImages/Brand X/Alamy; **245 r,** Spencer Grant/Photo Edit,Inc.; **246,** Yellow Dog Productions/Getty Images; **248 t,** Cre8tive Studios/Alamy; **248 b,** Chris Knorr/Design Pics/Corbis.

Interchapter Feature
Page 252 bkgrnd, iStockphoto.com; **253,** GlowImages/Alamy.

Chapter 8
Page 254 tl, Lawrence Wee/Shutterstock; **254 bl,** Opla/Shutterstock; **254 br,** S. Oleg/Shutterstock; **255 tl,** Opla/Shutterstock; **255 young woman,** Annett Vauteck/iStockphoto.com; **255 elderly woman,** iStockphoto.com; **255 tr hand,** Paul Maguire/Shutterstock; **255 tm,** Piligrim/Shutterstock; **255 br,** Catalin Petolea/Shutterstock; **256 tm,** Piligrim/Shutterstock; **257 embryo,** Dopamine/Photo Researchers, Inc.; **257 b,** Phase4Photography/Shutterstock; **258 l,** Ben Blankenburg/Corbis/JupiterImages; **258–259 r,** Keith Leighton/Alamy; **259,** Sandy Huffacker/Stringer/Getty Images News; **260 skydiver,** O.Furrer/F1online digitale Bildagentur GmbH/Alamy; **260 sky,** Goodshoot/JupiterUnlimited; **260 lock,** Adrian Brockwell/Alamy; **264 l,** Keystone/Stringer/Hulton Archive/

this is your book

you can write in it